Masters of War: History's Greatest Strategic Thinkers

Andrew R. Wilson, Ph.D.

THE
GREAT
COURSES·

PUBLISHED BY:

THE GREAT COURSES
Corporate Headquarters
4840 Westfields Boulevard, Suite 500
Chantilly, Virginia 20151-2299
Phone: 1-800-832-2412
Fax: 703-378-3819
www.thegreatcourses.com

Andrew R. Wilson, Ph.D.

Professor of Strategy and Policy
U.S. Naval War College

Professor Andrew R. Wilson is Professor of Strategy and Policy at the U.S. Naval War College in Newport, Rhode Island. He received a B.A. in East Asian Studies from the University of California, Santa Barbara, and earned a Ph.D. in History and East Asian Languages from Harvard University. His dissertation involved archival research in mainland China, Taiwan, and the Philippines and was funded by Foreign Language and Area Studies Fellowships.

Fluent in modern Mandarin, Professor Wilson also reads classical Chinese. At the Naval War College, he lectures on Asian military history, the classics of strategic theory, Chinese military modernization, and Sun Tzu's *The Art of War*. During his 15 years in Newport, he has won several awards for teaching and service. Prior to joining the Naval War College faculty in 1998, he taught Chinese history at Wellesley College and at Harvard University, where he was awarded the Derek C. Bok Award for Excellence in Graduate Student Teaching. He also has taught at Salve Regina University and has given guest lectures at many other colleges and universities.

Professor Wilson is the author of numerous articles on the Chinese diaspora, Chinese military history, Chinese sea power, and Sun Tzu's *The Art of War*. His books include *Ambition and Identity: Chinese Merchant Elites in Colonial Manila, 1880–1916*; *The Chinese in the Caribbean*; *China's Future Nuclear Submarine Force*; and *War, Virtual War, and Society: The Challenge to Communities*. At present, he is completing a new translation of Sun Tzu's *The Art of War* and a maritime history of premodern China. In addition to his teaching duties, Professor Wilson is a founding member of the Naval War College's Asia-Pacific Studies Group and its China Maritime Studies Institute.

Professor Wilson appeared in a documentary on The History Channel and has been interviewed on National Public Radio. He has lectured on military history, strategic theory, and international security in nearly two dozen countries and on six continents. In the United States, he has been invited to speak at the National War College, the National Defense University, the U.S. Naval Academy, the Naval Postgraduate School, and the Air War College. In addition, Professor Wilson has contributed to the curricula of military colleges in Ecuador, Brazil, Colombia, Mexico, Ethiopia, and Uganda.

Professor Wilson's other Great Course is entitled *The Art of War*. ∎

Table of Contents

Table of Contents

Table of Contents

SUPPLEMENTAL MATERIAL

Acknowledgment

This course, *Masters of War*, borrows its title and takes its inspiration from the pathbreaking work of comparative strategic analysis pioneered by my late colleague Michael I. Handel. It is my honor to dedicate this course to Michael's memory and to his legacy. ∎

Masters of War: History's Greatest Strategic Thinkers

Scope:

The Prussian military theorist Carl von Clausewitz wrote, "In the whole range of human activities, war most closely resembles a game of cards." Clausewitz did not mean that war was a game; rather, he knew that war was so fraught with chance that it was much more like a game of poker than a mathematical equation. Poker is a game of chance, but it is equally a game of skill. In war, the skill most essential to improving the odds of success is crafting good strategy, which hinges on objective strategic analysis. And the best way to hone one's skills in strategic analysis is to study the classics of strategic theory and to test their utility across a range of historical and contemporary cases. This is why the classics of strategic theory are still taught in preeminent security studies programs, such as those at Yale, MIT, and Georgetown University, institutions that produce the elite of our civilian strategists. The classics are also required reading for the elite of the world's militaries at staff colleges around the globe. That our professional military and senior civilians are students of the strategic classics should come as little surprise. What is surprising is that al-Qaeda is equally interested in enhancing strategic literacy. Its members obviously study Mao Tse-tung on guerilla war, but they also read Sun Tzu and Clausewitz. For al-Qaeda, good strategy is the only way that the weak can prevail over the strong.

Although warfare has changed immeasurably over the course of human history, the classics of strategic thought endure. From the hoplites and triremes of ancient Greece to the Special Forces and UAVs in today's Afghanistan, strategy has remained a question of using the means at our disposal to compel an enemy to bend to our political will. As such, the greatest works of strategic theory deal primarily with the human contest of wills that takes place within the machine of warfare. *Masters of War* offers a concise and rigorous overview of the greatest students of war, from the ancient classics of Thucydides and Sun Tzu to the Renaissance genius of Machiavelli and the 19th-century philosopher-soldiers Jomini and Clausewitz. We will also learn about the strategic specialists, including Alfred Thayer Mahan and Julian

Corbett on naval warfare; the air-power theorists of the 20th century; and the masters of insurgency and counterinsurgency war, including Mao Tse-tung, David Galula, and Roger Trinquier. We will place each theorist within his unique historical and strategic circumstances, show how his insights apply over a range of historical cases, and evaluate his contemporary influence. In the process, we will begin to discern the complements and contradictions within and among the classics of strategic thought. In the final section of the course, we move from specific theorists to more general subjects, including the strategic challenges of terrorism and counterterrorism, the role of morality in war, and the future of strategic thought.

To judge the depth and sophistication of a strategic theory, we need to see the theorist in the context of his time. In other words, how appropriate were his prescriptions to the problems of his own age? With the exception of the most recent works of strategic theory, none of the classics we will cover was written for a 21st-century audience; thus, before we try to gauge just how applicable they are in the contemporary world, it is a good idea to try to understand who these classics were written for and what alternative theories, or ways of war, they were written against. Moreover, many of the classics of strategy were written in response to dramatic institutional, social, and technological changes that were transforming war, including the introduction of gunpowder, the French *levée en masse*, the steam battleship, air power, and nuclear weapons. Situating these thinkers within their contemporary "revolutions" in military affairs will make us better educated consumers of the strategic literature of today's high-tech world.

Our criteria for greatness in the realm of strategic thought will not be based on the military success of our theorist but on the depth and sophistication of his analysis and on his enduring influence. We will test each theorist with a discussion of strategy in action—historical cases that exemplify the strengths and limitations of these classics. For example, when we examine Sun Tzu on espionage, we will also look at the greatest intelligence coup in military history, Operation Fortitude. With Jomini and Clausewitz, we will look at the campaigns of Napoleon Bonaparte. When we visit the sea-power theorists, we will ship out to Trafalgar, Tsushima, Guadalcanal, and Leyte Gulf. With our insurgents and counterinsurgents, we will look at China, Algeria, Vietnam, and Iraq. With the terrorists and counterterrorists, it will

2

be the IRA and al-Qaeda. We will have plenty of historical practice against which to test these theories

This course is more than just a survey of the history of strategic thought. Our masters of war have stamina and have made substantial and enduring contributions to the maturation of strategic thought. We will, therefore, remain watchful of how these classics continue to influence strategic debates today. This course will have an insidious effect on the way you think about policy, strategy, and war. By the end of the last lecture, you will never again be able to watch the nightly news or read the daily paper without thinking about Thucydides, or Machiavelli, or Mao. ■

Why Strategy Matters
Lecture 1

The Japanese attack on Pearl Harbor may have been a military masterpiece, but it was a catastrophically bad strategic choice, and in the end, bad strategy brilliantly executed is still bad strategy. The example of Pearl Harbor emphasizes an important truth: There is a significant element of chance in war, and success requires the development of skills that can enhance the odds in one's favor. As we'll learn throughout this course, military prowess matters, but the skill that is most essential to improving the odds in war is strategic analysis.

Introduction to Strategic Analysis

- Strategic analysis involves objectively weighing the risks and rewards of different courses of action—thinking through the chains of cause and effect in each action before making a move. The best way to develop skills in strategic analysis is to study the classics of strategic theory and test their utility across a range of historical cases.

- In this course, we'll look at these classics of strategic theory—such works as Sun Tzu's *Art of War* and Clausewitz's *On War*—and apply those "masters of war" to historical case studies and contemporary security challenges. This approach is similar to that used in the preeminent security studies programs in the United States and by the best and brightest military minds of our time.
  - The work of the Prussian general and military thinker Carl von Clausewitz played a significant role in what became the Weinberger-Powell doctrine, a set of political and military preconditions conceived as a litmus test for committing U.S. troops to foreign wars.

  - Donald Rumsfeld repeatedly invoked Clausewitz and Sun Tzu during his tenure as secretary of defense. And Rumsfeld's deputy, Paul Wolfowitz, a leading architect of the Iraq War, regularly endorsed Thucydides as a guide to strategy in the 21st century.

Defining Strategy

- The term "strategy" derives from the Greek word *strategos*: the elected post of general in classical Athens. The idea that Athenian generals—or *strategoi*—were also politicians is the critical piece of this concept.

  o The term "political general" is laden with negative connotations, but at the highest level of command, a general must be political, that is, he or she must appreciate the idea that war is a means to a political end.

  o We can define strategy, then, as the process by which political purpose is translated into military action.

- Effective strategy also demands constant management, reassessment, and adaptation, largely because war is interactive—the enemy gets a vote. The nature of the military profession is not, however, always conducive to producing dynamic and adaptable strategic thinkers.

  o Most of an officer's career is consumed with the demands of the tactical and operational levels of war. Most officers don't have much time to ponder the strategic and political implications of what they're doing. But at the highest levels of command, deep thinking is exactly what is needed.

  o This is not a new dilemma. In the 1800s, Clausewitz pointed out that the very things that made someone a fine junior officer could actually handicap his strategic judgment. All that emphasis on drill and repetition and the belief in right and wrong answers can stifle strategic imagination. Doctrine and method provide clarity and predictability, but strategy is the realm of fog, friction, and chance.

  o Clausewitz's successors in the German armies of World War I and World War II didn't understand the difference. They had mastered the science and doctrine of warfare but not the art of strategy. As a result, they regularly mistook tactical and operational brilliance for strategic wisdom. Japan was guilty of this at Pearl Harbor and so was the U.S. military in Vietnam.

Contrasting Patton and Eisenhower

- To clarify the distinction between strategic and operational thinking and to illustrate the connection between politics and war, let's draw a contrast between Patton and Eisenhower.

- Patton had a genius for war, but his genius was best suited to the operational level of war: commanding battles and leading campaigns, that is, subsets of the larger strategy.

- Eisenhower, on the other hand, had few of the warrior credentials of Patton. Instead, he was considered the finest staff officer in the U.S. Army. His genius is evident in the way he managed the Allied coalition and the intense personalities of Churchill, Montgomery, and Patton.

- If the roles were reversed—with Eisenhower in operational command and the bombastic Patton in charge of strategy—the Allied campaign after Normandy would have played out very differently and not for the better.

- Tactics and operations are about winning battles and campaigns; strategy is about winning wars, and as we saw in Vietnam, the former does not necessarily translate to the latter.

The Civil-Military Nexus

- Strategy evolves out of a dialogue between the political leadership and the military leadership, or what we might call the civil-military nexus. This is a tough relationship to make work. Military officers might be too "in the weeds" tactically, doctrinally, or operationally to think strategically. Political leaders might be too deferential to the senior military or feel themselves too ill-informed on military matters to offer their strategic input.

- The Athenians didn't have this problem: Their generals were also politicians and instinctively saw the connections between politics and war. But in the United States, where the civilian and the military are too often seen as discrete spheres, we need to appreciate the interconnection. It is the duty of the politicians to constantly play a role in crafting, implementing, and adjusting strategy.

- Wasn't civilian meddling in the conduct of the Vietnam War responsible for its loss? As we'll see, the complete opposite was the case. Civilians didn't meddle enough in the critical strategic choices in Vietnam.

- Franklin Roosevelt's planning for Operation Torch, the Allied landings in Axis-occupied North Africa, offers another example of this principle.
   o Army Chief of Staff George C. Marshall opposed the operation. He thought it would be a dangerous diversion of resources from the primary theater of the war, Western Europe, and that the operation would delay the invasion of France. These were strategically valid points, but FDR overruled Marshall based on larger strategic considerations.

   o To FDR, action in 1942 was critical to supporting America's allies, chiefly the British. Invading North Africa also demonstrated U.S. credibility to the Soviets; would convince the American people that the Europe-first strategy was feasible; and would serve to prepare the untested U.S. military for the more daunting tasks of liberating France and toppling the Nazi regime.

   o In FDR's reasoning, we see that strategy is not only the process by which political purpose is translated into military action, but it is also the process of seizing opportunities in the midst of war to link unanticipated military opportunities to desired political outcomes.

Considerations in Strategic Theory

- As we've said, the nature of any war is largely defined by its political purpose, and the strategy must be geared toward those ends. The political purpose might be as simple as seizing some piece of territory or forcing some form of modest political concession, or it might be broad and complex, as in the case of forcing a regime change.

- Great strategic theory recognizes three common truths: (1) War is a dynamic realm of chance, uncertainty, and interaction; (2) war serves a political purpose; and (3) the military is a subordinate instrument of policy.

- There are no formulas that, if followed to the letter, will lead to success in war. Beware of any theory that claims to be a step-by-step science of strategy.

- Strategic theory also involves net assessment, an objective analysis of the strengths and weaknesses of each belligerent with an eye toward identifying how these relative attributes might interact in a war. In addition to counting tanks or missiles, such an assessment must look at intangibles, such as the genius of the enemy's military commanders or the unique nature of the enemy's society.

- Another question we should ask about strategic theory is: Does it offer lessons about leadership, especially strategic leadership? We've already seen that the United States in World War II needed different types of leaders at different levels of the war—FDR, Marshall, Eisenhower, and Patton—and that was just in one war. As much as war can take many forms, so, too, can leadership in war.

- It's also important to look at how a strategic theory addresses the theme of how and why a war ends. An end to hostilities is obviously desirable in that it stops the bloodshed, but it should also result in a better state of peace for the victor.

- Finally, we should ask whether a theory is sufficiently grounded in history, because thinking historically accustoms the mind to critical analysis—to applying theoretical concepts to actual events.

Who Are Our Masters of War?
- Paradoxically, some of the great works of strategic theory come to us not from the victors of war but from the vanquished.
  - For example, Thucydides wrote his *History of the Peloponnesian War* after being cashiered for failing to defend the city of Amphipolis. Clausewitz was a POW for a year after the Prussian disasters of 1806. And Mao did some of his best work in a cave after the Long March.

  - Our criteria for greatness in the realm of strategic thought will not be based on military success but, rather, on the depth and sophistication of the analysis and on its enduring influence.

- We will fill our course with discussions of strategy in action, with historical cases that exemplify the strengths and limitations of each of the classics we will explore.
  - For example, when we examine the *Sunzi* on espionage, we will also look at the greatest intelligence coup in military history, Operation Fortitude.

  - With the naval theorists Alfred Thayer Mahan and Sir Julian Corbett, we will sail off to Cape Trafalgar, Tsushima Strait, and Leyte Gulf. With Mao and revolutionary war, it will be China, Vietnam, and even al-Qaeda.

- Finally, many of the classics of strategy were written in response to dramatic institutional, social, and technological changes that transformed war, such as the gunpowder revolution, the French *levée en masse*, the steam battleship, airpower, and nuclear weapons. We need to understand these contexts before we try to gauge how applicable the work is in the contemporary world.

- Warfare has changed immeasurably over the course of human history, yet the classics of strategic thought endure. The greatest works of strategic theory are primarily about the human contest of wills that takes place within the larger machine of warfare. In the next lecture, we'll begin with Thucydides's tale of the Peloponnesian War, one of the Western world's great works of history and its first classic of strategic thought.

Suggested Reading

Earle, ed., *Makers of Modern Strategy*.

Handel, *Masters of War*.

Heuser, *The Evolution of Strategy*.

Murray, Bernstein, and Knox, eds., *The Making of Strategy*.

Paret, ed., *Makers of Modern Strategy from Machiavelli to the Nuclear Age*.

Questions to Consider

1. Why is it important to have senior military officers who think strategically?

2. Give a one-sentence definition of military strategy. What distinguishes strategy from the tactical and operational levels of war?

Why Strategy Matters
Lecture 1—Transcript

By almost all measures Japan's attack on Pearl Harbor was a masterpiece. It was bold in concept and brilliant in execution. It was a masterpiece of deception: a masterpiece of tactical and operational surprise and a masterpiece of military innovation. It involved the brilliant use of carrier-based aircraft, a revolutionary military capability. Those planes inflicted tremendous damage on a fleet sitting in port. But I said, "By almost all measures." Pearl Harbor may have been a military masterpiece, but it was a catastrophically bad strategic choice. Yamamoto may have been a military genius, but he also launched his country on the path to total defeat. In the end, bad strategy brilliantly executed is still bad strategy.

But why you might ask start our course on the great strategic thinkers with an abject strategic failure? For one, we all learn more from our failures than from our successes. But I also mention Pearl Harbor because I want to emphasize a very important point right out of the gate—there is a huge amount of chance in war. Yamamoto was a gambler, and he viewed the attack on Pearl Harbor as a great gamble. In fact, he said it would require a miracle for Japan to win the war, but he was willing to take that risk. But it wasn't just a victory against the U.S. fleet at Pearl Harbor that was at stake.

Japan's leadership knew that the fate of their entire empire hinged on that one gamble. On the face of it, attacking the United States at those odds sounds insane, but even Carl von Clausewitz, that cool-headed Prussian theorist said war is "like a game of cards." In other words, war is a gamble. Clausewitz didn't mean that war was a game. After all, he had seen Napoleon shatter the Prussian army in 1806. So war was not a game to Clausewitz, but he knew that war was so subject to chance that it is much more like poker or blackjack than a scientific experiment.

But if war is largely a matter of chance, why would Clausewitz have written so extensively about strategy? Let's think about it. Poker and blackjack are games of chance, but they are also games of skill. Knowledge and experience can't guarantee success in cards, but they can significantly improve your odds. You learn the rules of the game, you work the probabilities, you try to read your opponents, and you might even count a few cards. To succeed in war requires developing similar odds-enhancing skills. Military prowess matters, but the skill that is most essential to improving the odds in this most dangerous game is strategic analysis.

Strategic analysis involves objectively weighing the risks and rewards of several different courses of action. You weigh your options by thinking through the chains of cause and effect in each course of action; you do that before you place your bets. But you can't wait until the cards are about to be dealt to start thinking in this way, you need to come to the table already adept at strategic analysis. But how does one develop those strategic analytical skills? The best way is to study the classics of strategic theory and to test their utility across a range of historical cases.

That's what we are going to do in this course. In the process you are going to get a view into what is taught at the preeminent security studies programs in the United States, places like Yale, MIT, and Georgetown—programs that produce the elite of our civilian strategists. We'll also be doing the kind of analysis that is expected of military officers attending staff colleges around the globe. At the Naval War College, where I work, we look at the classics of strategic theory—works like Sun Tzu's *The Art of War* and Clausewitz's *On War*—and apply those masters of war to historical case studies and to contemporary security challenges, like the wars in Iraq and Afghanistan and Libya.

Now maybe it surprises you that our best and brightest officers are spending time with these moldy old books. Maybe you don't think classical strategic thought or military history matters. If that's the case, I can give you a few examples that might change your mind. Colin Powell, who was National Security Advisor, Chairman of the Joint Chiefs, and later Secretary of State, described the first time he read Clausewitz as a revelation. In fact, Clausewitz played a big role in what became the Weinberger-Powell Doctrine: that set of political and military preconditions conceived as a litmus test for committing U.S. troops to foreign wars. If that's not enough, Donald Rumsfeld repeatedly invoked Clausewitz and Sun Tzu during his tenure as Secretary of Defense. And Rumsfeld's Deputy, Paul Wolfowitz, a leading architect of the Iraq War, regularly endorsed Thucydides as a guide to strategy in the 21st century.

But it's not just our officers and senior civilians who are students of the classics of strategic theory. Copies of Clausewitz have been found in Al Qaeda safe-houses. Bin Laden may have drawn some inspiration from Clausewitz in assessing the United States. After all, the Prussian talked about the overall strength of a nation at war being a function of their means and their will.

Where Al Qaeda was at a distinct disadvantage in terms of means, military means, bin Laden believed that they had the edge in terms of willpower. To bin Laden, American withdrawals from Vietnam in the '70s, Lebanon in the '80s, and Somalia in the '90s demonstrated a weakness of American will. To bin Laden American soldiers were paper tigers and Washington, D.C., readily abandoned distant battlefields at the first whiff of unacceptable costs in blood, treasure, and time. Or at least that's what bin Laden thought. The fact that Navy Seals, backed by the full power of America's intelligence services, found bin Laden in distant Pakistan, in the 10th year of the global war on terrorism proves just how wrong his assessment was. But it does show that our foes are trying to think strategically. But like Yamamoto, bin Laden mistook a dangerous gamble for an educated guess.

So the great strategic thinkers still matter and what you learn in this course will be highly relevant to today's strategic environment. But I am getting ahead of myself. Let me tell you a little bit more about my job. The course I teach at the Naval War College is called Strategy and Policy. That course is a lot of fun to teach. We rigorously apply the great works of strategy to the challenges of fighting and winning real wars. It is also a deadly serious course. Strategy and Policy was a response to America's failure in Vietnam. To many, defeat in Vietnam arose from a failure of strategic imagination. Like the Japanese at Pearl Harbor, we mistook the ability to win battles with the strategic vision necessary to win wars.

Admiral Stan Turner, who was the president of the War College in the early '70s, believed that the kind of intellectual vitality that had characterized the Navy in the Second World War, the age of officers like Ray Spruance, Bull Halsey, and Chester Nimitz, was in decline. Turner wanted the War College to produce strategically minded military officers who were the "match for the best … civilian strategists."

But to figure out what it means to be strategically minded, let's first define "strategy." The term "strategy" derives from the Greek word *strategos*: the elected post of general in classical Athens. That Athenian generals—or *strategoi*—were also politicians is the critical piece of this concept. The term "political general" is often laden with all sorts of negative connotations. Think of some of the famously incompetent politicians that Abraham Lincoln appointed to military command. Even today, "political general" is widely considered an insult to an officer's bona fides as a warrior. But at the highest levels of command a general must be political.

I do not mean political in a partisan sense, but rather in the sense of appreciating that war is a means to a political end. If we look at war that way, then we might define strategy as this: the process by which political purpose is translated into military action. Effective strategy also demands constant management, constant reassessment, constant adaptation. Strategy is not a crock-pot; you can't just set it and forget it.

This has a lot to do with the fact that war is interactive. The enemy gets a vote. As much as we are trying to compel an enemy to do our will, he is trying to do the same thing to us. So a good theorist—a master of war— will understand interaction and adaptation and will give some guidance on how to compensate for the fog, friction, chance, and uncertainty that are the handmaidens of war.

The nature of the military profession is not always conducive to producing dynamic and adaptable strategic thinkers. I don't mean this as an insult. It's an occupational hazard. Most of an officer's career is consumed with the demands of the tactical and operational levels of war. This is as it should be. Let's say that you're a logistician getting supplies to the army. Or you're the chief engineering officer on a nuclear submarine. You really don't have much time to ponder the strategic and political implications of what you're doing. But it's a different matter at the highest levels of command. At those levels, deep thinking is exactly what we need.

This is not a new dilemma. Back in the 1800s, Clausewitz pointed out that the very things that made somebody a fine junior officer could actually handicap his strategic judgment. All that emphasis on drill and repetition and the

belief in right and wrong answers can stifle strategic imagina
and methods provide clarity and predictability. But strategy, s
realm of fog, friction, and chance.

Clausewitz' successors in the German Armies of World War I a
War II didn't understand the difference. They had mastered the science and
doctrine of warfare, but not the art of strategy. As a result, they regularly
mistook tactical and operational brilliance for strategic wisdom. Japan was
guilty of this at Pearl Harbor and so was the U.S. military in Vietnam.

So we have these four interconnected levels of war: policy, strategy,
operations, and tactics. To clarify the distinction between strategic and
operational thinking and to illustrate the connection between politics and
war, let's draw a contrast between Patton and Eisenhower. Patton had a
genius for war, but his genius was best suited to the operational level of war:
the level of commanding the battles and leading the campaigns. Those are
subsets of the larger strategy.

Eisenhower, on the other hand, had few of the warrior credentials of Patton.
Instead, he was considered the finest staff officer, the finest administrative
officer in the U.S. Army. Ike's genius is evident in the way that he managed
the Allied Coalition and the intense personalities of Churchill, Montgomery,
and Patton. Imagine now if the roles were reversed with Ike in operational
command and the bombastic Patton at the strategic level. Had that been
the case, the Allied campaign after Normandy would have played out very
differently and not for the better.

To steal a football analogy, Patton might be a great quarterback, but you
want an Eisenhower as your coach. Or here's another example: There's a
famous exchange in the 1970s between Colonel Harry Summers and a North
Vietnamese colonel. Summers pointed out that the Vietnamese had "never
beat us on the battlefield." The Vietnamese officer responded, "That may be
so, but it is also irrelevant." In other words tactics and operations are about
winning battles and campaigns, strategy is about winning wars. The former,
those battles, do not necessarily translate into the latter, success in war: a fact
that Pearl Harbor amply demonstrates.

...rategy is not just up to the general. Strategy evolves out of a dialogue between political leadership and military leadership, or what we might call the civil-military nexus. This is a tough relationship to make work, and to make work well. Military officers are often too "in the weeds" tactically, doctrinally, or operationally to think strategically. Political leaders are often too deferential to the senior military or feel themselves too ill-informed on military matters to offer their strategic inputs.

The Athenians didn't have those problems. Their generals were also politicians and instinctively saw the connections between politics and war. Alexander of Macedon, Julius Caesar, and Frederick the Great didn't have these problems because they were both head of state and general-in-chief.

But in the United States, where the civilian and the military are often seen as occupying discrete spheres, we need to appreciate the interconnection. We need to see that it is the duty of the politicians to constantly play a role in the crafting, implementation, and adjustment of strategy.

At this point, you might be saying to yourself, wait a minute, wait a minute! Wasn't it civilians meddling in the conduct of the Vietnam War? Using the 8,000-mile screwdriver? Tying the hands of the generals? Wasn't that what lost us that war? Hopefully, by the end of this course I will have persuaded you that something like the complete opposite was actually the case. It wasn't that the civilians meddled too much in Vietnam; it was that they didn't meddle enough, especially in the critical strategic choices. They didn't make their voices heard.

How about a less controversial example? Let's go back to the summer of 1942. During that summer Franklin Roosevelt initiated the planning for Operation Torch, the Allied landings in Axis-occupied North Africa. FDR made that decision against—against—the advice of his Army Chief-of-Staff, George C. Marshall. Marshall thought this was a dangerous diversion of resources, a diversion from the primary theatre of the war, Western Europe. And Marshall judged correctly that Torch would delay the invasion of France, D-Day, from 1943 to 1944. These were strategically valid points and Marshall should be applauded for raising them to his commander-in-chief, but FDR overruled Marshall based on larger strategic considerations.

To FDR action in 1942 was critical to supporting America's allies, chief among them the British. The British were in a bind in North Africa. And FDR needed to support Churchill who was facing heat from the opposition at home. Invading North Africa also demonstrated U.S. credibility to the Soviets, who were absorbing the full-brunt of a German invasion. Getting into the fight in the near-term would also convince the American people that the Europe-First strategy was feasible. It would keep popular passions focused on Europe. Finally, attacking North Africa, the "soft-underbelly" of the Axis, was a good way to prepare the untested U.S. military for the more daunting tasks of liberating France and toppling the Nazi regime.

In FDR's reasoning, we see that strategy is not only the process by which political purpose is translated into military action, where strategy and operations derive from political objectives. It is also the process of adapting, of seizing opportunities in the midst of a war to link unanticipated military opportunities to desired political outcomes.

In 1942 FDR was doing exactly that. We also see at least three levels of political outcomes that make Operation Torch a good strategic choice: In the long-term it contributed to the ultimate defeat of the Axis. In the mid-term it cemented the Grand Alliance and kept it moving in the right strategic direction, and in the near-term it shored-up support on the U.S. and British home fronts.

So, the nature of any war will largely be determined by that larger political purpose, and your strategy must be geared toward that end, but there are many kinds of political objectives. The political purpose might be as simple as seizing some piece of territory or forcing some form of modest political concession from your enemy. Or it might be broad and highly complex, as in the case of what we call regime change—overthrowing the enemy's system of government and replacing it with something more to our liking. But the main point here is that good strategic theory recognizes the political purpose of war.

So now we have a working definition of strategy: the process by which political purpose is translated into military action. We have also seen three common elements of great strategic theory. A great strategic theory recognizes that: 1. War is a dynamic realm of chance, uncertainty, and interaction; 2. War serves a political purpose; and 3. The military is a subordinate instrument of policy.

But the list doesn't end there. Our goal in this course is to make you better-educated consumers of strategic theory. So as you walk around and kick the tires on each model we roll out, here are a few other issues you want to keep your eye on.

Watch out for the how-to manual. Many of our theorists offer general rules for winning, but they typically avoid the trap of laying out hard and fast maxims. There are no formulas that if followed to the letter will lead to success in war.

Beware of any theory that claims to be a step-by-step science of strategy. There is a lot of science in war: for example, ballistics, aeronautics, fluid dynamics, and chemistry. And, yes, mastery of those sciences is a critical requirement for success in modern war. But by the same token, there's a lot of science and engineering in a cathedral, but we would never assume that there is a hard or exact science to a Chartres or a Saint Peter's. A brilliant strategy and a beautiful cathedral are both designed to have a psychological impact on the minds and perceptions of an audience. In the end, they are both more art than science.

You might also ask: Does this theorist have something to say about net assessment? And what is net assessment? Net assessment at its most basic is an objective analysis of the strengths and weaknesses of each belligerent with an eye to how these relative attributes might interact in a war. This is "Know the enemy and know yourself."

But net assessment is much more than counting tanks or missiles or aircraft carriers. It also involves looking at intangibles such as the genius of the enemy's military commanders and the strength of his popular will. A strategist might also look into the unique natures of societies. Are they dynamic, expansionist, and risk-taking? Or are they traditional and conservative: content to defend what they currently have?

In 1941, the Japanese had a very clear understanding of the strengths and weaknesses of the United States Navy, but they failed utterly in understanding the industrial potential of the United States or the desire of the American people for retribution.

Or think about the First Gulf War. Sunzi's *The Art of War* expands on the simple dictum of "know the enemy, know yourself," with "know the weather, know the terrain." Now, knowing those things might be as simple as assessing your physical environment—mountains, seasonal conditions, and the like. But what if we take that dictum metaphorically, so that it includes an assessment of your political, social, and institutional environment? That broader environment will likely contain critical enablers and impediments to achieving your desired political ends.

In the first Gulf War President George H. W. Bush was able to put together a remarkably broad coalition in the international environment and keep the still-lurking Soviet Union from playing the role of spoiler. At the same time, maintaining the Arab coalition regionally, building a New World Order globally, and exorcising the ghosts of Vietnam domestically ended up limiting his options, especially when it came to how far Bush thought he could push Saddam Hussein as the war wound down. At the end of the day, net assessment is not just about predicting the *contest* between belligerents, it is also about understanding the *context* in which that *contest* takes place.

Another question we should ask about strategic theory is this: Does it offer lessons about leadership, especially strategic leadership? There is a lot of variation on this theme. We are going to run the gamut from the almost supernatural intellect of Sunzi's "clever combatant"; to the eloquence, principle, and restraint in Thucydides profile of Pericles; to the stamina, audacity, and tenacity of Mahan's hero Admiral Nelson; to the subtle cunning of a Machiavellian prince. We've already seen that the United States in World War II needed different types of leaders at different levels of the war: leaders like FDR, Marshall, Ike, and Patton. And that was just in one war. As much as war can take many forms, so, too, can leadership in war.

What's next? Well, as we look at various strategic theories in this course, we need to ask: How do these theories address the theme of how and why wars end? Ending a war is obviously desirable because it stops the bloodshed, but it should also result in a better state of peace, a better state of peace for the victor. But is this always the case? Our theorists (some definitely more than others) will ponder the problematic nature of peace, in which even a vanquished opponent, like Nazi Germany in the 1930s, or Saddam Hussein's Iraq in the 1990s, might simply view the last war's settlement as a temporary evil that must be endured until it is overthrown by rejuvenated force of arms.

And finally, ask yourself if this theory is sufficiently grounded in history. History is going to play a very important role in this course. A number of the masters we'll be studying—Thucydides, Jomini, Clausewitz, Mahan, and Corbett—were historians first. David Petraeus, to give you a contemporary example, did his doctoral dissertation on the historical lessons of Vietnam, a study that informed his approaches to counterinsurgency in Iraq and Afghanistan. And we've even seen that Osama bin Laden tried, tried and failed, to use recent history to predict American responses to Al Qaeda attacks. The great thing about history is that it is complex and contingent; it can stand in for personal experience. Most of all thinking historically accustoms the mind to critical analysis.

Critical analysis, to paraphrase Clausewitz, is the process by which theoretical concepts are applied to actual events. This is what we do at the Naval War College. We arm students with an arsenal of theoretical concepts and then throw them into combat. Well, actually we throw them into seminar rooms where we look at historical case studies. And we look at these cases less for what happened than for what could have happened. To borrow a television analogy—we aren't *CSI*, we aren't trying to figure out how the victim died. We are more like the show *House*—we are trying to figure out how to save the patient.

So we put our students into the shoes, or in the case of Thucydides into the sandals, of decision makers in the past and ask them, what would Mao do, what would Machiavelli do, what would Mahan do in this situation? What would you do? Short of declaring a war for the sake of experiment, historically grounded critical analysis is the best way to inculcate strategic imagination, strategic agility, in the minds of our military officers.

So with all those elements and themes in mind, which theorists make the list? Who are our masters of war? Paradoxically some of the great works of theory come not from the victors, but from the vanquished. The lessons of failure are often far more powerful, more enduring. For example, Thucydides wrote his history of the Peloponnesian war after being cashiered for failing to defend the city of Amphipolis. Clausewitz was a POW for a year after the Prussian disasters of 1806. And Mao did some of his best work in a cave after the disastrous Long March.

Our criteria for greatness in the realm of strategic thought will not be based on military success of these individual theorists, but rather on the depth and sophistication of the analysis and on its enduring influence. But, we will fill out our course with discussion of strategy in action, with historical cases that exemplify the strengths and limitations of each of these classics. For example, when we examine the Sunzi on espionage, we will also be looking at the greatest intelligence coup in military history, something called Operation Fortitude. With the naval theorists Alfred Thayer Mahan and Sir Julian Corbett, we'll be sailing off to Cape Trafalgar, Tsushima Strait, and Leyte Gulf. With Mao and his theory of revolutionary war, we'll look at China, Vietnam, and even Al Qaeda.

We will have plenty of practice against which to test these theories. We will also be taking a historically rigorous approach. Most of the classics we'll be looking at were not written for a 21st century audience. So, before we try to gauge just how applicable they are in the contemporary world to us we need to understand what audiences these classics were originally written for and in what context.

Keeping that historical context in mind has the added benefit of giving us some perspective. Many of the classics of strategy were written in response to dramatic institutional, social, and technological changes, changes that transformed war: things like the gunpowder revolution, the French *levée en masse*, the steam battleship, the introduction of airpower and nuclear weapons. As we listen to the hype these days about revolutionary new technologies and about the transformation of war, let's take a look back at how these great minds tackled the great military revolutions of the past.

But this is much more than just a course on the history of strategic thought. We will always keep an eye to how these classics continue to influence strategic debates—and actual war plans—today.

Warfare has changed immeasurably over the course of human history, and yet the classics of strategic thought endure. From the hoplites and triremes of Ancient Greece to the Special Forces and unmanned aerial vehicles in today's Afghanistan, strategy has remained a question of using the means at your disposal to compel an enemy to bend to your political will. The greatest works of strategic theory are primarily about the human contest of wills that takes place within that larger machinery of warfare. So as we begin our survey of history's greatest strategic thinkers, we will start at the beginning, with those hoplites and triremes, the soldiers and ships that populate Thucydides' tale of the Peloponnesian War, one of the Western world's first great works of history and its first classic of strategic thought.

I'll see you next time.

Thucydides on Strategy
Lecture 2

Thucydides's *History of the Peloponnesian War* is a gift that keeps on giving. It can be read as a window onto ancient Greek culture, a primer on international relations, or a chronicle of war and strategy. In this first of two lectures on Thucydides, we will look at the elements of his narrative that best exemplify the criteria of theoretical brilliance we laid out in Lecture 1: the use of history in the process of critical analysis, the recognition that war serves a political purpose, examination of the lessons of leadership, and more.

The Origins of the Peloponnesian War

- Thucydides identifies three immediate causes of the Peloponnesian War: (1) Athenian support of Corcyra in its war against Corinth, a Spartan ally; (2) economic sanctions imposed by Athens on the city of Megara, also a Spartan ally; and (3) the attack launched by Athens on the city of Potidea, a former Corinthian colony.

- Sparta used these events as pretexts for declaring war on Athens, but Thucydides viewed these three crises more as catalysts for war. The truest cause was the growth of the power of Athens and the alarm it inspired in Sparta. Thucydides thus uses the origins of this war to give us one of the most succinct appraisals of what motivates states to seek empire: the lethal trifecta of fear, honor, and interest.

- Thucydides also tells us that the different motivations that Sparta and Athens had for going to war directly influenced their radically different political objectives.
  - Sparta was highly militarized but also deeply reluctant to go to war; it went to war only for objectives of great value.

  - As a sea power with a large and often unruly maritime empire, Athens was regularly engaged in small wars of imperial policing.

- o Sparta's political objective was unlimited: "Free the Greeks," in other words, dismantle the Athenian Empire and liberate Greek city-states from Athenian domination.

- o For Pericles, the leading general of Athens, the goal was limited: Restore the status quo ante bellum and get back to the business of dominating the Greek world through commerce and cultural imperialism.

- o Pericles underestimated how scared and serious the Spartans were. He assumed that if Athens could hold out for a few years, then the Spartans would grow frustrated and return to the peace table.

The strategy of Pericles in the Peloponnesian War was designed to frustrate the Spartans to the point that they would sue for peace and accept Athenian domination of the Aegean.

Net Assessment

- To determine which of these objectives would exercise the greatest influence on the nature of the war, we need to gauge the strengths and weaknesses of each side, determine the relative values of the political objectives, and gauge the capacity of each belligerent to compel the other to do its political will.

- In Thucydides, the initial net assessments are contained in the speeches of the Athenian statesman Pericles and the Spartan king Archidamus.

- Pericles is more optimistic in appraising Athenian strengths, especially in terms of time and money. But he also gives us great insights into what he sees as Sparta's fundamental weakness, its economy. In particular, the Spartans depended on the helots, a conquered people, to provide the agricultural surplus that allowed them to maintain the only standing army in Greece, but the helots presented a constant threat of revolt.

- In contrast to the optimism of Pericles, the speech of King Archidamus predicts the difficulties of defeating Athens. For him, Athens was everything that Sparta wasn't: dynamic, expansive, rich, and seagoing. Archidamus believed that his countrymen had grossly underestimated how much pain the Athenians could bear. But the basis of Athenian power, its maritime empire, was also a vulnerability.

  o Athens was a democracy, but it demanded tribute from its allies to provide a collective defense and to maintain the largest fleet in Greece. The fact that Pericles spent the allied contributions on public works projects and festivals antagonized Athens' allies.

  o Further, Athenian power was dependent on market access. Athens exported wine and olive oil and imported timber and grain, and it needed silver to keep the empire liquid. To Archidamus, the only hope of freeing the Greeks lay in dismantling Athens' political economy. To do that, Sparta needed a fleet, and building one would take a long time and a good deal of allied assistance.

- Using the voices of Pericles and Archidamus, Thucydides masterfully lays out a series of questions that must be asked and objectively answered so that a strategist can confidently claim to know the enemy and himself.

Leadership
- Thucydides gives us numerous profiles in leadership: good, bad and middling. He rates Pericles highly. The statesman was blessed with the qualities of intellect, self-sacrifice, determination, and restraint. He had a workable strategy, and he was eloquent enough to convince the Athenians of the wisdom of his strategy.

- Later Athenian statesmen, among them Alcibiades and Nicias, fell short as leaders in the eyes of Thucydides.
  o Thucydides's portrait of Alcibiades is a fascinating study in contrasts. Like Pericles, he was intelligent, determined, and eloquent, but he was also vain, self-serving, and impetuous. His strategic proposals were brilliant, but they often served the best interests of Alcibiades, not Athens.

  o Nicias, the archrival of Alcibiades, had all the restraint and self-sacrifice of Pericles, but none of his imagination or eloquence. His opposition to Alcibiades's ambitious plans for the Sicilian expedition backfired; he became a victim of his own rhetorical sleight-of-hand and ended up as commander of the expedition.

Interaction and Adaptation
- Thucydides gives us a rich chronicle of strategic adaptation and innovation, highlighting the fact that strategic decision points often arise from chance or luck.

- The first stroke of luck in the Peloponnesian War was extremely bad for Athens. The city was ravaged by a plague that killed between a quarter and a third of its population. Among the victims was Pericles, and his death divided the citizens on the issue of war.

- Fate intervened again in the spring of 425, when a detachment of Athenians was forced ashore by a storm at the town of Pylos on the coast of the Peloponnese. Pylos was the homeland of Sparta's helots, and the Spartans feared the Athenian occupation there would incite a helot revolt.
  o A regiment of Spartan hoplites sent to oust the Athenians became trapped on the small island of Sphacteria. The Athenian demagogue Cleon defeated the Spartans there and took more than a hundred prisoners.

  o Desperate to get their warriors back, the Spartans offered terms, and it looked like the Athenians would achieve their initial political objectives using a slightly modified form of Pericles's strategy.

o Thucydides shows us, however, the natural tendency to overreach in moments of success. Cleon demanded even greater concessions from the Spartans, prompting one of their most innovative adaptations of the war: the plan of Brasidas to capture the city of Amphipolis, an Athenian ally and critical hub for trade.

o In taking Amphipolis, Brasidas scored a psychological blow against the Athenian Empire and threatened some of its crucial commodities. The result was an almost total inversion of initial policies and strategies. Cleon, the Athenian, became the advocate of the direct approach and an unlimited objective, while Brasidas, the Spartan, executed an indirect strategy in the hopes of a negotiated settlement.

o The two men met at the battle of Amphipolis, and both were killed. With the two most strident hawks out of the way, cooler heads in Athens and Sparta prevailed, and they hammered out a peace.

The Peace

- As noted in Lecture 1, a great strategic theory addresses the how and why of ending wars. Thucydides shows us just how difficult it is to make peace in the first place and how hard it is to make peace last.

- During the plague, the Athenians sought terms, but the Spartans had little incentive to negotiate with a reeling Athens.

- After Cleon's victory at Pylos, it was the Spartans' turn to seek terms, but Cleon demanded too many concessions.

- After Amphipolis, both sides were bloodied and exhausted, but both sides also had leverage: Athens still has Spartan POWs and

Brasidas's men still occupied Amphipolis. This is almost the ideal circumstance for a negotiated settlement: exhaustion and leverage on both sides at the same time.

- The Peace of Nicias might have lasted were it not for two factors: Brasidas's men refused to give up Amphipolis, and many in Sparta and Athens viewed the peace more as a strategic pause than a permanent settlement.

Social and Moral Implications of War

- In the next lecture, we'll look at the decision of the citizens of Athens to destroy the city of Melos in 416 B.C. From that point forward, the democratic system in Athens, the source of its strength, began to implode. By the end of the war with Sparta, the Athenians were at war with themselves.

- Even the Spartans were spiritually and culturally challenged by this protracted conflict. True to Archidamus's prediction at the beginning, this war was bequeathed to another generation and Sparta was changed forever.

- In the process of defeating Athens, Sparta's frailties and systemic flaws were exacerbated, in particular its helot problem and its excessively stringent eugenics program. In victory, Sparta was fundamentally weakened as a great power.

Lessons for the Elephant

- Most people read Thucydides from the Athenian perspective. His injunctions seem primarily about how a rambunctious democracy can avoid self-defeating behavior in the course of a protracted conflict. At the same time, Sparta's ultimate victory gives us a glimpse into how a land power can exploit its strengths and compensate for its weaknesses.

- Victory over the Athenians took decades and required the Spartans to build a navy, cultivate creative and audacious admirals, and guarantee Persian financial support. That process fundamentally transformed Sparta but also weakened it fatally.

- From 412 onward, the Spartans cobbled together a large fleet, built and manned largely by Spartan allies and paid for by the Persians but commanded by Spartans. This fleet compounded Athenian overstretch and strained Athens' maritime lines of supply.

- The admiral Lysander understood the stress that Athens was under and sought to increase it. He initially avoided battle with the Athenian fleet but seized every opportunity to nibble away at the empire.

- When Lysander finally struck, at Aegospotami in 405, he bested the Athenian fleet and won a war that had lasted 27 years.

- Sparta's hegemony was undone shortly afterward by its replacement of democratic regimes with oligarchic tyrannies and the mobilization of Persia against it.

- In the final analysis, Sparta's command of the seas was built on shaky foundations. Sparta had its fair share of brilliant admirals, but it lacked the commercial dynamism, the seamanship, and the shipbuilding capabilities that Athens enjoyed at the height of its power.

Suggested Reading

Hanson, *A War Like No Other*.

Kagan, *The Peloponnesian War*.

Plutarch, "Alcibiades" and "Lysander" in *The Rise and Fall of Athens*.

Strassler, ed., *The Landmark Thucydides*.

Strauss, "Sparta's Maritime Moment."

1. According to Thucydides, what were the causes of the Peloponnesian War? Do you agree that these causes are timeless?

2. What best explains Athens' ultimate defeat: Spartan strategy or Athenian mistakes?

Thucydides on Strategy
Lecture 2—Transcript

Welcome back to *Masters of War* and to our discussion of Thucydides, son of Olorus, an Athenian. Thucydides' history of the Peloponnesian War is one of those gifts that keeps on giving. I first read Thucydides as an undergraduate in Western Civ. In that course, this book was a window onto ancient Greek culture and institutions. When I was a graduate student, Thucydides was a primer on international relations theory. Now as a professor of strategy and policy I look at Thucydides as a chronicler of war and as a great student of strategy. Talk to anyone who teaches a case study on Thucydides and they will tell you that they could easily fill an entire semester with this incredibly rich book.

Ask The Great Courses! They have a wonderful 36-lecture course by Professor Kenneth Harl that gives you a blow-by-blow, year-by-year account of the epic struggle between Athens and Sparta.

In this course we'll confine our discussion of Thucydides to the next two lectures. In this first I will be looking at the elements of Thucydides' narrative that best exemplify those criteria of theoretical brilliance that I talked about last time. I won't be doing this as systematically for all of our masters, but in this case it is necessary because the theory is so tightly enmeshed in the story, the history, that it is often difficult to separate the two. A little structure is therefore necessary.

In our previous lecture I claimed that a great strategic theorist is historically conscious and uses the study of history to accustom the mind to critical analysis. In his *History of the Peloponnesian War*, Thucydides satisfies this criterion admirably. He says in the introduction: "It will be enough ... if these words of mine are judged useful by those who want to understand clearly the events which happened in the past and which (human nature being what it is) will ... be repeated in the future."

Thucydides was not content to merely relate the events of the war between Athens and Sparta. This isn't history for history's sake; it is history as a form of instruction. In particular, Thucydides (an Athenian) wanted to explain the causes of Athens' defeat, so that future generations might avoid a similar fate.

In the next lecture we will go into much more detail on just how influential and instructional this history has been, but for now, suffice it to say that my students find the Peloponnesian War to be the richest and most relevant historical case study that we cover. So as a strategic theorist, Thucydides is clearly historically conscious, but what about the other criteria from our last lecture?

I also said that a great strategic theory should recognize that war serves a political purpose. On this count Thucydides also scores very well. In fact, he awakens us to two critical factors: the political origins of war and the possibility that two belligerents, two combatants, can have radically divergent political objectives.

On the origins of war, Thucydides' breaks them down in terms of proximate and underlying causes. There are three proximate or immediate causes of the Peloponnesian War. Firstly, in the years leading up to the outbreak of the war in 431 B.C. Athens backed the city of Corcyra in its war against Corinth. Corinth was the founder of Corcyra; it was also a Spartan ally. The Spartans then viewed this as Athenian meddling in their affairs. Secondly, in 433 Athens imposed a series of harsh economic sanctions on the city of Megara. Megara was also a Spartan ally and it sits astride the land route between the Peloponnese and Attica. Megara was geo-strategically critical to Sparta. If Megara is in hostile hands Sparta cannot march its great army out of the Peloponnese and project power. Finally, in 432 the Athenians launched an attack on the city of Potidea, another former Corinthian colony. These were the three pretexts that the Spartans claimed for declaring war on Athens. They were important factors, but Thucydides viewed these three crises as more catalysts for the war. The truest cause lay deeper.

As Thucydides himself puts it: "The 'truest' cause" was "the growth of the power of Athens, and the alarm that this inspired in Sparta." The dynamism of the Athenians and their restless expansionism posed an existential threat to the conservative Spartans and threatened to undermine their alliance. If Athenian expansion was not checked now, then Sparta would soon find itself ringed by Athenian proxies. For Sparta this was a preventive war. If this were not enough, Thucydides uses the origins of this war to give us one of the most succinct appraisals of what motivates states to seek empire: the lethal trifecta of fear, honor, and interest. Fear, honor, and interest is what drives Athenian expansion and it is also what alarms Sparta so deeply.

The second factor that Thucydides raises is that the different motivations that Sparta and Athens have for going to war directly influence their radically different political objectives. Sparta was highly militarized, but it was also deeply reluctant to go to war. As a result, Sparta only went to war for objectives of great value. But Athens, the sea-power, has a large and often unruly maritime empire. Its navy is constantly out there patrolling, constantly engaged in small wars of imperial policing. War wasn't a big deal to Athens.

Sparta's political objective was therefore unlimited: it was grand, it was "Free the Greeks." In other words to dismantle the Athenian empire and liberate Greek city-states from Athenian domination. For Pericles, the leading strategos, or general, of Athens, the goal appears limited: restore the status quo ante bellum and to get back to the business of dominating the Greek world through commerce and cultural imperialism. Pericles underestimated how scared and serious the Spartans were. As a result, he assumed that if Athens could hold out for a few years, then the Spartans would grow frustrated and return to the peace table.

The question remains, however, which of these radically different political objectives would exercise the greatest influence on the nature of the war? Would it be a limited war or an unlimited war? To determine that, we need to gauge the strengths and weaknesses of each side to determine the relative values of those political objectives and to gauge the capacity of each belligerent to compel the enemy to do his political will.

This brings us to another criteria for strategic brilliance: A useful framework for assessing the likely nature of the coming conflict. Here again, Thucydides scores very well, especially in terms of giving very detailed examples of net assessment. And remember what we mean by net assessment: the objective analysis of the strengths and weaknesses of each belligerent with an eye to how these relative attributes might interact in a war. In Thucydides, the initial net assessments are contained in the speeches by Pericles, the Athenian statesman, and Archidamus, the King of Sparta.

Pericles is more optimistic in appraising Athenian strengths especially in terms of time and money. This is not surprising: Pericles is trying to sell the war to his fellow citizens, but he still gives us great insights, especially into what he sees as Sparta's fundamental weakness, its economy.

Sparta is what we call an elephant; it's lumbering and powerful, but Spartan power was built on a problematic foundation. Generations earlier, the Spartans had defeated a people known as Messenians. The Messenians, called helots by the Spartans, were forced to till the lands of Sparta. The helots provided the agricultural surplus that allowed Sparta to maintain the only standing army in Greece. The armies of all the other Greek city-states were composed of citizen volunteers. Spartans did not farm, they did not trade, they did not manufacture. They trained for war. This had traditionally given Sparta the decisive edge in the gruesome art of Hoplite battle where discipline was everything. As you can imagine the helots were a mixed blessing since there was a constant threat of revolt. The helots made Sparta awesomely powerful in war, but they also made Sparta profoundly insecure.

Pericles also assesses that the Spartans cannot sustain a protracted war. In fact, he thinks they have been hectored into declaring war by their allies, especially the Corinthians. The Spartan alliance is another vulnerability that might be attacked.

In contrast to the optimism of Pericles, the speech of King Archidamus predicts a very hard slog if the Spartans and their allies are going to defeat Athens. The Spartans, he says, will bequeath this war to their children. To Archidamus, Athens is what we call the whale. It was everything that Sparta wasn't: dynamic, expansive, rich, and sea-going. Archidamus feels that his countrymen have grossly underestimated how much pain the Athenians can bear. But at the same time he recognizes that the basis of Athenian power, its maritime empire, was also a vulnerability.

Athens was a democracy but it was anything but democratic in dealing with its empire. Instead, it was a kind of Athenian protection racket. Athens demanded tribute to provide for the collective defense and to maintain the largest fleet in Greece.

Pericles also spent those allied contributions on public works projects and on festivals. This made Athens the cultural center of the Greek world, but it also antagonized its allies. Athenian power was further dependent on market access. Athens exported wine and olive oil and imported timber and grain. It also needed silver to keep the empire liquid. To Archidamus, the only hope of freeing the Greeks lay in dismantling Athens' political economy. To do that, Sparta needed a fleet, it needed a navy, and that would take a long time and a lot of Allied help.

So here, by using the voices of Pericles and Archidamus, Thucydides masterfully lays out a series of questions that must be asked and objectively answered so that a strategist can confidently claim to know the enemy and to know himself.

True to the Athenian predilection for prudence and self-restraint, Pericles' strategy was designed to frustrate Sparta to the point that they would sue for peace and accept Athenian domination of the Aegean. This strategy involved refusing to meet the Spartans in a pitched land battle. Instead it involved conducting punitive raids along the Peloponnese. Pericles was pursuing what we call a "negative aim." He wanted to get back to the status quo as opposed to a "positive aim," Which would be to change the status quo.

Crafting military action to a negative aim is particularly difficult. It was that much harder because while self-restraint was a virtue among the Athenians they were also steeped in the Homeric tradition of martial heroism. Pericles had to restrain those heroic passions, and Thucydides was generally impressed by Pericles' restraint and by his ability to convince the Athenians to follow his lead.

At this point I want to combine two of the criteria I introduced last time: leadership and the subordination of military action to political purpose. Thucydides gives us numerous profiles in leadership: good, bad, and mediocre. After Themistocles, the savior of Athens in the earlier wars against Persia, Pericles rates second as a leader in Thucydides' eyes. As we have seen, Pericles is striving to subordinate his strategy to Athens' larger interests. He was also blessed with the qualities of intellect, self-sacrifice, determination, and restraint: the attributes that Thucydides feels are most desirable in a leader. True, not all students of the Peloponnesian War are fans of Pericles. Some view him as too headstrong and others as too optimistic. But for now, let's stick to Thucydides' take.

Pericles knows Athens and he knows Sparta. He is rational and objective, he has a workable strategy, he is eloquent enough to convince the Athenians of the wisdom of his strategy, and he has both the determination and restraint to see that his painful and protracted strategy is implemented. Later Athenian statesmen, among them Cleon, Alcibiades, and Nicias all fall short as leaders in Thucydides' eyes.

I'll come back to Cleon in a few moments, but here I want to jump ahead to look at the disastrous leadership competition between Nicias and Alcibiades. Alcibiades figures very prominently in the second half of Thucydides' history. In fact he was one of Thucydides' main sources on events in Athens. Actually both of them are in exile in Asia minor. But rather than simply parroting Alcibiades, Thucydides turns him into a fascinating study in contrasts. Alcibiades, like Pericles, is brilliant, determined, and eloquent. He is also vain, self-serving, and impetuous. His strategic proposals are brilliant, such as his push for an alliance with the city of Argos in 420 B.C., but they often appear serve the best interests of Alcibiades, not necessarily the best interests of Athens.

Alcibiades was also the architect of the initial plan for the Sicilian expedition, we'll come back to that the next lecture, but his archrival was the pious and conservative Nicias. Nicias had all of the restraint and self-sacrifice of Pericles, but none of his imagination or eloquence. He opposed Alcibiades; he opposed Alcibiades' ambitious plans at every turn until he became a victim of his own rhetorical sleight-of-hand. He ended up in command of a Sicilian expedition that he had opposed from the outset and which he felt had been cursed by the Gods. The end result was a disaster. Nicias is exactly the wrong kind of leader.

At this point Thucydides' account begins to read like a Greek tragedy, with the poorly led Athenians engaging in self-defeating acts that weaken them relative to Sparta and that undermine their own alliance. One could spend years mining Thucydides for the do's and don'ts of strategic leadership.

Thucydides also does a very good job of highlighting interaction and adaptation. Since his great history covers three decades and consumes eight books, Thucydides is particularly rich on this subject, and if you'll indulge me I want to take a bit of extra time on this topic and walk through the first decade of the Peloponnesian War (otherwise known as the Archidamian War). To be honest it takes a little while for the interaction and adaptation game to really get going. In the opening stages of the war it seems that not only are Athens and Sparta pursuing different political objectives, they also seem to be fighting two different wars.

In contrast to Pericles' indirect approach, the Spartans march straight into Attica every year like clockwork, ravaging crops and trying to compel the Athenians to meet them in a battle that the Athenians are destined to lose. The Athenians wisely refuse to comply, so the Spartans march home.

The contrast between the hammer-headed Spartans and the elegant Pericles makes for fascinating seminar discussion about the general principles of strategy. Is it better to seek decisive victory by going directly at the enemy's army and his capital? Or is it better to attack his strategy or his alliances, use the indirect approach? Thucydides allows us to ponder both of these approaches, but he also gives us a rich chronicle of strategic adaptation and innovation. "Think," Thucydides tell us, "of the great part that is played by the unpredictable in war." "The longer a war lasts," he says, "the more things tend to depend on accidents."

The first stroke of accident was one that brought extremely bad luck for Athens. With the people crammed behind the walls, plague ravaged the city, killing between a quarter and a third of the population. Among the victims was the patient and moderate Pericles. Without Pericles, the Athenians divide into basically three camps. One wants to negotiate with Sparta to end the war. Another, dominated by Nicias, wants to stick with the initial strategy. A third group wants to take the war more aggressively to the Spartans.

The Athenians waver back and forth until fate intervenes again. In the Spring of 425 a detachment of Athenians was forced ashore by a storm at the town of Pylos on the coast of the Peloponnese. At Pylos, the Athenians decide to build a stone fort.

This is the homeland of Sparta's helots, and many start fleeing to Pylos. Alarmed at the prospect of a Helot revolt, the Spartans try to oust the Athenians from their fort, but the regiment of Spartan hoplites gets trapped on a small island called Sphacteria. This was a trivial little sideshow, and it probably would have stayed that way except for the fact that luck intervened again and produced one of the quirkiest interaction dynamics in the whole war.

Back in Athens, the hawkish demagogue Cleon promises a quick victory over the Spartans trapped on Sphacteria. True to his word, Cleon not only defeats them, but he takes more than a hundred Spartan hoplites prisoner. This was a huge blow to Sparta's prestige: Spartans don't surrender! And it caused them to change their political objectives from "Free the Greeks" to "Free our Greeks."

Desperate to get their hoplite warriors back, the Spartans offer terms and it looks like the Athenians have achieved their initial political objectives using just a slightly modified form of Pericles' initial strategy. But Thucydides shows us the natural tendency to overreach in moments of success. Remember Cleon? Cleon, hero of Sphacteria, has parlayed military success into political power. He's a strategos now. He demands even greater concessions from the Spartans. Cleon doesn't seem to really want peace. He instead wants to hold onto the hostages to keep Sparta at bay while he goes on the offensive against Sparta's allies.

Still desperate, the Spartans make one of their most innovative adaptations of the war. It is probably my favorite part of the entire book. The Spartans approve a plan hatched by a general named Brasidas, who wants to take a rag-tag force of mercenaries, disgraced Spartans and freed Helots and march overland into the Athenian rear area. The objective seems primarily just to create trouble.

An atypical Spartan, Brasidas is creative, flexible, and eloquent and he succeeds far beyond anyone's expectations. His ultimate coup is the capture of the city of Amphipolis. Amphipolis is not just an Athenian ally, it is also a critical node in the grain, timber, and silver trades. In one fell-swoop, Brasidas scores a psychological blow against the Athenian empire and threatens three of its crucial commodities. It is because of his failure to protect Amphipolis that Thucydides was cashiered and sent into exile. It is no surprise that he seems fixated on it.

More important than his personal stake, Thucydides gives us an almost total inversion of the initial policies and strategies. Cleon the Athenian is now the advocate of the direct approach and an unlimited objective. Brasidas the Spartan is executing an indirect strategy in the hopes of a negotiated settlement. The two men meet at the battle of Amphipolis, and both are killed. With the two most strident hawks out of the way, cooler heads in Athens and Sparta prevail and they hammer out a peace: a peace named after the leading member of the Periclean faction, Nicias.

Thus, in the midst of this remarkable history of war, Thucydides takes the time to look into what motivates nations to seek peace and shows why a durable peace is often hard to achieve: which answers another one of our criteria for strategic brilliance. A great strategic theory will address the how and why of ending wars. Thucydides shows us just how difficult it is to make peace in the first place and how hard it is to make peace last.

During the plague, the Athenians sought terms, but it seems that the Spartans had little incentive to negotiate with a reeling Athens. After Cleon's victory at Pylos, it was the Spartans' turn to seek terms, but Cleon demanded too many concessions. After Amphipolis both sides are bloodied and exhausted, but both sides also have leverage: Athens still has those Spartan POWs and Brasidas' men still occupy Amphipolis. This is almost the ideal circumstance for a negotiated settlement. Exhaustion and leverage on both sides at the same time. In fact, on paper Athens came out of the Peace of Nicias very well, they still had their empire and their trade and could make good on their losses. It was Sparta that was making the biggest concession to get their POWs back. By renouncing their "free the Greeks" objective they also lost credibility with their allies.

So it is an uneven peace to begin with, but it might have lasted, if it weren't for two things. One, Brasidas' men refused to give up Amphipolis, hence that critical trade hub was still in hostile hands. Two, many in Sparta and in Athens viewed the peace more as a strategic pause than as a permanent settlement. Chief among these Athenian opportunists was the charismatic and ambitious Alcibiades. We'll spend more time on Alcibiades next time. In the meantime, Thucydides shows us repeatedly why the results in war are rarely final.

At this point I have gone over pretty much all of the criteria for theoretical brilliance that I talked about last time. But each one of our masters is going to go above and beyond that list in some way. Sunzi will show us the power of intelligence and deception. Clausewitz will discourse on genius. Thucydides goes above and beyond on many counts, but I want to end here on two: first is his examination of the social and moral implications of war and second are his lessons for the elephant: in other words how a land power can defeat a sea power.

First the social and morals strains of war: In the next lecture we'll look at Athens' moral turning point in 416 B.C., when the citizens are called on to debate the fate of the city of Melos. The Athenians decide that Melos must be destroyed. From that point forward, the democratic system in Athens, the source of its great strength and dynamism, begins to implode. By the end of the war with Sparta, the Athenians are at war with themselves.

But even the Laconic Spartans find themselves spiritually and culturally challenged by this protracted conflict. True to Archidamus' prediction way back at the beginning, this war was bequeathed to another generation and Sparta was changed forever.

In the process of defeating Athens, Sparta's frailties and systemic flaws were exacerbated, in particular its Helot problem and its excessively stringent eugenics program. The Spartans were breeding themselves into extinction. In victory, Sparta was fundamentally weakened as a great power.

What about Thucydides' Lessons for the Elephant? Most people nowadays read Thucydides from the Athenian perspective. Therefore his injunctions seem primarily about how a rambunctious democracy can avoid self-defeating behavior in the course of a protracted conflict.

At the same time, Sparta's ultimate victory provides a glimpse into how a land power can exploit its strengths, compensate for its weaknesses, and defeat a sea power. Thucydides died before he could finish the last chapter of his history and we must rely on Xenophon and Plutarch for this part of the story, but it is clear throughout that Sparta's maritime transformation was a critical sub-plot for Thucydides.

Victory over the Athenians took decades and required the Spartans to build a navy, cultivate creative and audacious admirals, and guarantee Persian financial support. That process fundamentally transformed Sparta, but also weakened it fatally.

We usually think of Sparta essentially borrowing a navy from Persia and not really developing the foundation of true sea power. There is some truth to this. The financial backing of the Persians was critical to keeping the Spartans afloat. The Spartans didn't have a commercial empire to match that of Athens. The Spartan navy was also less prestigious than the Spartan army, home to a collection of misfits, half-breeds, and other atypical Spartans. Nonetheless, Spartan sea power was anything but superficial especially under the leadership of an admiral named Lysander.

Back at the beginnning of the war, Sparta's fleet was only 20 triremes as compared to 300 in the Athenian navy. In the early part of the war, the Spartans were dependent on Corinth for a navy. Over time, however, some in Sparta began to appreciate that only a navy under Spartan command could defeat Athens. After the Athenian disaster in Sicily, the time seemed ripe for Sparta to go to sea.

From 412 onward the Spartans cobbled together a large fleet, built and manned largely by Spartan allies and paid for by the Persians, but commanded by Spartans. A large and credible fleet compounded Athenian overstretch and put even greater strain on Athens' maritime lines of supply. Lysander understood the stress that Athens was under and tried to increase it. He did this initially by avoiding battle with the Athenian fleet, but seizing every opportunity to nibble away at Athens' empire. But when the opportunity presented itself, Lysander struck. His greatest victory came at Aegospotami in 405 B.C., where he bested an Athenian fleet of 180 triremes. In the course of an afternoon, Lysander won a war that had lasted 27 years.

But look what happened next. With Athens laid low, Sparta seizes control of its empire and replaced democratic regimes with oligarchic tyrannies. This proved to be a crucial mistake. Oligarchy was highly unpopular and for the first decade following their victory, the Spartan army and navy were busy putting down rebellions. The Persians now mobilized for war against Sparta and even former allies like Corinth started to maneuver against Sparta. Lysander was killed in battle in 395, and by 394 Sparta's short-lived naval hegemony was completely undone.

What lesson can we glean from that? Well, in the final analysis, impressive though it was, Sparta's command of the seas was built on shaky foundations. Sparta certainly had its fair share of brilliant admirals, but it lacked the commercial dynamism, the seamanship, and the ship building that Athens enjoyed at the height of its power. A modern land power like China contemplating a challenge to American maritime hegemony would be well-served by studying the example of Sparta. Here we see what it takes for an elephant to become whale. And we see that to beat the whale, a land power must become like the whale in all of the attributes of deep and sustainable maritime power.

Such a process requires fundamental transformations and can very easily threaten social upheaval. According to Thucydides, Archidamus saw this coming and grasped its significance. Therefore, in addition to the rich history and challenging theoretical insight, Thucydides' *History of the Peloponnesian War* anticipates the nature and use of sea power, a subject to which we will return in later lectures on Mahan and Corbett. It also provides potential lessons for emerging great powers in the 21st century.

But when we come back, we'll be looking at the depth, the breadth, and the often contradictory influence of Thucydides on Western strategic thought.

I'll see you then.

Thucydides as a Possession for All Time
Lecture 3

In this lecture, we will look at two vignettes from Thucydides's *History*, the Sicilian expedition of 415 to 413 B.C. and the Melian Dialogue of 416. We will also look at two contrasting interpretations of each vignette to gain an understanding of why this rich and ancient text still influences conflicting sides of contemporary debates about policy and strategy.

Background on the Sicilian Expedition

- In 421 B.C., the Athenians and the Spartans had concluded a peace treaty, but to the Athenian politician Alcibiades, the idea of peaceful coexistence with an unbroken Sparta was unrealistic. Only a major blow at Sparta's great hoplite army could shatter its grip over its Peloponnesian allies, and Alcibiades had a plan for achieving this objective.

- He cobbled together an alliance of Athens, Argos, and some other states to meet the Spartans in a battle at Mantinea (418 B.C.) that, it was believed, would break the Greek stalemate. Nicias opposed the scheme, and in the end, Athens committed only a small force, resulting in an indecisive battle.

- In 416 B.C., a delegation from allies in Sicily arrived in Athens to beg for aid against the rising power of two city-states: Selinus and Syracuse. These were both Dorian cities, which meant they had something of a cultural bond with Sparta and a potential hostility to Ionian Athens. Humbling Selinus and Syracuse presented another opportunity for Alcibiades to break the stalemate and lead a grand campaign.

- A campaign to Sicily had a number of elements in its favor, primarily the fact that its cities were fabulously wealthy. Further, the city of Segesta, in the western part of Sicily, was an ally of Athens and claimed it would cover the costs of the expedition. Syracuse, the strongest power in Sicily, would be inclined to side with Sparta in a war against Athens, and it was a major sea power. Athens saw value in a preventive war to check the rise of this potential naval competitor.

- Alcibiades lobbied hard for an expedition of 60 triremes to sail to Sicily, recruit allies, and either intimidate or beat Syracuse into submission.
  o The plan passed easily, and a shared command was selected that included both the bold Alcibiades and the prudent Nicias.

  o At a later assembly, Nicias spoke out against the intemperance of the expedition, but in 415, Athens sent more than 130 triremes and several thousand hoplites to Sicily. A second deployment of an additional 73 triremes and 5,000 more hoplites followed in 414.

  o By September 413, all of the hoplites were either dead or prisoners, and the triremes were either sunk or captured by the Syracusans and their Peloponnesian allies.

Conflicting Viewpoints

- The results in Sicily were a catastrophic combination of excessive caution and excessive bravado. Prudence and audacity are both necessary in war, but in the case of Sicily, the pendulum swung dangerously back and forth between these two virtues. An expedition boldly conceived by Alcibiades but cautiously executed by Nicias was the worst of all possible combinations.

- Thucydides's account of the Athenian disaster at Sicily is the richest, most detailed, and most dramatic section of his *History*.
  o Thucydides's take is that post-Pericles Athens was ruled by the mob and manipulated by political hacks, such as Alcibiades. Despite the claims of supporting allies in Sicily, the true objective was the outright conquest of the island.

- o Machiavelli agreed with Thucydides's critique of Athenian depravity. According to him, ancient Athens had become imbalanced. Democracy is good, but it must be balanced with elements of oligarchy: a powerful elite, such as the Roman Senate, and an executive element, such as Sparta's kings or Rome's consuls.

- The most prominent contemporary students of Thucydides challenge his account. According to the eminent Yale historian Donald Kagan, the Sicilian expedition was not an example of democracy out of control. Rather, it was a prudent, reasonable, and fairly low-risk strategy of imperial policing that was disastrously bungled by the cowardly and disingenuous Nicias.

- Sicily has become a test case for determining when it is a good idea to open or contest a new theater in an ongoing struggle, with several factors weighing both in favor of and against the expedition. The same questions that we ask about Sicily can also be applied to Vietnam and the U.S. invasion of Iraq. Was our democracy deranged, or was Iraq a good idea poorly executed?

The Melian Dialogue
- If Sicily is the military and strategic highpoint of Thucydides's *History*, then the Melian Dialogue is the moral and spiritual low point.

- In 416 B.C., the island of Melos was viewed as critical to Athens; its neutrality was considered more of an aid to Sparta than to Athens, and a potential Spartan ally in the Aegean was a potential liability for Athens. Thus, Athens sent a large force to Melos to present an ultimatum: submit to Athens and pay tribute or be destroyed.

- Thucydides's account of the negotiations between the Athenians and the Melians is one of the highlights of the *History*. The Melians appeal to justice, but justice, according to the Athenians matters only in disputes between states of equal power. In all other relations, the strong do what they will and the weak suffer what they must.

- The Melians decided to resist the Athenian force, but the city was eventually taken, all the men were killed, and all the women and children were sold into slavery. The city was then repopulated with Athenian colonists.

Interpreting the Melos Incident
- Two schools of political science have fixated on the Melian dialogue: the realists and the neoconservatives.

- In general, political realists view international relations as a state of anarchy, a realm of conflict and competition where calculations of relative power and self-interest almost invariably trump morality or justice.
  - Many of Thucydides's most important disciples, including Thomas Hobbes, Machiavelli, and the influential political scientist Hans Morgenthau, see an implicit endorsement of the realist perspective in his *History*, particularly in the Melian Dialogue.

  - Melos was technically neutral, but there were hints that it might have been aiding Sparta. Given this fact, the Athenian political demands seem fairly reasonable: If Melos became an Athenian ally, it could retain control of its domestic politics and enjoy the benefits of Athenian protection and free trade in the Aegean.

  - Further, the Athenians believed they couldn't back down from Melos precisely because of its weakness. If the Melians weren't punished for their defiance, dozens of other subject cities might be emboldened to revolt against Athens. We see here parallels to the Cold War and the domino theory.

- Neoconservatives have a radically different take on the Melian Dialogue. Leo Strauss, a political philosopher at the University of Chicago, saw a mirror for understanding the past, present, and future of America in the rise and fall of Athens.

o   In the decades after the Persian wars, Athens was a great force for good in the Greek world; it spread democracy and prosperity and held the barbaric Persians at bay.

o   Over time, however, Athens lost its way. Its great democracy was undermined by selfishness, moral depravity, and self-serving politicians. Its foreign policy became morally bankrupt, and its empire became a tyranny. The Melian Dialogue represents the depth of this tyrannical depravity.

o   The fact that the Athenians disdained morality and justice in favor of self-interest shouldn't be taken as an endorsement of realism but as an indictment of naked self-interest divorced from morality. Brutish imperialism de-legitimized a once just and good empire and began to drive Athens' natural allies into the camp of its blood enemies.

o   From a neoconservative perspective, what this meant for Athens—and what it potentially means for the United States— is that a foreign policy based on pure realism, a foreign policy based on cold-blooded calculations of relative power, undermines the power and legitimacy of a hard-won empire.

o   This is not an indictment of the Athenian Empire then or of American hegemony now. To neoconservatives, the root of the disparity between the earlier good Athens and the evil Athens on display at Melos lay in the moral collapse of the Athenian democracy. Athens' empire collapsed because its foreign policy had become immoral. Its foreign policy was immoral because its internal politics had become immoral.

o   Neoconservatives are concerned that a similar moral collapse may threaten the greatness of the United States on the world stage. What this means for war and strategy is that war can be just and can enhance a nation's power, but only if its purpose and conduct conform to the nation's core values.

Suggested Reading

Hale, *Lords of the Sea.*

Kagan, *The Peace of Nicias and the Sicilian Expedition.*

———, *Thucydides: The Reinvention of History.*

Strassler, ed., *The Landmark Thucydides*, Books V–VII.

Strauss, "Thucydides: The Meaning of Political History."

Walling, "Thucydides on Democratic Politics and Civil-Military Relations."

Questions to Consider

1. Was the Sicilian expedition a sound strategic choice? If so, why? If not, why not?

2. Which interpretation of Thucydides do you find most persuasive: the realist interpretation or the neoconservative interpretation? Why?

Thucydides as a Possession for All Time
Lecture 3—Transcript

As we heard in the last lecture, Thucydides wanted his great history to serve as a reflection on the enduring issues of war, strategy, and statecraft. It was intended to serve as a mirror to aid in good governance, good policy, and good strategy; a reflection on the good and bad decisions of the past. Or, as Thucydides puts it: his history was meant to be "a possession for all time." And if we take the legions of medieval and modern Thucydides fans at their word, then Thucydides succeeded admirably. For example, George Marshall famously said, "I doubt seriously whether a man can think with full wisdom and with deep convictions regarding certain of the basic issues today who has not at least reviewed the period of the Peloponnesian War and the fall of Athens."

Colin Powell had a Thucydides quotation framed and hung over his desk in the Pentagon when he was Chairman of the Joint Chiefs and over his desk at the State Department when he was Secretary of State. What was this quotation that Powell found so important? "Of all manifestations of power, restraint impresses men most."

Today we'll be looking at two vignettes from Thucydides' *History of the Peloponnesian War*, the Sicilian Expedition of 415 to 413 B.C. and the Melian Dialogue of 416. We will also be looking at two contrasting interpretations of each vignette. Hopefully this will give you a good idea of why this rich and ancient text can still influence conflicting sides of contemporary debates about policy and strategy.

In the last lecture I brushed past the Sicilian expedition in the interests of a general survey of Thucydides thoughts on war and strategy. Today we will return to Sicily in more detail, but we will be coming at it from two radically different perspectives. The first is a Machiavellian perspective that sees the decision to attack Sicily, particularly the city of Syracuse, as an archetype of a democracy deranged by demagogues and mob rule. The second perspective is one that we often employ at the Naval War College and is one that many contemporary interpreters of Thucydides gravitate toward. This perspective examines Sicily as a test case for the merits of opening a new theatre in an ongoing war.

First a little background on Sicily. As you will remember, in 421 B.C. the Athenians and Spartans concluded a peace treaty; the peace of Nicias. This agreement called for essentially a return to the status quo, albeit with a few minor modifications. Nicias, the Athenian statesmen, and Pleistoanax, one of the two Spartan kings, sincerely believed that peace between these two great powers was in the best interest of all. Others saw it merely as a strategic pause.

The charismatic and ambitious Alcibiades was one of the latter. To Alcibiades, peaceful coexistence with an unbroken Sparta was unrealistic. Only a major blow at Sparta's center of gravity, its great hoplite army, could shatter Sparta's grip over its Peloponnesian allies. Alcibiades came up with a particularly novel and relatively low-risk way of doing this. Argos, a perennial rival of Sparta, was perhaps the second greatest land power in the Greek world. The Argives were coming to the end of a peace treaty with Sparta and a new war was likely. Blessed with a brilliant strategic imagination and a gift for diplomacy, Alcibiades cobbled together an alliance of Athens, Argos, and other like-minded states to meet the Spartans in a battle that almost everyone believed would break the Greek stalemate. This was the Battle of Mantinea in 418 B.C.

In Alcibiades scheme, Argos and the other allies would provide the bulk of the hoplites and Athens would anchor the line. Nicias knew what was afoot and attempted to sink the Argive alliance as a way to protect the peace that bore his name. To Nicias, the political risks of reigniting a war with Sparta vastly outweighed whatever potential benefits might be gained by joining Argos. Alcibiades looked at it the other way around, low risk, high reward. In the end, Athens committed only a small force, not enough to swing the battle. The result was an indecisive battle that solved nothing.

Frustrated by that result, Alcibiades cast about for alternatives. In 416, a delegation from allies in Sicily arrived in Athens to beg for aid against the rising power of two city-states: Selinus and Syracuse. The two dominant ethnic groups in classical Greece were the Dorians and the Ionians, and the rivalry between Athens and Sparta roughly came down along this ethnic divide. Why is that important? Well, Syracuse and Selinus were Dorian cities, this meant that they had something of a cultural bond with Dorian Sparta and a potential hostility to Ionian Athens. Humbling Selinus and Syracuse presented another opportunity for Alcibiades to break the stalemate and lead a grand campaign.

For decades Sicily had been a kind of promised land for the Athenians. Its cities were fabulously wealthy; rich in grain, gold, and horses. Remember that Athens access to grain and precious metals was vulnerable to interdiction. This was why Amphipolis was so strategically significant. If Athens could control Sicily, however, it would have redundant sources of supply. Its imperial position would be unassailable. In fact, back in the 420s the Athenians had sent an expedition to Sicily to gauge pro-Athenian sentiment. That expedition met with mixed results, but many Athenians still longed to dominate Sicily. If anything the fall of Amphipolis only increased Athenian interest in Sicily.

A campaign to Sicily had a couple of other items in its favor. The city of Segesta, in the western part of Sicily, was an ally of Athens. And the Segestans claimed that they had more than enough money to cover the costs of the expedition, with the promise of additional loot after the defeat of Syracuse and Selinus. The Athenians sent a delegation to Segesta to investigate the claims. The ambassadors were dazzled by the fabulous gold adornments of each Segestan house they visited. Apparently they failed to notice that the Segestans had been moving the gold from house to house just prior to each Athenian visit.

Okay, so the Segestans were playing the Athenians, but a campaign in Sicily still made some strategic sense. Syracuse is the strongest power in Sicily. It is also Dorian city and is therefore inclined to side with Sparta and Corinth against Athens. Finally, Syracuse was a major sea power, with a large fleet. Therefore, some Athenians saw value in a preventive war against the rising power of Syracuse. Such a war would check the rise of a potential naval competitor and a possible ally of Corinth and Sparta.

Alcibiades lobbied hard for an expedition of 60 triremes to sail to Sicily, recruit allies, and either intimidate or beat Syracuse into submission. This is low risk, high reward. The plan passed easily and as was Athenian tradition, a shared command was selected including both the bold Alcibiades and the prudent Nicias.

But Nicias had second thoughts. At a later assembly, Nicias spoke out against the intemperance of the expedition and the self-serving aspirations of Alcibiades. With stunning eloquence, however, Alcibiades dismantled all of these counterarguments. Desperate to torpedo the whole affair, Nicias then tried to sober up the Athenians by arguing that if they were to go to Sicily, they would need a vastly bigger armada and a major contingent of ground troops. The ploy backfired and the assembly voted overwhelmingly to approve Nicias' recommendations. In the end Athens sent more than 130 triremes and several thousand Athenian and allied hoplites to Sicily in 415. A second deployment of an additional 73 triremes and 5,000 more hoplites followed in 414. By September 413, all of the hoplites were either dead or prisoners and the triremes either sunk or captured by Syracuse and its Peloponnesian allies.

What you end up with in Sicily is a catastrophic combination of excessive caution and excessive bravado. Prudence and audacity are both necessary in war, but in the case of Sicily the pendulum swings dangerously back and forth between these two virtues. An expedition boldly conceived by Alcibiades but cautiously executed by Nicias was the worst of all possible combinations. Thucydides account of the epic Athenian disaster at Sicily is the richest, most detailed, and most dramatic section of his *History*.

Where you come down on the Sicilian expedition will probably depend on who you blame for the disaster. Do you blame the vain and devious Alcibiades and the Athenian mob? Or do you blame Nicias? Nicias, who finds himself in sole command of an expedition that he opposed from the outset and which he felt had been cursed by the gods; Nicias, who is reduced to strategic paralysis and who prefers to die with honor in Sicily than face condemnation in Athens. Regardless of which side you come down on, you will find yourself in illustrious company.

If you blame Alcibiades, the demagogue, and the mob you are in the camp of Thucydides and Machiavelli. Thucydides' take is that post-Pericles Athens is ruled by the mob and manipulated by political hacks like Alcibiades. Despite the claims of supporting allies in Sicily, the true objective is the outright conquest of the island. This fires the passions of the Athenians and it promises everlasting income to the professional rowers of Athens who man the merchant fleet and the navy and who vote in the assembly. The tragic and gruesome details of what happens to the Athenians in Sicily only magnify the depravity of the initial decision to launch the expedition. In contrast we have the people of Syracuse. Syracuse is something of a hero in this story. Syracuse is a younger and more moderate version of Athens. The Syracusans deserve to win their war against the rapacious invader from Athens.

In contrast to Spartan balance, Athens' pure democracy breaks down into mob rule. Then demagogues like Alcibiades who are gifted speakers can sway the mob to endorse policies and strategies that suit their own personal interests. So that's one way of looking at the Sicilian debacle: Blame Alcibiades and Athenian mob rule.

If on the other hand you blame Nicias for both the scale of the expedition and the flawed execution of the Sicilian campaign, then you find yourself in the company of many of the most prominent contemporary students of Thucydides. Among this group is Donald Kagan, the eminent Yale historian and classicist who finds another interpretation in Thucydides' account.

According to Kagan, the Sicilian expedition is not an example of democracy out of control. Rather we have what looks like a prudent and reasonable, and even fairly low-risk strategy of imperial policing and modest expansion that is bungled into disaster by the cowardly and disingenuous Nicias.

That brings me to the issue of how we treat Thucydides at the Naval War College. The Peloponnesian War entered our curriculum in the mid-1970s when the U.S. military was still coming to grips with the loss in Vietnam. Vietnam could not be discussed objectively in seminar, but Athens, Sparta, and Sicily could. In this context the struggle between Athens and Sparta stood in for the Cold War and Sicily stood in for Vietnam.

Sicily became a test case for figuring out when it is a good idea to open or contest a new theatre in an ongoing struggle. A favorite question of mine is "Was Sicily a good idea badly executed or a bad idea?" Good idea means did it make sound strategic sense? We can all agree that the execution was badly botched and violated many of the principles of war, but even with the disaster was it still a good idea to aid Segesta and to check the rise of Syracuse? Forty years after its introduction it is still a lively debate.

So, what makes Sicily a good strategic choice? For one, resources: There's grain, gold, and horses (very rare in Greece). Two, credibility: You're supporting allies; you have a moral obligation to liberate fellow democrats from the yoke of Syracuse. Three: You're checking a rising power who might one day might ally with your enemies and perhaps use his growing arsenal of triremes (of mass destruction) to attack you. Then there's passion: This is an outlet for the restless energies of the Athenians.

But what makes Sicily a bad strategic choice? One, there's distance: It's far away; the logistics would be a nightmare. Two, the ally: Segesta? That ally might be playing you. Three: A preventive war against Syracuse actually makes an enemy out of a neutral. And finally, passions: Passions and vanity might be getting the better of reason.

We can ask these same questions about Vietnam and a similar debate could be raised about the United States' decision to invade Iraq in 2003. Was our democracy deranged, was passion manipulated by demagogues? Or was Iraq a good idea poorly executed? A near total disaster averted only by the assignment of a new general, David Petraeus?

If you think this is just academic musing in some seminar room, think back to how these conflicting interpretations of Thucydides actually informed the Iraq debate. Remember Colin Powell, Secretary of State, talking about the importance of restraint. Paul Wolfowitz, deputy to Donald Rumsfield, much more of the Kagan school, he highlighted the favorable conditions for transforming Iraq.

Now that we've examined the Sicilian expedition, let's turn to another part of Thucydides' *History*. If Sicily is the military and strategic crescendo, the climax, of Thucydides' great history, then the Melian Dialogue is its moral and spiritual low point.

Melos lies in the Aegean Sea a couple of hundred miles to the southeast of Athens. It is actually kind of a backwater. Even today the population of the island is less than 5,000 people. In 416, however, Melos was viewed as critical to Athens. This is three years before the Sicilian defeat and, remember, we are still within the Peace of Nicias. In other words, a truce exists between Athens and Sparta. We are also fresh off the indecisive battle of Mantinea. Melos has some ties to Sparta, it's a Dorian island, but it has been technically neutral throughout the first 15 years of the Peloponnesian War. In the eyes of the Athenians, however, Melos' neutrality is more of an aid to Sparta than to Athens. A potential friend of Sparta in the Aegean is a potential liability for Athens.

In 416 Athens sends a force of 38 ships and nearly 2,000 warriors to play hardball with the Melians. They present Melos with an ultimatum: submit to Athens and pay tribute or be destroyed. The Melian leaders ask for a private meeting with the Athenian delegation. What follows in Thucydides' account is a masterpiece of classical Greek point–counterpoint, a highly stylized exchange between anonymous Athenians and equally anonymous Melians. This is the Melian Dialogue of 416 and it is really one of the highlights of an already great piece of literature. In general, the Melians appeal to justice. They appeal to what is right. After all the Athenians are asking a free and neutral people who have not actively fought against Athens to submit to the Athenian yoke.

The Melians ask, "Why is it good for us to be the slaves as for you to be the masters?" The Athenians respond, "You, by giving in, would save yourselves from disaster; we, by not destroying you, are able to profit from you." So the Melians counter, "Well, will you not agree to our being neutral, friends instead of enemies, but allies of neither side?" "No," the Athenians said, "because it is not so much your hostility that injures us; it is rather the case that, if we were on friendly terms with you, our subjects would regard that as a sign of weakness in us, whereas your hatred is evidence of our power."

In perhaps the most famous part of the dialogue, the Athenians rebuff the Melian appeal to justice. Justice they say only matters in disputes between states of equal power. In all other relations the strong do what they will and the weak suffer what they must.

The Melians, seeing that there is no chance of getting the Athenians to back down, trust their fate to the gods and maybe to their distant Spartan cousins and decide to resist the huge Athenian force that has landed on their shores. The gods and the Spartans ignore their pleas. The city is eventually taken, all the men are put to the sword and all of the women and children are sold into slavery. The city is then repopulated with Athenian colonists and, from an Athenian perspective, the Melos problem is solved.

When you look at the grand scope of the three-decade struggle between Athens and Sparta, the Melos incident is only a blip on the radar, but Thucydides pays an awful lot of attention to it. The vignette closes the fifth of his eight books. Because Thucydides thinks it matters, his students and critics have also paid an awful lot of attention to Melos and the Melian Dialogue. In particular two schools of political science fairly fixate on the Melian Dialogue: The realists and the neo-conservatives.

Let's start with the realist take on the Melian Dialogue. To realists, and there are many different schools of political realism, but in general realists view international relations as a state of anarchy, a realm of conflict and competition where calculations of relative power and, most important, self-interest almost invariably trump morality or justice.

Many of Thucydides' most important disciples, folks like Thomas Hobbes, Machiavelli, and the influential political scientist Hans Morgenthau, to name just a few, see in his *History of the Peloponnesian War* an implicit endorsement of the realist perspective. Nowhere is this more the case than in the Melian Dialogue, where the Athenians deride the morality and justice arguments of the idealistic Melians and claim instead that "might makes right."

There is a lot of merit to this interpretation, right? Melos is in the Aegean, smack dab in the middle of Athens sphere of influence. Yes, it is technically neutral but there were hints that they might have been aiding Sparta. In addition, even if they were strictly neutral, Melian neutrality can easily be seen as a direct benefit to Sparta. Given that rationale, Athenian political demands look fairly reasonable, some might say appealing to the Melians. Become an ally, pay us tribute and you can keep your lives and your city. You can also keep control of your domestic politics. In addition, you are now part of the Athenian protection racket and the Aegean free trade zone. Your tribute helps pay for the navy that secures the Aegean you now have access to markets across the Greek world. Not a bad trade, especially given that the alternative is extermination.

Of course, we need to remember that many Greeks viewed any cession of political sovereignty as equal to slavery. If the Melians submit they become slaves and they have willingly forsaken the justness of their cause for the narrow self-interest of survival. Well, if those are the Athenian carrots, the Athenian stick might also be reasonable, rational, realist.

"Why do you threaten to destroy us if we do not submit?" The Melians ask. "We are nobodies. We are weak." The Athenians reply: "It is precisely because you are weak that your defiance demands your destruction. If you were strong and we backed down, that wouldn't really hurt our reputation. But if you are weak and we back down, then we are the ones who look weak. Reputation is everything. If we don't punish you for your defiance then other weak states, dozens of our subject cities perhaps, may be emboldened to revolt against Athenian hegemony."

Think here of the natural parallels to the Cold War and to the domino theory. Could the United States have tolerated Soviet proxies in the Caribbean and Latin America? Could the Soviets have tolerated the Czechs or the Poles diverging from the policies of Moscow? Great powers often feel compelled to resort to war to prevent that first domino from falling.

Realists of all stripes, therefore, point regularly to the Melian Dialogue as the first and perhaps the purest exposition and endorsement of the central tenets of realism in international relations. Neo-conservatives see something radically different in the Melian Dialogue.

In a 2003 essay in the *Weekly Standard*, Irving Kristol wrote that thanks to the work of scholars like Donald Kagan and Leo Strauss, Thucydides had become the favorite neo-conservative text on foreign affairs. We have already seen that Kagan challenges Thucydides own interpretation of Sicily to make the case that foreign expeditions, especially those that support allies and check aggressive rising powers, can be sound strategic choices. Leo Strauss was a University of Chicago political philosopher who re-imagined the story of the Peloponnesian War as a great tragedy, the hero of which is Athens itself. To Strauss, Athens in the decades after the Persian War was a great force for good in the Greek World. It spread democracy, it spread prosperity, it expanded civilization, and it held the barbaric Persians at bay.

It can do all of that because it is first and foremost well governed and because Athenians remain true to their moral principles and to their concepts of justice. Athenians were rightly proud of this exceptionalism and Athens' neighbors were rightly drawn to it as a model worthy of emulation and rightly accepted that Athens deserved her empire. During its rise, therefore, the Athenian empire was a beacon of morality and justice. And it was indispensible to the collective security of the Greek world. At the same time, Athens' greatness created enemies that had to be dealt with.

To Strauss, the rise and fall of Athens was a mirror for understanding the past, present, and future of America and the American empire. Neo-conservatives have carried the analogy even further.

Over time heroic Athens loses its way. There is some inkling of this during the time of Pericles, but post-Periclean Athens completely loses its moral compass. Its democracy is undermined by selfishness, moral depravity, and self-serving politicians. By extension, Athenian foreign policy becomes morally corrupt and its empire becomes a tyranny. The Melian Dialogue represents the depths of this tyrannical depravity.

The very fact that the Athenians disdain morality and justice and trumpet self-interest shouldn't be taken as an endorsement of realism, it should be taken as an indictment of naked self-interest divorced from morality. It helps that the Melian Dialogue takes place behind closed doors. Most of the other speeches in Thucydides are public and the speakers usually make some nod toward justice or morality. At Melos, we see the Athenians for what they have truly become.

Athens naked realism at Melos is emblematic of the unabashed self-interest of the now-corrupted Athenians. Brutish imperialism delegitimizes a once just and good Athenian empire and begins to drive Athens' natural allies into the camp of its blood enemies.

The Melians warn the Athenians that they are on a slippery slope that may very well end in terrible retribution. Thucydides may be foreshadowing the cruel fate that the Athenians meet in Sicily three years later.

The Melians also hold up the mirror of Athens past, the great heroic Athens, Athens that defied the Persians, Athens the beacon of freedom, they hold that mirror up to the tyrannical Athenians that they are meeting that day. Had they listened to the Melians, the Athenians might have been able to save themselves. Instead the Athenian delegation to Melos mocks the gods, they mock morality, and they mock the very things that made Athens great. They deserve whatever fate they get.

From a neo-conservative perspective what this means for Athens, and what it potentially means for the United States, is that a foreign policy based on pure realism, a foreign policy devoid of morality and values, a foreign policy based on cold-blooded calculations of relative power, undermines the power and legitimacy or your hard-won empire.

But this is not an indictment of the Athenian empire then or of American hegemony now. The early Athenian empire was just, it was good, and it was deserved. At Melos, however, Athens was unjust, evil, and deserving only of condemnation. To neo-conservatives the root of the disparity between good Athens and evil Athens lay in the moral collapse of the Athenian democracy. Athens' empire collapsed because its foreign policy had become immoral. Its foreign policy was immoral because its internal politics had become immoral.

Neo-conservatives today are concerned that a similar moral collapse may threaten the greatness of the United States, especially on the world stage.

What this means for war and strategy is that war can be just and can enhance your power, but only if its purpose and conduct conform to your core values. For example, from a neo-conservative perspective the war in Iraq was morally right, not because of realist rationales of checking aggression or securing resources, but because it promised to liberate the Iraqi people.

I am not going to tell you where I come down on any of these debates, either Sicily or the Melian Dialogue, but I encourage you to take the time read the Melian Dialogue and the section in Thucydides on the Sicilian expedition and decide for yourself if one, the other, or none of these interpretations satisfy.

Even if you can't make up your mind, a few hours spent in a virtual conversation with Thucydides will be time very well spent. And if you think you've heard the last of Thucydides, don't worry, he'll be haunting many lectures to come.

When next we meet, however, we'll be moving from ancient Greece to ancient China and delving into Sunzi's *The Art of War*. We'll be trading hoplites and triremes for crossbows and chariots. In many ways, ancient Greece and ancient China could not possibly have been more different in politics, in geography, in culture, in religion, and in warfare. Moreover, both of those ancient worlds were radically different from our own. And yet both Sunzi and Thucydides are required reading in the best civilian and military strategy programs today. I assume you already have a sense for why this is the case with Thucydides and in the next two sessions we'll see why the Sunzi may also rank as "a possession for all time."

I'll see you then.

Sun Tzu's *The Art of War*
Lecture 4

S un Tzu's *Art of War* is the world's most widely read and most frequently quoted (and misquoted) work of strategic theory. As one of the great books on leadership, it is required reading in military academies and business schools. Interestingly, the name of the book is not *The Art of War* but more accurately translated as *Master Sun's Military Methods*. More than a book about war, it is, thus, about the totality of the military as an institution and an instrument. In this lecture, we'll examine the history of the book, discuss the basic elements of its theory on the use of the military, and explore how a "superior general" might put this theory into practice.

What Is the *Sunzi*?

- The standard version of the *Sunzi* comprises 13 essays attributed to Master Sun. Given that they purport to be the words of a master, they appear to be statements of truth, free from the extensive supporting analysis and historical examples that we will see in Clausewitz and Machiavelli.

- Because the *Sunzi* is written in a terse style, individual passages read as discrete pearls of wisdom that are easily divorced from the rest of the text. For example: "The Supreme Excellence is to achieve victory without resort to battle."

- The *Sunzi* is a coherent and intellectually challenging strategic theory. The arguments build to a rhetorical crescendo; the language is consistent and purposeful; and the author mercilessly pushes a theoretical agenda.

History behind the *Sunzi*

- The *Sunzi* begins: "Master Sun said: 'The use of the military is the greatest affair of the state. It is the terrain of life and death, the path of survival and ruin. It must be studied.'" This statement is obvious from a 21st-century perspective, but why did the author feel obligated to make such a statement and to make it his opening salvo?

- The Zhou kingdom (1100–256 B.C.) consisted of several hundred feudal states that declared their loyalty to the Zhou king as the universal sovereign. From the 8th century onward, the authority of the king was buttressed by the growing military power of neighboring dukes, who came to be called hegemons.

- The first hegemon of the northern state of Qi implemented a series of institutional reforms that transformed Qi from a loose confederation of clans into a bureaucratically managed autocracy. In the process, the duke dramatically increased Qi's military power, which he used to defend the northern frontier and control the ambitious Chinese states to the south.

- Along with these institutional innovations came changes in the nature of war. In the 7th century, war was seasonal and highly ritualized, and battles between chariot-mounted aristocrats might involve only a few thousand men on both sides. By the end of the 6th century, there were infantry armies of more than 100,000.

- It was at this moment that the general Sun Wu appeared. Sun Wu was born in Qi, but he made his name in the service of the southern state of Wu against its western neighbor, Chu. In 509 B.C., Sun Wu achieved a dramatic victory over Chu, but the triumph of Wu proved short-lived. The state was ultimately conquered by one of its southern neighbors.

- In the two centuries after the fall of Wu, war accelerated in scale, breadth, and lethality. In the Warring States era (5th–3rd centuries B.C.), we see ever larger and better organized states. By the 4th century, when the *Sunzi* was written (c. 330–320 B.C.), only seven large states remained. In other words, it was composed in a context in which multiple states were large and lethal enough to compete for control of all of China.

- We would think that such dramatic changes in the scale and scope of warfare would demand a complete reappraisal of the military ethos, but aristocratic values of heredity, privilege, and personal valor still prevailed. The *Sunzi*, with its anti-heroic bent, was an argument against that fundamental contradiction.

- The *Sunzi* is not just a critique of aristocratic pretensions, however; it is also an assault against moral philosophers, like the Confucians, whose goal was to restore harmony within China's social and political institutions by returning to the moral tenets of the founders of the Zhou dynasty. In contrast to Confucian morality and ritual, the *Sunzi* claims that the professional management and use of mass infantry armies is "the greatest affair of the state."

The *Sunzi* as a Work of Strategic Theory

- The *Sunzi* makes three major claims: (1) that the text contains the wisdom of Sun Wu, who deserves the title of master (*zi*), a thinker on par with the greatest philosophers; (2) that the sole purpose for the existence and employment of the military is to increase the wealth and power of the state; and (3) that the general must wield the military with the same skill and autonomy with which a master swordsman handles his weapon.

- We can see these three claims in stark relief in the very first line of the text and peppered throughout the book. For example, on the purpose of the military, the *Sunzi* says, "If it does not profit the state, do not use the military." On the autonomy of the general, it says, "The ruler who has able generals and who does not interfere in their affairs will be victorious."

- With the historical background we now have, we realize that what initially sound like bland platitudes are actually part of a radical and relentless sales pitch that demands a coldly rational, anti-heroic, and almost superhuman approach to war.

- The author of the *Sunzi* was not satisfied with the way in which states were conducting wars, and he didn't approve of the criteria for command. Thus, the *Sunzi* presents a revolutionary ideal that is vastly superior to the aristocratic/heroic ideal that sees battle as ritual and to the Confucian disdain for military affairs.

- As much as the *Sunzi* is an elaborate assault on amateurish, vain aristocrats and on naïve Confucian moralists, it is also a spirited delineation and defense of the realm of authority and expertise that defines the professional general.

Theoretical Prescriptions
- From the three major claims of the *Sunzi*, we can derive the three core theoretical prescriptions of the book: Be efficient, avoid protraction, and value the commander's intellect and skill above all else.

- In order for a state to survive and to win wars, it must make efficient use of its resources, while always keeping an eye on the ultimate benefit to the state. Chapter III of the *Sunzi* lays out a continuum from the most to the least efficient strategies that moves from attacking the enemy's strategy to attacking its alliances, armies, and finally, cities.

- The second of the *Sunzi*'s core theoretical prescriptions is to avoid protraction. This is an important theme in the work. In fact, all of Chapter II is concerned with the dangers and costs of protracted operations. Protraction poses a mortal danger to both belligerents, from which neither side benefits.

- The third prescription of the *Sunzi* places an emphasis on the intellectual, as opposed to the heroic, qualities of the commander. The intellectual qualities enable the general to master the totality of the military as both an institution and an instrument and are critical to the successful performance of net assessment.
  o The first chapter of the *Sunzi* gives us five categories of net assessment to determine the nature of a looming conflict: (1) the spiritual strength of a state, that is, its ability to mobilize, to make sacrifices, and to resist the enemy's attempts at subverting

its resolve; (2) the environment; (3) the terrain; (4) command, that is, the talent of the general, the pivotal figure who must manipulate these elements; and (5) method—logistics, staffing, discipline, and organization.

o With the *Sunzi*, command is no longer based on aristocratic pedigree; it is an intellectual enterprise, based on the ability to test and process these five elements and craft strategy in accord with their subtle variations.

Theory into Practice

- The first key to putting this theory into practice is to have superior intelligence and, at the same time, to limit an opponent's access to intelligence.

- The second key is operational initiative. Keep the enemy off balance by employing both conventional and unconventional forces and through deception. Use intelligence and deception to distract, anger, or win over the opposing general. Take the war to the enemy by invading its territory to multiply the stresses on its institutions and society.

- The third key is knowing when and where to deliver the decisive blow. Create and exploit the situation where you can make the best use of your resources. Know how to position your troops to maximize their destructive impact on the enemy.

- The successful commander must study the field of engagement, weigh the strengths and weaknesses of the military forces, plumb the will and intentions of the adversary, and gauge the mood of the troops.

Modern Applicability

- The *Sunzi* provides the modern soldier, businessperson, and sports coach with a wealth of advice that is intensely appealing but often difficult to follow in practice.

© Jupiterimages/Pixland/Thinkstock.

The promise of big rewards at low risks explains the appeal of the *Sunzi* in the world of business.

- In reading the *Sunzi*, we should ask ourselves whether it deemphasizes the interactive nature of war, whether its apparent faith in the clarity and utility of espionage and intelligence is realistic, and whether war or business or sports can be as rational and antiseptic as the text seems to promise.

- The *Sunzi* highlights many of the enduring tensions between the military and the politicians it serves, but it is essential not to confuse the judicious exercise of political authority over the military with the amateurish interference of a Warring States aristocrat in the serious business of war.

- The *Sunzi* does not have a monopoly on wisdom, but reading it carefully and understanding the author's larger purpose can be a marvelous educational experience and may improve the chances of success in any field.

Suggested Reading

Meyer and Wilson, "*Sunzi Bingfa* as History and Theory."

Sun Tzu, *The Art of War* (translated by Samuel B. Griffith).

————, *The Art of Warfare* (translated by Roger Ames).

Questions to Consider

1. Does placing Sun Tzu's *The Art of War*, or any other strategic classic, in its historical context increase or decrease its contemporary utility?

2. What are the most important qualities of Sun Tzu's ideal military commander?

Sun Tzu's *The Art of War*
Lecture 4—Transcript

Sun Tzu's *The Art of War* is the world's most widely read work of strategic theory. Among our masters, it's the most frequently quoted (and misquoted). As one of the great books on leadership, it is required reading in military academies, staff colleges, and even business schools. It has spawned an entire cottage industry of pop strategy manuals claiming Sunzi's relevance to sports, business, and in one case even romance. It has been quoted in many films and on television shows as varied as *The Simpsons* and *The Sopranos*.

So what is it about this short, spare book written well over 2,000 years ago that inspires so much interest? One expert to called it the concentrated essence of wisdom on the conduct of war. Why?

Before I answer that, I am going to let you in on a couple of secrets. The first is that the name of the book is not *The Art of War*. Rather *Sunzi bingfa*, its Chinese title, which I am pronouncing in modern Mandarin, is more accurately translated as *Sun* (a surname) *zi* (the master) *bing* (military) and *fa* (method). *Master Sun's Military Methods*. This book is about much more than war. It is about the totality of the military as an institution and as an instrument of statecraft.

The second secret is that this text was not written by Master Sun, the general named Sun Wu who lived at the end of the 6th century B.C. That is why I refer to the book by its title, *Sunzi* or *The Sunzi*, rather than saying Master Sun says this, or Master Sun says that. Instead, what is happening is that an anonymous 4th century author has appropriated Sun Wu's military credentials.

That author calls General Sun "master" because he wants to claim that the military is on par with governance, morality, and ritual: the traditional topics of other Chinese masters, such as Master Kong Fu, Kongfuzi, who you know as Confucius. This claim of master status for General Sun is important if we are to understand why this seemingly bland collection of platitudes is actually a revolutionary manifesto on generalship.

So now that I've let you in on a couple of secrets about the book, let's think about the *Sunzi*'s appeal. One reason that it is so potent derives from the promises of winning without fighting and achieving strategic surprise through deception and maneuver. These were obviously appealing to western audiences in the aftermath of World War I and World War II and perhaps are even more so today when our adversaries appear less and less vulnerable to the conventional, to the American way, of war.

The promise of big rewards at low risks also explains the *Sunzi*'s appeal in the world of business. In addition, the pithiness of the *Sunzi* makes it a useful tool for would-be strategists, those guys who want to validate their theories with reference to the classics. This can lead some people to cherry-pick the text. You know, something like peppering their Powerpoint presentations with pithy platitudes plucked from these pages. At least, I am glad that they are reading it.

Finally some of the current fascination with this ancient classic can be attributed to interest in and concerns about the rise of China. Some may seek in the pages of this book insight into the strategic inclinations of the People's Republic of China.

There is nothing wrong with reading the *Sunzi* from any of these perspectives, but I think that before we try to apply this ancient book to our contemporary problems we might want to arm ourselves with a bit more background. The *Sunzi* wasn't written for us, so before we try to gauge its contemporary utility it is a good idea to understand who it was written for and what it was written against.

As such, I have divided my comments today into three overlapping topics. The first is an examination of the history of the book. Here, I am not just talking about the unique historical conditions that gave rise to this particular view on strategy and war, but also about the fact that this book is a reaction against those historical conditions.

This is not to say that only those with an encyclopedic knowledge of ancient China can understand this book. But a little knowledge goes a long way. A little knowledge of the *Sunzi* as a historical artifact and as a historical event will make you a better-educated and more objective consumer of its theoretical and practical content. After we've examined the history, we'll discuss the basic elements of the *Sunzi*'s theory on the use of the military. Then, as our third topic, we'll talk about the "Superior General" and how he might put that theory into practice.

So let's begin with the book as a historical artifact and historical event. What is the *Sunzi* anyway? The standard version of the book comprises 13 essays attributed to Master Sun. Given that they purport to be the words of a Master, they appear to be statements of truth, free from the extensive supporting analysis and numerous historical examples that we will see in Clausewitz and Machiavelli.

In addition, the *Sunzi* is written in a very terse style. As such, individual passages read (in both English and Chinese) as discrete pearls of wisdom that are easily divorced from the rest of the book. For example, and I quote, "The Supreme Excellence is to achieve victory without resort to battle." That may sound great, but when taken out of context is about as useful as advising a rookie Wall Street investor to buy low and sell high.

Many versions of the *Sunzi* also intersperse commentaries with the original text. When a translation is formatted like this, we tend to lose sight of its original coherence. In actuality the *Sunzi* is a coherent and intellectually challenging strategic theory. The arguments build to a rhetorical crescendo, the language is consistent and purposeful, and the author mercilessly pushes a theoretical agenda.

Master Sun says, "The use of the military is the greatest affair of the state. It is the terrain of life and death, the path of survival and ruin, it must be studied." That's how the book starts.

This statement is obvious from a 21st-century perspective, but why did our author feel obliged to make such a statement, and make it the opening salvo of this book?

To answer that requires a brief digression into Chinese history. From 1100–256 B.C. China was ruled by a dynasty called the Zhou. Under the early Zhou, the kingdom consisted of several hundred feudal states, which declared their loyalty to the Zhou king as the universal sovereign. The moral basis of Zhou rule, known as heaven's mandate, derived from the king's benevolence and from his role as the ultimate arbiter between Heaven and Earth. From the 8th century on, however, the Zhou's moral authority had to be buttressed by the growing military power of neighboring dukes, rulers who came to be called hegemons (they were the protectors of the Zhou order).

The first hegemon was the duke of the northern state of Qi. The duke of Qi implemented a series of institutional reforms that transformed Qi from a loose confederation of clans into a bureaucratically managed autocracy. In the process, the duke dramatically increased Qi's military power, which he used to defend the northern frontier and to control the rambunctious and ambitious Chinese states to the south. This was the job of the hegemon.

Along with these institutional innovations, war was changing. In the 7th century war was seasonal and highly ritualized. Battles between chariot-mounted aristocrats might involve a few thousand men on both sides, but by the end of the 6th century we have infantry armies of more than 100,000. That's when General Sun Wu appears.

Sun Wu was born in Qi and hence was an expert on the institutional and organizational revolution that had made the Duke of Qi the first hegemon. But it was in the service of the southern state of Wu that he made his name. In the late 6th century, Wu was locked in a contest for dominance with its western neighbor, Chu.

King Helü of Wu had the services of an able minister, Wu Zixu, himself an exile from Chu. Wu Zixu's two notable qualities were his eye for talent and his unremitting desire for revenge against Chu (the king of Chu had killed his father).

In 509 B.C., Wu Zixu convinced the king, King Helü, to entrust his armies to Sun Wu who achieved a dramatic victory over Chu. That victory elevated the King of Wu to the status of hegemon, but Wu's triumph proved short-lived. Helü's successor weakened the kingdom through a series of protracted wars.

In the end, Wu was ultimately conquered by one of its southern neighbors, that state in turn was ultimately destroyed by a resurgent Chu.

To anyone reading the *Sunzi* when it appeared in the late 4th century, 200 years later, this great tragic drama of Wu would have come immediately to mind. In the two centuries that followed the fall of Wu, war accelerated in scale, breadth, and lethality. In the Warring States era, which spans the 5th to 3rd centuries B.C., we see ever larger and better-organized states. By the 4th century, only seven very large states remained. This is when the *Sunzi* was written, around 330–320 B.C. So here's the context that we need to understand. The *Sunzi* was composed in an era where multiple states were large and lethal enough to compete for control of all of China. We have every reason to believe that each of these states could raise an army comprising hundreds of thousands of men.

China's famous terracotta warriors, a 7,000-man army of the afterlife, guard the tomb of the king who succeeded in unifying all of China in the late 3rd century. They are a graphic reminder of the centrality of war and the scale of the military in this period and to the bureaucratic sophistication of the warring states.

Now, you would think that such dramatic changes in the scale and scope of warfare—armies of several hundred thousand men, armed with standardized weapons, and requiring huge logistical support—would have demanded a complete reappraisal of the military ethos. Instead, old aristocratic values of hereditary privilege and personal valor still prevailed. The *Sunzi*, with its anti-heroic bent, is an argument against that fundamental contradiction.

For the aristocrat combat is the venue in which he can display his martial virtues and settle family vendettas, blood feuds. By contrast, the *Sunzi* claims, and I quote, "to reject battle and yet force the submission of the enemy's troops is the supreme excellence." This injunction was an affront to the aristocratic warrior. Victory without combat precluded displays of valor and completely subverted the primary purpose of war. In contrast to the aristocratic amateur, the *Sunzi* gives us the methodical professional.

But the *Sunzi* is not just a critique of aristocratic pretensions; it is also an assault against moral philosophers, like the Confucians, who were vying for the attention of the rulers of the warring states.

The interview that Confucius had with the Duke of Wei sums up his attitude toward the military affairs. I quote,

> Duke Ling of Wei asked Confucius about military formations. Confucius answered, "I have, indeed, heard something about the use of sacrificial vessels, but I have never studied the matter of commanding troops." The next day Confucius departed.

Confucius was the first "master," the first "zi," and his goal was to restore harmony within China's social and political institutions by returning to the moral tenets of the founders of the Zhou dynasty.

Like the author of the *Sunzi*, the Confucians asserted that their education, not their aristocratic pedigree, qualified them to serve at the highest levels of government, but the similarity ends there. Confucius dismissed the militaristic obsessions of the duke of Wei; a Sunzian would have been delighted by them.

Given this historical dynamic, Sun Wu, the 6th-century general, is an exceptional choice as the source of this 4th-century book. This is a culture where legitimacy was quantifiable in terms of antiquity. The fact that Sun Wu was a contemporary of Confucius is priceless. It gives Sun Wu, or *Sunzi*, credibility and justifies the claim that General Sun is also a master. In contrast to Confucian morality and ritual, the *Sunzi* claims that the professional management and employment of mass infantry armies is "the greatest affair of the state."

So now that we've placed the *Sunzi* in historical context, let's move to a discussion of the book as a work of strategic theory. And for starters let's ask how a Sunzian would have responded to the duke of Wei's questions about military formations.

The *Sunzi* makes three major claims. The first is that the text contains the wisdom of Sun Wu, who deserves the title of master (*zi*), a thinker on par with the greatest philosophers. The duke would have been taken aback by the impudence of that assertion. The second claim is that the sole purpose for the existence and employment of the military is to increase the wealth and power of the state. The duke would have agreed, albeit only in part. Remember, he is an aristocrat. The third claim is that the general must wield the military with the same skill and autonomy that a master swordsman handles his own weapon. The duke would have bridled at the general's primacy over the ruler in matters of war.

We can see these three claims in stark relief in the very first line of the text "The use of the military is the greatest affair of the state. The terrain of life and death, the path of survival and ruin, it must be studied." We also see these concepts peppered throughout the book. For example, the purpose of the military is to increase the wealth and power of the state. "If it does not profit the state, do not use the military." On the autonomy of the general we have this line: "The ruler who has able generals and who does not interfere in their affairs will be victorious." And finally on the primacy of the general, we have this famous passage: "The commander who understands the military is the arbiter of the people's destiny, the master of security and peril for the realm and for the dynasty."

Armed with just a bit of the historical background we begin to realize that what sounded initially like bland platitudes (buy low, sell high), are actually part of a radical and relentless sales pitch. The pitch is particularly relentless in its demands for a coldly rational, anti-heroic, and almost super-human approach to war. This is because the author was not satisfied with the way that states were conducting their wars. And he definitely didn't like the criteria for command.

The *Sunzi* presents a revolutionary new ideal against which military commanders must be measured. It is an ideal, but the military is now the state's largest and most expensive instrument. The very existence of the military affects every aspect of state and society. Therefore, the *Sunzi*'s new ideal is vastly superior to the aristocratic/heroic ideal that sees battle as ritual and it is vastly superior to the Confucian disdain for military affairs.

74

But as much as the *Sunzi* is an elaborate assault on amateurish, vain aristocrats and on naïve Confucian moralists, it is also a spirited delineation and defense of the realm of authority and expertise that defined the professional general.

From the three claims I just outlined, we can derive the three core theoretical prescriptions of the book: Be efficient, avoid protraction, and value the commander's intellect and skill above all other things.

Let's look at each of these theoretical prescriptions in turn. First: Be efficient. In order for a state to survive and to win wars, it must make efficient use of its resources while always keeping an eye on the ultimate benefit of the state. The rulers of the warring states, to whom this book is pitched, were vying for ultimate mastery over ancient China. They want to seize Heaven's mandate. That end could not be achieved if resources were wasted in ill-conceived campaigns or in wars dictated by passions and aristocratic pretensions. The downfall of the state of Wu proves that the use of the military can be a path to both survival and ruin!

So what strategies put the state on the path to survival and ultimately to greater power? Chapter III of the *Sunzi* lays out a continuum from the most to the least efficient strategies: Attacking the enemy's strategy; attacking his alliances; attacking his armies; and last, attacking his cities.

"The superior approach is to attack the enemy's strategy." You attack the enemy's strategy by convincing him that his ways and means are insufficient to achieving his ends. We saw Pericles' do this by denying the Spartans their hoplite battle.

"Second to this is to sever his alliances." After attacking his strategy you might try to attack the ties that bind states to each other, but also that hold them together internally. In the American Revolution the British tried repeatedly to drive a wedge between the colonies in order to suppress the revolution.

"Next to this is attacking the enemy's army." After attacking the alliances you might try to attack the enemy's army. This was Sparta's preferred strategy: seek a decisive result. But in the *Sunzi* the costly expenditure of blood and treasure in combat comes *third* in the list of efficient strategies. In other words, combat implies a failure to find more efficient means toward your ends.

"Last is to attack the enemy's walled cities. Attacking a walled city is only a last resort." There may be some moral qualms here as siege brings the war to the civilian population, but more importantly sieges are impractical. They are long and expensive and an encamped army invites disease. Moreover, by laying siege what do you give up? You give up maneuver and initiative. Attacking a walled city is thus a sure sign that you have gotten yourself into a protracted war.

Which brings us to the second of the *Sunzi's* core theoretical prescriptions: Avoid protraction. This is a very important theme in the book. In fact all of Chapter II is concerned with the dangers and costs of protracted operations. Protraction poses a mortal danger to both belligerents, from which neither side benefits. But we need to ask if this is always the case. After all, George Washington consciously employed a Fabian strategy designed to frustrate the British, to buy time to win allies and to build up enough strength for a final decisive blow.

But remember the historical context. Two Chinese warring states are like heavyweight boxers. They have pummeled each other for 15 rounds. Would they have the strength to defend themselves against a third boxer who has just entered the ring? Remember what happened to the kingdom of Wu, exhausted by those wars? But also remember the aristocratic warrior. He likes battles and the sieges. They give him the chance to prove his valor. In contrast, the *Sunzi* rails against the notion that combat and battle are ends in themselves. They are just one means to an end.

The third core prescription of the *Sunzi* places an emphasis on the intellectual, as opposed to the heroic, qualities of the commander. The intellectual qualities enable the general to master the totality of the military as both institution and instrument. These intellectual qualities of the commander are also critical to the successful performance of net assessment. Remember that we defined net assessment as knowing the enemy, knowing yourself, and knowing your environment.

In the first chapter the *Sunzi* gives us five categories of net assessment to determine the nature of a looming conflict. The first category is called the Way, or the Dao. This is the spiritual strength of a state: its ability to mobilize for war, to face the necessary sacrifices, and to resist the enemy's attempts at subverting that resolve and cohesion. The second category is Heaven, literally the climate. All the phenomena that obtain above us, the environment in which we are operating. The third is terrain, that is, developing an intuitive grasp of geography so that the army may move across the land in the most natural and efficient way possible. The fourth is command, the talent of what we would call the professional general, the new role that this book is creating, the pivotal figure who must manipulate all of these elements. And the fifth is method, that's logistics, staffing, discipline, and organization. Those processes that the general employs to keep the army a sharply honed weapon that is infinitely responsive to his will.

Do you see how the *Sunzi* is revolutionizing the ancient Chinese attitudes toward war? Command should no longer be based on aristocratic pedigree; it is an intellectual enterprise, based on the ability to test and process the five elements I just named and to craft strategy in accord with their subtle variations. Whereas the aristocrats were born to command, the Sunzian general has earned his command based on his intellect and on his mastery of the new means of war. And these new standards are more than just axiomatic platitudes like "buy low, sell high," they are an ideal that a commander must pursue.

This explains the structure of the book. Chapter I identifies the critical calculations, those five factors, that must be made prior to war. Chapter II lays out the costs and dangers of mobilizing a state for war, Chapters III through XII showcase the nearly supernatural skill of the commander in organizing his troops, maneuvering the army, exploiting terrain and weather, gathering intelligence, shaping his forces, and manipulating the enemy. Finally, Chapter XIII explains how all of this is possible, through the deft use of spies, of espionage.

So, if that's the theory in a nutshell, what does this mean in practice? The first key in practice is information superiority, a popular buzz phrase. Have superior intelligence, superior knowledge of the environment, and at the same time limit your opponent's ability to know the true nature of the situation. This can be at the highest levels of politics and strategy. Or valuable intelligence can be something as seemingly trivial as the dust clouds stirred up by an army on the move.

The second key is operational initiative. The *Sunzi* tells us: "If I am able to determine the enemy's formations while I conceal my own then I can concentrate and he must divide." Keep the enemy off balance by employing both conventional and unconventional forces, infantry and cavalry. Keep him off balance through deception and feigned maneuvers and by feeding him false information through doubled agents. Use intelligence and deception to distract, anger, or win over the opposing general. You can use your superior discipline to exploit his character flaws. Take the war to the enemy by invading his territory to multiply the stresses on his institutions and on his society.

The third key is knowing when and where to deliver the decisive blow. Create and exploit the situation where you can make the best use of your resources. Know how to position your troops in the terrain to maximize their destructive impact on the enemy. Only then can a commander deliver the decisive blow with lightning speed. I quote: "That the striking hawk is able to shatter the body of its prey is a matter of timing." The hawk is the ideal hunting machine. It is an analogy for the "superior general": A commander who has the edge in information superiority, operational initiative, and timing.

To exploit these attributes, the successful commander must study the field of engagement, weigh the strengths and weaknesses of the military forces, plumb the will and intentions of his adversary, and gauge the mood of the men. But the general is more than a processor of intelligence; he is a source of information. Like an unmarried maiden shuttered in her father's house, and in stark contrast to the strutting aristocratic warrior, the Sunzian commander is metaphorically shuttered, a mystery to friend and foe alike. The only information that the enemy can glean about him is that which is fed to him.

As you can see the *Sunzi* provides the modern soldier, business person and sports coach with a wealth of advice that is at once intensely appealing but often very difficult to follow in practice. And I would add that there may be many elements of the *Sunzi* that you might not wish to approximate in practice. Here I think we need to stay attuned to what are ideal types, that is, what we should aspire to, versus what we can realistically hope to achieve.

A couple of things to be on-guard for: As you read or reread the *Sunzi* ask yourself if it is too one-sided in that it does not give enough emphasis to the interactive nature of War. Ask yourself if the author's apparent faith in the clarity and utility of espionage and intelligence at all levels of war is realistic. Ask yourself if war or business or sports can be as rational and antiseptic as the text seems to promise. Can war be drained of passion and deep-seated hatreds, be they personal, national, ethnic, or religious?

For me whose job it is to prepare military officers for the unique challenges of senior leadership, I am most concerned that some may be inspired by the *Sunzi* to attempt to liberate the military from political oversight. The author of the *Sunzi* draws a sharp line between the general and the ruler and he is jealously protective of the autonomy of the general.

The *Sunzi*, therefore, highlights many of the enduring tensions between the military and the politicians that they serve. I quote: "The ruler who has able generals and who does not interfere in their affairs will be victorious." But attempting to approximate that ideal type in practice can prove catastrophic. Rather it is essential not to confuse the judicious exercise of political authority over the military, which is critical to good strategy, with the amateurish interference of a warring states aristocrat in the serious business of war.

The enduring popularity of the *Sunzi* is testimony to the evocative power of a book that speaks compellingly to readers far removed in space, time, and culture from its origins.

I hope that I have whetted your appetite for the book and persuaded you that reading it against the historical situation it was designed to address makes the text more interesting, more vital, and ultimately more useful when dealing with the problems of today.

The *Sunzi* does not have a monopoly on wisdom, but reading it carefully and understanding the author's larger purpose can be both a marvelous educational experience and may very well improve your chances of success in any field.

I'll see you next time.

Sun Tzu through Time

Lecture 5

If a great work of strategic theory is a "possession for all time," then the *Sunzi* gives Thucydides a run for the money. It was incorporated into the Chinese strategic canon more than 2,000 years ago, making it perhaps the most consistently applied and historically significant classic of them all. To highlight the *Sunzi*'s historical impact, this lecture covers four topics: the place of the *Sunzi* in China's strategic culture, the *Sunzi* in feudal and modern Japan, the embrace of the *Sunzi* in the West, and a case study of the most brilliant example of the *Sunzi* in action— World War II's Operation Fortitude.

The Place of the *Sunzi* in China

- Given the *Sunzi*'s status in the canon of Chinese—and world— strategic literature, it might seem strange that it received a negative response in ancient China. But recall that the *Sunzi* represented a forceful assault on the aristocratic pretensions of the warrior elite and on the naïve moralism of the Confucians. This assault didn't go unanswered.

- One school of thought rejected the *Sunzi* outright, while another tried to moderate some of its more extreme prescriptions.
  - The most prominent rejector was Xun Qing (Xunzi), an important successor of Confucius. In his "Debate on the Principles of Warfare," Xun Qing lays out an extended critique of the *Sunzi*, in which he rejects the autonomy and authority of the professional commander and asserts the sole legitimacy of the ruler in all matters of governance, including war.

  - A more subtle critique of the *Sunzi* is offered in the *Wuzi* (*The Military Methods of Master Wu*). The *Wuzi* is attributed to Wu Qi, a minister and general who lived a century after Sun Wu. He tries to strike a middle course among three poles: the extreme anti-heroic and amoral approach of the *Sunzi*, the moral compass sought by the Confucians, and the martial virtue craved by the aristocracy.

- Despite its force and appeal, the *Sunzi* did not dominate strategic thought in China. Instead, it sparked a debate about the role and utility of military force in statecraft and in society. The *Sunzi*, the *Wuzi*, and other works also enshrined the necessity to think holistically and strategically about the use of force.

- The centrality of the *Sunzi* in Chinese strategic thought has inclined some to conclude that it represents the epitome of Chinese strategic culture. In particular, some people, including many in contemporary China, would have us believe that the concept of "winning without fighting" has defined Chinese military history, but we can point to many examples in which winning by fighting was a necessity.

- It's also true that Chinese tradition was under intense assault for most of the 20th century. The Communists dismissed the *Sunzi* as anachronistic and naïve. Today, a renewed interest in the classics is developing in China, but the move back to tradition is tentative and often superficial.

The *Sunzi* in Japan

- The *Sunzi* probably made its first appearance in Japan in the 8th or 9th century A.D. and, by the 11th century, was widely quoted in military texts. Even in the 19th and 20th centuries, when Japan was embracing foreign military models, the *Sunzi* remained required reading among military officers. Ironically, this Chinese text was viewed as central to maintaining Japanese national character in a modern world.

- For some among the samurai, however, the *Sunzi*'s anti-heroic and amoral approach to the use of the military ran completely counter to their cultural ethos. An aphorism from the Tokugawa period (17th–19th centuries) argues that although the *Sunzi* is important, a true warrior reads the *Wuzi*. Given the *Wuzi*'s attempt to bring heroism and morality back into war, we should not be surprised by its relative popularity among the samurai.

- When Japan emerged from its isolation in the late 19th century, its leaders looked both to foreign models and the classics to craft a new military ethos. The *Sunzi*'s emphasis on intelligence, surprise, and deception became crucial elements of the new Japanese way of war.
  - o When these tools were kept subordinate to sound strategy and policy, Japan proved successful, as we can see from its successes in both the Sino-Japanese War and the Russo-Japanese War.

  - o By the 1930s, however, deception and surprise had become almost ends in themselves. In the attack on Pearl Harbor, we see a brilliant example of operational deception and surprise but one that also had catastrophic strategic implications.

The Embrace of the *Sunzi* in the West
- The first European translation of the *Sunzi* was published in Paris in 1782 by a French Jesuit missionary who had served in China. More translations followed in the early 20th century, but these were not widely read beyond a small group of China experts. Western interest in the *Sunzi* did not really spike until the late 1940s, inspired by Mao's victory in the Chinese civil war and the advent of the Cold War.

- After the Communists won China's civil war and Mao's guerilla strategy began to be exported to the Third World, many people became

For Mao, winning without fighting, the most problematic axiom in the *Sunzi*, was inconceivable.

interested in the "Chinese way of war." Indeed, U.S. General Samuel B. Griffith claimed that Mao was the *Sunzi*'s most important disciple, but Mao's strategic outlook seems far more European than classically Chinese.

- Cold War tensions between the United States and the USSR also made the *Sunzi* an appealing strategic guide. From the late 1940s onward, attacking the enemy's strategies and alliances was far more attractive than the obvious thermonuclear implications of attacking the armies or cities of the opposing superpower.

- By the 1980s, the *Sunzi* had escaped from the realm of security studies and began to appear in business school curricula and American pop culture. Today, interest in the *Sunzi* is at an all-time high.

The *Sunzi* in Action
- The execution of Operation Fortitude in World War II tracks almost exactly with chapter XIII of the *Sunzi*, which is entitled "The Use of Spies." The chapter describes five types of spies and the "divine skein" of their recruitment and manipulation. Fortitude was the Allied scheme that convinced Hitler that the Normandy landings were a diversion and that the real invasion would come at the Pas de Calais.

- The Nazis were relentless in rooting out enemy infiltrators and traitors. As a result, living agents and internal spies working for the Allies were relatively few. Great Britain and the United States were at pains to craft a divine skein out of doubled agents and disinformation.
  - In the 1930s, a group of Polish engineers and mathematicians managed to build an Enigma machine in reverse, which they shared with the British. Churchill immediately grasped the significance of the ability to read German radio traffic. True to the *Sunzi*, he accorded significant funding to what came to be called Ultra, which opened the way for the Allies to weave their own divine skein.

  - With a mix of Ultra intercepts and good detective work, MI5 managed to co-opt Germany's entire espionage ring in

Britain by 1941. This created the wellspring of doubled agents from which the divine skein could be sewn. Remarkably, the Germans never realized that their espionage network had been completely compromised.

o As much as knowing what the Germans were doing was important, knowing what the Germans thought the Allies were doing was even more strategically significant. Because of Ultra, the Allies knew whether or not the Nazis believed their disinformation campaign.

• The basic premise of Fortitude, divided into Fortitude North and Fortitude South, was to convince the Germans that major Allied invasions were planned for Norway and the Pas de Calais in France.
o Misinformation spread through doubled agents was reinforced by radio transmissions *from* and well-publicized appointments *to* entirely fictitious military headquarters.

o The northern feint was convincing enough to tie down nearly 30 German divisions in Scandinavia, a theater of marginal importance. The real coup, however, was Fortitude South, which invented a fictitious army under Patton in southeast England.

o The deception masters served up to German reconnaissance all the evidence of an army preparing for an assault on occupied France. Patton's fictional army even bought up thousands of Michelin Guide maps for the Calais area.

o Fortitude South convinced Hitler and Field Marshal von Rundstedt that the attack would be at Calais sometime in August of 1944.

o When the Allies began to land in Normandy on June 6, Hitler thought it was a diversion and would not reinforce with the troops that were committed to Calais. Three weeks later, Hitler was still convinced that a second assault force was coming from Dover.

- Despite the brilliance of the deception, Fortitude did not allow the Allies to win without fighting. But were it not for the divine skein of intelligence and deception embodied in Fortitude South, a successful Allied invasion of France in 1944 may well have been inconceivable.

The Success of Operation Fortitude
- The *Sunzi* gives us a straightforward explanation for the efficacy of Operation Fortitude: The Allies knew Germany's general inclinations and the structure of its intelligence gathering and could, therefore, use its own institutions against it. Ultra also exploited the Germans' arrogance over the purported superiority of their encryption technology.

- Further, the British and Americans understood that their divine skein hinged on turned agents. MI5 and the FBI made excellent use of these assets.

- The deception story was also plausible. Attacks on Norway and the Pas de Calais made military sense, and the fictitious armies made credible noise in preparing for those assaults. That was enough to reinforce what was essentially a sound German assessment.

- Finally, Allied civil and military leadership appreciated the importance of espionage and deception and went to great pains to fund and man Ultra and Fortitude but also to keep them absolutely secret.

- As much as Fortitude can be viewed as a model of intelligence, deception, and surprise, it should also serve as a cautionary tale.
  ○ Fortitude was a necessary preparation for Operation Overlord, but a massive amphibious invasion was still required to oust the Germans from France and to drive on Berlin.

  ○ Moreover, the more the Germans fell back, the muddier the intelligence picture became, and brute force overcame elegant deception. Fortitude was a spectacularly successful part—but only a part—of a comprehensive Allied strategy for victory in Europe.

o It's also true that the circumstances of Ultra and Fortitude may be too ideal to try to repeat in all but the rarest cases. Despite our contemporary revolution in information technology, it would be arrogant to assume that we could lift the fog of war as completely as the Allies did in this case.

Suggested Reading

Cubbage, "German Misapprehensions Regarding Overlord."

————, "The Success of Operation Fortitude."

Sawyer, *The Seven Military Classics of Ancient China.*

Warner, "The Divine Skein."

Questions to Consider

1. What does it mean to know the enemy and to know yourself?

2. Was Operation Fortitude too perfect of an intelligence coup to serve as a model?

Sun Tzu through Time

Lecture 5—Transcript

If a classic of strategic theory is "a possession for all time," then the *Sunzi* gives Thucydides a run for the money.

The *Sunzi* was incorporated into the Chinese strategic canon more than two thousand years ago, that potentially makes this book the most consistently applied and historically significant classic of them all. To highlight the *Sunzi*'s historical impact, I will be covering four topics in today's lecture: the first is the place of the *Sunzi* in China's strategic culture. The second is the *Sunzi* in feudal and modern Japan. The third is the embrace of the *Sunzi* in the West. And fourth is a case study of the most brilliant example of the *Sunzi* in action: World War II's Operation Fortitude.

Let's start with the *Sunzi*'s place in Chinese history and in Chinese strategic culture. We have seen just how appealing and persuasive the *Sunzi* can be. But this does not mean that it appealed to the majority of Chinese readers when it appeared in the late 4th century B.C.

In fact, there was a negative response to the *Sunzi* in ancient China. This might seem strange given the *Sunzi*'s status in the canon of Chinese (and world) strategic literature. But remember the last lecture: the *Sunzi* represents a forceful assault on the aristocratic pretensions of the warrior elite and on the naïve moralism of the Confucians. This assault didn't go unanswered.

There were two primary responses to the *Sunzi*: one school that rejected it outright and the other that tried to moderate some of its more extreme prescriptions. Among the rejecters, the most prominent was a philosopher by the name of Xun Qing (known to posterity as Xunzi, or Master Xun). Xun Qing was Confucius's second most important successor, after Mencius, who we talked about last time. In his 'Debate on the Principles of Warfare', Xun Qing lays out an extended critique of the *Sunzi*. The essay describes an oral contest between Xun Qing and the Lord of Linwu, a military commander.

In this debate, the Lord of Linwu offers strategic prescriptions that parrot the *Sunzi*, and Xun Qing counters with arguments in defense of the moral doctrines of Confucius. Xun Qing, Master Xun, was the most prominent scholar, teacher, and writer of his day, the leading guardian of the legacy of Confucius. The fact that he would devote an entire essay to an extended rebuttal of the *Sunzi* testifies to that book's influence and its controversial nature.

Xun Qing's responses contain very little detail about the conduct of war. Instead, he returns consistently to the moral qualities of the rulers, the uprightness of the state's institutions, and the people as the keys to success. Yet the very existence of this debate speaks to the change that had taken place in warring states' intellectual culture. A new space was opened up in which military matters could and should be examined and discussed. The military was no longer a subject on which an aspiring Master could remain silent. Remember, Confucius walked out on the duke of Wei, the duke who asked him about military formations. Xun Qing can't ignore the military, but he does have to reject the core tenet of the *Sunzi*—namely, that the professional commander is autonomous and supremely authoritative when it comes to matters of the military. Instead, Master Xun asserts the sole legitimacy of the ruler in all matters of governance, including war.

A more subtle critique of the *Sunzi* is offered in the pages of a book called the *Wuzi*: The Military Methods of Master Wu. The *Wuzi* is attributed to Wu Qi, a minister and general who lived a century after Sun Wu. At first glance, there seems little difference between these two ancient Chinese masters. Many maxims in the *Wuzi* seem to be lifted straight out of the *Sunzi*, and throughout history the texts of Sun and Wu have been mentioned in the same breath. But a close reading exposes some critical differences.

Yes, like Sun Wu, Wu Qi's military credentials are impeccable. But the book attributed to him tries to strike a middle course between three poles: the extreme anti-heroic and amoral approach of the *Sunzi*, the moral compass sought by the Confucians, and the martial virtue craved by the aristocracy. The *Sunzi* does not expand on the issue of the moral influence of the king, and at times it seems downright hostile to the ruler. By contrast the *Wuzi* returns the ruler to a central position and elevates fundamentally Confucian virtues of benevolence, righteousness, propriety, and the Dao, or moral influence.

Like the *Sunzi*, the *Wuzi* recognizes that mass warfare is the new reality, but a state that is not virtuously ruled will be unable to leverage its total potential in war. As to the issue of martial virtue, the *Wuzi* puts more of a human face on the soldiers and officers. In the *Sunzi*, the general is the master manipulator and the men simply pawns in his game. In the *Wuzi*, the heroism, pride, personality, and the individual talents of the officers and men matter. In many ways the *Wuzi* accepts the new reality that motivates the *Sunzi*, but seeks to make it more palatable to an ancient Chinese audience.

Therefore, despite its force and appeal, the *Sunzi* did not dominate strategic thought in China. Instead, it sparked a vibrant debate about the role and utility of military force in statecraft and in society. This happens very early in the history of China. This should lead us to admire the dynamism and breadth of ancient Chinese strategic thought. Especially noteworthy is the concept that battle was only a means to an end, not an end in itself.

These classics also enshrined the necessity to think holistically and strategically about the use of force. While contemporaries in the West were certainly pondering the same topics, Thucydides for example, it was not until the Renaissance, only 500 years ago, that a similar canon of strategic thought coalesced in Europe. In short, China had a 1,500-year head start in cultivating those habits of strategic analysis and critical thinking that I think are so crucial.

For 2,000 years the *Sunzi*, along with the *Wuzi* and other military classics, were required reading for military officers and for much of the period from the 11th to the 19th centuries were the basis for the imperial military exams in China. The centrality of the *Sunzi* in Chinese strategic thought has, however, inclined some to conclude that the *Sunzi* represents the be all and end all of Chinese strategic culture.

In particular some people, including many in contemporary China, would have us believe that the concept of "winning without fighting" has defined Chinese military history. Certainly, there are abundant examples of nifty stratagems through all of those dynasties that ruled, but there are also abundant examples of actual wars by and between Chinese states. Winning without fighting may have been desirable or appealing, but winning by fighting was often a necessity.

Moreover, when you think about continuity, Chinese tradition was under intense assault for most of the 20th century. Part of that tradition included the *Sunzi*, which was dismissed by the Communists as anachronistic and naïve. I am not saying that there isn't still a glimmer of *Sunzi* in modern China, but this ancient master shares the stage with many foreign ideologies and military doctrines.

A renewed interest in the classics is developing in China, as is interest in the great campaigns and great commanders of Chinese history, but in my opinion the move back to tradition is tentative and often superficial. Case in point, a recent Chinese Defense White Paper quoted from the *Sunzi*, most likely as a way to ease the concerns of its neighbors. But when some foreign experts raised the point that deception is a pivotal concept in the *Sunzi*, the next version of the White Paper didn't mention this ancient classic.

In addition, the People's Liberation Army holds a biannual conference on the *Sunzi*, inviting foreign students of the book and foreign military personnel to share in discussions of its historical and contemporary relevance. And while the quality of the scholarship presented at these conferences has improved, it is still primarily a propaganda event. Above all, the conference seems to be an effort to leverage the global popularity of the *Sunzi* as a way to elevate China's cultural status, but also to calm foreign friends by emphasizing the *Sunzi*'s apparent disdain for conflict.

Let's turn from China now and explore the *Sunzi* in Japan. During the first millennium A.D., Japan borrowed heavily from Chinese culture. This included architecture, written language, religion, statecraft, and strategic thought. The *Sunzi* probably made its first appearance in Japan around the 8th or 9th century, and by the 11th century was widely quoted in military texts. The 17th century ninja manual of Natori Masazumi, called the *Shoninki*, makes extensive use of the *Sunzi*'s discussion of the five types of spies, and even expands on their character and use.

Even in the 19th and 20th centuries when Japan was embracing foreign military models, the *Sunzi* remained required reading among army and navy officers. Ironically, this Chinese text was viewed as central to maintaining Japanese national character in a modern world. So we see in Japan a rich history of engagement with and commentary on the *Sunzi*. For some among the samurai, however, the *Sunzi*'s anti-heroic and amoral approach to the use of the military ran completely counter to their cultural ethos. An aphorism from the Tokugawa period, 17th to 19th centuries, argues that while the *Sunzi* is important, a true warrior reads the *Wuzi*. Given the *Wuzi*'s attempt to bring heroism and morality back into war, we should not be surprised by its relative popularity among the samurai.

In Japan, as in many places, only selective elements of the *Sunzi* were embraced. Given Japan's relative isolation and the flexible language of the *Sunzi*, it was easy for Japanese interpreters to twist the text to serve the interests of the samurai class and the state. When Japan emerged from its isolation in the late 19th century, its leaders looked both to foreign models and the ancient classics to craft a new military ethos. The *Sunzi*'s emphasis on intelligence, surprise, and deception became crucial elements of the new Japanese way of war.

When these tools were kept subordinate to sound strategy and policy, Japan proved very successful, as we can see from its successes in both the Sino-Japanese War and the Russo-Japanese War. By the 1930s, however, deception and surprise had become almost ends in themselves. In the attack on Pearl Harbor we see a brilliant example of operational deception and surprise, but one that also had catastrophic strategic implications.

Turning from Asia to the West: The first European translation of the *Sunzi* was published in Paris in 1782. Despite some dubious claims to the contrary, it was unlikely that Napoleon Bonaparte had the time or the patience to read this early version. More translations followed in the early 20th century, but these were not widely read beyond a small group of China experts. Western interest in *Sunzi* did not really spike until the late 1940s.

The peak in interest was inspired by two events: The first was Mao Tse-tung's stunning victory in the Chinese Civil War. The second was the advent of the Cold War. After the Communists won China's Civil War and Mao's guerilla strategy started to be exported to the third world, a lot of people got interested in the "Chinese Way of War." Is there such a thing? In fact, one of the first truly excellent translations of the *Sunzi* was the one published by U.S. Marine Corps General Samuel B. Griffith. Griffith's version made a noble effort to compare the *Sunzi* with the strategic writings of Mao Tse-tung. Griffith claimed Mao as the *Sunzi*'s most important disciple. I am not persuaded by that.

While Mao had certainly read the *Sunzi*, his strategic outlook was far more European than classically Chinese. Much of Mao's military inspiration came through Lenin, who plagiarized willfully from the European masters: especially Jomini and Clausewitz. As a result of this foreign influence, Mao saw revolution as an act of violence by which one class overthrew another. For Mao, winning without fighting, that most problematic axiom in the *Sunzi*, was inconceivable.

But while many of his parallels are forced, Griffith raised provocative questions about continuities in Chinese strategic culture and his version is still required reading at many of America's senior service colleges. Regardless of the success of the Mao/*Sunzi* comparison, Griffith's *Sunzi* makes for a worthwhile read in and of itself. As we will see, for military officers steeped in a tradition of Jomini and Clausewitz, the *Sunzi* provided an attractive and provocative counterpoint.

Cold War tensions between the United States and the Soviet Union also made the *Sunzi* an appealing strategic guide. From the late 1940s onward attacking the enemy's strategies and alliances were far more attractive than the obvious thermonuclear implications of attacking the armies or cities of the opposing superpower.

By the 1980s the *Sunzi* had escaped from the realm of security studies and began to pop up in business school curricula and in American pop culture. At the same time, China began opening to the outside world and some exciting new archeological discoveries were made, including finding a nearly intact version of the *Sunzi* in a Han Dynasty tomb. Today, interest in the *Sunzi* is at an all-time high, and we are at the beginning of a rich and varied interrogation of this ancient classic.

Having surveyed the incredible impact (both positive and negative) of the *Sunzi* on the theory and practice of strategy through time, I'd like to close with a case study of the *Sunzi* in action. As you can probably imagine, even a superficial study of military history yields a host of examples of generals who succeeded or failed in war based on the degree to which they followed Master Sun's prescriptions. In fact, a recent book entitled *Sun Tzu at Gettysburg* explores a range of such cases from western military history.

In my own *Sunzi* course (at the Naval War College) the final student project is a similar exercise. I challenge the students to explain the outcome of a specific battle or campaign from a Sunzian perspective, but I do not limit them to war. They are free to examine cases from sports, business, and even film. The only requirement is that they are serious and rigorous in their application of the *Sunzi*'s maxims.

In that spirit, I am going to look at a case of perhaps the most masterful intelligence, deception, and surprise campaign in history, Operation Fortitude. Now, it's unlikely that the architects of Fortitude actually read the *Sunzi*, but the execution of that deception campaign tracks almost exactly with Chapter XIII of the *Sunzi*—which is entitled "The Use of Spies."

Intelligence, deception, and surprise percolate throughout the *Sunzi*'s 13 chapters. In the first chapter we are introduced to the concept of net assessment where you collect and process strategic and operational intelligence. We are also introduced to the critical importance of denying the enemy accurate intelligence about you, in other words, deception.

In the subsequent chapters we see intelligence gathering at the tactical and operational levels of war. Likewise we see surprise—the ability to meet the enemy's fewer numbers with your superior force and the outsized psychological impact that can follow from surprise. It is the final chapter, however, that explains how this almost supernatural knowledge is obtained— namely, through the use of spies.

The *Sunzi* describes five types of spies: local spies—these are the natives of the enemy's state; internal spies are enemy officials on our payroll; doubled agents are those enemy spies sent into our midst that we then turn to our cause; expendable—or dead spies—are our own agents who spread disinformation to the enemy, they are called dead because they are meant to be captured; and finally, living agents are those who return with information on the enemy's dispositions.

The recruitment and manipulation of these five varieties of agents constitutes what the *Sunzi* calls a "divine skein" or "spirit web." This divine skein is an inscrutable network of information and disinformation that can be spread wide and then drawn in to ensnare the opponent.

So let's take a look at this theory in practice. In the early stages of World War II, the areas of intelligence, deception, and surprise were all dominated by the Axis. Nazi Germany's attacks on Scandinavia, France, and the Soviet Union caught their adversaries largely unaware. In Asia, Japan's attacks on Pearl Harbor, the Philippines, and Singapore were all masterworks of operational surprise.

The allies, however, ultimately gained the hard-won upper hand in the intelligence battle. As you probably know, code breaking and misinformation allowed the U.S. Navy to anticipate the Japanese attack on Midway and to inflict unrecoverable damage on the Japanese navy.

In Europe, we see in 1943 a great example of brilliant misinformation. This was Operation Mincemeat, the basis for the book and film "The Man Who Never Was." For Mincemeat, the British dressed a corpse as a Royal Marine and dumped the body off the coast of Spain hoping the Nazis will find it. On the body were fake Allied plans for the invasions of Greece and Sardinia designed to draw the Germans away from the actual invasions of Sicily and Italy. Not only was the corpse dressed as a Royal Marine, British intelligence created an entire life-story for the dead man including a fiancé, an overbearing father, and overdue bills and library books. The Germans bought the deception completely and even after the Allies landed in Sicily it took the Germans two weeks to realize that Sardinia and Greece were a ruse.

Remember *Sunzi*'s "dead spy," the expendable agent employed to spread disinformation to the enemy? In Operation Mincemeat we have a very literal case of the dead spy. But the crowning jewel of Allied intelligence and deception in World War II—and perhaps the gold standard in the history of warfare—has to be Operation Fortitude. Or to be even more specific, Fortitude South, the scheme that convinced Hitler that the Normandy landings were a diversion, and that the real invasion would come at the Pas de Calais.

As far back as the *Sunzi* we have most of the elements of World War II intelligence gathering and deception. The one major change was signals intelligence. Wireless communications were a great boon to military operations, but since they were out there in the ether they could be heard by everyone. The Germans were pioneers in the use of wireless to coordinate their land and sea campaigns and employed the enigma machine, the most sophisticated encryption device ever invented.

The Nazis were also relentless in their counterintelligence operations, that is, in rooting out enemy infiltrators and traitors. As a result living agents and internal spies working for the Allies were relatively few. As for local spies, the French and Dutch resistance movements did provide important information to the Allies in the lead up to D-Day, but that tended to be primarily tactical and operational intelligence. Obviously once the Allies landed in France, local spies grew in importance, but prior to June 1944 Great Britain and the United States were at pains to craft their divine skein out of doubled agents and disinformation. This was a very shaky foundation indeed, but chance intervened.

In the 1930s a group of Polish engineers managed to build an enigma machine in reverse, something called a "bomb," which they shared with the British. Churchill immediately grasped the significance of reading German traffic and true to the *Sunzi*'s admonition, treated what came to be called Ultra with the greatest liberality of funding and with the utmost of secrecy. Ultra was invaluable at the operational level of war, especially in countering the U-Boats and in disrupting German logistics in the Mediterranean and North Africa. But more importantly Ultra opened the way for the Allies to weave their own divine skein.

According to Chapter 13 of the *Sunzi*: "It is essential to seek out enemy agents who have come to spy, bribe them to serve you."

With a mix of Ultra intercepts and good detective work, MI5 ultimately co-opted Germany's entire espionage ring in Britain. In fact, by mid-1941 German infiltrators parachuting into England were being met by British intelligence agents the very moment they touched down. But rather than imprisoning German spies or putting them on trial, MI5 turned the spy ring into a sophisticated disinformation campaign. They turned entire German spy network; got it working actively for the Allies. This created the wellspring of doubled agents from which the entire divine skein was sewn.

What's even more remarkable is that the Germans never realized that their network had been completely compromised. The British knew the extent of their success because the Ultra intercepts allowed them to read German communications and to gauge how much of the disinformation was believed by the Third Reich.

The *Sunzi* tells us that it is through doubled agents that local and internal spies are recruited. But as we have seen that was almost impossible for Britain to do inside the Third Reich. Fortunately, Ultra gave the Allies a live feed on German actions and inclinations.

As much as knowing what the Germans were doing was important, knowing what the Germans thought the Allies were doing was even more strategically significant. Because of Ultra, the Allies knew whether or not the Nazis believed the disinformation campaign. This double cross was the key to the success of Operation Fortitude. The Allies knew the enemy, knew what the enemy wanted to believe, and manipulated those beliefs in a master stroke of deception and surprise.

The basic premise of Fortitude, divided into Fortitude North and Fortitude South, was to convince the Germans that major Allied invasions were planned for Norway and the Pas de Calais in France.

As the *Sunzi* points out: "If the enemy must defend everywhere, then he will be weak everywhere."

Misinformation spread through doubled agents was reinforced by radio transmissions from and well-publicized command appointments to entirely fictitious military headquarters.

Fortitude North conjured up Fourth Army under General Sir Andrew Thorne based in Scotland and Northern Ireland. The success of the Northern feint is evident in the fact that it was convincing enough to tie down nearly 30 German divisions in Scandinavia, a theatre of marginal importance. The real coup, however, was Fortitude South, which invented First U.S. Army Group under George Patton in Southeast England. In Chapter 9 of the *Sunzi* we have the superior general keeping his eyes and ears tuned to the movements and moods of the enemy army. The Allies played on the German's hunger for exactly that kind of intelligence.

Patton's fictitious army not only had a big radio presence, but the deception masters served up to German reconnaissance all of the sights, sounds, and smells of an army preparing for an assault on occupied France. Patton's fictional army even bought up thousands of Michelin Guide maps for the Calais area.

Fortitude South convinced Hitler and Field Marshall von Rundstedt that the attack by the Allies would be at Calais sometime in August of 1944. Only Rommel smelled a rat in Allied movements but he could not convince Hitler and von Rundstedt. When the Allies began to land in Normandy on June 6, Hitler thought it was a diversion and would not reinforce with the troops, about 20 divisions worth, that were committed to Calais. Three weeks later, Hitler was still convinced that a second assault force was coming from Dover.

As we know from history and from film, the Allied assault on Normandy was hard enough as it was. No matter how brilliant the deception it did not allow the Allies to win without fighting, but were it not for the divine skein of intelligence and deception embodied in Fortitude South, a successful Allied invasion of France in 1944 may well have been inconceivable.

Given the information mania of our current day, we may rightly be drawn to Operation Fortitude as a model of using intelligence, deception, and surprise as an essential component of victory in war. But, from that perspective we need to ask why Fortitude worked. The *Sunzi* gives us a straightforward explanation: the Allies knew the enemy's general inclinations and the structure of their intelligence gathering and could therefore use the enemy's own institutions against him.

Ultra also exploited German arrogance over the purported superiority of their encryption technology, the enigma machine. The British and Americans also understood that their divine skein hinged on turned agents. MI5 and the FBI made excellent use of these assets.

The deception story was also plausible. Attacks on Norway and the Pas de Calais made military sense, and the fictitious armies readying for those assaults made a lot of credible noise. That was enough to reinforce what was essentially a sound German assessment.

Finally, Allied civil and military leadership appreciated the importance of espionage and deception and went to great pains to fund and man Ultra and Fortitude, but also to keep them absolutely secret. Of the tens of thousands of people involved in the ruse, only a few dozen knew the entire plan.

As much as Fortitude can be viewed as a model of intelligence, deception, and surprise, it should also serve as a cautionary tale. In the first place, Fortitude was a necessary preparation for Overlord, but a massive amphibious invasion was still required to oust the Germans from France and to drive on Berlin. Moreover, the more the Germans fell back, the muddier the intelligence picture became and brute force overcame elegant deception. Fortitude was a spectacularly successful part, but only a part, of a comprehensive Allied strategy for victory in Europe. In the second place, the circumstances of Ultra and Fortitude may be too ideal to try to repeat in all but the rarest cases. The success of the deception ultimately relied on a highly cooperative adversary. The Germans couldn't believe that their codes could be broken and could not conceive that their agents had been turned.

In still other ways the Nazis failed to appreciate the interactive nature of espionage and failed to understand that the Allies might know as much about them, as they believed they knew about the Allies.

Despite our contemporary revolution in information technology, it would be arrogant to assume that we could lift the fog of war as completely as the Allies did in this case. A simplistic reading of the *Sunzi* and its embrace of espionage might, however, encourage exactly that kind of arrogance.

As we have seen already in this course and unfortunately as we will see many times in subsequent lectures, relying on only one element of a single strategic theory as the key to victory, in this case the key being deception and surprise, may in fact be the first step on the path to ruin.

Machiavelli's *The Art of War*
Lecture 6

I n his most famous and most controversial work, *The Prince*, Niccolò
Machiavelli argued that the most important areas of study for a ruler were
the rules and disciplines of war. War, he said, was the "sole art" of the
ruler and one of the main means by which a prince could rise to power and
maintain his position. Machiavelli wrote two subsequent volumes on exactly
these topics: books on the rules and disciplines of war and the mechanics and
merits of military power. In this lecture and the next, we'll look at those two
books, *The Art of War* and *Discourses on Livy*.

Machiavelli's Life

- Machiavelli was born in Florence in 1469. His father, a lawyer,
  introduced the young Niccolò to the world of Greek and Roman
  history. As a boy, he took an avid interest in ancient history,
  especially in Livy's account of the early Roman Republic.

- For the first 25 years of his life, Machiavelli's Florence was ruled
  by the Medici family, but in 1494, the French king, Charles VIII,
  invaded Italy and ousted the Medicis. In 1498, Machiavelli had a
  hand in bringing to power Piero Soderini and was rewarded with
  important positions in the new government.

- In his guise as a diplomat—a spy—Machiavelli gained firsthand
  knowledge of the chaos and intrigue of Italian politics. He witnessed
  the rise and fall of the brilliant and ruthless Cesare Borgia. In fact,
  Borgia became one of the models for *The Prince*, and his military
  reforms inspired Machiavelli's own military projects.

The Chaos of Italy

- Charles VIII's invasion of Italy sparked a multilateral tug-of-war
  for control of the Italian peninsula. From the 1490s to the 1550s, the
  kings of France, England, and Spain, along with the pope and the
  Holy Roman Emperor, all vied to dominate the Italian states. The

Italian states themselves were forced to ally with these superpowers and against one another.

- In the face of these outside powers and their Italian allies, Florence was virtually powerless. Machiavelli believed that the republic needed a strong military to ensure its survival as an independent state with an independent foreign policy.

- Unfortunately, like many Italian states, Florence relied on mercenaries for its defense. These professional soldiers (*condottieri*: "contractors") were expensive and, because they worked for profit, disinclined to risk their assets—their soldiers and heavy cavalry—in decisive battles. As a result, Italian wars tended to drag on.

- Machiavelli was dissatisfied with the *condottieri* and wanted to put Florence's fate in the hands of a Florentine commander with a Florentine citizen-army. His ideas gained greater appeal in light of the republic's protracted efforts to retake the city of Pisa using *condottieri*.

- In 1505, after yet another failed assault on Pisa, Soderini ordered Machiavelli to begin recruiting a militia from the agricultural districts around Florence. The new militia proved crucial in retaking Pisa in 1509 but was unable to defend the city of Prato or Florence itself in 1512. In the purge that followed the return of the Medicis to Florence, Machiavelli was imprisoned and tortured.

The Roman Model
- In his forced retirement from government, Machiavelli returned to the study of ancient history and its lessons for contemporary Italy. In particular, he looked to Roman history and the model of the Roman Republic.

- In his view, a republic was the best and most stable form of government because it embodies stabilizing tensions. In republican Rome, such tensions existed among the two consuls, the aristocratic/oligarchic Senate, and the tribune of the plebs.

- Machiavelli appreciated the intimate link between society and the military. The fact that Florentine society had been demilitarized and had outsourced its defense to mercenaries represented fundamental weaknesses of the republic. In contrast, the very basis of the Roman Republic was the Roman citizen-army: the legions.
  - The command structure of the legions mirrored the political structure of the republic, making them a kind of incubator of republican virtue. The legions stabilized the republic internally and defended it externally.

  - In addition, long-serving citizen-soldiers were both better soldiers and better citizens; a stronger army and stronger republic could direct their energies outward, toward conquest and empire.

- Even with the catastrophic failure of the militia at Prato, Machiavelli remained committed to the merits of the citizen-army. Unlike a militia, a long-serving citizen-army would give Florence greater freedom of action in its foreign affairs and would decrease its dependence on powerful allies.

Overview of *The Art of War*

- *The Art of War* is structured as a Socratic dialogue in the style of Plato. Participating in the dialogue is a group of Florentine noblemen, led by Cosimo Rucellai, and the *condottiero* Fabrizio Colonna. Colonna, who acts as the spokesman for Machiavelli's ideas, takes the role of Socrates, and Rucellai and his guests are the interlocutors.

© Jupiterimages/Goodshoot/Thinkstock

The Art of War echoes the views expressed in *The Prince* on the merits of military power: A strong military is the foundation of a viable state.

- In this long conversation, Colonna and the Florentines range over the breadth and scope of recorded history. In the process, they test which ancient tactics and strategy are best suited to which particular military challenges. Machiavelli acknowledges that contemporary Italy is not the same as ancient Rome, but he still makes a powerful and specific argument about the Roman institutions that would best serve the security and stability of Florence.

- There is a tendency to view *The Art of War* as dry, preachy, and excessively strident. As the only major work published during Machiavelli's life, it seems to lack the snide humor of his more famous works. The Socratic structure is also seen as too one-sided, with the excessively deferential Florentines simply receiving wisdom at the feet of Colonna.

Structure of *The Art of War*
- *The Art of War* is divided into a preface and seven chapters. In the preface, Machiavelli speaks in his own voice about the interconnection of politics and war and the intimate relation between the military and civilian order.
  o Machiavelli's views on the merits of military power are similar to those expressed in *The Prince*: A good military is the foundation of a viable state. Without good arms, a state cannot build good institutions and cannot defend itself. Without good arms, the prince cannot see his vision become a reality.

  o On the topic of the interdependence of strong political institutions and military might, Machiavelli offers a counterargument to the *Sunzi*. Rather than a general who is removed from the political elite, Machiavelli argues for one who is a member of the elite. A general should be as comfortable with politics as he is with war and strategy.

- Book I of *The Art of War* is an extended discussion of *virtu*, the skill and prowess of the general. *Virtu* gives the general the ability to assess and adapt to the endless complexity of the battlefield. *Virtu* in war also encompasses aggressiveness and the pursuit of decisive battle.

- Book II deals with armaments and military formations. Colonna holds forth on the merits of the Roman legion, but he wants to combine that structure with more contemporary innovations.
  - He seems to recognize the advent of what the British historian Geoffrey Parker called the "military revolution"—the 16th-century innovations that included improvements in artillery and musketry, increases in the size of European armies, the expansion of state bureaucracies, and the beginning of real logistics.

  - These changes spelled the end of religiously inspired wars fought by small armies of knights and opened the era of mass war and power politics.

- In Book III, we see the hybrid Roman/modern army in action.

- Book IV bears more than a passing resemblance to some of the middle chapters of the *Sunzi*. It covers marching the army through various types of terrain and weather and deals with the ways in which a commander can raise and manipulate the morale of his men to tactical advantage.

- Book V concerns the demands of marching an army into enemy territory. A good army has clear orders and minimal logistics. It is arrayed so as to defend against attack from all directions, and it is careful to avoid traps and ambushes.

- Book VI is a detailed discussion of how to encamp an army—not surprisingly, in Roman fashion. We also hear Colonna's thoughts on why prostitution and gambling should be banned in military camps. The discussion then turns to espionage and counterespionage.

- Book VII deals with the strengths and weaknesses of different styles of fortifications, methods of attacking fortifications, and the capabilities and limitations of artillery.

Book III: A Fictional Battle

- The bulk of Book III is devoted to an extended discussion of a fictional battle in which the advantages of the hybrid Roman/modern army are on full display. The chapter stands out in gripping vividness compared to the often dry detail of the rest of the book.

- Some have seen this central chapter as Machiavelli's chance to re-fight the Battle of Prato with the army that *The Art of War* envisions. There may be some merit to that view, but Machiavelli was too consistently interested in influencing policy in the present to linger too much on what might have been in the past.

- Decisive battle was the centerpiece of Machiavelli's entire approach to strategy, and a decisive battle is the centerpiece of his *Art of War*. All the other elements covered in the book—recruitment, training, formations, espionage, and so on—come together in this great clash of arms.

- In the opening stages of the battle, the victorious army takes out the enemy's artillery. The main body then moves with precise order and discipline to close with the enemy. The enemy collapses in the face of this onslaught and falls into a rout. The whole affair seems predestined, and many of Machiavelli's detractors are right to point out that such a mechanistic view of battle is simplistic and dangerous.

- We should note, however, that this perfect battle is meant to be a clash of opposites. On one side is an army that has perfected the mechanics of war and embraced the model of ancient Rome. On the other side is an army that has ignored the lessons of the past and the present.

- Despite its strengths, *The Art of War* is primarily tactical in its focus, dealing with the mechanics of military power rather than with strategy at the higher level. To comprehend the full range of Machiavelli's insight on the purpose and conduct of war and to understand the strengths and weaknesses of his strategic injunctions, we will next turn to his other great military work, *Discourses on the First Decade of Titus Livy*.

Suggested Reading

Gilbert, "Machiavelli: The Renaissance of the Art of War."

Hornqvist, "Machiavelli's Military Project and the *Art of War*."

Machiavelli, *The Art of War* in *The Chief Works and Others*.

Questions to Consider

1. In what ways is Machiavelli's *The Art of War* similar to Sun Tzu's *The Art of War*? In what ways is it different?

2. Why do you think Machiavelli used Fabrizio Colonna as his spokesman? Was Colonna a good choice?

Machiavelli's *The Art of War*
Lecture 6—Transcript

In his most famous and most controversial work, *The Prince*, Niccolo Machiavelli argued that the most important things for a ruler to study were the rules and disciplines of war. War, he said was the "sole art" of the ruler and one of the main means by which a prince could sustain his power. War was also perhaps the only means by which a would-be prince could rise to that rank. These were not the idle musings of a dilettante. Machiavelli wrote two subsequent volumes, much longer than *The Prince*, on exactly these topics: books on the rules and disciplines of war, on the mechanics and merits of military power (in other words the topics that he had identified as the most critical to the prince). Those books, Machiavelli's *The Art of War* and his *Discourses on Livy* will be the subject of our next two lectures.

Although he is much more famous as a political philosopher and as author of *The Prince*, Niccolo Machiavelli can easily be counted as one of the West's most insightful and influential military thinkers. Like many great strategic theorists, Machiavelli sensed a sea-change coming in the nature of warfare. The feudal system was coming to an end and with it the military centrality of the hereditary knights. Moreover, the gun-powder revolution was beginning to sweep Europe. Machiavelli sensed that these social and technological revolutions were going to have far-ranging consequences for the nature of warfare and statecraft. But Machiavelli was not merely an observer of these revolutionary trends. As we'll see, he was personally involved in the effort to recruit and train a Florentine militia in the tumultuous early years of the 16th century.

So we are already getting the sense that, pun intended, Machiavelli was a Renaissance man. He was a Renaissance man in the modern sense of the phrase. He was a bureaucrat, a diplomat, a political philosopher, a biographer, a playwright, a poet, a satirist, and a military theorist. He was also a Renaissance man in the historical sense of the term. He believed in reason and rationality. He was a humanist who believed that society and knowledge progressed or regressed based on human creativity—and not on the basis of some divine intervention. And Machiavelli was a student of ancient history, especially of ancient Greece and Rome. He believed, like many in the Renaissance, in the immense value of antiquity to the present. To Machiavelli the future could be a perfect synthesis of the best of the past and the promise of the present. Both of his great works on military and strategic theory are imbued with these beliefs.

In this lecture I will be talking primarily about *The Art of War*, which Machiavelli published in 1521. But before we get to the manuscript, let's spend a little time learning about the man. Machiavelli was born in Florence in 1469. His father, a lawyer, introduced the young Niccolo to the world of Greek and Roman history. As a young boy Machiavelli took an avid interest in ancient history, especially in Livy's account of the early Roman Republic.

For the first 25 years of his life, Florence was ruled by the Medici family. But in 1494, the French King, Charles VIII, invaded Italy and ousted the Medicis. In the chaos that followed, the rabidly moralistic Dominican friar, Girolamo Savonarola, seized power in Florence and launched a crusade to purify the city of its moral corruption. Machiavelli had a hand in Savonarola's overthrow in 1498 and was rewarded with important positions in the new government of Piero Soderini. Throughout his years in the Republic's government, Machiavelli continued to write on a range of issues and to comment on Roman texts.

These literary works complemented his busy duties as a diplomat and reformer of the Florentine military. In his guise as diplomat, or more accurately I should say in his guise as spy, Machiavelli gained first-hand knowledge of the chaos and intrigue of Italian politics. Machiavelli got to see the brilliant and ruthless Cesare Borgia in action during his rise to power and was also there to witness Borgia's downfall. Borgia became one of the models for *The Prince* and his military reforms inspired Machiavelli's own military projects.

Now, in the era of Machiavelli's political service, Italy was a total mess. Charles VIII's invasion of Italy had sparked a multilateral tug of war for control of the Italian Peninsula. From the 1490s to the 1550s, the kings of France, England, and Spain, along with the Pope and the Holy Roman emperor, all vied to dominate the Italian states. The Italian states themselves were forced to ally with these superpowers and against one another.

Let's look at the military realities of Renaissance Italy. In the face of these outside powers and their Italian allies, Florence was virtually powerless. Machiavelli wanted to reverse Florence's decline and his diplomatic experience deeply influenced his actions as a military reformer. To Machiavelli, Italy's political crisis was an outgrowth of its military weakness. If Florence was going to survive as an independent state and to have an independent foreign policy, then it needed a strong military. Unfortunately, Florence did not really have its own army.

Like many Italian states, the Florentines preferred to forgo the expense and complications of having their own military forces and their own defense bureaucracy. Instead, the Republic relied on mercenaries. These armies-for-hire were commanded by the *condottieri*, the professional military leaders working under a contract, called a *condotta*, for the Republic (*condotta*, contract, *condottieri*, contractors).

One of the biggest problems with this system was that mercenaries were expensive and this often required the Florentines to borrow from the kings of France and Spain to pay for these levies of troops. This undermined Florentine political independence.

Another problem was that these contracts were for a fixed term. In other words they often required painful and costly renegotiation. Think of it as a military version of baseball's free-agent system. Renegotiation was common because the Italian wars rarely reached a decisive resolution and tended to drag on. Working for profit, the *condottieri* were disinclined to risk their assets, in other words their soldiers and heavy cavalry, in bloody but decisive battles. Machiavelli regularly ridiculed the mercenary way of war, describing grand, day-long battles between well-paid and magnificently-equipped armies in which only one or two men die, and usually by accident, not at the hands of the enemy; his anti-mercenary rant in Chapters 12 and 13 of *The Prince* is well worth a read.

Despite Machiavelli's jabs, armies for hire were more powerful and more professional than what most Italian states could put into the field. As such, they were a major force in Italian wars and in Italian politics. But Machiavelli was dissatisfied with the contractors and wanted instead to put

Florence's fate in the hands of a Florentine commander leading a Florentine citizen army.

Machiavelli's ideas gained a greater appeal in light of the Republic's protracted efforts to retake the city of Pisa. Under the Medicis, Pisa had been ruled by Florence, but the city had gained its independence in 1494. Without Pisa and its easy access to the sea, Florence was unlikely to remain a great power contender for long. Reliance on mercenaries, however, had delayed Pisa's recapture and strained the Republic's finances.

In the early 1500s Machiavelli was acting as secretary of the government office responsible for military matters. During his tenure, the *condottieri* had repeatedly proven incapable of capturing Pisa.

In 1505 after yet another failed assault on Pisa, Soderini ordered Machiavelli to begin recruiting a militia from the agricultural districts around Florence. That new militia proved crucial to the final retaking of Pisa in 1509. Machiavelli's views on the merits of the citizen army seemed vindicated. In 1512, however, a 3,000-man Florentine force, including 1,000 of Machiavelli's militiamen, was tasked to defend the city of Prato against a combined army of the Pope, the Holy Roman Emperor, the king of Spain, and the Medicis. Now, a militia is a long way from a citizen army. So, facing a mass of professionals, the Florentines panicked and tried to flee. Many of them were among the thousands slaughtered at Prato.

After the fall of Prato, Machiavelli mustered what was left of the militia to defend Florence against the advancing Medicis. The militia faltered again, and the Florentine Republic was finished. The triumphant Medicis retook the city and purged the government of Republicans. Machiavelli was imprisoned and tortured in 1513. He was lucky to make it out alive.

Machiavelli returned to government only briefly at the very end of his life, but he put his forced retirement to good use. Not only did he write *The Prince*, Machiavelli also returned to the study of ancient history and its lessons for contemporary Italy. In particular he looked to Roman history and to the model of Republican Rome.

Why the Roman Republic? Machiavelli was deeply enamored of the model of the Roman Republic. In his view, the Republic was the best and most stable form of government. It was stable because it was mixed. Our own Republic was in part founded on the same mixed model. The United States is not a pure democracy like ancient Athens with all of its volatility; we have three branches of government, a system of checks and balances. In a similar way, republican Rome had stabilizing tension between its executives, the two consuls, its aristocratic/oligarchic senate, and the voice of the people with the Tribune of the Plebs.

Living in chaotic times, Machiavelli was naturally drawn to the Roman model of political stability and stamina. Obviously the social and political implications of Machiavelli's views on republicanism are beyond the scope of this lecture, but I can recommend the terrific course that Professor William Cook put together for The Great Courses, called "Machiavelli in Context." For our purposes, I will primarily focus on the influence of the Roman model on Machiavelli's military and strategic thought.

Machiavelli appreciated the intimate link between society and the military. Florentine society had been de-militarized and they had outsourced their defense to mercenaries. These were fundamental weaknesses of the Florentine Republic. In contrast, the very basis of the Roman Republic was the Roman citizen army: the legions. The command structure of the legions mirrored the political structure of the republic, making them a kind of incubator of Republican virtue. The legions therefore stabilized the republic internally and defended it externally. In addition, long-serving citizen soldiers made for better soldiers (in other words they were a match for mercenaries) and they were better citizens. Better citizens, in turn, made for a stronger and more stable republic. Ideally, those better citizens would not be tempted to use their military training in domestic politics. Instead a stronger army and stronger republic could direct its energies outward, toward conquest and empire.

Even with the catastrophic failure of the militia at Prato, Machiavelli remained committed to the merits of the citizen army. If anything, the Florentine Republic's embrace of the Roman analogy had been much too little and far too late.

Unlike a militia, a long-serving citizen army recruited from and exclusively loyal to the Florentine Republic would give Florence greater freedom of action in its foreign affairs and would decrease its dependence on powerful allies. Machiavelli thus gives us some idea as to how a middle-ranked power can defend and ultimately expand its power and interests. This is the argument that he begins to lay out in *Dell'arte della guerra, The Art of War.*

Where Thucydides often reads like a Greek tragedy and the *Sunzi* like a series of lectures, Machiavelli's *The Art of War* is structured as a Socratic dialogue in the style of Plato. Participating in the dialogue is a group of Florentine noblemen, led by Cosimo Rucellai, and the formidable *condottiero*, Fabrizio Colonna. Colonna, who acts as the spokesman for Machiavelli's ideas, takes the role of Socrates and Rucellai and his guests the role of interlocutors. Over seven chapters Colonna consistently stresses the value of antiquity to the point of arguing for the establishment of modern legions on the model of the Roman Republic.

But Machiavelli is not a fan of anachronism for its own sake. The value of antiquity is not limited to its mythic authority, but extends to its accessibility as a practical guide to strategy and tactics. Machiavelli is imitating the ancient style of a Platonic dialogue in a contemporary setting to make an ancient argument with contemporary relevance.

As an author he follows the literary style of the ancients in the same way that he hopes his contemporary readers will copy the ancient Roman models of order, discipline, and *virtu*—*virtu* brings adaptability or one might say strategic agility. It is a very long conversation, in which Colonna and the Florentines range over the breadth and scope of recorded military history. In the process they test which ancient tactics and strategy are best suited to which particular military challenges. Machiavelli acknowledges that contemporary Italy is not the same as ancient Rome, but he still makes a powerful and very specific argument about the Roman institutions that would best serve the security and stability of Florence.

Colonna is an interesting choice as Machiavelli's mouthpiece. Colonna, who died in 1520, just prior to the publication of *The Art of War*, was a Roman mercenary captain who served the Holy League in the war that had ended both the Florentine Republic and Machiavelli's political career. It might seem odd to have this arch-mercenary serve as a spokesman for the citizen army. In fact, at one point Cosimo Rucellai asks Colonna exactly that: "Why," Rucellai asks, do "you [Colonna] condemn those who do not imitate the ancients [when] on the other hand, in matters of war you have [not] employed any of the ancient methods?" In other words, with all due respect Don Fabrizio, why don't you practice what you preach?

Colonna's response has a very contemporary ring. He basically says that you go to war with the army you have, not the army you wish you had. As yet, there had been no enlightened prince who had built an army on the model of Rome, hence a general like him had not had the opportunity to wage war as it should be waged.

There is a tendency to view *The Art of War* as dry, preachy, and excessively strident. As the only major work published during Machiavelli's life, it seems to lack the snarky humor of his more famous works. The Socratic structure is also seen as too one-sided, with the excessively deferential Florentines simply in receive mode at the feet of Colonna. I agree in general with this later characterization, but I still think there is plenty of snark and humor in this book. The choice of Colonna is brilliant and shocking. The mute deference of the Florentines serves only to showcase their ignorance, and by extension Florence's ignorance, of military affairs. Machiavelli also mocks the popular antiquarianism of his contemporaries. The superficial interest in the ancients was all the rage, but Machiavelli was all about the substantial relevance of the past to the present.

The conversation between Colonna and the Florentines is set in the famous Rucellai gardens, which you can visit in Florence today. Those classically inspired gardens had become the center of intellectual ferment in Renaissance Florence. The Florentine elite would meet in the peace and quiet of the gardens to discuss the great issues of the day.

Into that sylvan paradise marches the warlord Fabrizio Colonna to lecture these dilettantes. And how does he start the conversation? He insults their superficial antiquarian pretentions. The garden was famous for its trees, ancient and rare specimens that the Rucellai family had tended with great care. "Wouldn't it have been better," Colonna says, "to imitate the ancients in the strong and rugged things, not in the soft and delicate."

The model of the ancients does not lie in ruminating on great issues in the comfort of a splendid garden, it lies in bold action in the real world. And with that, Colonna opens the discussion. *The Art of War* is divided into a preface and seven chapters. In the preface, Machiavelli speaks in his own voice about the interconnection of politics and war and the intimate relation between the military and civilian order. Those of you familiar with *The Prince*, will already have a good idea of Machiavelli's views on the merits of military power. A good military is the foundation of a viable state. Without good arms, a state cannot build good institutions and cannot defend itself. Without good arms the prince cannot see his vision become a reality. This was the lesson of recent Florentine history.

Machiavelli was suspicious of a system in which the politicians deferred to professional soldiers on military matters. In his appreciation of matching military action to political ends and of the social function of the military, Machiavelli was leaning on the ancients to make an argument that was ahead of his times.

On the topic of the interdependence of strong political institutions and military might, Machiavelli offers a counterargument to the *Sunzi*. Remember, the author of the *Sunzi* was defining and defending the expertise and autonomy of the general. Italy has lots of professional soldiers, maybe too many, and they have too much autonomy. Machiavelli is trying to reverse that trend.

On the surface therefore Machiavelli's *The Art of War* and the *Sunzi* seem to make similar arguments about the autonomy of the military commander; a general who is free from the meddling of the politicians. But Machiavelli doesn't draw as stark a distinction between the rulers and the generals. In his own career Machiavelli had moved back and forth between military and civilian jobs and his ideal general would be a member of the Florentine political elite. In other words, a general should be as comfortable with politics as he is with war and strategy.

After establishing these views in the preface, Machiavelli refrains from direct comment throughout the rest of the book. The remaining seven chapters are the conversation between Colonna and the Florentine elite.

Book I is an extended riff on the virtues of *virtu*, the skill and prowess of the general. On this topic, Machiavelli's commander sounds a lot like the *Sunzi*'s clever combatant. His *virtu* gives him the ability to assess and to adapt to the never-ending complexity of the battle-field. *Virtu* in war also has to do with aggressiveness and the pursuit of decisive battle. It is only through bold and decisive actions that great things can be achieved.

In addition, Book I covers issues such as recruiting the citizen army, the role of the army in the political life of the state, and the paired dangers of, on the one hand, complete peace-time de-mobilization and, on the other, of a perpetual war-footing. Demobilization threatens the state externally, leaves it defenseless, while a perpetual war-footing threatens the state internally.

Book II deals with armaments and military formations. Colonna holds forth on the merits of the Roman legion, but he wants to combine that structure with more contemporary innovations like the Swiss square, itself a modern version of a legion. And he wants to integrate firearms into the units.

Coming from a heavy-cavalry commander like Colonna, this focus on the infantry is kind of surprising, but Colonna seems to appreciate that the days of armored knights mounted on heavily armored chargers are quickly coming to an end.

With the turn of the 16th century we have the advent of what Geoffrey Parker called "The Military Revolution." This involved improvements in artillery and musketry, a huge increase in the size of European armies, the expansion of state bureaucracies, and the advent of real logistics. This changed the very nature of warfare. It spelled the end of religiously inspired war fought by small armies of knights, the medieval period, and opened the era of mass war and power politics.

But if we view Machiavelli's argument from the perspective of our own military technological revolution, the Roman analogy looks pretty silly.

In an age of precision-guided munitions, aircraft carriers, and GPS, the organization and tactics of a Roman legion are something akin to quaint artifacts, of interest only to reenactors or the producers of the next Russell Crowe movie. In the early 16th century, however, the disciplined, rigidly ordered, but tactically flexible legion was a particularly useful model for the new infantry armies. That modern–Roman hybrid army in action is the topic of Book III, but I'll return to that section in a minute.

Book IV bears more than a passing resemblance to some of the middle chapters of the *Sunzi*. It covers the army marching through various types of terrain and weather in search of advantage over an out-maneuvered adversary. Book IV also deals with the morale of the men and the ways in which the commander can raise and manipulate morale to tactical advantage. As much as the prince and the general display their respective *virtu*, the officers and foot-soldiers have their own brand of *virtu*.

Book V concerns the demands of marching an army into enemy territory. A good army has clear orders and minimal logistics. It can defend against attack from all directions and it is careful to avoid clever traps and ambushes.

Book VI is a detailed discussion of how to encamp an army. Not surprisingly Colonna's modern camp is laid out in Roman fashion with those classic intersecting roads and the division into four wards. We also hear Colonna's thoughts on why prostitution and gambling should be banned in military camps. The topic then turns to espionage and counterespionage, again tracking very closely with our Chinese master.

The final book, Book VII, deals with the strengths and weaknesses of different styles of fortifications, a subject on which Machiavelli had written earlier. The last book also covers different methods of attacking fortifications, especially regarding the capabilities and limitations of artillery. Lastly, in his summation, Colonna offers a list of his general principles, 27 in all, which, if we are to believe Machiavelli, he enumerates off the cuff. Colonna then closes the discussion by returning to Cosimo Rucellai's "practice what you preach" question.

It would be easy, Colonna argues, for a ruler of a large enough state to restore the ancient military ways, but none of the Italian states had done that. Why not? For Colonna there were none of what he called "wise princes" who had followed this simple model, this simple Roman model. Instead, the Italians were in his words "the shame of the world." Their military weakness made them pawns rather than players in the game of power politics.

Obviously, there is a lot more depth and detail in Machiavelli's *The Art of War* than this short summary would imply. The discussion ranges far and wide and is peppered with countless supporting examples from ancient, medieval, and Renaissance military history. Machiavelli was probably showing off a little and may even have been preemptively bludgeoning his critics with history and promoting his military credentials. At one point Colonna singles out Machiavelli's 1506 militia ordinance for overwhelming praise. But regardless of his motivations, Machiavelli was relentless on the value of history to the solution of contemporary problems.

Ultimately, it was recent history, the rise and fall of the Florentine republic that most concerned Machiavelli. With that in mind, let's go back to Book III of *The Art of War*. Book III contains some general military prescriptions, but the bulk of it is devoted to the extended discussion of a fictional battle in which the advantages of the Roman–modern hybrid are on full display. The chapter in itself stands out in gripping vividness as compared to the often dry detail of the rest of the book.

All of these strengths notwithstanding, *The Art of War* is primarily tactical in its focus. In other words it deals primarily with the mechanics of military power, the grammar of war, rather than the merits of military power and with strategy at the higher level, the logic of war. To comprehend the full range of Machiavelli's insight on the purpose and conduct of war, and to understand the strengths and weaknesses of his strategic injunctions, we need to look to another book. So in our next lecture we'll turn from *The Art of War* and pick up our discussion with Machiavelli's other great military work, his *Discourses on the First Decade of Titus Livy*.

I'll see you then.

Machiavelli's *Discourses on Livy*
Lecture 7

S omebody very smart once said, "If you want a new idea, read an old book." Machiavelli could not have agreed more. He drew many innovative ideas for solving the problems of 16th-century Italy from old books. Machiavelli's *Art of War* was very much inspired by his reading of an old book by Vegetius. In this lecture, we will spend time on Machiavelli's reading of an even older book, his *Discourses on the First Decade of Titus Livy*, a text that serves as his manifesto on republican empire and his exposition on the importance of *virtu*.

Titus Livius

- Titus Livius, known as Livy, was a Roman whose formative years coincided with the Roman civil wars, first between Caesar and Pompey and then between Brutus, Marc Antony, and Octavian Caesar (Emperor Augustus).

- Livy appears to have been a friend and confidant of Augustus, writing an official history of Rome commissioned by the emperor himself. It is to that monumental history, *Ab urbe condita libri*, that Livy owes his fame and the affection of Machiavelli.

- The first 10 books (the first "decade") of Livy's work cover the first 450 years of Roman history, from the mythical founding of the city in the 8th century B.C. to the conquest of Italy and Rome's emergence as a Mediterranean empire.

Overview of the *Discourses*

- Machiavelli's *Discourses* were probably mostly written after *The Prince* and before *The Art of War*. We can therefore view the *Discourses* as a kind of downward expansion on *The Prince*, taking policy in *The Prince* down to the level of political institutions and strategy in the *Discourses*. In the same way, *The Art of War* is a downward expansion on the *Discourses*, linking political institutions and strategy to military institutions, operational doctrine, and tactical methods.

- For Machiavelli, the early history of Rome serves as a kind of laboratory for studying human nature and human motivations in action, illustrating the patterns of history, the types of challenges that states might face, and the options for dealing with those challenges. Machiavelli makes creative use of Livy's history to inculcate readers with the habits of political and strategic judgment they will need in the highest civilian and military posts.

- Machiavelli is also writing to his fellow Florentines in particular.
  o As we've seen, *The Art of War* was a call for Florence to follow the ancients in the military arts. The *Discourses* is a call to the Florentines to follow the Romans in political organization—most critically, in their strategic behavior.

  o If Florence was to survive and ultimately to thrive, modeling its armies on Rome was not enough. The Florentines also had to model their strategies on the audacity and adaptability of the Romans; they had to replicate Rome's strategic *virtu*.

  o To make his case, Machiavelli tries to shock his audience into realizing the valuable lessons of Rome by showing the glaring dichotomy between ancient Roman *virtu* and contemporary Italian corruption. Specifically, he highlights the contrasts between Florence, a state corrupted in its institutions and a slave to the caprices of *fortuna*, and early Rome, a state blessed with strong institutions and a master of its own destiny.

Fortuna and *Virtu*

- The term *fortuna* in Machiavelli's writing can be defined as fate; it is what lies beyond man's control. Although *fortuna* makes human existence a constant struggle, it is not purely malevolent or capricious. Struggle gives birth to conflict, which can result in creativity.

- *Virtu* is a more problematic concept. In its simplest sense, *virtu* involves adapting to current circumstances and acting appropriately. It should not be confused with virtue or morality; in some instances, *virtu* may be the exact opposite of morality. It is *virtu* that allows men and states to contend with, and capitalize on, *fortuna*. *Virtu* is about insight, adaptability, efficacy, and the will to act; it is strategic agility.

- *Virtu* varies with circumstances, at different levels of society, and at different levels of war. Thus, we have the *virtu* of states and their rulers in determining policy and crafting strategy; the *virtu* of the general at the level of strategy and operations; and the discrete *virti* of the officers and men, that is, the operational and tactical levels of war.

- Machiavelli wasn't the first to highlight *virtu* as a counterpoint to *fortuna*, but he was among the first to systematically link all these levels and types of *virtu* together. If anything, the rise of Rome as portrayed by Livy is, to Machiavelli, a study in the optimization of individual and institutional *virtu* in action.

- Ultimately, *fortuna* places men and states within the roiling currents of history; *virtu* is what allows men and states to harness those currents and become the masters of their own destiny.

The Structure of the *Discourses*

- The *Discourses* is divided into three books, each with numerous chapters in which Machiavelli discusses particular historical vignettes or trends from ancient Rome. He then matches those with examples—or, more often, counterexamples—from contemporary Italy that contrast the *virtu* of the Romans with the depravity and corruption of the Italians.

- The first book of the *Discourses* is concerned mostly with Roman political institutions. Here, the Roman Republic, as characterized by Machiavelli, is an ideal balance of monarchy, aristocracy, and democracy. Rome was, therefore, politically stable, but the dynamic tension of its institutions also made it strategically nimble.

- Book II looks at how Rome used its homegrown military power to defend itself and then used offensive wars to grow and prosper. Book III deals primarily with the deeds of great Roman citizens and how their *virtu* benefited Rome.

The Policies and Strategies of Republican Imperialism

- In the *Discourses*, war is divided into four basic categories: offensive and defensive, and limited and total. In general, Machiavelli favors the offensive both strategically and operationally.
  - He tells us that weaker states—those that are less politically cohesive and robust—are better off going on the offensive. Taking war into the heart of an enemy's territory enables such states to reduce their own burdens of defense and multiply the burdens on the enemy. Offensive war also offers the chance of a decisive result in the near term.

  - Constitutionally stronger states are better off on the defensive. They are better able to bear the burdens of a protracted defense.

- In Book II, Machiavelli expands on the different types of wars by introducing the distinction between limited and total war.
  - A limited war is waged to expand the power and influence of the state. The populations of the conquered territory are generally treated humanely and are either allowed to live with their own laws or incorporated into the winner's state.

  - A total war is a cruel and frightful zero-sum affair in which a nation seeks to seize a new homeland and either drive out or exterminate the indigenous population.

- Republics must be especially vigilant and prepared for the almost inevitable possibility of war.
  - Machiavelli claims that republics invite wars because foreign princes are either eager to conquer a fledgling republic or are frightened into a preventive war against an expanding republic. War is also more likely for a republic because it is a more dynamic and expansive system of government than a monarchy.

o   Machiavelli is one of the first thinkers to show us why different types of political systems tend to have significantly different strategic inclinations.

The Conduct of War

- Both the *Discourses* and *The Art of War* were arguments against the prevailing notion that ancient tactics and strategy were irrelevant in an age of modern armies and gunpowder weapons.

- The *Discourses* stresses the tactical and operational *virtu* of the Roman infantry legion, manned by citizen-soldiers and motivated by religion and love of Rome. The legion could easily adapt its shape to the terrain and to the enemy. It was designed to accept tactical defeat and then fall back, regroup, and counterattack.

- Many critics of Machiavelli point to his obsession with infantry and the legion as emblematic of his hopeless anachronism. Machiavelli seems to downplay, if not disparage, the importance of artillery and the range and lethality of musket fire. This criticism misses the larger point that Machiavelli finds contemporary analogies to the legions of Rome.

- Machiavelli's ideal commander has his own brand of *virtu*—that flexibility and adaptability necessary to contend with *fortuna*. He is a greedy consumer of intelligence, not shy about using methods of deception to weaken an enemy, and on campaign, he is bold. At the same time, he is sensitive to opportunities for termination of war.
  o   Given that the general is often responsible for everything from planning, to leading, to terminating the campaign, Machiavelli favors the Roman system that gave commanders a great deal of autonomy—freedom from control by a distant government.

  o   At the same time, republican generals were also members of the civilian elite and served for fixed terms; this served to check the tendency toward military necessity hijacking national interest.

The Relevance of Machiavelli Today

- Machiavelli's books on strategy and war were a watershed in the evolution of Western strategic thought. He was ahead of his time in his call to subordinate military action to political ends, a concept that dominates strategic thought today. Unfortunately, his apparent efforts to free war from ethical considerations lost him many potential students.

- Later in this course, we will look at several states that meet Machiavelli's definition of a republic: France, Great Britain, and the United States. All seem to validate Machiavelli's point about the innate expansionism of republican empires, but they also point to the dangers of imperial overstretch. In fact, some recent scholarship seems to prove that democracies are far more belligerent than less representative systems of government.

- Note that America seems to have followed something of a Machiavellian trajectory. Alexander Hamilton, for example, talked explicitly about building the country into a republican empire, strong in institutions, strong in military power, and in control of sufficient territory so that it might be both secure and vigilant.

Like Machiavelli, Alexander Hamilton was a staunch advocate of the republican empire.

© iStockphoto/Thinkstock.

- The paired concepts of the citizen-army and the republican empire probably find their fullest exposition in the history of the United States. As we look forward in the 21st century, we might ask ourselves a few questions: Where is the United States relative to the point of imperial overstretch? What are the implications of our move away from a citizen-army to a professional military? Finally, how might Machiavelli assess our current state of affairs?

Suggested Reading

Heuser, *The Strategy Makers*.

Machiavelli, *Discourses on Livy* in *The Chief Works and Others*.

Najemy, "Society, Class, and State in Machiavelli's *Discourses on Livy*."

Pocock, *The Machiavellian Moment*.

Questions to Consider

1. Was the Roman Republic a good model for Renaissance Florence?

2. How do the *Discourses* differ from *The Art of War*? What is the significance of those differences?

Machiavelli's *Discourses on Livy*
Lecture 7—Transcript

Somebody very smart once said, "If you want a new idea, read an old book." Machiavelli could not have agreed more. Machiavelli read a lot of old books and drew from them many innovative ideas for solving the problems of 16th-century Italy. As a Renaissance man he was not alone in this endeavor; rediscovering the wisdom of the ancients and applying it to contemporary problems was one of the core objectives of Renaissance humanism. Machiavelli's *The Art of War*, which we discussed last time, was very much inspired by his reading of an old book by Vegetius. Today we will be spending time on Machiavelli's reading of an even older series of books; his *Discourses on the First Decade of Titus Livy*: A text that serves as Machiavelli's manifesto on Republican Empire and his exposition on the importance of *virtu*.

Titus Livius, or Livy as we usually call him, was a Roman whose formative years coincided with the Roman civil wars, first between Caesar and Pompey, and then the wars between Brutus, Marc Antony, and Octavian Caesar, later to become Emperor Augustus. In fact, Livy appears to have been a friend and confidant of Emperor Augustus, acting as mentor to the emperor's grandnephew Claudius, and writing an official history of Rome commissioned by Augustus himself. It is to that monumental history, *Ab Urbe Condita Libri*, that Livy owes his fame and the affection of Machiavelli.

Like Machiavelli, Livy came of age in a time of chaos and war, and he had seen a great prince in action. For Machiavelli the prince was Cesare Borgia, for Livy it was Augustus. Like Machiavelli 1,500 years later, Livy believed that Rome, like Florence, could be restored to morality, to unity, and to greatness through an understanding and imitation of the past. As with many of the classics of Greece and Rome, only a fraction of Livy's history has survived. Of its 142 books, only 25 are still complete, but there are summaries of the others.

It is the first decade, or first 10 books of Livy, that Machiavelli *Discourses* upon. Those first 10 books cover the first 450 years of Roman history. They begin with its mythic foundation in the 8th century. The stories of Romulus,

Remus, and the She Wolf. The middle chapters follow Rome's rise from a village on the Tiber to a major power in Italy and its rebirth after the Gallic invasion of the early 4th century. The last five chapters deal with Rome's conquest of Italy and its emergence as a Mediterranean power.

A lot of ink has been spilled about the timing of and Machiavelli's motivations for writing the *Discourses* as well as its relation to the far more controversial *The Prince*. I am going to shy away from those debates and instead look at the *Discourses* as a complement to *The Art of War*. It is pretty certain that the *Discourses* were mostly written after *The Prince* and before *The Art of War*, that's during the first decade of Machiavelli's political exile. We can therefore look at the *Discourses* as a kind of downward expansion on *The Prince*; taking policy in *The Prince* down to the level of political institutions and strategy in the *Discourses*. In the same way, *The Art of War* is a downward expansion on the *Discourses*, linking political institutions and strategy to military institutions, operational doctrine, and tactical methods. This really clarifies those levels of analysis and those levels of war.

Therefore, to understand Machiavelli's contributions to strategic thought, we need to see *Discourses* and *The Art of War* as paired texts. One way to see the different levels of analysis that Machiavelli is tackling is to look back to the masters that we have discussed so far. Book I of the *Discourses* is largely about the same issues as Thucydides' *History of the Peloponnesian War*. Book II and Book III of the *Discourses* and Machiavelli's *The Art of War*, are quite similar to Sunzi's *The Art of War*. Machiavelli's interest in Livy's history of early Rome does not spring from the interesting narrative, the how and what of Roman history; he is much more interested in the reasons why Rome became great.

The early history of Rome, like Thucydides' account of the Peloponnesian War, serves as a kind of laboratory for studying human nature and human motivations. We see the patterns of history, the types of challenges that a state might face, both internally and externally. We see as well a menu of options for dealing with these challenges. Machiavelli is making creative use of Livy's history of Rome to inculcate readers with the habits of critical political and strategic judgment that they will need in the highest civilian and military posts.

But it is even more focused than that. Machiavelli is writing to his fellow Florentines. We've seen that *The Art of War* is a call for Florence to follow the ancients in the military arts. The *Discourses* are a call to the Florentines to follow the Romans in political organization, but most critically in their strategic behavior.

If Florence was to survive and ultimately to thrive, modeling its armies on Rome was not enough, they also had to model their strategies on the audacity and adaptability of the Romans; they had to replicate Rome's strategic *virtu*.

To make his case Machiavelli tries to shock his audience into realizing the valuable lessons of Rome by showing in the sharpest contrasts the glaring dichotomy between ancient Roman *virtu* and contemporary Italian corruption. Specifically he wants to highlight the contrasts between Florence, a state corrupted in its institutions and a slave to the caprices of *fortuna* and the model of early Rome, a state that was blessed with strong institutions and that was master of its own destiny.

Contemporary Italians didn't look very good when held up to the mirror of ancient Rome. They looked even worse because they were willfully ignorant of the political circumstances (*fortuna*) in which they found themselves and willfully ignorant of the possible strategic solutions (*virtu*) that can be gleaned from the ancient Romans.

Now, I have mentioned these two concepts, *virtu* and *fortuna*, before, but it is worthwhile to take a little time to discuss what Machiavelli meant by them. The *Discourses*, as with almost all of Machiavelli's writings, are chock full of these two concepts. *Fortuna* is the easier one to define. *Fortuna* is variously characterized as a perverse and volatile goddess, a torrent of water sweeping away everything in its path, or even the hand of the Christian god. Simply put *fortuna* is fate, unforeseen circumstances, luck, fog, friction, what have you. *Fortuna* is what lies beyond man's control, and Machiavelli credits *fortuna* with about 50 percent of what happens in the course of human history. But *fortuna* is not purely malevolent or capricious, it is what makes human existence a constant struggle. That struggle gives birth to conflict, and conflict can give rise to creativity.

The other 50 percent of human history is attributable the more problematic concept of *virtu*. We shouldn't confuse *virtu* with virtue or morality. In fact, in some instances *virtu* is the exact opposite of morality. In its simplest sense *virtu* involves adapting to the current circumstances and acting appropriately. In some cases this might involve acting morally, in others it might involve bashing in your brother's skull with a shovel as in the case of Romulus killing Remus. It is this, how should I say it, moral flexibility, that draws the most fire from Machiavelli's critics. To many readers, Machiavelli's concept of *virtu* is morally repugnant.

Morality aside, it is *virtu* that allows men and states to capitalize on and even to contend with *fortuna*. *Virtu* is about insight, adaptability, efficacy, and the will to act. Intellect (honed by the study of history) probes the potentialities of the moment, adaptability shapes action in accord with those potentialities, and willpower or decisiveness carries the plan into action. *Virtu* is strategic agility.

As much as *virtu* can vary with circumstances, it varies at different levels of society; rulers, princes, have *virtu*; institutions have *virtu*; citizens have their own *virtu*. It also varies at the different levels of war. Thus we have the *virtu* of states and their rulers in determining policy and crafting strategy; this is a big topic in *The Prince* and in much of the *Discourses*. We also have the *virtu* of the general at the level of strategy and operations, a topic spread across the *Discourses* and *The Art of War*. And finally we have the discrete *virti* of the officers and men, that is the operational and tactical levels of war. This is the core of *The Art of War*.

Machiavelli wasn't the first to highlight *virtu* as a counterpoint to *fortuna*, but he was among the first to systematically link all of these levels and types of *virtu* together. If anything, the rise of Rome as portrayed by Livy is to Machiavelli a study in the optimization of individual and institutional *virtu* in action. Good policy and good strategy are great, but they are nothing without good arms. Good arms are unsustainable in the absence of good policy or in the presence of weak institutions or poor leadership. You need to have *virtu* at all levels to be successful in war.

Ultimately, *fortuna* places men and their states within the roiling currents of history; *virtu* is what allows men and states to harness those currents and become the masters of their own destiny, and this is why *virtu* is Machiavelli's core strategic concept.

So let's see how *virtu* is handled in Machiavelli's *Discourses*. The *Discourses* is divided into three books: Each book contains numerous chapters (60 in the first book alone) in which Machiavelli discourses on particular historical vignettes or historical trends from ancient Rome. He then matches those with examples, or more often counterexamples, from contemporary Italy that contrasts the *virtu* of the Romans with the depravity and corruption of the Italians.

Machiavelli reserves a particular condemnation for the Catholic Church. The church to him is a double evil. In the first place it teaches submission to God's will and a kind of meek fatalism, the opposites of *virtu*. Roman religion glorified action and decisiveness. In the second place, the Catholic Church did not practice what it preached; the popes (among them Borgias and Medicis) were as much players in power politics as the dukes of Italy and the kings of France and Spain.

So that is what Machiavelli wants to contrast to the Roman Republic, the condition of Italy. The first book of the *Discourses* is concerned mostly with internal Roman politics, with Roman political institutions. Here, the Roman Republic, as characterized by Machiavelli, is an ideal balance of monarchy with the consuls, aristocracy with the senate, and democracy with the tribunes representing the plebeians (or the common people). Rome was therefore politically stable, but the dynamic tension of its institutions also made it strategically nimble. We have already seen how institutions matter in war and strategy. Remember, Machiavelli thought balanced institutions helped Sparta endure the strains of the Peloponnesian War. Athens on the other hand, unhinged by mob rule, drove itself off a cliff.

The third book deals primarily with the deeds of great Roman citizens and how their *virtu* benefitted Rome; it also contains several chapters on military leadership. It is Book II, with a few elements of Book III thrown in, that we'll be looking at today. These are the parts of the *Discourses* where

Machiavelli looks to how Rome used its homegrown military power to defend itself and then used offensive wars to grow and prosper. It is about a small to medium-sized power coming to dominate a region. Machiavelli's ultimate goal was a unified and powerful Florence, a state that could rid Italy of foreign troops and foreign influence, and perhaps a state that could unify Italy under Florentine domination. If Rome had done it, why not Florence?

According to Machiavelli's reading of Livy, the early Roman Empire was built by good leaders operating within good institutions and employing good citizen soldiers. All of these Roman institutions and Roman individuals possessed different qualities of *virtu*. Rome waged its wars to increase these advantages and to increase its power and strategic ability. The peoples and areas they conquered were transformed into mirror images of Rome and incorporated into the Roman state.

Roman soft power, its culture and institutions, were spread by Roman hard power, the legions. And this one-two punch amplified both hard and soft power. Those states that Rome annexed became "more Roman than Rome," as in the case if Livy's hometown of Padua, and they revitalized the Republic. But war could also be a path to ruin. The *Discourses* is full of warnings about overextension, but prudence notwithstanding, Book II of the *Discourses* is best seen as a manifesto on the merits of republican imperialism.

So this brings to the issue of Machiavelli on the policies and strategies of Republican Imperialism. In the *Discourses*, war is divided into four basic categories: offensive and defensive and limited and total. In general, Machiavelli favors the offensive both strategically and operationally, but he is by no means obsessed with the offensive. He tells us that weaker states are better off going on the offensive. By weaker Machiavelli means constitutionally weaker, that is, less politically cohesive and robust. At first glance this is kind of counterintuitive, but it does make sense. If your institutions are weak and your people are not terribly loyal, then you stand no chance of defending yourself against a powerful adversary. But if you go on the offensive, and take the war into the heart of the enemy's territory, you reduce the burdens on your own state and multiply the burdens on the enemy. Offensive war also offers the chance of a decisive result in a shorter period of time. The weaker side can't sustain a protracted war. So the lesson is pretty simple: if you are a weak republic, you either expand or you die. But if you are a constitutionally stronger state, strengthened in the crucible of wars fought and won before, then you might be better off on the defensive. Strong states are better able to bear the burdens of a protracted defense. Think about Pericles' argument in the Peloponnesian War

Machiavelli sums this up in a nifty little maxim: "A ruler who has people well-armed and equipped should wait and wage a defensive war. A ruler who has poorly armed subjects should meet the enemy as far away from home as he can."

In Book II, Chapter 8, Machiavelli expands on the different types of wars by introducing the distinction between limited and total war. Naturally, this distinction arises from the motivations for the war itself. A limited war is waged to expand the power and influence of the state. The populations of the conquered territory are generally treated humanely and they are either allowed to live with their own laws or incorporated into the winner's state, given Roman citizenship. A total war is a cruel and frightful zero-sum affair in which a nation driven by famine or invasion seeks to seize a new homeland and either drive out or exterminate the indigenous population; Hitler's quest for lebensraum, or "living room" in Eastern Europe would fall into this category, as would the Gallic invasions of Italy in the 4th century. Wars can also be set in motion by chance, or by the machinations of an ally. As a result, war in the *Discourses* seems almost inevitable.

A republic must be especially vigilant and prepared for war. But why was this especially the case for republics? Because republics are going to end up fighting more wars. Way back in Book I of the *Discourses*, Machiavelli claims that republics invite wars because foreign princes are either eager to conquer a fledgling republic or are frightened into a preventive war against an expanding republic. War is also more likely for a republic because the republic is a more dynamic and expansive system of government, more expansive and dynamic than monarchies. People motivated by patriotism will seek to glorify the state through war and expansion. Kings and aristocrats are more interested in maintaining the status quo.

Embracing republicanism then seems a formula for constant war, but for Machiavelli this is both an acceptable risk and a necessary crucible for sustaining republican *virtu*. At the same time a republic must be cautious not to get overextended. Territorial expansion must enhance strength, not diminish it. This is why a mixed republic that balances prudence with audacity is the superior form of government. A state possessed of *virtu* will know when to expand and when to stand pat.

Like Thucydides, Machiavelli is interested in showing us why different political systems tend to have significantly different strategic inclinations. If we are to believe Machiavelli, republics tend to make different strategic choices than monarchies.

As he expands on the ways that different states wage wars, Machiavelli argues against yet another bit of conventional wisdom, the idea that money wins wars. The richer side does not always win. Gold, he says, is not the "sinew" of war. After all Athens was rich and they lost to cash-strapped Sparta. Persia was immensely rich, and yet they fell to an upstart like Alexander. Gold is good, but robust institutions are better. And good citizen soldiers are better than mercenaries, because they are motivated by glory and love of country, not gold. But, good soldiers can still get gold whenever they want.

When it comes to the actual conduct of war, the *Discourses* stresses many of those same issues that we saw in Sunzi's *The Art of War*. The *Discourses* and *The Art of War*, Machiavelli's that is, both argued for the relevance of ancient tactics and strategy, even in an age of modern armies and gunpowder weapons. The *Discourses* stresses the tactical and operational *virtu* of the Roman infantry legion, a legion manned by citizen soldiers and motivated by religion and love of Rome. Primed for glory, the legion was also inherently flexible.

It could easily adapt its shape to the terrain and to the enemy. It was also designed to accept tactical defeat and then fall back, regroup, and counterattack. This was a distinct improvement over the Greek hoplite phalanxes, which fought until one side broke. A Roman legion would force the enemy to throw waves of infantry and cavalry against the lethal shield wall. If the wall did start to crumble, the legion could draw back to a more defensible position and start all over. As much as Rome had political and strategic stamina and flexibility, the legion had operational and tactical stamina and flexibility.

Many critics of Machiavelli point to this obsession with infantry and with the legion as emblematic of his hopeless anachronism. Machiavelli seems to downplay, if not disparage, the importance of artillery and cavalry and the range and lethality of musket fire. This is a fair criticism, but it misses the larger point that Machiavelli is seeing contemporary analogies to the legions of Rome, especially among the Swiss and the Germans, who seemed to have copied the spirit (or concept) of the legion rather than its exact form or fighting style. In addition, and this is particularly useful to us today, Machiavelli is not dazzled by the latest and greatest in technology or tactics. He accepts them, but only as incremental rather than transformative changes in the nature of war or strategy. Technological advance does not repudiate the value of an old book, in fact, it reinforces the value of an old book.

On the issue of command, Machiavelli is less systematic than he is on other topics and we have to root around Books II and III of the *Discourses* for a picture of Machiavelli's ideal commander. Obviously this general has his own brand of *virtu*, that flexibility and adaptability necessary to contend with *fortuna*.

Machiavelli's general is also a greedy consumer of intelligence, on the terrain, the weather, and on the political conditions in the opposing state. Nor is the general shy about using all methods of deception and deceit to weaken an enemy. On campaign he is bold, he avoids half-measures and he is willing to embrace risk in pursuit of short, sharp, violent, and decisive blows against the enemy. And yet at the same time he is acutely sensitive to opportunities for ending a war. He has to sense that critical juncture where the enemy has taken just enough punishment to quit and his side has just enough combat energy left, just enough leverage left, to close the peace deal.

When it comes to enforcing that deal, Machiavelli tends to favor a generous peace. In Book II, Chapter 23, he relates the story of the city of Privernum, which had revolted against Rome, but because the citizens had behaved as men should, the Romans forgave them and allowed them to become Roman citizens. Contrast this to Athens' extermination of Melos. And yet elsewhere in the *Discourses* it would seem a Carthaginian solution may be called for. Machiavelli tells us, in war termination be cruel or be kind as the situation merits, but always avoid half measures. The middle course invariably leads to disaster. As to abiding by the terms of the peace treaty, making the result final, well that, too, depends on whether it suits your long-term interests, yet another example of *virtu* in action.

Finally, given that the general is often responsible for everything from planning, to leading, to terminating the campaign, Machiavelli favors the Roman system that gave commanders a great deal of autonomy, freedom from control by a distant government. But, at the same time, republican generals were also members of the civilian elite and served for fixed terms. This naturally served to check the tendency toward military necessity hijacking national interest and of generals becoming ambitious and wanting to seize absolute power.

Thus, although he had come to the study of politics from the study of war, Machiavelli was first and foremost a statesman and only second a military commander. He never wavered in his commitment to the close interconnection between operations, strategy, and state policy.

Machiavelli's books on strategy and war were a watershed in the evolution of Western strategic thought. He was ahead of his time in his call to subordinate military action to political ends, a concept that found its fullest exposition in the works of Clausewitz and which dominates strategic thought today. Unfortunately, Machiavelli's apparent efforts to free war from ethical considerations lost him many potential students. Machiavelli's real contributions are often overshadowed by the moral repugnance that his name invokes. When we think about Machiavelli and the meaning of Machiavellian we think about cold-blooded, ruthless, calculating, might makes right, the end justifies the means, and all of that. We might want to think of him in a couple of other ways.

As we read the *Discourses* we see Machiavelli as the advocate of republican empire. As we have seen republics both de-stabilize the balance of power and tend to be more expansionist than monarchies. A republic needs territory, resources, and population if it is to survive. Those things may very well have to be taken by force. Later in this course we will be looking at several states that meet Machiavelli's definition of a republic: revolutionary and Napoleonic France, Great Britain, and the United States. All of them seem to validate Machiavelli's point about the innate expansionism of republican empires, but they also point to the dangers of imperial over-stretch.

Closer to home, it seems as if America followed something of a Machiavellian trajectory. In fact, Alexander Hamilton, often caricatured as an arch-Machiavellian in a conventional sense of the phrase, was actually much more of a republican imperialist. He understood that the new United States was viewed with suspicion by the great powers. He talked explicitly about building the country into a republican empire, strong in institutions, strong in military power, and in control of sufficient territory so that, he said, it might be both secure and vigilant.

Another point of great relevance throughout modern history and potentially to America today, is Machiavelli's advocacy of an army composed of true citizen-soldiers.

It is hard to draw any direct cause and effect between Machiavelli's writings and the appearance of citizen-armies or even the notion of republican empire, but while Machiavelli might not have directly inspired these developments, he certainly anticipated them and provided ample justification for developing citizen armies. In fact, while Machiavelli is now known for *The Prince*, it was the *Discourses* and *The Art of War* that had the greatest influence in the first two centuries after his death. Both books were in wide circulation by the end of the 16th century and provided some of the broadest and most systematic exposition on the subjects of tactics, operations, and strategies. Machiavelli might not have been absolutely right about all these things, but he could not be ignored. No less a luminary than Voltaire opined that: "Machiavelli taught Europe the art of war; it had long been practiced, without being known."

Machiavelli's emphasis on the citizen-army anticipated the nationalization of war that would take place in the 18th and 19th centuries, although he could not possibly predict the scope of those revolutionary mobilizations.

The paired concepts of the citizen-army and the republican empire probably find their fullest exposition in the history of the United States. As we look forward into the 21st century we might ask ourselves a few questions. Where is the United States relative to the point of imperial overstretch? Are we at it? Beyond it? Short of it?

What are the implications of the fact that in the last three decades we have moved away from a citizen-army, to a professional military, and a professional military that is increasingly dependent on contractors for many of its core functions? In other words, as we look forward into the 21st century we might ask ourselves how Machiavelli might assess our current state of affairs.

The Napoleonic Revolution in War
Lecture 8

The Battle of Jena, which took place in 1806 between the Prussians and the French, was a masterpiece of classic Napoleonic tactics—the use of terrain, superior numbers, and superior firepower to sweep the field of the enemy. The Battle of Auerstaedt, fought on the same day as Jena, highlighted the superior morale and leadership of the French *grande armée*. The two masters of war we'll consider in the next part of the course, Antoine-Henri de Jomini and Carl von Clausewitz, were both present at Jena, and both immediately understood the larger significance of these two battles: Prussia's status as a Great Power and its reputation for military acumen were shattered on that day.

The God of War
- Carl von Clausewitz, a 26-year-old Prussian aide-de-camp at the time of Jena, later referred to Napoleon as the "god of war."
  - Clausewitz realized that the way Napoleon commanded and the way his armies fought were the culmination of a fundamentally new way of war: a transformation of warfare unleashed by the French Revolution.

  - Napoleon was the god of war because he embodied the French state and controlled French foreign policy. As emperor and national hero, he funneled the passions and hatreds of the French people, and as commanding general, he brilliantly wielded the *grande armée* on the field.

- The Prussians at Jena and Auerstaedt couldn't have been more different than the French. Their leadership was divided, and they suffered from weak command and control of their various units. Further, they had only superficially embraced the kind of warfare— the tactics, maneuver, coordination, and logistics—that the *grande armée* had long since mastered.

- A decade later, however, the Prussians were part of the coalition of Great Powers that forced Napoleon to abdicate. They did so by adopting many of the political and military reforms that had made the French army so formidable.

Warfare in the *Ancien Régime*

- As we saw in our lectures on Machiavelli, war in the Renaissance was primarily the domain of mercenaries, hereditary aristocrats, and poorly trained local levies. Standing armies tended to be relatively small, although they could bulk up during actual campaigns. War was constant and protracted, though rarely intense.

- Not much changed over the next 200 years. Even in the 18th century, the military forces of the major European powers were still significantly handicapped. The exception was Prussia under Frederick the Great, but even Frederick could not completely overcome the systemic problems of the European military system.
  - Armies in the 18th century were larger than those of the Renaissance but still small relative to the populations of their respective states.

  - Because monarchs avoided conscripting peasants, who were engaged in agriculture, the manpower pool typically included unproductive members of society—criminals, vagrants, and so on. Armies were fleshed out with foreign mercenaries.

  - To minimize the social disruptions of maintaining a standing military, *ancien régime* rulers tried to keep society and the military separate. Soldiers in the enlisted ranks served for very long terms, in some cases up to 30 years.

  - Given the questionable mettle of these foot soldiers, desertion was another major problem. To prevent mass desertions, armies marched slowly, in mass formations, and in daylight.

- o   Other challenges presented themselves in combat. Poor training and the technical problems of early gunpowder weapons demanded rigid and linear tactics.

- There were some efforts at tactical and technological reforms and the professionalization of some sectors of the officer corps under the likes of Frederick the Great, but in general, an *ancien régime* army was a slow and unwieldy mass of disgruntled and terrorized soldiers led by untrained and unimaginative aristocrats.

- Not surprisingly, 18th-century wars tended to be frequent but just as frequently indecisive. Few rulers, again with the exception of Frederick the Great, were willing to commit finite resources to decisive battles.

- The European balance-of-power system also argued against decisive wars. Any state that seemed poised to fundamentally change the status quo would invariably be met by a coalition of other powers intent on maintaining the balance of power.

The *Levée en Masse*

- The event that transformed warfare during the era of the French Revolution and the rise of Napoleon Bonaparte was the *levée en masse*. Initially an act of desperation in the face of foreign invasion, the *levée en masse* had two results: a massive French army of more than 700,000 men and an unprecedented nationalization of the French war effort.

- In 1793, France faced a coalition of all the major European powers intent on reversing the revolution. In response, the Committee of Public Safety promulgated the *levée en masse*, which put the entire French nation on a war footing.

- To feed and equip its massive new army, the committee nationalized and centrally coordinated arms manufacture, provisioning, and supply. To train the army, new units were interspersed with veteran units or, in some cases, paired with veteran noncommissioned officers for training as they marched toward the front. The French learned to mass the green troops in large columns, using them to screen their well-trained mobile units.

- French troops were broken down into divisions of multiple brigades that could move along different roads quickly and converge on the battlefield. Desertions prevented traditional armies from using this tactic, which meant that the French were suddenly lighter, faster, and more flexible than their enemies.

- In the area of command, the new regime inherited a tradition of innovation from the old that included the use of divisions, columns, and skirmishers. The French military built on that legacy of innovation and paired it with ambitious and audacious new blood in its officer corps.

- The fact that the new French army was both larger and more flexible inclined French commanders to be bolder and less risk-averse than their opponents. Nowhere was this more the case than with Napoleon Bonaparte.

The Rise of Napoleon
- The child of minor Corsican nobility, Napoleon Bonaparte was a 20-year-old artillery officer in the French army at the outbreak of the revolution in 1789. By 1793, he was a brigadier-general.

- Napoleon's precocious genius for war was clearly on display during the 1796–1797 Italian campaign, where he smashed the Austrians, France's staunchest enemies, and then deftly negotiated the Treaty of Campo Formio.

- He also had a genius for political intrigue, which was apparent in 1799 when he abandoned his army in Egypt and returned to Paris to seize power as first consul. In 1804, he declared himself emperor.

- In the hands of Emperor Napoleon and his gifted marshals, the raw, mass conscript armies of the revolution and the *levée en masse* were transformed into the most lethal fighting force the world had ever seen, the *grande armée*.

o The *grande armée* first saw action in the campaigns of 1805–1806, where Napoleon scored success after success at Austerlitz, Jena, and Auerstaedt.

o By 1807, Napoleon had used the *grande armée* to force the submission of all his continental enemies.

Nearly every element of *ancien régime* warfare, from the tactical to the strategic levels, would change with the French Revolution and the rise of Napoleon Bonaparte.

• Napoleon wasn't much of a military reformer, but he didn't have to be. By the time the *grande armée* was formed in 1803/1804, France had been at war for more than a dozen years, and its men were generally well combat-tested. Among Napoleon's modest innovations were the expansion of the artillery, the closer integration of the artillery and the infantry, and the expansion of the corps system.

Strategic Implications of the Transformation

• The *grande armée* allowed Napoleon to build a strategy based on speed, maneuver, firepower, shock, and pursuit.

• In many ways, the Napoleonic way of war was very Sunzian in execution. Napoleon and his marshals carefully planned all the mundane elements of a campaign and were voracious consumers of intelligence. But ultimately, Napoleon's goal was not to win without fighting; he sought to inflict the most decisive blow possible on the enemy's army.

- Whereas 18th-century wars were rarely decisive, Napoleon's *grande armée* could now inflict shocking casualties on its adversaries, along with strategic and psychological blows directed at the enemy's means and will.

- The size and operational depth of Napoleon's forces also meant that they could sustain heavy losses themselves and still be combat-effective and able to pursue the retreating enemy. This prevented the enemy from regrouping and compounded its strategic paralysis. Ultimately, the *grande armée* could threaten an enemy capital.

- For both Napoleon and Clausewitz, this "principle of continuity" was the key to Napoleon's quick, decisive victories. The psychological shock of a dramatic battlefield reversal was compounded by the highly credible threat that the emperor could inflict additional costs. In the early years of Napoleon's rule, this combination was usually sufficient to induce a European ruler to accept the emperor's terms.

- The battles of Jena-Auerstaedt, along with the ensuing march to Berlin, distill the essence of Napoleonic strategy. The *grande armée* effectively struck three centers of gravity: It overwhelmed the enemy army in the field, it seized the enemy's political capital, and by its speed, it foreclosed the possibility of allied intervention on behalf of a reeling enemy. Napoleon did the same to the Austrians the following year.

- At the peak of his powers, Napoleon married military genius with diplomatic acumen. He used diplomacy to isolate potential adversaries, in other words, to attack their alliances. But even after humiliating an adversary in battle, he would generally offer generous terms to soften the blow and facilitate capitulation.

Napoleon's Downfall
- As much as the *grande armée* was the great enabler of French success, it also proved the path to Napoleon's ruin. Over time, his enemies mastered many of the elements of the French military

revolution and, as a result, began to shift the qualitative balance between their forces and the *grande armée*.

- Better diplomacy and a growing consensus among the Great Powers that Napoleon had to be reined in also made for a more cohesive coalition. It was no longer easy for Napoleon to isolate his enemies and defeat them.

- For all of that, it was Napoleon's own blunders—putting his brother on the throne in Spain and invading Russia with a weaker version of the *grande armée*—that accelerated his fall. These paired disasters fundamentally undermined the military power of France and, with it, the political power of Napoleon.

- For all of the tactical and organizational innovations embraced by the *grande armée*, the core of the transformation of war in the Napoleonic era was, as Clausewitz noted, political—driven by the revolution in France and the nationalization of war.

Suggested Reading

Chandler, *The Campaigns of Napoleon*.

———, *Jena 1806*.

Esdaile, *The Peninsular War*.

Paret, "Napoleon and the Revolution in War."

Questions to Consider

1. Why were the armies of revolutionary France so revolutionary?

2. What were Napoleon's greatest strengths? What were his greatest weaknesses?

The Napoleonic Revolution in War
Lecture 8—Transcript

At 6:30 on the morning of October 14, 1806, Napoleon Bonaparte threw a force of 55,000 French soldiers against what he thought was the main Prussian army. The battle took place northwest of the city of Jena. From the start the 38,000 men of the Prussian force were outnumbered and outfought by the superior training, organization, and unity of command of Napoleon's army.

Nothing seemed to go the Prussian's way. When one of the French commanders, Marshal Ney, recklessly attacked Prince Hohenlohe's main body with only 3,000 cavalry and light infantry, Napoleon was able to maneuver his four corps to both rescue Ney and to start to turn the Prussian flanks. Napoleon's veterans, his maneuver forces, it seemed could turn on a dime to counter every Prussian move, and the French emperor could use his hard-drilled artillery to pummel the hapless Germans.

Early in the afternoon, Prince Hohenlohe ordered a retreat, but this quickly disintegrated into a rout as the desperate Prussians tried to flee from the relentless attacks of Napoleon's cavalry. In less than eight hours at Jena the Prussians and their Saxon allies had lost 25,000 men killed, injured, or captured, and they had surrendered more than 100 cannon. By comparison, the French suffered 5,000 casualties and were ready to give chase to the retreating Prussians.

As if the thrashing at Jena wasn't bad enough, it turned out that the main Prussian army, a force of 63,000 men under the Duke of Brunswick, was actually further to the north, outside the city of Auerstaedt. That army was taking a beating from the French as well.

Jena was a masterpiece of classic Napoleonic tactics, such as using terrain, superior numbers, and superior firepower to sweep the field of the enemy. Auerstaedt, which was fought on the same day as Jena, highlighted instead the superior morale and leadership of the French *grande armée.*

Initially out-numbered more than 2:1, the French Marshal Louis Nicolas Davout still threw his rigidly disciplined III Corps against the Prussians at Auerstaedt. The French withstood spirited but uncoordinated Prussian counterattacks, and gradually gained the upper hand. When the Duke of Brunswick was killed early in the battle, command of the Prussian forces fell to the poorly prepared King Frederick William.

Cohesion on the Prussian side quickly evaporated and despite still superior numbers, the King's first command was a total disaster. The Prussians suffered an additional 12,000 casualties and 3,000 POWs to the 7,000 killed or injured for the French. In the two weeks that followed the paired battles of Jena and Auerstaedt the remnants of the Prussian resistance crumbled. On October 26th Napoleon's *grande armée* marched into Berlin unopposed.

The two masters of war we'll consider in this part of the course were present at Jena. Baron Antoine-Henri de Jomini was on the staff of Marshal Ney, the same Marshal Ney whose premature attack on the Prussian line almost sank Napoleon's entire battle plan. The other master was Carl von Clausewitz—a 26-year-old aide-de-camp on the staff of the elderly Prince August Ferdinand. Clausewitz was one of the more than 25,000 Germans taken prisoner that day. Both he and Jomini understood immediately the larger significance of those two battles.

It was more than Prussia's army that was shattered at Jena and Auerstaedt. It was also Prussia's status as a Great Power. The Prussia of Frederick the Great, with its reputation for military acumen, was humiliated on that October day.

When Napoleon met King Frederick William III to agree to terms in the summer of 1807, the Prussian king was forced to hand over half of his territories and half of his subjects to the French emperor.

Given the remarkable speed and decisiveness of the Prussian campaign, it is no surprise that Clausewitz referred to Napoleon as the "god of war." He did this, not because he worshipped the French emperor, but rather because to Clausewitz the way Napoleon commanded and the way his armies fought were the culmination of a fundamentally new way of war: a transformation of warfare unleashed by the French Revolution.

Napoleon was the god of war because he embodied the French state and controlled French foreign policy. As emperor and national hero he funneled the passions and hatreds of the French people, and as Commanding General he brilliantly wielded the *grande armée* on the field brilliantly.

The Prussians at Jena and Auerstedt couldn't have been more different. Their leadership was divided and they suffered from weak command and control of their various units. To make matters worse, they had only superficially embraced the kind of warfare—the tactics, maneuver, coordination, and logistics—that the *grande armée* of France had long-since mastered.

The Prussians were also a remarkably cooperative adversary for Napoleon. They rushed into a war for which they were ill prepared, a war in which the military and material support of allies like Britain and Russia had yet to arrive. And yet a decade later, Prussia was part of the coalition of great powers that forced Napoleon to abdicate. In order to do that Prussia and its allies had been forced to adopt many of the political and military reforms that had made the French Army so formidable. Napoleon's adversaries also had to build a cohesive alliance if they were going to stand a chance against the god of war.

In fact, our two masters were involved in reversing the Napoleonic tide. In a shattered Prussia a small group of military reformers, Clausewitz among them, worked to persuade the humiliated king that not only did they need to reform their military institutions; they needed to figure out how to tap the latent potential of the entire Prussian nation. As for Jomini, he ultimately left the French Army and served as an advisor to the Russian tsar in the final stages of the war against Napoleon.

That brings us to the question of what was so revolutionary about the way the French fought. So, to understand the scale and nature of the Napoleonic Revolution in warfare, let's first take a look back at the nature of warfare before the French Revolution, in what we call the *ancien régime*.

As we saw in our lectures on Machiavelli, war in the Renaissance was primarily the domain of mercenaries, hereditary aristocrats, and poorly trained local militias. Standing Armies tended to be relatively small, numbering in the low tens of thousands. But they could bulk up, growing to more than 50,000, but only during actual campaigns. Nonetheless, wars were constant and although they were long wars, they were rarely intense or decisive wars.

Not much changed over the next 200 years. Even in the 18th century the military forces of the major European powers were still significantly handicapped. The significant exception was Prussia under Frederick the Great, but even the great Frederick could not completely overcome the systemic problems of the European military system.

Armies in the 18th century were larger than those of the Renaissance, numbering 100,000 to 300,000 men, but that was primarily a result of population growth and modest improvements in the bureaucratic capacity of the major powers. Armies were still very small relative to the populations of their respective states.

The typical manpower pool was also a big problem. Since agriculture was still the basis of national power, 18th-century monarchs didn't like to conscript peasants, that is, the more productive members of society. Instead they conscripted the unproductive members of society, folks like criminals and vagrants and fleshed out the rest of their armies with foreign mercenaries.

To minimize the social disruptions of maintaining a standing military, *ancien régime* rulers tried to keep society and the military separate. To join the army was like being torn out of society. Soldiers in the enlisted ranks served for very long terms, in some cases 8, 10, 20, and even 30 years. Military service was a life sentence.

Given the questionable mettle of these foot soldiers, desertion was another major problem. Hence draconian discipline was called for, but so, too, was concentration of forces. Marching at night, or along multiple roads, both desirable from an operational point of view, only offered more opportunities for soldiers to desert. To prevent mass desertions, armies marched slowly, in mass formations, and in the daylight. Obviously this slowed their movements and increased their logistical problems.

When it came to actual combat, there were yet other challenges. Poor training and the technical problems of early gunpowder weapons demanded rigid and linear tactics. For example, long, difficult-to-maneuver lines of infantry would draw up only a few dozen yards from each other. At the command, they would start pouring out round after round of inaccurate musket fire until one or the other army broke.

But it wasn't just the foot soldiers that were a problem. At the top you have officers that were almost exclusively drawn from the aristocracy. This is that same privileged but incompetent class of preening amateurs that the *Sunzi* so roundly denounced.

There were some efforts at tactical and technological reforms and the professionalization of some sectors of the officer corps under the likes of Frederick the Great. But in general an *ancien régime* army was a slow and unwieldy mass of disgruntled and terrorized soldiers led by untrained and unimaginative aristocrats. Not surprisingly, 18th-century wars tended to be frequent, but just as frequently indecisive. Few rulers, again with the exception of Frederick the Great, were willing to commit finite resources to decisive battles. In other words even when battles were fought they were unlikely to result in the numbers of losses to either side that would cause a ruler to permanently renounce his political objective.

Lastly, the European balance of power system argued against decisive wars. Any state that seemed poised to fundamentally change the status quo would invariably be met by a coalition of other powers intent on maintaining the balance of power.

Nearly every element of *ancien régime* warfare, from the tactical to the strategic levels, would change with the French Revolution and the rise of Napoleon Bonaparte. The event that transformed warfare in this era was the *levée en masse*. Initially an act of desperation in the face of foreign invasion, the *levée en masse* resulted in two things: a massive French army of more than 700,000 men and an unprecedented nationalization of the French war effort. Flush with revolutionary enthusiasm French armies had initially done pretty well in 1791 and 1792. By in 1793, however, France faced a coalition of all of the major European powers intent on reversing the revolution.

There were enemies closing on every front.

Confronted with the possibility of total defeat, the Committee of Public Safety, the government of France, promulgated the "*levée en masse*" designed to put the entire French nation on a war-footing. This passage from the very first article of the *levée en masse* invokes exactly what the revolutionary leaders had in mind: (It is worth quoting at length.)

> Until the enemy is driven from the soil of the Republic, all Frenchmen are in permanent requisition for the service of the armies. The young men shall go to battle; the married men shall forge arms and transport provisions; the women shall make tents and clothing and shall serve in the hospitals; the children shall turn old linen into lint; the aged shall betake themselves to the public places in order to arouse the courage of the warriors and preach the hatred of kings and the unity of the Republic.

The *levée en masse* enabled France to do what no other European power could, make war the domain of the individual citizen. But the levee itself was not the answer to France's strategic dilemma; it was only the first step. Now they needed to figure out how to feed, equip, train, move, and command an army of nearly 800,000 men.

To feed and equip the new army the Committee nationalized and centrally coordinated arms manufacture, provisioning, and supply. In some cases, notably when they operated beyond the borders of France, French armies could rely on supplies taken from the enemy. That's what the *Sunzi* tells us to do—take food from the enemy and increase the stress on his economy and society—but you still need to rely on your own government for guns, ammunition, and uniforms.

To train the army, new units were interspersed with older veteran units. And training got even more creative than that. In the crisis days of the early 1790s, small squads of new recruits would be paired with a veteran non-commissioned officer who would train them in rudimentary tactics of infantry war as they marched toward the front. This was the most basic type of basic training.

So what do you do with these raw recruits fresh off the farm? Young men who can only manage lowest common denominators of left face, right face, and forward march? One thing you can do with them is mass the green troops in large columns where all they had to do were those rudimentary things. This gave the French army a sudden boost in firepower. You then screen your main force with well-trained mobile units that harass the enemy's main body. Think about it! You now have a one-two punch of mass complemented by mobility. From very early on, we can see that the new French military was making virtues out of necessities.

Moving these armies also proved a monumental challenge, but here, too, the French made a virtue out of necessity. French units could not move en masse, so they were broken down into smaller divisions of multiple brigades that would move along different roads and converge on the battlefield. Traditional armies could not do this because of desertions, so the French were suddenly lighter, faster, and more flexible than their enemies.

This leaves us with the issue of commanding these armies. Much of this innovation can be credited to the talent and creativity of the French officer corps. Prior to the revolution, elements of the French military were among the most innovative officers in Europe.

The new regime therefore inherited a tradition of innovation, including the use of divisions, columns, and skirmishers. The Revolution, in turn, drove many aristocratic officers into exile. Interestingly, though, that loss of personnel—combined with the dramatic increase in the size of the French military—actually transformed the French officer corps into an innovative meritocracy. You see that existential crisis that France faced was another catalyst for creativity.

The French military built on the legacy of pre-Revolutionary innovation and paired that with ambitious and audacious new blood. The divided command structure put a premium on individual initiative and the fact that the new French army was both larger and more flexible, inclined French commanders to be bolder and less-risk averse than their opponents. Put another way, whereas the ancient Athenians preferred the prudence of Pericles, the modern French were producing a generation of Cleon's and Alcibiades'. Or to paraphrase the *Sunzi*, revolutionary France made the military the most vital affair of the state, and in the hands of clever and young combatants it proved the savior of the Revolution and the French nation. Nowhere was this more the case than with Napoleon Bonaparte.

The child of minor Corsican nobility, Napoleon Bonaparte was a 20-year-old artillery officer in the French army at the outbreak of the Revolution in 1789. By 1793 he was a brigadier-general. Bonaparte's precocious genius for war was clearly on display during the 1796–1797 Italian Campaign. In Italy, Napoleon smashed the Austrians, France's staunchest enemies, and then deftly negotiated the Treaty of Campo Formio. He also had a genius for political intrigue, which was apparent in 1799 when he abandoned his army in Egypt and returned to Paris to seize power as First Consul. In 1804 he declared himself emperor.

In the hands of Emperor Napoleon and his gifted marshals the raw, mass conscript armies of the revolution and the *levée en masse*, were transformed into the most lethal fighting force the world had ever seen, the *grande armée*. The *grande armée*, technically refers to the personal command of the emperor, in the same way that Air Force One technically refers to any Air Force aircraft that the president is on. But *grande armée* in this context is no mere honorific, it refers to the large mass of the best units that the French had, commanded by Napoleon.

It was originally formed for the invasion of England, but the fickle tides and awful weather of the English Channel scuttled that ambitious plan. Instead the *grande armée* first saw action in the campaigns of 1805–1806 where Napoleon scored success after success at Austerlitz, Jena, and Auerstaedt. By 1807 Napoleon had used the *grande armée* to force the submission of all of his continental enemies.

Crucial to this monumental achievement was the lethality and flexibility of the French Army. Despite his genius for battle, Napoleon was not much of a military reformer. But he did not have to be because he was fortunate to inherit the Army of the Republic. By the time the *grande armée* was formed in 1803–1804 France had been at war for more than a dozen years. French officers and enlisted men were generally well combat tested. Moreover nationalistic enthusiasm still ran very high in France. As a result Napoleon had fresh batches of highly motivated recruits to salt in with his veterans and a tested method of rapidly indoctrinating them into French tactics. This gave Napoleon's armies a degree of sustainability and resilience that other generals could only dream of.

Among Napoleon's modest innovations was the expansion of the artillery, not surprising given his early experience as an artillery officer, and the closer integration of the artillery with the infantry. He also expanded the corps system. Corps were essentially self-contained armies comprised of infantry, divisions of main line and skirmishers, as well as organic contingents of cavalry and artillery. The *grande armée* was divided into multiple corps. Under the leadership of an audacious marshal, a corps was capable of acting alone, as we saw with Marshal Davout's III corps at Auerstaedt, or in coordinated attacks as with Napoleon's IV, V, and VII Corps at Jena.

A corps was also very nimble for its size. It was less logistically cumbersome, in large part because they seized provisions on the march, and they had integrated cavalry to scout and clear routes of advance. Even in enemy territory the *grande armée* could march 30 miles a day and could keep up a blistering pace for weeks at a time. For example, in less than six weeks in 1805, the *grande armée* marched from Boulogne, on the West Coast of France, all the way to the Danube in Austria and they were still ready to fight.

Now let's consider some of the strategic implications of what we've learned about Napoleon and his army. The *grande armée* allowed Napoleon to build a strategy based on speed, maneuver, firepower, shock, and pursuit. 0In many ways, the Napoleonic way of war was very Sunzian in execution. Napoleon and the marshals were arch professionals who carefully planned all of the mundane elements of a campaign involving logistics, personnel, and morale of the men. They were also voracious consumers of intelligence, using local spies and their own cavalry to develop knowledge of the enemy. They also did everything in their power to conceal their own movements and plans. But ultimately, Napoleon's goal was not to win without fighting, but rather to inflict the most decisive blow possible on the enemy's army. There were few bloodless victories.

But whereas 18th-century wars were rarely decisive, Napoleon's *grande armée* could now inflict shocking casualties on its adversaries. These were strategic and psychological blows directed at the enemy's means and will. The size and operational depth of Napoleon's forces also meant that they could sustain big losses themselves and still be combat effective and able to pursue the retreating enemy. This prevented the enemy from regrouping and compounded their strategic paralysis. Ultimately the *grande armée* could threaten the enemy capital.

This was what Clausewitz called the Principle of Continuity, which is building on operational success to maintain military and political pressure on the opponent. For both Napoleon and Clausewitz this was the key to Napoleon's quick decisive victories. The psychological shock of a dramatic battlefield reversal was compounded by the highly credible threat that the emperor could inflict additional costs. In the early years of Napoleon's rule these were usually sufficient to induce a European ruler to accept the emperor's terms.

The battles of Jena and Auerstaedt, along with the ensuing march to Berlin, distill the essence of Napoleonic strategy. The *grande armée* effectively struck three centers of gravity: it overwhelmed the enemy army in the field, it seized the enemy's capital, and by its very speed it foreclosed the possibility of allied intervention on behalf of, say, the Prussians. Napoleon did the same to the Austrians the following year.

Here it is important to point out, that at the peak of his powers Napoleon married military genius with diplomatic acumen. He used diplomacy to isolate potential adversaries, in other words to attack their alliances. But even after humiliating an adversary in battle, he would generally offer generous terms to soften the blow and facilitate capitulation. Late in his career, however, Napoleon increasingly neglected soft power elements and tried to substitute military success for political success. Let's think about that. As much as the *grande armée* was the great enabler of French success, it also proved the path to Napoleon's ruin. As readers of the *Sunzi*, this shouldn't really surprise us.

Over time, Napoleon's enemies mastered many of the elements of the French military revolution and as a result began to shift the qualitative balance between their forces and the *grande armée*. Perhaps more significant, European rulers made some tentative steps toward leveraging the national passions of their populations. This meant that the armies of Russia and Austria, for example, were not only modernizing. They also could suffer the numbers of casualties that a fight with Napoleon entailed and still stay in the war against France. Better diplomacy and a growing consensus among the great powers that Napoleon had to be reined in also made for a more cohesive coalition. It was no longer as easy for Napoleon to isolate his enemies and defeat them in detail.

For all of that, it was ultimately Napoleon's own blunders in Spain and Russia that accelerated his fall. In 1808 Napoleon put his brother Joseph on the Spanish throne and the country rose in revolt. As we will see in a later lecture on the Sir Julian Corbett and the Peninsular War, the British made masterful use of the Spanish uprising to bleed Napoleon in Spain. At any one point between 1808 and 1813 Napoleon was forced to commit between 200,000 and 450,000 troops to Spain and Portugal. The "Spanish ulcer" ultimately cost the emperor 300,000 men killed in action or lost to disease. According to Napoleon himself: "That unfortunate war destroyed me; it divided my forces, multiplied my obligations, undermined my morale."

With the losses in Spain, the new *grande armée* that Napoleon mobilized for the invasion of Russia in 1812 was a shadow of its earlier incarnation. At nearly 700,000 men it was larger than the earlier *grande armée*, but now more than half of the recruits were not French and the core of veterans needed to stiffen the raw recruits had been significantly reduced. Napoleon managed to get his battle with the Russian army at Borodino in September 1812, but the czar refused to capitulate. Of the nearly 700,000 who set off with Napoleon, less than 100,000 made it out of Russia.

We will revisit this cautionary tale throughout the course. As long as war and combat are kept subordinate to well-conceived policy, nations have a greater chance of success. When war is viewed as an end in itself, disaster invariably ensues.

The paired disasters of Spain and Russia in which the emperor mistook military genius for strategic wisdom fundamentally undermined the military power of France and with it the political power of Napoleon. Following Napoleon's final defeat at Waterloo in 1815, the leaders of Europe tried to build a system that would reverse the clock and prevent another French Revolution and another Napoleon from happening. This was understandable but it was also naïve.

At the same time, the military officers of Europe and the United States were also attempting to master the lessons of the French way of war, the use of flexible combined arms manned by citizen soldiers and commanded by professional officers.

For all of the tactical and organizational innovations embraced by the *grande armée*, I agree with Clausewitz that at its core the transformation of war in the Napoleonic era was first and foremost political. It was the political revolution in France and the nationalization of war that were driving all of these other changes.

To quote Clausewitz:

> In 1793 a force appeared that beggared all imagination. Suddenly war again became the business of the people—a people of thirty million, all of whom considered themselves to be citizens. ... The people became a participant in war; instead of "just" governments and armies, ... the full weight of the nation was thrown into the balance. ... Nothing now impeded the vigor with which war could be waged, and consequently the opponents of France faced the utmost peril.

Carl von Clausewitz and Baron Antoine Henri de Jomini were among the first generation of historians and strategic analysts who tried to make sense out of the trauma of the Napoleonic era. And as we'll see in our next couple of lectures, these two masters had a fundamentally different way of interpreting this trauma. Jomini viewed combat and tactics in the age of Napoleon as an important, but still evolutionary advance in warfare and strategy. To Jomini, Napoleon was not a harbinger of ominous and irreversible changes in the nature and the scale of war. He was merely the apotheosis of war's eternal nature.

For Clausewitz, on the other hand—and despite the best efforts of the statesmen of Europe—the genie of total war was out of the bottle, and out of the bottle forever.

Baron Jomini as a Strategist
Lecture 9

Carl von Clausewitz and Baron Antoine-Henri de Jomini were among the first generation of historians and strategic analysts who tried to make sense of the trauma of the Napoleonic era. But as we'll see in this lecture and the next, these two masters had a fundamentally different way of interpreting that trauma. Jomini viewed combat and tactics in the age of Napoleon as an important but still evolutionary advance in warfare and strategy. To Jomini, Napoleon was not a harbinger of ominous and irreversible changes in the nature and the scale of war; he was merely the apotheosis of war's eternal nature.

The Life of Jomini

- Jomini was a prolific military historian and strategic analyst. A French-speaking Swiss, he had prepared for a business career but got caught up in the romance and excitement of the revolutionary changes sweeping Europe at the end of the 18th century.

- In 1801, at the age of 22, Jomini moved to Paris, where he began his study of military history and the art of strategy.

- In fact, it was his scholarship that brought Jomini to the attention of Napoleon Bonaparte. Jomini's first major work, *A Treatise on Great Military Operations*, compared the campaigns of Frederick the Great to those of France's revolutionary armies, especially Napoleon's brilliant Italian campaign of the 1790s.
  - In this work, Jomini's theoretical principles are interspersed with detailed discussions of the mechanics of military operations, including logistics, marches, maneuver, morale, and the use of concealment.

  - For Jomini, the study of military history and the great commanders and campaigns of the past was a test of the military principles that he felt best explained victory and defeat.

- o Frederick and Napoleon had mastered these principles and used them against adversaries who had lost sight of the eternal patterns of war. Almost all of Jomini's subsequent writings used the successes and failures of Napoleon as proofs of his core concepts.

- Jomini's participation in the greatest campaigns of the Napoleonic era gave him unprecedented insight into the great military and political leaders of his day.
  - o He believed that the Napoleonic revolution in warfare represented a return to the ways in which wars should be fought.

  - o In contrast to Clausewitz, who argued that the French Revolution had fundamentally transformed war, Jomini tried to explain Napoleon's successes and failures in accordance with what he viewed as immutable principles of military strategy.

- In 1813, a mix of professional frustrations and personal principles compelled Jomini to abandon Napoleon and join the Russian Army. He retained his Russian commission until his death in 1869.

The Appeal of Jomini

- Most of our masters to this point in the course were long dead before their views got much of a hearing, but Jomini enjoyed the blessing and the curse of interacting with his fans and detractors in his own lifetime.

- Jomini's popularity is partially explained by the fact that he wrote in French, which all educated Europeans read, unlike Clausewitz, who wrote in German. Jomini also outlived the Prussian by several decades and produced multiple versions of his strategic principles.

- Further, Jomini's "great captains" approach represented an appealing and recognizable look at the consummate masters of the art of war. This approach applied to Napoleon was particularly satisfying to a traumatized European population. In Jomini's estimation, the phenomenon of Napoleonic war was not a harbinger of ominous and irreversible changes in the nature and scale of war but merely the apotheosis of war's eternal nature.

- Finally, Jomini was popular because his search for guiding principles of war found an enthusiastic audience among the emerging class of professional military officers.

Jomini's Core Theoretical Tenets
- From the early 1800s to his death in 1869, Jomini hammered again and again on a deceptively simple lesson: "That all strategy is controlled by invariable scientific principles; and that these principles prescribe offensive action to mass forces against weaker enemy forces at some decisive point if strategy is to lead to victory."

- Jomini's best known and most frequently translated work is his *Summary of the Art of War*, written in 1838. In it, he argued that the eternal key to victory lay in the ability to maintain a concentration of one's own forces and to throw that larger mass against smaller elements of the enemy's forces at a series of what he calls decisive points.
  o Concentration of forces capitalizes on what Jomini termed "interior lines of communication." Army units kept in close proximity with good communications and supply both behind them and between them could converge in a rapid and coordinated manner on a logistically isolated part of the enemy's army or its frontier fortifications.

  o The French corps moving quickly along multiple roads and converging on outnumbered elements of the enemy was exactly what Jomini prescribed.

- True to his Enlightenment inclinations, Jomini was also an operational and theoretical optimist. Operations could be controlled and scripted with a high degree of certainty, and strategic theory could serve as a practical guide for action in war.

- Jomini's theory has been condemned by modern-day pundits for its apparent simplicity and its self-serving character. Though it's true that Jomini was analytically monomaniacal and personally ambitious, he was also a serious student of the serious realities of war.
  - If we read him carefully, we can see that he was fully aware of the fog, friction, and chance of war. He was not blindly attached to the idea that war could be reduced to mathematical calculations, and much of his early work was concerned with showing the limits of a purely scientific approach to war.

  - He also possessed an encyclopedic knowledge of war in the 18th and 19th centuries and had firsthand experience of Napoleon in action. He understood both the emperor's operational and tactical genius and his strategic and political failings. As a staff officer, he was intimately involved in making Napoleon's strategic genius an operational reality.

Specifics of Jomini's Strategic Thought
- Jomini doesn't try to lay down absolute laws of war, but he does insist both that general rules apply and that military leaders ignore these rules at their peril. One may accuse him of being formulaic, but Jomini makes the important point that the rules of war can offer practical guidance.

- Nor was war an end in itself for Jomini. In fact, the opening chapters of the *Summary* deal at length with the larger political purpose of war and the other instruments of national power, such as diplomacy, that exist side by side with the military.

- Jomini saw that different political objectives call for different strategic objectives in war. In fact, he was harshly critical of Napoleon on this point.
  - The emperor invariably aimed for the destruction of the enemy's army in a decisive battle, but this objective makes sense only in the pursuit of an unlimited political objective, such as in the Jena campaign.

- o Napoleon's search for decisive battle in Russia was, to Jomini, counterproductive and catastrophic.

- Ultimately, for Jomini, a well-planned and well-executed campaign offers a much greater chance of success, regardless of its objective. Planning for all kinds of wars hinges on mastering the same principles and applying them to fit the circumstances of each unique contingency.

- Jomini also took some tentative steps toward explaining why some wars come to quick and decisive ends while others are protracted and indecisive. In this discussion, we see some shades of Machiavelli's critique of the mercenary wars of Renaissance Europe.
  - o At the height of his powers, Napoleon was able to discern precisely how much and what kind of pain was needed to bring about a quick end to a war. The speed, mass, and lethality of the *grande armée* made that strategic vision a reality.

  - o Yet when Napoleon began to substitute operational success—in other words, the winning of battles—for strategic vision, as was the case in Spain and Russia, France became bogged down in wars it could not win and could no longer afford.

Jomini's Enduring Value
- Much more so than his immediate predecessors, who focused primarily on the tactical level of war and on the techniques of logistics and marches, Jomini was concerned with all of the levels of war and with their interconnection.
  - o His *Summary* deals at length with many of these subspecialties, including logistics, morale, training, tactics, and military intelligence, but he never loses sight of how the mastery of all these means remains subordinate first to strategy and then to the achievement of a political end.

  - o In this sense, Jomini was critical to the invention of modern strategy, the linkage between the modern way of war and its political purpose.

- Moreover, the clarity and felicity with which Jomini deals with these subspecialties and with the levels of war laid out much of the vocabulary of the modern military profession, including such terms as interior versus exterior lines and concentration of force.

- Jomini is also exceptionally insightful on military intelligence. In fact, when it comes to its value, collection, and analysis, Jomini goes even further than the *Sunzi* on the subject of espionage and is delightfully specific about what it means in practice.

- More evidence of Jomini's enduring value comes in his discussion of leadership. It is true that to Jomini all of the "great captains" of the past are master practitioners of his core principles, but as much as Jomini was inspired by the Enlightenment and the promises of reason, man with all his gifts and flaws still mattered, especially in war.
  o Theories mean nothing if intelligent men do not, in Jomini's words, "apply them, with map in hand, to hypothetical wars, or to the brilliant operations of great captains."

  o By engaging in these types of mental exercises, one could achieve *coup d'oeil*—strategic intuition—what Jomini calls "the most valuable characteristic of a good general."

- Jomini was also aware of the likely tension between the master practitioners of war and their political masters. His take on this issue perhaps argues for too strict a delineation between politics and strategy: that the government must not meddle in matters that only educated and experienced officers can understand.

- Jomini was an innovative thinker who immeasurably advanced the systematic study of strategy and inspired intense debates about strategy and operations. He tirelessly emphasized the importance of history and self-education to the cultivation of consummate military leadership. He understood that although war was not subject to rigid scientific laws, one could still identify rules and principles that are of direct value to its practitioners.

Suggested Reading

Brinton, Craig, and Gilbert, "Jomini."

Heuser, *The Evolution of Strategy*.

Jomini, *The Art of War*.

———, *Jomini and His Summary of the Art of War*.

Shy, "Jomini."

Questions to Consider

1. What were Jomini's objectives in writing military theory? Did he achieve those objectives?

2. What are the parallels between Jomini's theories and Machiavelli's *The Art of War* and Sun Tzu's *The Art of War*?

Baron Jomini as a Strategist
Lecture 9—Transcript

At the beginning of the Jena campaign, Emporor Napoleon summoned Antoine Henri Jomini, a young Swiss officer serving on the staff of Marshal Ney. The emperor complimented Jomini on his works of military analysis and on his insight into what Napoleon called "the true principles of war." The emperor went on to inquire about the Prussian military, which was a topic that Jomini knew well from his studies of Frederick the Great. Jomini asked for four days to put together his notes on the Prussians and for permission to rejoin Napoleon at the town of Bamberg. The shocked emperor shot back, "Who told you I am going to Bamberg?!"

Somehow, it seems, Jomini had learned of Napoleon's secret plan to stage at Bamberg for the drive into Prussia. Jomini coolly replied that he had not been told about Bamberg, but rather that he had divined that Bamberg was where the emperor would naturally move next. It was, he said, "The map of Germany" that told him that Bamberg was the next logical step in the Jena campaign.

Now, as we'll see, Jomini was quite the self-promoter. So it should come as little surprise that this precocious anecdote, in which a 27-year-old staffer gets the better of Napoleon Bonaparte, actually comes from Jomini himself. But even if we might doubt its veracity, the Bamberg story is important for what it tells us about Jomini as a theorist. Jomini had an enduring faith in the principles of war and their timeless relevance to the planning of military operations. The principles of war dictated the move to Bamberg. In Jomini's analysis, Napoleon's adherence to the principles of war explained his incredible successes. His abandonment of those principles explained his ultimate defeat.

We've seen that both Clausewitz and Jomini served in the Jena campaign, but they come at their study of war and strategy from very different perspectives. You might ask, why? Well for one, Jomini was on the winning side and Clausewitz on the losing side. Clausewitz was trying to explain a shocking defeat, where Jomini was sketching out a textbook victory.

Second, Jomini was inspired by the Enlightenment and by the belief that reason can discern sense even in the chaos of war. Clausewitz, as we will see, muddied the positive doctrines of the enlightenment with a hefty dose of pessimistic German romanticism. But I am getting ahead of myself. Who is this supremely confident staff officer who presumes to predict the plans of Napoleon, the god of war?

Baron Antoine Henri Jomini was a truly prolific military historian and strategic analyst. A French-speaking Swiss, Jomini had prepared for a business career but got caught up in the romance and excitement of the revolutionary changes sweeping Europe at the end of the 18th century.

In 1801, at the age of 22, Jomini moved to Paris where he began his study of military history and the art of strategy. Unlike Clausewitz who came to the study of strategic theory in the midst of his military career, Jomini's formative works of scholarship predated his military service.

In fact, it was his scholarship that brought Jomini to the attention of Marshall Ney and of Napoleon Bonaparte. Jomini's first major work, titled *A Treatise on Great Military Operations*, compared the campaigns of Frederick the Great to those of France's Revolutionary Armies, and especially to those of Napoleon's brilliant Italian campaign of the 1790s.

In this, as in most things, Jomini was being very entrepreneurial; he wanted to sell books to a wide audience; an audience eager to make analytical sense out of the exploits of great commanders. Jomini also desperately wanted to serve in the army of Napoleon.

His theoretical principles are therefore interspersed with detailed discussions of the mechanics of military operations, including logistics, marches, maneuver, morale, and the use of concealment. For Jomini, the study of military history and of the great commanders and campaigns of the past was a test of the military principles that he felt best explained victory and defeat.

Frederick and Napoleon had mastered these principles and used them against adversaries who had lost sight of the eternal patterns of war. In fact, almost all of Jomini's subsequent writings used the successes and failures of Napoleon as proofs of his core concepts. More than just an historian in uniform, Jomini's business training, much like that of Alexander Hamilton, made him a good staff officer, a talent that the huge *grande armée* needed in spades. Working on a staff meant that Jomini spent most of his time at headquarters. And his participation in the greatest campaigns of the Napoleonic Era gave him unprecedented insight into the great military and political leaders of his day. He served with distinction in the Austerlitz, Jena, Eylau, and Friedland campaigns, all in close proximity to Napoleon, and he accompanied Marshal Ney on the ill-fated Iberian campaign.

In his search for the eternal principles of war Jomini did not turn a blind eye to the Napoleonic revolution in warfare with its greatly increased speed, firepower, and mass. In fact, to Jomini, this was a return to the ways that wars should be fought. The indecisive wars of the *ancien régime* were the exception to the eternal nature of war. To Jomini, Frederick the Great was in fact a lesser general than Napoleon because Frederick could not have the same audacity and almost careless disregard for casualties as the French emperor.

We see, therefore, that in contrast to Clausewitz, who argued that the French Revolution had fundamentally transformed war, Jomini tried to explain Napoleon's successes and failures in accord with what he viewed as immutable principles of military strategy, principles that could be traced back through the victories of the great captains all the way back to Julius Caesar and Alexander of Macedon.

In 1813 a mix of professional frustrations and personal principles compelled Jomini to abandon Napoleon and to join the Russian Army. He retained his Russian commission until his death in 1869, and between his monumental works of history and strategic analysis, he served also as military tutor and aide-de-camp to the future Czar Nicholas I. In the annals of 19th-century war and diplomacy, few could match Jomini's experiences or his impressive roster of highly placed friends (and enemies).

Nor is it easy to imagine any strategic theorist achieving Jomini's level of influence in his own lifetime. Most of our masters to this point in the course were long dead before their views got much of a hearing. Jomini enjoyed the blessing and the curse of interacting with his fans and detractors in real time. His immense knowledge of history and his prolific writings tended to quiet most of his contemporaries, and he was a great commercial success in his own day.

But why was Jomini so popular? For one, he wrote in French, which all educated Europeans read, unlike Clausewitz who wrote in German. Jomini also outlived the Prussians by several decades and produced multiple versions of his strategic principles. Secondly, Jomini wrote in an appealing and recognizable genre, something called the "great captains" approach, looking the consummate masters of the art of war, folks like Alexander, Caesar, and Frederick the Great. The "great captains" motif applied to Napoleon was additionally appealing to a traumatized European population. In Jomini's estimation, the phenomenon of Napoleonic War was not a harbinger of ominous and irreversible changes in the nature and the scale of war, but merely the apotheosis of war's eternal nature. Finally, Jomini was very popular because his search for guiding principles of war found enthusiastic audiences among the emerging class of professional military officers, officers eager to define and delineate the profession of arms.

As we will see a few lectures from now, Jomini remained a hot commodity long after his death, and his thoughts on strategy and military operations have had a global influence. But what is it about his precepts that are so attractive and popular? In contrast to Clausewitz, whose theory evolved over the course of his life, Jomini claimed to have come upon his core theoretical tenets at the age of 18. From that point on, he never wavered in his belief. And I quote: "That all strategy is controlled by invariable scientific principles; and that these principles prescribe offensive action to mass forces against weaker enemy forces at some decisive point if strategy is to lead to victory."

From the early 1800s to his death in 1869, Jomini hammered again and again on this deceptively simple lesson. Jomini's best known and most frequently translated work is the *Précis de l'art de la guerre* or *Summary of the Art of War* written in 1838. The *Summary*, in fact, was an updated version of a two-volume study commissioned by Czar Nicholas I that Jomini reworked for a larger market appeal.

In the *Summary*, as elsewhere, Jomini argued that the eternal key to victory lay in the ability to maintain a concentration of one's own forces and to throw that larger mass against smaller elements of the enemy's forces at a series of what he calls decisive points.

Concentration of forces would capitalize on what he termed interior lines of communication. Army units kept in close proximity with good communications and supply both behind them and between them could converge in a rapid and coordinated manner on a logistically isolated part of the enemy's army or potentially his frontier fortifications: in other words converging on one after another of these decisive points. It sounds a lot like the *Sunzi* doesn't it? "If I am concentrated and the enemy divided, it is like a grindstone thrown against an egg."

The *grande armée* at the peak of its lethality was thus the apotheosis of a style of operations based on masses of men brought to bear rapidly at these decisive points.

French corps moving quickly along multiple roads and converging on outnumbered elements of the enemy was exactly what Jomini prescribed. But as we have seen already, to do this required training, flexible organization, initiative, discipline, morale, speed, and superior intelligence of the enemy. It also often required ruses or feints to confuse or unbalance the enemy. In this and in many other ways, Jomini and the Sunzi have a great deal in common.

All of that complexity notwithstanding, Jomini's goal was to "guide" a commander "in the task of directing operations in the midst of the noise and tumult of battle." We'll see in the next lecture that Clausewitz wrote with an eye to the long-term intellectual development of military officers. Clausewitz wanted a dog-eared copy of *On War* left on the bookshelf at home amidst dozens of books on military history. Jomini is much more about the here and now of war and strategy. He wanted his books to be in the traveling libraries of the great captains of the future.

True to his Enlightenment inclinations, Jomini was also an operational and theoretical optimist. Operations could be controlled and scripted with a high degree of certainty and strategic theory could serve as a practical guide for action in war. "Tactics," he says, "is the art of using these masses [troops] at the points to which they shall have been" brought "by well-arranged marches at the decisive moment and at the decisive point of the field of battle."

Jomini, therefore, was relentless and consistent in his teachings, but we need to avoid treating him as something of a parody, or as a lesser theorist of strategy. Even today, pundits will latch onto a Jominian maxim like the one I just quoted to rail against the superficial and simplistic "Jominian" way of war. To them, Jomini is all about mechanics and formulas.

An even worse condemnation of Jomini's theory, beyond its apparent simplicity, is its self-serving character. Jomini is variously called a hustler, a huckster ,and a charlatan who pandered to his audience to sell books and to cement his reputation. This is unfair. Jomini was analytically monomaniacal and personally ambitious, but he was also a serious student of the very serious realities of war. If we read him carefully we can see that he was fully aware of the fog, friction, and chance of war. In fact, he was not blindly attached to the idea that war could be reduced to mathematical calculations and much of his early work was concerned with showing the limits of a purely scientific approach to war.

He also possessed an encyclopedic knowledge of war in the 18th and 19th centuries. He had first-hand experience of Napoleon in action. He understood both the Emperor's operational and tactical genius and his strategic and political failings. And, as a staff officer he was intimately involved in making Napoleon's strategic genius an operational reality.

As one of the two greatest interpreters of Napoleon, Jomini deserves our respect. This is why Jomini's thoughts on how best to use a Napoleonic-style army are still read at our military academies and war colleges. The Napoleonic way of war was the model for European and American militaries well into the 20th century and in many ways still influences military doctrines today. For the Soviets in Afghanistan and the U.S. Army in Desert Storm, Jomini still mattered. Whether or not all of his theoretical prescriptions stand the test of time, Jomini cannot be lightly dismissed.

So what are some of the specifics of Jomini's strategic thought that deserve our attention? First, Jomini isn't trying to lay down absolute laws of war. But he does insist both that general rules apply and that military leaders ignore these rules at their peril. One may accuse him of being formulaic, but Jomini makes the important point that the rules of war can offer very practical guidance.

"Theories," Jomini says, "cannot teach men with mathematical precision what they should do in every case; but they point out the errors which should be avoided." Ultimately, he claims, "these rules thus become, in the hands of skillful generals commanding brave troops, means of almost certain success." Nor was war an end in itself for Jomini. In fact, the opening chapters of the *Summary* (a response to Clausewitz' *On War* most likely) deal at length with the larger political purpose of war and of the other instruments of national power, such as diplomacy, that exist side by side with the military.

Jomini was not as concerned with the causes or the nature of war as was say Thucydides, but he was aware that war could take many forms and could be fought in dramatically different environments and for a range of diverse political objectives. Different political objectives in turn called for different strategic objectives in war. Strategy must vary to match the political objectives of a war. There was no one size fits all strategy appropriate to every single war. In fact, Jomini was harshly critical of Napoleon on this very point. The emperor invariably aimed for the destruction of the enemy's army in a decisive battle.

Such an objective makes strategic sense when you are pursuing an unlimited political objective, such as in the case of the Jena campaign. Napoleon needed to crush Prussia and impose harsh terms, and to do that he needed to crush Prussia's armies. But in wars fought for lesser objectives, the capture of strategically valuable terrain paired with the harassment of the enemy might be sufficient to compel an enemy to bend to your political will. Napoleon's relentless search for decisive battle in Russia was to Jomini counterproductive and catastrophic.

Ultimately for Jomini a well-planned and well-executed campaign offers a much greater chance of success regardless of its objective. Planning for all kinds of wars hinged on mastering the same principles and applying them as fit the circumstances of each unique contingency. As he puts it in the *Summary*: "An army is ruined if forced to adhere to precisely the same style of tactical maneuvers in every country it may enter and against every different nation."

So Jomini has several points to make about the causes of war and an awful lot to say about the conduct of war. In addition, Jomini took some tentative steps toward explaining why some wars come to quick and decisive ends while others are protracted and indecisive. In this discussion we see some shades of Machiavelli's critique of the mercenary wars of Renaissance Europe, which simply dragged on with no decisive result.

At the height of his powers, Napoleon was able to discern precisely how much and what kind of pain was needed to bring about a quick end to a war. The speed, mass and lethality of the *grande armée* made that strategic vision a reality. Yet when Napoleon began to substitute operational success, in other words the winning of battles, for strategic vision, as was the case in Spain and Russia, France became bogged down in wars it could not win and which it could no longer afford. Jomini draws a sharp contrast between Napoleon's masterpieces, "the beautiful operations of Marengo, Ulm, and Jena" and "the Russian War in 1812."

Even if Napoleon could replicate those "beautiful operations" in Russia he could not have won. The theatre of war was too big, the *grande armée* was too spread out and the Russians had too much room to maneuver and too much time to recover.

Jomini is equally important in the degree to which he contributed to the maturation of the military profession in the 19th century. He may have been eclipsed by other theorists in terms of analytical sophistication, but his work was still path-breaking. He was one of the first strategic theorists to systematically embrace all of the elements of the new way of war and he managed to make sense of them for a wide audience.

Much more so than his immediate predecessors who focused primarily on the tactical level of war and on the techniques of logistics and marches, Jomini was concerned with all of the levels of war and with their inter-connection. His *Summary* deals at length with many of these sub-specialties, including logistics, morale, training, tactics, and military intelligence, but he never loses sight of how the mastery of all of these means remains subordinate first to strategy and then to the ultimate end, the achievement of a political end. In this sense, Jomini was critical to the invention of modern strategy, the linkage between the modern way of war and its larger political purpose.

Moreover, the clarity and felicity with which Jomini deals with these sub-specialties and with the levels of war, laid out much of the vocabulary of the modern military profession. Contemporary military jargon owes much to Jomini such as interior versus exterior lines and concentration of force. One could only wish that the modern variant of military jargon was as clear and as elegant as that of its originator.

Jomini is also exceptionally insightful on military intelligence. In fact when it comes to its value, its collection and its analysis, Jomini goes even further than the *Sunzi* on the subject of espionage.

Many of Napoleon's spectacular military successes were preceded by what jargoneers today call "intelligence preparation of the battle-space." Jomini is delightfully specific about what that meant in practice: "A general should neglect no means of gaining information of the enemy's movements." He "should make use of reconnaissances, spies, and bodies of light troops commanded by capable officers." And he should "Select intelligent officers who can elicit important information from prisoners and deserters." But, he warns, "Perfect reliance should be placed on none of these means." And Jomini concludes on a cautionary note. In the absence of perfect intelligence, hedge your bets: He says: "As it is impossible to obtain exact information by the methods mentioned, a general should never move without arranging several courses of action."

Without knowing it, Jomini was improving on the *Sunzi*. When it comes to espionage, he values it, but he is skeptical, and where the *Sunzi* asks for a leap of faith on the value of intelligence, Jomini can give us concrete examples of its strengths and its limitations. If anything, Jena and Auerstadt were initially intelligence failures. Napoleon misjudged that he was meeting the bulk of the Prussian Army at Jena, and Marshal Davout stumbled into Auerstadt at a huge numerical disadvantage. The French, however, proved far more capable of recovering from these missteps and gaining and maintaining the information edge as that October day progressed.

More evidence of Jomini's enduring value comes in his discussion of leadership. It is true that to Jomini all of the great captains of the past are consummate technicians, master practitioners of his core principles, but as much as Jomini was inspired by the Enlightenment and the promises of reason, man with all his gifts and flaws still mattered, especially in war.

Theory meant nothing if intelligent men did not, in Jomini's words "apply them, with map in hand, to hypothetical wars, or to the brilliant operations of great captains." By engaging in these types of mental exercises, one could acquire a strategic *coup d'oeil*. This *coup d'oeil*, literally a glimpse, or the bat of the eye, is strategic intuition, and it is what he calls "the most valuable characteristic of a good general." Without *coup d'oeil*, without strategic intuition, theory is useless.

Intellect and personal qualities matter in leadership. Jomini tell us that to be a great general you need to be able to do two things: you need to be able to draw up a good plan of operations and you need to have the determination to carry it out. You can learn how to be a good planner, but determination usually depends on personal attributes.

Great leaders need to anticipate interaction. They have to realize that war is not a game of chess. When an ordinary general, a general lacking in genius, determination, and *coup d'oeil*, faces of against a skillful, active, and enterprising enemy, an enemy whose movements are a perfect riddle, then you see the stark difference between an ordinary man and a military genius.

Jomini was also aware of the likely tension between the master practitioners of war and their political masters. This had not been a problem for Napoleon, especially after 1802. For post-Napoleonic militaries that were commanded not by the head-of-state but rather by one of the growing cadre of professional military men problems were likely to ensue.

Jomini's take on this issue was that the government must not meddle in matters that only educated and experienced officers understood.

Or in the words of the master himself:

> A general whose genius and hands are tied by an Aulic Council [the ruling council in Vienna] five hundred miles distant cannot be a match for one who has liberty of action, other things being equal ... interfered with and opposed in all his enterprises [he] will be unable to achieve success, even if he have the requisite ability. It may be said that a sovereign might accompany the army and not interfere with his general, but, on the contrary, aid him with all the weight of his influence.

What Jomini is saying is that if the ruler chooses to accompany the army on campaign, to be present on the battlefield, then his sole purpose is to magnify the gravitas of the general. It is here that I have my only big disagreement with Jomini. I sympathize with the desires of the military profession to keep amateur politicians out of their area of expertise, but Jomini goes too far. He argues for too strict of delineation between politics and strategy. This is all the more shocking given that his archetypes are men like Caesar, Frederick, and Napoleon! They embodied policy and strategy! Unfortunately, far too many students of Jomini have selectively latched on to this notion to argue that once a war begins, the politicians should stay out of the business of strategy.

All of our masters have had their detractors, but perhaps none as virulent as the critics of Baron Jomini. Hopefully, today I have convinced you that this brilliant, vain, and ambitious man deserves inclusion among the masters. Jomini was an innovative thinker who immeasurably advanced the systematic study of strategy. He influenced generations of professionals and amateurs and inspired intense debates about strategy and operations. He tirelessly emphasized the importance of history and self-education to the cultivation of consummate military leadership. He understood that while war was not subject to rigid scientific laws, one could still identify rules and principles that are of direct value to the practitioners of war.

Jomini certainly appealed to an audience of professional military men, officers inclined to seek semi-scientific conclusions. He might even be faulted for pandering to those inclinations, but he was not at fault for them having those inclinations. Nor is he to blame for the fact that subsequent generations of self-styled "Jominians" have emphasized what they felt was important in the works of the master.

For all of his stridency about the immutable principles of war, Jomini was also nuanced and contingent; he backed up his theories with personal experience in some of the most epic wars in human history. His ideas could not be ignored, and they certainly were not ignored by our next master, Carl von Clausewitz. We'll see that Clausewitz frequently disagreed with Jomini, but if anything we'll also see that the Jomini forced Clausewitz to raise his theoretical game.

I'll see you next time.

Clausewitz's *On War*
Lecture 10

Carl von Clausewitz was born under the *ancien régime* but came of age during Prussia's two-decade struggle with revolutionary France. He joined the army at the age of 12 and was still in uniform when he died 39 years later. During the course of his career, Clausewitz saw a good deal of combat, earned a solid reputation as a staff officer, and developed an abiding interest in history and philosophy. He was also a passionate advocate of military reform, although his agenda met with only limited success. It is his written work, especially *On War*, that cements his place in the pantheon of strategic thinkers.

Studying the Past to Prepare for the Future
- In *On War*, Clausewitz argued that the revolutionary changes that had taken place in the Napoleonic era demanded an entirely new way of thinking about war, as well as an entirely new way of preparing Prussia to fight the wars of the future. Paradoxically, this preparation for the future should be based on the study of history.

- To Clausewitz, history is not just about learning what happened in the past; it stands in for experience and can help us objectively evaluate courses of action in light of their alternatives.

- The rigorous study of history also allows us to test general theoretical concepts. Theory is "intended to provide a thinking man with a frame of reference … to guide him in his strategic choices." Theory provides useful analytical tools that can help us confront complex problems; testing these theoretical principles against history keeps us honest.

- At the same time, Clausewitz bridled at the idea that something as complex and contingent as war could be subject to hard-and-fast theoretical maxims: "Theory cannot equip the mind with formulas for solving problems. … But it can give the mind insight into the great mass of phenomena and of their relationships."

Absolute War v. War in Reality

- The distinction between theory as a frame of reference and theory as a prescriptive guidebook for waging war has created confusion over the years. That confusion is compounded by the tension in Clausewitz's work between the Enlightenment principles of reason and scientific thinking and the uncertainty and irrationality of German romanticism. This tension is best seen in his discussion of absolute war versus war in reality.

- In a nod to Newton, Clausewitz works toward what war looks like in reality by starting with the ideal or abstract nature of war. What would war look like in a vacuum, free from all constraints, such as rationality and material limitations?

In *On War*, Clausewitz borrowed the scientific methods of such Enlightenment thinkers as Isaac Newton, but he remained skeptical that the rational approach could be applied to human interaction.

- In the "pure concept," war would always be for the most unlimited objectives and involve a total effort; in other words, destroy the enemy's armed forces, occupy its country, and exterminate its population.

- Some have interpreted this Newtonian approach as either Clausewitz's belief in a science of war or his advocacy of absolute war. Both interpretations are wrong. Absolute war is an abstraction that is meant to help us to better understand war in reality.

- In reality, war does not usually achieve its absolute form primarily because war is political; it is fought for some political object. There is no political objective that justifies absolute war.

- Further, war is a physical contest, fought by human beings in the real world; it involves fear, passion, and genius, as well as fog, friction, and chance. These factors naturally shape the nature of a war and prevent it from reaching its pure concept.

The Paradoxical Trinity

- From this Newtonian methodology, Clausewitz derives one of the most seductive, creative, and confusing tools of strategic analysis ever conceived: the paradoxical trinity, Clausewitz's tool for net assessment.

- Every war, Clausewitz says, is characterized by three dominant tendencies: (1) "primordial violence, hatred, and enmity, which are to be regarded as a blind natural force"; (2) "the play of chance and probability within which the creative spirit is free to roam"; and (3) "its element of subordination, as an instrument of policy, which makes it subject to reason alone."

- We can see why this is a "paradoxical trinity": If the passions aroused by war are a blind natural force, how can war remain subject to reason? The same goes for the creative spirit (the genius of the general): What is there to prevent a spectacular military success achieved through a stroke of that genius from influencing policy?

- As a political instrument, war must serve a rational political purpose, but by its very nature, war may be dominated by passion and hatreds or by unforeseen events on the battlefield or strokes of genius. Political leaders and military commanders must always strive to keep passion and chance subordinate to reason.

- Clausewitz overlays the trinity on a nation at war, converting it from an abstraction into a practical tool of net assessment.

o To determine the likely nature of a looming conflict, all that's needed is to apply this simple model: Figure out how the three dominant tendencies (passion, genius, and reason) of one belligerent will interact with the three dominant tendencies of another belligerent.

o To make those determinations, one must calculate how the people, the military, and the government interact in the enemy's state and in one's own.

The Political Aims of War
- To Clausewitz, war was a continuation of the political competition between states by military means. War's violent nature makes it a unique form of political competition, but we can never lose sight of its political purpose.

- Although war may have a unique grammar—meaning that war and combat are governed by military considerations—ultimately, war and politics serve the same logic.

- Clausewitz addresses a spectrum of wars for varying political aims, from limited wars—conducted to wrest concessions from an adversary or to prevent a challenge to the status quo—to unlimited wars—conducted to overthrow a regime.

- The types of government institutions, the character and inclinations of the populations, and the larger environment also contribute to the unique nature of a conflict. A war between two dictatorships will likely be much different than a war between two democracies, even though the political objectives might be similar.

Clausewitz on Strategy
- From net assessment emerges a list of strategic targets, or what Clausewitz calls "centers of gravity" These might include the enemy's army, its capital, its main ally, or in the case of popular uprisings, its people. A state might have several potential centers of

gravity that may shift over time depending on the political objective being pursued.

- Once the center of gravity is determined, Clausewitz looks for ways to strike it for maximum strategic and political effect. "Two basic principles ... underlie all strategic planning," he says: "act with the utmost concentration and with the utmost speed."
  - o This is a prescription for dominating that part of the trinity where combat takes place: the realm of chance and probability.

  - o The superior general masses his forces for a rapid and decisive blow against the enemy's center of gravity. Once he has shattered that center of gravity, he pursues the beaten enemy.

- Clausewitz also tells us that war is inherently interactive—as much as we use force to compel an enemy to do our will, our enemy is doing the same to us.

- Finally, while Clausewitz advocates mass at the decisive point, he is aware that one mass trying to overwhelm an enemy's mass often causes war to escalate. Even after they have conducted net assessment and strategic planning, it is still incumbent on the general and the politician to keep war from getting out of control.

The Culminating Points of Attack and Victory
- Clausewitz's principle of continuity demands that we follow up a battlefield victory with a continuation of the offensive to exert maximum military and psychological pressure on the adversary. The antithesis of this principle is the culminating point of the attack, beyond which it is counterproductive to advance—doing so invites defeat.

- The culminating point of attack is the point at which the remaining strength of the attacker is "just enough to maintain a defense and wait for peace." Going past it shifts the advantage to the defender, who gets stronger relative to the attacker.

- Passing the culminating point of victory isn't just pushing an offensive too far; it's pushing political objectives too far. It may actually increase the enemy's will to resist and invite third-party intervention on the enemy's behalf.

- With these culminating points, Clausewitz explains why military success does not always lead to success in war. He also reemphasizes the idea that war serves a political purpose; hence, victory can be declared only when that purpose is achieved.

Why Wars End
- On the topic of why wars end, Clausewitz offers another of his deceptively simple maxims: "No one starts a war … without first being clear in his mind what he intends to achieve by that war and how he intends to conduct it. The former is its political purpose; the latter its operational objective."

- If we take this prescription literally, then a war is over when we have achieved our operational objective. This, however, can only be the case if we have accurately predicted the enemy's center of gravity and have inflicted sufficient harm upon it to convince the enemy to capitulate.

- Those factors are almost impossible to determine with accuracy in advance; therefore, the decision to end a war ultimately lies with the defeated side: "Once the expenditure of effort exceeds the value of the political object, the object must be renounced and peace must follow."

- Of course, such decisions are often not rational. Limited wars are especially difficult to terminate. Even when war is brought to a formal end, Clausewitz understands this result is inherently unstable, given the political nature of war.

Politicians and Military Leaders
- Clausewitz's thoughts on the proper relationship between politicians and military leaders in the making of strategy are among the most

brilliant ever penned: "Subordinating the political point of view to the military would be absurd, for it is policy that has created war. ... No other possibility exists, then, than to subordinate the military point of view to the political."

- But Clausewitz doesn't argue that generals should simply acquiesce to political domination. Crafting strategy is a dynamic conversation between politicians and military leaders that is constantly tested, reviewed, and adapted throughout a conflict.

Suggested Reading

Clausewitz, *On War.*

Paret, "Clausewitz."

Rothfels, "Clausewitz."

Strachan, *Clausewitz's On War.*

Questions to Consider

1. Is the center of gravity a useful strategic concept? What is the difference between culminating point of attack and culminating point of victory?

2. What is the difference between a limited and an unlimited war? How do Clausewitz's core concepts differ in a limited versus an unlimited war?

Clausewitz's *On War*
Lecture 10—Transcript

Earlier in the course I mentioned that *Sunzi* is frequently quoted in film and television. That's not the only master to make it onto the big screen. I can honestly say that my first exposure to Carl von Clausewitz was not in graduate school, but actually in the 1995 film *Crimson Tide*. In the movie, Gene Hackman is the captain of a ballistic missile submarine. He tells a new subordinate (played by Denzel Washington) that when he was "at the Naval War College" he studied "metallurgy and nuclear reactors, not 19th-century philosophy." But then he goes on to quote Clausewitz anyway "War," he says "is a continuation of politics by other means."

I still get a kick out of the fact that both Clausewitz and the Naval War College got the nod in *Crimson Tide*. But more importantly here we have contemporary naval officers. Yeah, they're fictional, but they are having an intelligent conversation about a long dead Prussian Army officer. That alone should get you interested in Clausewitz's masterpiece *On War*.

Today I will tell you a little bit about who Clausewitz was, and how and why he wrote *On War*. Then I want to spend the majority of our time looking at the central tenets of Clausewitz's theory as they relate to the planning, waging, and ending of wars. Along the way, I will mirror Clausewitz's approach, starting with the simple and moving to the complex.

Simple things first: Carl von Clausewitz was a German, or more precisely a Prussian, and he lived through a great turning point in history. Clausewitz was born under the *ancien régime*, but came of age during Prussia's two-decade struggle with Revolutionary France. His father had served under Frederick the Great and young Carl joined the army in 1792, at the age of 12. He was still in uniform when he died 39 years later. In the intervening years Clausewitz saw a lot of combat, earned a solid reputation as a staff officer and as an educator, and developed an abiding interest in history and philosophy.

Clausewitz was also a passionate advocate of military reform. His take on the disasters at Jena and Auerstaedt was that the Prussian military and the

Prussian state were hopeless anachronisms. Only sociopolitical reform in Prussia could liberate the energy and talent of the Prussian people. Only that release of energy could give Prussia the military power equal to its great ambitions.

Clausewitz wasn't a revolutionary, but he did believe that Prussia had to embrace some elements of the French Revolution: the nation at arms. Visionary though it was, Clausewitz's reform agenda was highly controversial and met with only limited success. It is his written work, especially *On War*, that cements his place in the pantheon of strategic thinkers.

In *On War*, Clausewitz argued that the revolutionary changes that had taken place in the Napoleonic era demanded an entirely new way of thinking about war, as well as an entirely new way of preparing Prussia to fight the wars of the future. But Clausewitz goes about this in an interesting way. He is thinking about revolutionary changes in war, and yet he tells his readers to go back and read recent history. In fact, one way to look at *On War* is a primer for how a military officer should approach the study of war in the 18th and 19th centuries.

Clausewitz's point was simple: No matter how much experience an officer had, no matter how abundant his combat experience had been, it was insufficient to prepare him for higher levels of military leadership. In some cases personal experience, because it is by definition personal, can be a liability to broader strategic thinking. Therefore, an officer must immerse himself in the study of history.

Clausewitz was not alone in this. Napoleon famously said that "generalship is acquired only by experience and the study of the campaigns of all great captains." To Clausewitz, history is not just about learning what happened in the past, history stands in for experience and can help us objectively evaluate courses of action in light of their alternatives. Remember, this is critical analysis. *On War* is therefore a kind of a guide for would-be strategists. It shows them how they should study the past for guidance in the future. On this front, however, *On War* can be very frustrating. Clausewitz makes many references to history, but like many geniuses he simply assumes that his readers know what he is talking about. But Clausewitz isn't trying to confuse his readers. Instead he is providing what he calls "a frame of reference," a theoretical template for making sense out of the chaos of war.

The rigorous study of history allows us to test general theoretical concepts. Theory, as he says, is "intended to provide a thinking man with a frame of reference ... to guide him in his strategic choices ... not lead him by the hand." Theory provides useful analytical tools that can help you confront complex problems. At the same time, testing these theoretical principles against history, keeps you honest. If your nifty strategic maxim doesn't hold up to historical scrutiny, it should be jettisoned. At the same time Clausewitz bridled at the idea that something as complex and contingent as war could be subject to hard and fast theoretical maxims: "Theory cannot equip the mind with formulas for solving problems. ... But it can give the mind insight into the great mass of phenomena and of their relationships."

The distinction between theory as a frame of reference—a way to develop critical thinking—as opposed to a prescriptive and predictive guidebook for waging war has created a good deal of confusion over the years. That confusion is compounded by Clausewitz's own methodology in *On War*. One scholar has described Clausewitz as a child of the Enlightenment but a man of the Romantic Era. What this means is that Clausewitz was influenced by Enlightenment concepts and in *On War* he borrowed methods from the Enlightenment. Enlightenment thinkers tried to bring a rational, if not scientific, approach to human interaction. Reason and science are about certainty and predictability. But Clausewitz is a skeptic. "Earlier theorists," he tells us, tried subject war to "principles, rules, or even systems ... factors that could be mathematically calculated." Clausewitz seems at first to embrace this idea, but then muddies the science of the Enlightenment approach with the uncertainty, unpredictability, irrational, and non-rational aspects of German romanticism.

Think of it this way: Jomini is more in the Enlightenment camp. He is laying out formulas for how to win a war. Clausewitz is trying to get soldiers to think about different formulas for winning different types of wars. "In war," he says, "everything is uncertain and variable, intertwined with psychological forces and effects, and the product of a continuous interaction."

The Enlightenment versus romanticism tension is best seen in Clausewitz's discussion of absolute war versus war in reality.

In a nod to Newton, Clausewitz works toward what war looks like in reality by starting with the ideal or abstract nature of war. What would war look like in a vacuum, free from all constraints, such as rationality and material limitations? In the "pure concept," war would always be for the most unlimited objectives and involve a total effort, in other words destroy the enemy's armed forces, occupy his country, and exterminate his population. Some have interpreted this Newtonian approach as either Clausewitz's belief in a science of war or his advocacy of absolute war. Both are wrong. Absolute war is an abstraction (the simple) that is supposed to help us to better understand war in reality (the complex). In reality, war does not usually achieve its absolute form. Why not? For one, and most importantly, war is political; it is fought for some political object. There is no political objective that justifies absolute war.

Two, war is a physical contest, fought by human beings in the real world. In the real world you have fear, passion, and genius. You also have fog, friction, chance, and uncertainty. These factors will naturally shape the nature of a war and prevent it from reaching its pure concept. From this methodology, Clausewitz derives one of the most seductive, the most creative, and in some cases the most confusing tools of strategic analysis ever conceived: The paradoxical trinity. Where Thucydides gave us the speeches of Pericles and Archidamus and the Sunzi laid out those five fundamental factors, Clausewitz offers the trinity as his tool for net assessment.

Every war, he says, is characterized by three dominant tendencies. The first is "primordial violence, hatred, and enmity, which are to be regarded as a blind natural force." The second is "the play of chance and probability within which the creative spirit is free to roam." The third is "war's element of subordination, as an instrument of policy which makes it subject to reason alone." We see now why this is a "paradoxical trinity." If those passions aroused by war are a blind natural force, how can war remain subject to reason? The same goes for the creative spirit, by which he means the genius of the general. What is there to prevent a spectacular military success achieved through a stroke of that genius from influencing policy? Isn't that what Cleon tried to do after Pylos?

As a political instrument, war must serve a rational political purpose, but by its very nature war may be dominated by passion and hatreds or conversely it may be dominated by unforeseen events on the battlefield or by strokes of genius. Political leaders and military commanders must always strive to keep passion and chance subordinate to reason.

Always the pragmatic theorist, Clausewitz does not propose the trinity as an abstraction to inspire academic musings; instead, he overlays the trinity on a state, a nation at war. This converts the trinity from an abstraction into a practical tool of net assessment. "The passions that are to be kindled," he tells us, "must already be inherent in the people." "The scope which the play of courage and talent … realm of probability and chance depends on the particular character of the commander and the army." "But," he cautions, "the political aims are the business of government alone." This is why Napoleon is the god of war to Clausewitz, he is the trinity incarnate. As emperor he is French policy, as field commander he dominates the realm of chance and probability, and as hero of the French people he feeds on and channels their passions and primordial hatreds.

So to figure out the likely nature of a looming conflict, all you have to do is apply this very simple model, the trinity. Figure out how the three dominant tendencies (passion, genius, and reason) of one belligerent will interact with the three dominant tendencies of another belligerent. And you figure that out by calculating how the people, the military, and the government interact in one state and how they will interact with the people, the military, and the government in another state. Piece of cake, right? No it's not, but Clausewitz considers it the obligation of military and political leaders to determine "the kind of war on which they are embarking." This is not a naïve assumption that the nature of a war can be determined with a high degree of clarity, but it must be attempted.

Since war is subordinate to policy he says the first thing to examine is "our political aim and that of the enemy." Then "we must gauge the strength and situation of the opposite state. We must gauge the character and abilities of its government and people and do the same in regard to our own." If that weren't enough, he says that "we must (also) evaluate the political sympathies of other states." In other words it is both the contest and the context.

So let's start where Clausewitz tells us to, with the political aims of the war. War to Clausewitz was a continuation of the political competition between states by military means. War's violent nature makes it a unique form of political competition, but we can never lose sight of its political purpose. War, he says, might have a unique grammar, by which he meant that war and combat are governed by military considerations, which are the specialties of the generals, but ultimately that war and politics serve the same logic.

We have already seen that political aims can vary greatly, and Clausewitz does a pretty good job of sketching out the possible range. He starts with a simple contrast between two extremes of war. At one end of the spectrum we have his "absolute war," a conflict dominated exclusively by passions and hatred. At the other end, we have what he calls "war by algebra." This is a conflict that is determined not by violence, but by a comparison of the relative strengths of each side. In other words, it's deterrence. Neither of these would be war by Clausewitz's definition. "Absolute war" serves no rational political purpose and "war by algebra" does not involve bloodshed.

His spectrum for war actually falls between these two extremes. What we get is a spectrum between limited and unlimited wars. If you're looking to wrest some concessions from an adversary or to prevent him from challenging the status quo, then you are in a limited war. If you want to overthrow his regime, then the war is unlimited.

The 1990–1991 war against Iraq was a limited war. The 2003 Iraq War was unlimited, sought to overthrow the regime. So Clausewitz believes that political objectives are a major determinant of the nature of any particular war, but obviously not the sole determinant. The types of government institutions, the character and inclinations of the populations, and the larger environment all contribute to the unique nature of a conflict. A war between two dictatorships will likely be a lot different than a war between two democracies even though the political objectives might be similar.

The international context also matters: A war between North and South Korea in the 1950s at the height of superpower competition in the Cold War would be very different from a war between the two today. So, once you have worked through this trinitarian assessment of the two belligerents, or the two rival coalitions, and factored in the international context and its likely impact of the military contest, you can start thinking about the best strategy for achieving your political objectives.

Here's where we get to Clausewitz on strategy. From net assessment emerges a list of strategic targets, or what Clausewitz calls "centers of gravity." They are: the enemy's army; his capital if it is center of social, professional, and political activity; it could be the enemy's main ally, if that ally is indispensable; and finally, and only in the case of a popular uprisings, the center of gravity might be the people.

We have seen another list like this in the *Sunzi*: Attack the enemy's strategy first, the enemy's alliances second, the army third, and his cities last. But Clausewitz has little patience for the idea of "winning without fighting" involved in those first two. His is a book about war, not about deterrence or "war by algebra."

"Kind-hearted people" he says (fools, in other words) might think that you can "disarm or defeat an enemy without too much bloodshed." But for Clausewitz war is violence; and violence begets violence.

Clausewitz is not a bloodthirsty warmonger, but he is a realist. If the political objective is worth fighting for, then the other side is probably not going to give it up without a fight. So he gives us another one of these simple concepts, the center of gravity, that thing you need to hit with enough force to compel the enemy to do your will.

Back in high school we could all figure out the center of gravity or the center of mass of an inanimate object. But how do you figure out the center of gravity of a state at war? A state might have several potential centers of gravity that might shift over time. The relevant center of gravity might depend on the political objective being pursued. For example, in 1991 our political objective was liberating Kuwait. As a result Iraq's center of gravity was probably the Iraqi Army occupying Kuwait. If the objective is unlimited, for example, toppling Saddam Hussein, then the center of gravity is probably Baghdad, the political and cultural center of the country. After the fall of Saddam in 2003 the center of gravity shifted to the people. We had an entirely different war on our hands.

So, a simple concept derived from the physical sciences, but it turns out to be something that can be very complex. Nonetheless once a center of gravity is determined, Clausewitz looks for ways to strike it for maximum strategic and political effect. "Two basic principles … underlie all strategic planning," he says, "act with the utmost concentration and with the utmost speed." This is how you dominate that part of the trinity where combat takes place: the realm of chance and probability. The superior general masses his forces for a rapid and decisive blow against the enemy's center of gravity. Once he has shattered that center of gravity he pursues the beaten enemy.

This is essentially what had happened at Jena and Auerstadt. The French smashed the Prussian Army though a mix of mass, speed, and audacity and then kept the pressure up on the reeling Prussians. This doesn't happen all on its own, it often requires brilliant leadership, genius. Is Clausewitz a blind adherent to mass and brute force? No! He understood that Napoleon's victories did not derive solely from the mass of his armies. They had as much to do with the brilliance and audacity of Napoleon and his marshals. He tells us first that "The maximum use of force is in no way incompatible with the simultaneous use of intellect." Brains and brawn. And follows that up with: "What genius does is the best rule." That's not very helpful, is it?

Fortunately, he does not leave it there. Genius may be innate, you either have it or you don't, but it can be honed through the study of history. It must also be paired with absolute determination, much the same way as Jomini. So genius is easy: nature, nurture, and moral courage. In other words, the ability to make an intuitive judgment under stress and with imperfect information and the courage to see that decision implemented.

On the point of genius, it is useful to contrast the clever combatant in the *Sunzi*, the human supercomputer to Clausewitz' informed, but also intuitive, genius. A lot of this has to do with their different attitudes toward military intelligence: the *Sunzi* is hungry for intelligence at all levels of war, from the high political down to the dust trails stirred up by the enemy. This is the data you feed into the supercomputer.

Clausewitz likes political and strategic intelligence, but the more you get down to the operational and tactical levels of war, the more you find that intelligence is often uncertain and contradictory. Operating in this fog, it is only the inner glimmer of genius that the general can rely on.

Okay! We have done everything that Clausewitz has told us to do. We have accurately determined the nature of the war. We did this based on the competing political objectives and the strengths and weaknesses of both sides. We have also assessed the international context. We have determined the enemy's center of gravity and we are massing our forces with a genius at the helm. At this point Clausewitz warns us that we still have to confront, fog, friction, and interaction.

War is the province of uncertainty; Clausewitz says that three-quarters of the things that you need to know in a war lie hidden in a fog. War is also inherently interactive, so as much as we are using force to compel an enemy to do our will, he is doing the same to us. And finally, while Clausewitz advocates mass at the decisive point, he is also aware that my mass trying to overwhelm my enemy's mass often causes war to escalate. So even after they have done all of that net assessment and strategic planning, it is still incumbent on the general and the politician to keep war from getting out of control. All of these complementary and contradictory facets of war coalesce in two of my favorite concepts in *On War*: the culminating point of attack and the culminating point of victory.

I mentioned Clausewitz's principle of continuity in our discussion of Napoleon. That principle of continuity demands that we follow up a battlefield victory with a continuation of the offensive so as to exert maximum military and psychological pressure on the adversary. The antithesis of the principle of continuity is the culminating point of the attack, which warns that not only is it counterproductive to advance beyond that culminating point, but also that doing so invites defeat. The culminating point of attack is the point at which the remaining strength of the attacker "is just enough to maintain a defense and wait for peace." Going past that culminating point shifts the advantage to the defender who is getting stronger relative to the attacker. This is an operational concept, but Clausewitz elevates it to the level of strategy with a short chapter on the culminating point of victory.

Passing the culminating point of victory isn't just pushing an offensive too far, it's pushing your political objectives too far. Passing the culminating point of victory may actually increase your enemy's will to resist, and invite third party intervention on his behalf. Napoleon passed both his culminating point of attack and his culminating point of victory when he invaded Russia. The United States passed both in Korea when MacArthur advanced toward North Korea's border with China. With these culminating points, Clausewitz explains why military success does not always lead to success in war. He also reemphasizes that war serves a political purpose; hence, victory can only be declared when that purpose is achieved. So he is leading us to the topic of why wars end.

Here we have another of those deceptively simple maxims: "No one starts a war—or rather, no one in his senses ought to do so—without first being clear in his mind what he intends to achieve by that war and how he intends to conduct it. The former is its political purpose, the latter its operational objective." If we take this prescription literally, then a war is over when we have achieved our operational objective. This, however, can only be the case if we have accurately predicted the enemy's center of gravity and have inflicted sufficient harm upon it to convince him to capitulate. That is almost impossible to determine with absolute accuracy in advance, therefore the decision to end a war ultimately lies with the defeated side.

"Once the expenditure of effort exceeds the value of the political object, the object must be renounced and peace must follow." But how often are decisions going to be this cold-blooded and rational? It is little surprise then that wars, especially limited wars, are very difficult to terminate. In war, there is almost never this clear crossover point.

And even when war is brought to a formal end, Clausewitz understands that since the result is ultimately political that it is inherently unstable. "The defeated state," he says, "often considers the outcome merely a transitory evil, for which a remedy may still be found."

In the final analysis if you want to end a war on the most advantageous terms, you have to nail both the culminating point of attack and the culminating point of victory. To do that takes both military and political genius, and this is where I think that Clausewitz goes above and beyond.

Clausewitz's thoughts on the proper relationship between politicians and the military in the making of strategy are among the most provocative and brilliant ever penned.

> Subordinating the political point of view to the military would be absurd, for it is policy that has created war. Policy is the guiding intelligence and war only the instrument, not vice versa. No other possibility exists, then, than to subordinate the military point of view to the political.

That is a very strident demand, but given Prussia's own dysfunctional civil-military coordination that culminated in the disasters of 1806, it makes sense. It makes even more sense in light of Napoleon's self-destruction, when military considerations were divorced from political logic. Nor is Clausewitz arguing that generals should simply acquiesce to political domination. The politicians should not "summon soldiers … and ask them for purely military advice," he warns.

Crafting strategy is a dynamic conversation between the politicians and the military leaders that is constantly tested, reviewed, and adapted throughout a conflict, from the planning stages, through the execution, and down to the making of peace. Politicians who are ignorant of what military force can and cannot achieve are as dangerous as military commanders who are ignorant of what is and what is not politically feasible. This is why Clausewitz's *On War* is a crucial book for both the military and for senior civilians.

We'll come back to that in the next lecture. In the meantime, I have a confession to make. Carl von Clausewitz is really the master's master. Most of those big criteria that I brought up in the first lecture, historical perspective, political purpose, net assessment, leadership, interaction, and war termination? I obviously didn't come up with those. They are all derived from Clausewitz's *On War*.

On War is the first and fullest exposition of what we now call strategic theory. For all those masters that predate Clausewitz we have been looking for glimmers that anticipate his frameworks. In all of our subsequent discussions we look at what later theorists add and how close they come to the standards set by Clausewitz.

So go pick up a copy of *On War*. At 700 pages you will get a physical workout, but it is the mental exercise that is the most rewarding. I'll see you next time.

Jomini and Clausewitz through the Ages
Lecture 11

It would not be an exaggeration to say that Clausewitz and Jomini are the two most influential strategic theorists of the modern era. At first, Jomini was the more popular of the two, but over time, Clausewitz has caught up to, and perhaps overtaken, the Swiss author. Today, they continue to profoundly influence operational doctrine and strategic thought around the world. In this lecture, we'll look at the reputations of these two authorities and at their views on the important question of the proper roles of civilian and military leaders in planning and conducting wars.

Jomini's Influence

- As we saw in an earlier lecture, Jomini's menu of guiding principles for strategy and operations found an enthusiastic audience among the emerging class of professional military officers, who were eager to define and delineate the profession of arms.

- His writings provided the theoretical foundations, core principles, educational focus, and vocabulary for the military profession. The *Summary of the Art of War* was, therefore, widely considered the greatest military textbook of the 19th century.

- In the United States, Jomini's early fans included General Winfield Scott, who based his campaign plan in the Mexican-American War on the principles of Jomini, and the West Point professor Dennis Hart Mahan, whose lectures relied heavily on Jomini and influenced such students as William Tecumseh Sherman and Henry Halleck.

- The poor performance of the West Point Jominians in the Civil War tarnished Jomini's prestige in the United States. The bloody stalemate of the First World War, however, reignited interest in Jomini's concepts of maneuver warfare. The first generation of air-power theorists, writing in the 1920s and 1930s, were also drawn to Jomini's "decisive points."

- Today, it may seem that Jomini lost out to Clausewitz and to the *Sunzi* in American war colleges and military academies. His original works are still read, but quite often, if Jomini gets attention, it is as a negative example: an object lesson in being too mechanical and prescriptive.

- He has not, however, become irrelevant. In fact, a great deal of what Jomini thought about strategy and operations has come to deeply imbue U.S. operational doctrine. The U.S. Army's *Operations Manual*, FM 3-0, puts forward nine principles of war, all of which are variations on themes laid out by Jomini.

Clausewitz's Influence

- As a member of the reform faction in Prussia, Clausewitz was uniquely situated to affect the Prusso-German school of strategy, but he often ran afoul of his military and civilian superiors. His premature death, compounded by the incomplete nature and analytical density of *On War*, further limited his overall impact.

- But after Prussia's shocking victory over France in 1871 and especially with praise for Clausewitz from Helmuth von Moltke, the Prussian chief of staff, interest in *On War* began to increase across Europe.

- In the early 1900s, Clausewitz's appeal was primarily among political theorists, including Lenin and Mao Tse-tung, who were drawn by his arguments about the political character of war. In the West, Clausewitz won many fans in Britain, but after World War I, he was unfairly tarred with the brush of German militarism and fell out of favor.

- It wasn't until the 1970s that military officers in the United States got much exposure to Clausewitz, but he is widely studied today. Two critical events account for this sea change: (1) the appearance in 1976 of an exceptional English translation of *On War* by Michael Howard and Peter Paret and (2) the founding of academic departments in strategy and policy, giving military officers exposure to experts who understand and appreciate Clausewitz.

- The influence of Clausewitz on the U.S. military took yet another step forward in 1982, when Colonel Harry Summers published *On Strategy*, a Clausewitzian postmortem on America's failure in Vietnam. Summers's work found an instant readership in the military. Not content with simply understanding failure, Clausewitz might be useful in preventing future defeats.

- Finally, it seemed that Clausewitz might get to play a role in the planning and execution of war. Colin Powell's reading of Clausewitz was a significant influence in what became the Weinberger-Powell doctrine: the set of political and military preconditions proposed as a litmus test for committing U.S. troops to foreign wars.

- Clausewitz's distinction between limited and unlimited wars also filled an analytical vacuum in a military geared almost exclusively for fighting a big war with the Soviet Union but intellectually unprepared for the unique challenges of fighting and winning wars for limited political objectives, such as Vietnam.

- The Gulf War of 1990–1991 was the first test of the Americanized Clausewitz in action. The framing of the limited political objectives, the bounding of strategy within those objectives, the search for centers of gravity, and the fear of culminating points permeated the American conduct of that war.

Military and Civilian Roles in War

- Both Clausewitz and Jomini are frequently invoked in the often-heated debates about the proper roles of military officers and civilians in planning, executing, and terminating wars.

- One of the reasons that Jomini tends to be more popular than Clausewitz among military officers is that Clausewitz demands a high degree of political oversight in the conduct of war: "Policy is the guiding intelligence and war only the instrument, not vice versa.

... No other possibility exists, then, than to subordinate the military point of view to the political."

- Jomini seems to lean more toward the *Sunzi*, with the professional's hostility toward the meddling of the amateurs back in the capital: "A general whose genius and hands are tied by a [Ruling] Council five hundred miles distant cannot be a match for one who has liberty of action ...."

- Jomini is emblematic of what has come to be called the "normal theory" of civil-military relations. This theory accepts that war serves a political end, but it falls to the professional military to determine the best way to fight a war in pursuit of those political ends.

- The military profession is unique for a number of reasons, not least the fact that it is a profession of violence.
  o Fortunately, members of the military do not spend the majority of their time doing what they are trained to do, which means that the military is among the most self-reflective of the professions.

  o At the same time, military officers do not enjoy the same degree of autonomy as other professionals. In American history, this has created a great deal of tension between the serving military and the civilians in government.

  o The U.S. Army, in particular, traditionally took the more Jominian view of a clear point of separation between political and military considerations.

  o At first glance, this principle seems to be validated by history. For example, in the assessment of many, the inability of politicians to stay out of the spheres of strategy and command was what doomed American efforts in Vietnam.

Countering the Normal Theory
- A distinctly Clausewitzian counterargument to Jomini and the normal theory was developed in 2002, with the publication of a book

called *Supreme Command: Soldiers, Statesmen, and Leadership in Wartime* by Eliot A. Cohen, a professor of strategic studies.

- Cohen's thesis was that the normal theory represented a dangerous dereliction of the duties of the political leader, central to which was the judicious supervision of the execution of war. If politicians stay out of military affairs, they lose the ability to maintain the subordination of military action to political ends, and once wars are freed from political control, they tend to escalate toward Clausewitz's extreme.

- To make his case, Cohen used four models of civilian leadership in war: Lincoln in the Civil War, Clemenceau in World War I, Churchill in World War II, and Ben-Gurion in Israel's war of independence. All four leaders relentlessly pestered their military commanders and offered their own operational and sometimes tactical suggestions.

© iStockphoto/Thinkstock.

Abraham Lincoln has been cited as a model of civilian leadership in war, highlighting the idea that Jomini's normal theory represents a dereliction of the duties of politicians.

- In crafting his argument, Cohen takes his marching orders from Clausewitz: "Political considerations do not determine the posting of guards or the employment of patrols. But they are influential in the planning of war, of the campaign, and often even of the battle."

- With the exception of tactical minutiae, almost every action in war can have political significance; thus, every significant decision can and should be subject to political oversight. Military officers need to recognize this fact and to welcome it. This is what Cohen calls the "unequal dialogue."

- In general, Cohen's argument is persuasive, but he tends to neglect the military side of the civil-military equation. The danger of too narrow a definition of the unequal dialogue is that it can become an unequal monologue, with the military simply acquiescing to political oversight at all levels of war.

- In the end, Clausewitz tells us that as much as civilians need to familiarize themselves with what militaries can and cannot do, senior military leaders need to be knowledgeable of the strategic and political consequences of military action. They need to respectfully push back on issues of strategy and, possibly, even policy.

- Ultimately, it is a question of how deep and what kind of political oversight is necessary. The answer to that question, as with almost all questions related to strategy and war, is dependent on the nature of the war and the scale of political objectives.

Summing Up Clausewitz and Jomini

- The fact that Eliot Cohen's Clausewitzian view of the subordination of military action to political oversight has had real-world influence in policy circles in this country and has set off new debates about civil-military relations should alert us to the enduring significance and influence of Clausewitz and Jomini.

- That influence is best discerned by looking at the different levels of war. Clausewitz is most relevant to understanding the nexus of policy and strategy, while Jomini's interest in eternal principles of warfare best suits the tactical and operational levels of war.

- This "level-of-war" breakdown is a useful framework, but we should not simply view Clausewitz and Jomini as two sides of the same coin; significant differences exist between these two theorists.
  o Most significant is the disparity between their philosophical assumptions. Jomini, the Enlightenment theorist, believes that even with all of war's complexity, practical prescriptions for action are still possible. Clausewitz, the German romantic

pessimist, is ever mindful that even though one side might win all the battles, it can still lose the war.

o   We are the inheritors of both philosophical traditions, and even today, we have yet to come down on one side or the other.

Suggested Reading

Calhoun, "Clausewitz and Jomini."

Cohen, *Supreme Command*.

Handel, *Masters of War*.

Huntington, *The Soldier and the State*.

Questions to Consider

1. What are the main areas of agreement and disagreement between Jomini and Clausewitz?

2. What challenges does a democracy, such as the United States, face in trying to implement Cohen's unequal dialogue?

Jomini and Clausewitz through the Ages
Lecture 11—Transcript

It would not be an exaggeration to say that Clausewitz and Jomini are the two most influential strategic theorists of the modern era. At first, Jomini was the more popular of the two, but over time Clausewitz has caught up to and perhaps overtaken the Swiss author. Today, they continue to profoundly influence operational doctrine and strategic thought in the United States and around the world.

It is pretty easy to understand why Jomini had an initial edge in popularity over Clausewitz. We have already seen that Jomini's approach and style were very appealing. By employing the "great captains" genre, Jomini attracted a broad audience of professionals and amateurs. You'll recall that Jomini treated Napoleon as part of a military tradition that went back to Alexander and Julius Caesar. Napoleon didn't represent a sea-change in the scale and lethality of war. This was comforting to European audiences.

Clausewitz's vision was a good deal more ominous. Clausewitz is also a tougher read. His style can be convoluted, and he didn't pepper *On War* with a lot of gripping descriptions of battles. The posthumous publication of Napoleon's memoirs in the 1820s, in which the emperor praised Jomini, gave the Swiss theorist yet another boost.

Jomini's works were translated into all of the major languages and became required reading in Europe's military academies and staff colleges. He was even popular in Germany. Jomini appealed in particular to the professional military, those engineers and logisticians, who were drawn toward his semi-scientific maxims. As I noted last time, Jomini is not at fault for the fact that his readers often focused on what look like absolute laws of war, nor should we blame him for the interpretations of subsequent generations of so-called "Jominians," who emphasized what they felt was important in the master.

The most important thing is that Jomini's menu of guiding principles for strategy and operations found an enthusiastic audience among the emerging class of professional military officers who were eager to define and delineate the profession of arms. In his writings, Jomini provided the theoretical foundations, the core principles, the educational focus, and the vocabulary for the modern military profession. The *Summary of the Art of War* was, therefore, widely considered the greatest military textbook of the 19th century. Nor was his influence limited to Europe's armies.

Sir Julian Corbett, the great British maritime theorist, also read his Jomini, and applied many of Jomini's points about amphibious warfare to his analysis of Wellington's peninsular campaign.

In the U.S., Jomini's early fans included General Winfield Scott and the West Point professor Dennis Hart Mahan. Scott was fluent in French and had traveled in Europe toward the tail end of the Napoleonic wars. He was deeply impressed with the French way of war and carried Jomini's works with him throughout his career. Scott's greatest professional achievement came in the Mexican War of 1846–1848.

By his own admission, Scott had based his campaign plan on the principles of Jomini. Landing forces at Veracruz in 1847, Scott guaranteed interior lines of supply from the sea. He then began to march inland, outmaneuvering and defeating Mexican units in detail and seizing a series of decisive points along the way. Scott then launched an audacious campaign to threaten and ultimately take Mexico City. Reviewing this campaign, Jomini went so far as to say that Scott's planning and execution of the Mexican War was "brilliant" in his estimation.

In Mexico then, the United States had a successful test of Jomini in practice, but they also had a lot of Jomini in theory. Dennis Hart Mahan, the top cadet at West Point, followed up his graduation from the Academy with four years of study in France. He returned to West Point in the 1830s as an instructor of military engineering and military sciences, but his interests ranged over the entire scope of military operations. Understandably, West Point was already a hotbed of interest in Napoleon and the Napoleonic way of war. Dennis Hart Mahan's lectures, which relied heavily on Jomini, influenced many of his students, among them William Tecumseh Sherman and Henry Halleck. In fact, Halleck's *Elements of Military Art and Science*, which borrows at length from Jomini's *Summary*, became the primary textbook at West Point in the 1850s.

Nor was the United States Navy immune to the charms of Jomini. As we will see in the subsequent block on the sea-power theorists, Dennis Hart Mahan's son, Alfred Thayer Mahan sought in the history of naval warfare the same kinds of guiding strategic principles that Jomini had discerned. He also read the master when he was preparing for his lectures at the Naval War College. Mahan was not a slave to Jomini, but he was very Jominian in his emphasis on concentration, and on decisive battles followed by relentless pursuit. In fact, Mahan's boss at Newport, Admiral Stephen B. Luce, was even more Jominian than his protégé.

Unfortunately, the poor performance of the West Point "Jominians" in the Civil War tarnished Jomini's prestige in the United States. The bloody stalemate of the First World War, however, reignited interest in Jomini's concepts of maneuver warfare. The first generation of air-power theorists, writing in the 1920s and 1930s, were also drawn to Jomini's "decisive points." Soviet armor doctrine in the Cold War was decidedly Jominian as well.

But coming back to the United States, it seems at first glance that Jomini lost out to Clausewitz and to the *Sunzi*. His original works are still read in our war colleges and military academies, but quite often if Jomini gets attention, it is as a negative example, an object lesson in being too mechanical and prescriptive. In other words, he is the model of how not to think about the dynamic realm of strategy and operations.

But while Jomini does not get as much overt attention as he did in the past, this does not mean that he has become irrelevant. In fact, a great deal of what Jomini thought about strategy and especially what he thought about operations has come to deeply imbue U.S. operational doctrine. In fact, it's often hard to tell where Jomini ends and where modern military doctrine begins. As an example, let's look at Field Manual 3 (FM-3): The United States Army's Operations Manual. FM-3 puts forward nine principles of war all of which are variations on themes laid out by Jomini, and perhaps tracing back to Halleck's textbook from 1846.

I'll just mention a couple of these principles: FM-3 says that a military campaign will have a decisive operational objective; this is exactly the same as Jomini's decisive point. The same goes for the third principle in FM-3: overwhelming mass at the decisive point. There is also the principle of offensive action, take the offense and seize the initiative. Again these sound like platitudes, but they found their fullest exposition in Jomini. And finally, we have an emphasis on operational security. You deny the enemy knowledge about you, while you find out as much as you can about him. Even if a young army lieutenant has never heard of Jomini, she is still expected to learn his principles.

Let's turn our attention now to Clausewitz. As a member of the reform faction in Prussia, Clausewitz was uniquely situated to affect the Prusso-German school of strategy, but he often ran afoul of his military and civilian superiors. His premature death, from cholera, compounded by the incomplete nature and analytical density of *On War* further limited his overall impact. Jomini may actually have found a more receptive audience in late 19th-century Germany than Clausewitz, the native son. But after Prussia's shocking victory over France in 1871, and especially with praise for Clausewitz from Helmuth von Moltke's, the Prussian chief of staff, interest in *On War* began to increase across Europe. By the turn of the last century numerous translations had appeared.

So in the early 1900s Clausewitz's appeal was growing modestly, but ironically it was primarily among political theorists who were drawn by his arguments about the political character of war. Most military officers were too busy trying to master new technologies and new tactics to think too many deep thoughts about the gestalt of war. Philosophers and political theorists were another story. Not least among the early fans of Clausewitz was Lenin, who cribbed much of his best strategic insight from *On War*. Mao Tse-tung also read his Clausewitz, both in a Chinese translation of *On War* and in his study of Lenin.

Back in the West, Clausewitz won many fans in Britain, but after World War I he was unfairly tarred with the brush of German militarism and fell out of favor. Fortunately anti-Clausewitz sentiment was not universal in Britain. The British theorist who best appreciated and made the best use of Clausewitz was arguably Sir Julian Corbett, whose strategic thought we'll explore in another lecture.

On the whole, though, *On War* did not have much influence for more than a century after it was published. And the main reason for this was the fact that Clausewitz did not provide much in the way of prescriptions about the conduct of war. Clausewitz's approach also required his readers to study a lot of history. This made him an even harder sell. So while there were lots of self-professed Jominians running around, the best we can say for most of this period is that the Prussian had a lot of intuitive followers, intuitive Clausewitzians. People who never read the master, but who just kind of naturally got it. Many people point to Ulysses S. Grant as a great example of one of those intuitive Clausewitzians.

With the curse of hindsight, most Clausewitz mavens in the past, and even those today, don't get much beyond lamenting that general so-and-so was too Jominian and not Clausewitzian enough. In other words, the ideas of Jomini played a role in the planning and execution of wars, whereas Clausewitz's ideas were primarily used by those performing the postmortems on failed military campaigns.

It was not until the 1970s that military officers in the United States got much exposure to Clausewitz. He was percolating around in civilian strategy circles, especially in the work of Bernard Brodie, the Clausewitz of the nuclear age, who we will meet a few lectures from now, but the U.S. military was pretty much a Clausewitz-free zone. Nowadays, however, a military officer who hasn't read his Clausewitz is the exception.

Two critical events account for this sea-change. The first was the appearance in 1976 of a truly exceptional English translation of *On War* by Michael Howard and Peter Paret. That version comprises an elegant rendering of Clausewitz's often turgid prose and includes introductory essays, an index, and most importantly, chapter summaries (i.e., cliff's notes). The second event was the founding of academic departments like my own. For really the first time, military officers had a systematic exposure to civilian academics and especially to civilian strategy experts who understood and appreciated Clausewitz. At the same time, military officers had more opportunities to pursue Master's and Doctoral degrees at civilian universities where their professors introduced them to the likes of Thucydides, Sunzi, Machiavelli, and Clausewitz.

The influence of Clausewitz on the U.S. military took yet another step forward in 1982 when Colonel Harry Summers published *On Strategy*, a very Clausewitzian postmortem on America's failure in Vietnam. Summers' work found an instant readership in the military. Not content with simply understanding failure, Clausewitz might be useful in preventing future defeats.

Finally, it seemed that Clausewitz might get to play a role in the planning and execution of war. Colin Powell, himself a Vietnam veteran, described his first reading of *On War* as a revelation. In fact, Powell's reading of Clausewitz played a big role in what became the Weinberger-Powell Doctrine, that set of political and military preconditions that General Powell and former Secretary of Defense Caspar Weinberger proposed as a litmus test for committing U.S. troops to foreign wars.

Clausewitz's distinction between limited and unlimited wars also filled an analytical vacuum in a military geared almost exclusively for fighting a big war with the Soviet Union, but that military was intellectually unprepared for the unique challenges of fighting and winning wars fought for limited political objectives, like Vietnam.

The Gulf War of 1990–1991 was the first test of the Americanized Clausewitz in action. The framing of the limited political objectives, the bounding of strategy within those objectives, the search for centers-of-gravity and the fear of culminating points permeate the American conduct of that war. In fact, nothing is more Clausewitzian than former Defense Secretary Dick Cheney's justification for not removing Saddam Hussein from power. Cheney explained that going into Iraq would undermine the U.S.–led coalition and might lead to escalation, in other words, it meant passing the culminating point of victory. He also asked if going to Baghdad met the test of the value of the object: "How many dead Americans is Saddam worth?" Cheney asked. "Our judgment was not very many."

There you have a civilian explaining the political rationales for not going further militarily. And this brings us to a topic where Clausewitz has a lot of relevance and where Jomini is also frequently invoked, that is, in the often heated debates about the proper role of military officers and civilians in the planning, execution, and termination of wars. So if you think these long-dead Army officers don't matter, you've got another thing coming.

One of the reasons that Jomini has tended to be more popular among military officers than Clausewitz was because Clausewitz demanded a high degree of political oversight into the conduct of war. Remember that he says in Book Eight, Chapter 6, "Policy is the guiding intelligence and war only the instrument, not vice versa." He goes on: "No other possibility exists than to subordinate the military point of view to the political."

Political oversight does not extend to the "posting of guards" he says, but it can and should influence everything down to "the planning of a battle." In this manner Clausewitz hews closer to the line advocated by Machiavelli.

Jomini seems to lean more toward the *Sunzi*, with the professional's hostility toward the meddling of the amateurs back in the capital. Here's Jomini on the subject:

> A general whose genius and hands are tied by a [Ruling] Council five hundred miles distant cannot be a match for one who has liberty of action, other things being equal. ... Interfered with and opposed in all his enterprises [he] will be unable to achieve success, even if he have the requisite ability.

Jomini is emblematic of what has come to be called the "normal theory" of civil–military relations. The normal theory accepts that war serves a political end, but it falls to the professional military to determine the best way to fight a war in pursuit of those political ends.

I want to take a moment here to talk about the unique nature of the military profession. The military is unique for a lot of reasons. In the first place it is a profession of violence.

In the second place, and this is fortunate, the military does not spend the majority of its time doing what it is trained to do. Doctors and lawyers spend most of their workday treating patients and preparing briefs. Professional soldiers train and prepare for war, but actual fighting is relatively rare.

Obviously the last 10 years are an exception. But usually this means that the military is among the most self-reflective of the professions. What I mean by that is that they have the time and the advanced education to think deep thoughts about the larger purpose of war.

But at the same time, military officers do not enjoy the same degree of autonomy as other professionals. Hospital administrators rarely second-guess the professional judgment of doctors, but military officers do not have absolute freedom to exercise their professional judgment. In American history this has created a great deal of tension between the serving military and the civilians in government. The U.S. Army, in particular, traditionally took the more Jominian view of a clear point of separation between political and military considerations.

A 1936 Army handbook, *The Principles of Strategy for an Independent Corps or Army in a Theater of Operations*, put it this way:

> Politics and strategy are radically and fundamentally things apart. Strategy begins where politics end. All that soldiers ask is that once the policy is settled, strategy and command shall be regarded as being in a sphere apart from politics. ... The line of demarcation must be drawn between politics and strategy.

Pretty strident, isn't it? And at first glance isn't this principle borne out by history? In the assessment of many, the inability of politicians to stay out of the spheres of strategy and command was what doomed American efforts in Vietnam. In the words of General Westmoreland, the ground commander in that war: "A major problem was that Washington ... forced us to fight with [only] one hand." And we all know that one definition of the mantra of "no more Vietnams," and trust me there are a lot of different definitions, but one of the more popular was that when America goes to war, the military should have two free hands.

By the 1990s it had become obligatory for senior military and senior civilians to invoke the negative example of Vietnam and claim "Never again!" In 1990, Secretary of Defense Cheney and Chairman of the Joint Chiefs of Staff Colin Powell told the troops in Saudi Arabia that in the coming war that

"There won't be any restrictions placed upon running a first-class military operation. ... They won't have their hands tied behind their back." No more Vietnams. But if you read-up on Operation Desert Storm, you'll find that there was a very high degree of political oversight and the politicians absolutely put restrictions on what the military could do. And yet, public statements like this seemed obligatory despite what was really going on.

The second President Bush made a similar invocation in the context of Operation Iraqi Freedom.

> The thing about the Vietnam War that troubles me, as I look back, was it was a political war. We had politicians making military decisions, and it is lessons that any president must learn, and that is to set the goal and the objective and allow the military to come up with the plans to achieve that objective.

Jomini and the Normal Theory seemed to have won the day, but there was a distinctly Clausewitzian counterargument developing. In 2002, Eliot A. Cohen, a professor at Johns Hopkins University and later an advisor to the Bush administration, published a book called *Supreme Command: Soldiers, Statesmen and Leadership in Wartime.*

Cohen's thesis was that the normal theory represented a dangerous dereliction of the duties of the statesmen; central to those duties was the judicious supervision of the execution of a war. If a politician stayed out of military affairs he lost the ability to maintain the subordination of military action to political ends.

One reason that this would be dangerous is that once they are freed from political control, wars tend to escalate toward Clausewitz's extreme. In contrast to letting the generals exercise complete professional autonomy, the Normal Theory, it was incumbent on the statesman to be knowledgeable about military affairs, and to question, and even second-guess the military judgments of the soldiers. Finally, the civilians had to stay engaged throughout the conflict.

To make his case, Cohen used four models of civilian leadership in war: Lincoln in the Civil War, Clemenceau in World War I, Churchill in World War II, and Ben-Gurion in Israel's War of Independence. All four leaders relentlessly pestered their military commanders and offered their own operational and sometimes tactical suggestions. In crafting this argument, Cohen takes his marching orders from Clausewitz, specifically Book Eight, Chapter 6, of *On War*. In that very short section of his masterpiece, Clausewitz gives the statesman license to, as Cohen puts it, inject "himself in any aspect of war-making."

Remember what Clausewitz said: "Political considerations do not determine the posting of guards or the employment of patrols. But they are … influential in the planning of war, of the campaign, and often even of the battle." Let's look at this from a theoretical perspective. With the exception of tactical minutiae, almost every action in war can have political significance. Every significant decision can and should be subject to political oversight. Military officers need to recognize this fact and to welcome it. This is what Cohen calls the "Unequal Dialogue," and we have seen it already in FDR's decision to overrule Marshall on the decision to invade North Africa.

But Cohen's book is primarily written from the perspective of the statesman. If anything, Cohen was trying to overcome the disinclination of post-Vietnam political leaders to meddle in military affairs. To Cohen this was the mis-learned lesson of Vietnam, not that the politicians had meddled too much, but that they had not meddled enough in the critical strategic debates. From Cohen's perspective, Westmoreland's lament that he had one hand tied behind his back was disingenuous. On the contrary, President Johnson had not done enough to challenge the strategy that Westmoreland conceived and executed with hardly any inputs from Washington.

In general I am persuaded by Cohen's argument, but since he is writing from the statesman's perspective, he tends to neglect the military side of the civil–military equation. The danger of too narrow a definition of the unequal dialogue is that it can become an unequal monologue, with the military simply acquiescing to political oversight of all the levels of war.

As usual, Clausewitz has another counterargument: "The assertion that a major military development, or the plan for one, should be a matter for *purely military* opinion is unacceptable and can be damaging. Nor is it indeed sensible to summon soldiers ... and ask them for *purely military advice*."

What Clausewitz was saying, and what I hope my students learn from him, is that as much as the civilians need to familiarize themselves with what militaries can and cannot do, the senior military leaders need to be knowledgeable of the strategic and political consequences of military action. They need to be able to respectfully push back on issues of strategy and possibly even policy. Passive acquiescence will breed a cadre of officers of great tactical and operational skill, but no strategic imagination. We cannot afford to have that happen.

Ultimately, it is a question of how deep and what kind of political oversight is necessary. The answer to that question, as with almost all questions related to strategy and war, is "It depends." It depends on the nature of the war and the scale of the political objectives. In Europe in 1944 and 1945, Eisenhower didn't need much political oversight of the operational details of his campaigns. But, in a war where escalation is a distinct danger, as Secretary of Defense Cheney believed in 1991, then a more invasive political influence may be called for. We have to hope that senior civilians and senior military officers get the answer right. At the end of the day, I would prefer too much civilian meddling to not enough civilian meddling.

The fact that Eliot Cohen's decidedly Clausewitzian view of the subordination of military action to political oversight has had real-world influence in policy circles in this country and has set off another round of debate about civil–military relations should hopefully alert you to the enduring significance and influence of Clausewitz and Jomini.

That influence is best discerned by looking at the different levels of war. Clausewitz is most relevant to understanding the nexus of policy and strategy. This is largely why Clausewitz is taught with such rigor and enthusiasm in the senior staff colleges in the United States, like my own Naval War College, where officers are preparing to move out of the operational level of war to positions of higher leadership, in other words, to the level of strategic leadership. In this formulation, Jomini's interest in eternal principles of warfare best suits the tactical and operational levels of war. That is the level of planning and executing campaigns. Those operations serve strategic objectives, but that level is naturally subordinate to those strategic objectives.

The fact that Jomini's maxims on internal lines, sequential operations, and decisive points still permeate operational doctrine in the United States and around the world seems to prove this point.

At the Naval War College we have the luxury of spending our time on Clausewitz and on the higher logic of war because our military students have already mastered the grammar of war. In other words, they have mastered their Jomini; we get to complement that with a rigorous examination of Clausewitz and Sunzi.

Jomini has helped make my students professionals in the application of violence, reading Clausewitz (and my brilliant teaching of course), is what makes them strategic thinkers. This "level of war" breakdown is a useful framework, but at the same time let's not simply view Clausewitz and Jomini as two sides of the same coin: because there *are* significant differences between these two theorists. Most significant is the radical disparity between their philosophical assumptions. Jomini, the Enlightenment theorist, believes that even with all of war's complexity, that practical prescriptions for action are still possible; this appeals to the scientists and engineers among us. Clausewitz, the German Romantic pessimist, is ever mindful that even though you might win all of the battles, you can still lose the war.

Today we are the inheritors of both philosophical traditions, and even today we have yet to come down on either side: the optimists of the Enlightenment or the pessimists of romanticism. The U.S. military, the most professional, the most technologically advanced, and the best-educated the world has ever known, still finds it easier to win battles than to win wars.

From Sail to Steam—The Sea-Power Revolution
Lecture 12

In our discussion of the Peloponnesian War, we got a glimpse of the fundamental social, political, and cultural distinctions between land powers and sea powers—elephants and whales. We also got some inkling of the various ways in which a navy can be used, such as commerce raiding, amphibious landings, and decisive fleet-on-fleet battles. With this lecture, we turn our attention more fully to the sea and look at the revolution in naval warfare and maritime trade that took place over the century between the end of the Napoleonic Wars and the beginning of World War I.

From Sail to Steam
- The transition from sail to steam is bracketed by two epic naval engagements: Lord Nelson's triumph at Trafalgar in 1805 and Admiral Togo's defeat of the Russians at Tsushima in 1905.
  - Each battle looks like a classic example of victory at sea: a victory won through superior seamanship, communications, and gunnery and the audacity of a brilliant admiral.

  - But they took place in two radically different worlds. When Alfred Thayer Mahan and Sir Julian Corbett began writing about naval history and naval strategy in the 1890s, the maritime world was in the midst of a total transformation: a transformation from sail to steam.

- The changes that took place in the century between these two epic battles represent not just advances in military technology but a transformation in the global economy. Although the process of globalization had begun back in the late 15th century, it accelerated dramatically in the 19th century, as did the competition among would-be sea powers.
  - With a general state of peace emerging in Europe after 1815, the energies of European countries and, to some extent, the United States were directed outward in search of markets and colonies.

- o In the Opium Wars of the mid-19th century, the British succeeded in cracking open the lucrative China market. Not only did this expand the opportunities for trade, but it also liberated the massive amounts of silver that had been piling up in China for two and a half centuries. Japan and Korea were forced open soon afterward.

- o After this point, the cycle of growth accelerated. Growing global demand for the products of Western manufacturing accelerated the industrial revolution, increasing both production and the impetus to find more foreign markets. At the same time, demand for raw materials increased, as did the need for commercial shipping.

- • None of these demands could be met without certain technological advances, as well as advances in medicine. Railroads further accelerated the commercial exploitation of newly opened frontiers, and Western arms technology, notably the breechloader, greatly facilitated the colonial enterprise.

- • The next big advance in the maritime revolution was steam propulsion, but the transition from sail to steam in commercial shipping wasn't particularly rapid, nor was it complete.
  - o Sailing vessels were remarkably fast and economically competitive throughout the 19th century. In contrast, early steamships were expensive and inefficient and required vast stores of coal and frequent stops for refueling.

  - o Steamships found their first real niche in the mail and passenger business between Suez and India. On these voyages, steam vessels had advantages in speed, could steam into the prevailing winds, and could navigate the narrow Suez Canal under their own power.

  - o In terms of global shipping, the advantages of steam began to gradually win out, but it was probably not until the 1880s that the total tonnage of steam-powered ships edged out sailing ships.

The Calculus of Sea Power

- The transition to steam also transformed the calculus of sea power. In the age of sail, timber, cloth, hemp, and sailors were the raw materials of sea power. But by the end of the 19th century, any nation that could harness enough iron ore, coal, and talented engineers could compete on the high seas.

- If 19th-century maritime power was to be measured in wooden ships, then the British would have been at a distinct disadvantage, having cut down their forests to defeat Napoleon. Britain, though, had great comparative advantages in coal, iron, and steel production and still ruled the waves.

- The communications revolution that had begun with the expansion of global shipping took a quantum leap forward with the addition of telegraphy and submarine telegraph cables.
  - In the 1850s, the British were experimenting with cables across the English Channel; a decade later, they enjoyed direct and nearly real-time communications with continental Europe, North America, and India.

  - Two decades after that, a global network of telegraphy sped diplomatic cables, military orders, financial transactions, and news around the planet.

  - This was true globalization. Whereas maritime commerce in the age of sail had involved small cargoes of precious goods, steamships could move all manner of commodities in bulk. In addition, the leap forward in global communications guaranteed that these cargoes would make it to the markets where they were in highest demand.

- As the world approached the turn of the 20th century, maritime commerce and competition flourished. The world's oceans had become a great global commons, a largely ungoverned space through which the lifeblood of national power and prosperity flowed. Any nation that sought its fortunes in global trade could ill-afford to neglect its navy.

The Military Side of Sea Power

- On the military side of the sea-power revolution, it wasn't so much steam power as the screw propeller that transformed naval warfare.
  - o Side and stern paddle wheelers had demonstrated some utility in midcentury conflicts, but in general, paddle propulsion was inefficient, cumbersome, and vulnerable. It also got in the way of gunnery.

  - o The screw propeller, which was fully submerged and mounted along the midline of a ship, was much more efficient and much less vulnerable to enemy fire.

  - o The installation of these propeller shafts in lighter-but-stronger steel-hulled ships and their attachment to high-pressure boilers represented the coming-of-age of the modern steamship. The boilers allowed for the mechanization of the ship itself; steam pressure pumped the bilges, powered the steering, and maneuvered the guns.

- One of the most important drivers of naval transformation in the 19th century was the revolutionary improvement in gunnery.
  - o At the time of Trafalgar, success in naval battle depended more on rates of fire than range or accuracy, but the size and complexity of the guns meant that even the best crews could manage only two shots a minute.

  - o The new breech-loaded and rifled naval guns offered greater range, higher rates of fire, and improved lethality over the muzzle-loaded, smooth-bore cannon of Lord Nelson's navy.

The Reconfiguration of the Modern Warship

- The convergence of steel construction, steam power, and advanced gunnery resulted in the complete reconfiguration of the modern warship.

- The first-generation steam-powered ships were wooden, but the advent of exploding shells increased interest in armoring these ships, and by the late 1850s, iron-hulled ships were coming into vogue. The first and most important of this second generation of large steam warships was the HMS *Warrior*.

- The first all-steam warships were smaller vessels, such as the CSS *Virginia* and the *Monitor*. The *Monitor* also sported a turret, which gave her two big guns a broader field of fire, and the turret could be turned to protect the gun ports during reloads.

- Fewer guns, bigger holds, and advances in steam propulsion ultimately spelled the end of steam/sail hybrid battleships, such as the *Warrior*. In 1871, the Royal Navy launched HMS *Devastation*, exclusively steam powered and sporting a pair of two-gun turrets.

- The battleships and armored cruisers that Togo had at the Battle of Tsushima were even more advanced. Togo's flagship, the *Mikasa*, had a top speed of 18 knots, and with full coal bunkers, she could cruise for 7,000 nautical miles at a speed of 10 knots.
  - The main guns of *Mikasa* could fire three armor-piercing, 800-pound shells every two minutes, and with their telescopic sights and advanced range-finders, they could accurately hit targets 6,000 meters away.

  - *Mikasa* also had what was called a mixed battery, including smaller broadside guns and swivel guns on deck to defend against close attack, and she was armed with torpedoes.

  - To complement its offensive punch, *Mikasa* was belted above and below the waterline with nine inches of steel armor.

  - Finally, every ship in Togo's fleet was equipped with a radio-telegraph set that kept Togo in contact with his subordinates and with ground stations.

Admiral Togo's flagship, the *Mikasa*, represented the best of what came to be called the pre-Dreadnought battleships.

- As much as gunnery was becoming concentrated onboard, naval power was being concentrated in fewer, bigger ships. In 1810, the Royal Navy had 156 ships of the line; in 1914, it had 72 battleships and heavy cruisers. This shift would force military and political leaders to reconsider their willingness to "risk the fleet."

- The modern battleship vastly complicated the business of operating a navy. In the age of sail, barring major damage, ships needed to stop only for food and water, but a steam navy required elaborate logistics for coal and spare parts, as well as provisions.

- The new complexities of naval warfare also required a new breed of naval officers. The world's navies were forced to embrace new skill sets in naval warfare and to create training and educational institutions to hone their operational edge.

Changes after Tsushima

- As much as things had changed between Trafalgar and Tsushima, the changes in naval warfare of the decades ahead would be even more rapid and dramatic.

- A year after Tsushima, the Royal Navy commissioned the HMS *Dreadnought*. Compared to *Mikasa*, *Dreadnought* was bigger, better armed and armored, and faster. Ironically, the spectacular performance of Togo's big guns at Tsushima spelled the end of mixed-battery battleships like *Mikasa*. The age of the all-big-gun *Dreadnought* had begun.

- The battleship remained at the center of the fleet, but also in development were all manner of new ship types and weapons systems, including destroyers, submarines, and mine-layers, along with advanced mines, self-propelled torpedoes, and aircraft.

- Although steam and steel had transformed navies by the end of the 19th century, major naval wars were rare.
  - Whereas Clausewitz could look back on the Napoleonic revolution in warfare, our next two masters, Alfred Thayer Mahan and Sir Julian Corbett, were still in the midst of the sea-power revolution.

  - With the Russo-Japanese War of 1904–1905, they had a test case of both the power of modern naval technology and of what they viewed as the enduring principles of naval strategy.

Suggested Reading

Brodie, *Sea Power in the Machine Age.*

Corbett, *Maritime Operations in the Russo-Japanese War, 1904–1905* (especially pp. 382–411 in volume II).

Gray, *The Leverage of Sea Power.*

Mahan, "Retrospect upon the War between Japan and Russia."

Tucker, *Handbook of 19th Century Naval Warfare*.

Questions to Consider

1. How did technological innovations transform global commerce? How did they transform naval warfare?

2. Who would have been more out of his element: Nelson at Tsushima or Togo at Trafalgar?

From Sail to Steam—The Sea-Power Revolution
Lecture 12—Transcript

So far in our course, we've primarily been talking about land warfare theorists. In the next few lectures I want us to dip our heads into salt water, and to think about the enduring principles of Naval Strategy. Back in the Peloponnesian War we got a glimpse of the fundamental social, political, and cultural distinctions between land powers and sea powers, between elephants and whales.

We also had some inkling of the various ways you can use a navy, things like commerce raiding, amphibious landings, and decisive fleet-on-fleet battles. In today's lecture I am going to look at the revolution in naval warfare and maritime trade that took place over the century between the end of the Napoleonic Wars and the beginning of World War I. This will lay out the background for the sea-power theories of Alfred Thayer Mahan and Sir Julian Corbett.

The transition from sail to steam is bracketed by two epic naval engagements. The first was Lord Nelson's triumph at Trafalgar in 1805, the second was Admiral Togo's shellacking of the Russians at Tsushima in 1905.

Trafalgar was the culmination of a trans-Atlantic game of cat and mouse that began in early 1805. Napoleon had ordered the French Navy to go to sea in an attempt to lure the Royal Navy away from the English Channel. Remember, Napoleon had plans to invade England with his *grande armée*. The naval ploy was boldly conceived, but it ended catastrophically for France.

Lord Nelson pursued the French Admiral Villeneuve from Toulon on the French coast, all the way to the Caribbean and then back again. Back in European waters Nelson and Villeneuve both joined up with naval fleets that were already there.

A major battle was brewing in the late summer of 1805, but by this time Napoleon had already abandoned his plans for a cross-channel invasion and was moving east. Villeneuve was ordered to sail for the Mediterranean to support the Emperor against his central European foes.

Villeneuve never made it. On October 21, Nelson's fleet of 27 ships-of-the-line, those big two- and three-deck ships you see in the movies, met a combined Franco-Spanish armada of 33 ships near Cape Trafalgar off the southwest coast of Spain. Villeneuve tried to make for the port of Cadiz, but Nelson's fleet, divided into two lines, literally smashed into Villeneuve's ragged formation, unloading double broadsides on the French and the Spanish ships.

Nelson had taken great risks. He had divided his fleet and his firepower into those two lines, but he was using a new signal system that allowed him to coordinate his preparations for the battle much better than the French. Superior British seamanship also gave Nelson the weather-gauge and command of the engagement.

Nelson put his own flagship, HMS *Victory*, at the head of the northern line of advance, using the mass of the immense ship to shield the smaller vessels behind. In the course of the battle, Nelson was fatally wounded by musket fire, but the British victory was total. Of Villeneuve's 33 ships, 16 were captured and two more were destroyed. By November, all but 11 of the French ships were captured or out of action. French naval power never truly recovered.

A century later, in May of 1905, the Asian version of Trafalgar took place in the Tsushima straits between Japan and Korea. The Russo-Japanese War had begun in February of 1904 with a surprise Japanese attack on Russia's naval base at Port Arthur. That attack had wounded the Russian fleet, but had not crippled it. As a result, for the next 15 months, Admiral Togo Heihachiro, the Japanese naval commander, had an awful lot on his plate.

In fact, he had four different and often competing missions. He had to blockade the Russian Navy at Port Arthur. He had to support amphibious landings and resupply the Japanese Army for their operations in Korea and Manchuria. He had to defend Japanese trade from Russian commerce-raiders operating out of their other naval base at Vladivostok. And he had to prepare for a possible fleet engagement with yet another Russian fleet that had steamed out of the Baltic Sea in October 1904. By May 1905, the first three of those tasks were essentially complete and Togo could focus his energies on meeting the Baltic fleet.

Although he was at a disadvantage in terms of mass and firepower, Togo was in a generally favorable position. Where the Russians had been through a grueling 18,000-mile journey, Togo's force was both battle-tested and well-rested. The Japanese were also operating out of home ports and were primed for battle. The Russians were in transit and were laden with the requirements of a long journey, including mountains of coal piled on their decks.

On the night of May 26th one of Togo's scouts caught sight of a Russian hospital ship, fully lit up in the night. Alerted to the Russian approach by wireless telegraph, the Japanese fleet sortied from port. In a series of brilliantly executed maneuvers Togo's nimble and fast-firing ships quickly incapacitated the Russian battle line, sinking seven big battleships in the process. Togo lost only three small craft and 117 men killed in action as compared to a total of 34 Russian ships and more than 4,000 Russian sailors lost. Tsushima stands as perhaps the most lop-sided naval battle in history.

Each battle looks like a classic example of victory at sea. A victory won through superior seamanship, superior communications, superior gunnery, and the audacity of a brilliant admiral. But they take place in two radically different worlds. When Alfred Thayer Mahan and Sir Julian Corbett began writing about naval history and naval strategy in the 1890s, the maritime world was in the midst of a total transformation, a transformation from sail to steam.

So before we turn to our sea-power theorists, let's take some time to examine what exactly had changed in the century between these two epic battles. And while we do this let's keep in mind that we are not just talking about changes in military technology, we are talking about a transformation of the global economy, a globalization.

Globalization had begun long before the 19th century. In fact it had begun back in the late 15th century with the dawning of the European Age of

Discovery. Access to global markets and command of maritime trade had underwritten the great power rise of sea powers like Holland, Portugal, and Spain. But it was 19th-century Britain that was the ultimate sea power.

As much as Britain's Royal Navy was a fearsome instrument of war, it was the wealth derived from maritime trade that was the true basis of British power. When Napoleon tried to deny Britain access to European consumers with his flawed "continental system," it proved much too little and much too late. Continental Europe was just too addicted to the goods that the British sold.

Britain emerged from the Napoleonic Wars with a dominant position in world trade. But the process we now call globalization dramatically accelerated in the 19th century, as did the competition among would-be sea powers.

With a general state of peace emerging in Europe after 1815, after Napoleon's final defeat, the energies of European countries, and to some extent the United States, were directed outward in search of markets and colonies. In the Opium Wars, a series of minor conflicts in the mid-19th century, the British succeeded in cracking open the lucrative China market. Not only did this expand the opportunities for trade, but it also liberated the massive amounts of silver that had been piling up in China for two-and-a-half centuries.

Japan and Korea were forced open soon after. At this point, the cycle really starts to accelerate. Growing global demand for Western manufactures accelerated the industrial revolution. This increased production and with it the impetus to find more foreign markets. At the same time it increased demand for raw materials, which required greater access to and control over the sources of those raw materials. And third it required a dramatic increase in commercial shipping. None of these things could have happened without certain technological advances.

One of the least appreciated, but most important of the technological advances that underwrote the explosion in maritime trade was medicine. During the wars of the late 18th and early 19th centuries, shipboard medicine in Britain's Royal Navy improved dramatically. The prevention or cure of scurvy and the host of other maladies that had historically ravaged naval crews meant that British tars in the 19th century were actually healthier than their relatives living onshore. Those military medical advances migrated to the commercial fleets by mid-century. Merchant ships went to sea with a stocked medicine chest and formulas for curing common ailments.

On land, the prevention and treatment of tropical diseases, especially malaria, allowed Europeans to penetrate deeper into the hinterland of places like Africa and India. Railroads further accelerated the commercial exploitation of these newly opened frontiers and western arms technology, notably the introduction of the breech-loading rifle, greatly facilitated the colonial enterprise.

The next big advance in the maritime revolution was steam propulsion, but the transition from sail to steam in commercial shipping wasn't very rapid, nor was it complete. Sailing vessels were remarkably fast and economically competitive throughout the 19th century. In contrast, the early steamships were expensive and inefficient and required vast stores of coal and frequent stops for refueling.

Steamships found their first real niche in the mail and passenger business between Suez and India. When the Suez Canal opened in 1869, steamships quickly dominated the routes between Europe and Asia. On these voyages, steam vessels had advantages in speed, they could steam into the prevailing winds, and they could navigate the narrow canal under their own power.

In terms of global shipping, the advantages of steam began to gradually win out, but it was probably not until the 1880s that the total tonnage of steam-powered ships edged out sailing ships. Ultimately advances in steam technology, the replacement of the side or rear paddle with propeller screws and improvements in hull design and ship construction gave the iron-hulled and steel-hulled steamship the economic advantage. But only as long as there was a global network of commercial coaling stations.

The transition to steam also transformed the calculus of sea power. In the age of sail it was timber, cloth, hemp, and sailors that were the raw materials of sea power. By the end of the 19th century any nation that could harness enough iron ore, coal, and talented engineers could compete on the high seas. But Britain still ruled the waves. As much as the sea-power revolution created challenges for Britain, the transition to steam actually perpetuated the Pax Britannica.

The British had cut down their forests to defeat Napoleon. If 19th century maritime power was to be measured in wooden ships, then the British would have been at a distinct disadvantage, especially relative to the United States with it limitless old-growth forests. Britain, though, had great comparative advantages in coal, iron, and steel production. They also enjoyed a technological edge and the drive born of their global imperial responsibilities. Finally, the British led the communications revolution.

Obviously the expansion of global shipping improved global communications. That's how the mail traveled. By the 1860s, global mail routes were larger and more consistent than at any point in human history. The communications revolution took a quantum leap forward with the addition of telegraphy and submarine telegraph cables. In the 1850s the British were experimenting with cables across the English Channel. A decade later the statesmen, merchants, bankers, and insurance agents of London enjoyed direct and nearly real-time communications with Continental Europe, North America, and India. Two decades after that, there was a global network of telegraphy that sped diplomatic cables, military orders, market analyses, financial transactions, and the latest news across the planet.

This was true globalization. Whereas maritime commerce in the age of sail had involved small cargoes of precious goods, steamships could move all manner of commodities in bulk. In addition, the leap forward in global communications guaranteed that these cargoes would make it to the markets where they were in highest demand.

Therefore, as the world approached the turn of the 20th century there was an immense flourishing of maritime commerce and competition. The world's oceans had become a great global commons, a largely ungoverned space through which the lifeblood of national power and prosperity flowed. It didn't take a genius to see that a nation that sought its fortunes in global trade could ill-afford to neglect its navy.

Turning to the military side of the sea-power revolution, it wasn't so much steam power as the screw propeller that transformed naval warfare. Side and stern paddle wheelers had demonstrated some utility in mid-century conflicts. For example, during the Opium War the steam gun-ship *Nemesis* sailed up the Yangzi River to threaten China's southern capital at Nanjing. The shocked and humiliated Mandarins had no choice but to accede to British demands.

In general, however, paddle propulsion was inefficient, cumbersome, and vulnerable. It also got in the way of gunnery. The screw propeller which was fully submerged and mounted along the mid-line of a ship was much more efficient and much less vulnerable to enemy fire.

When these propeller shafts were installed in lighter-but-stronger steel-hulled ships and attached to high-pressure boilers, the modern steamship had come of age. But those boilers did more than drive the ship, they allowed for the mechanization of the ship itself. Steam pressure pumped the bilges, powered the steering, and maneuvered the guns. And oh what guns they were!

As you can imagine, one of the most important drivers of naval transformation in the 19th century was the revolutionary improvement in gunnery. This mirrored developments ashore with the invention of modern artillery.

Back in 1805, Nelson's *Victory* sported 104 muzzle-loaded smooth bore cannon: guns that fired round shot. A full broadside from the *Victory* would send 1,000 pounds of metal hurtling at an enemy ship. As a result, success in close battle depended more on rates of fire than range or accuracy, but even fast firing was no mean feat.

For example, a 32-pound gun, which fired a 32-pound ball, was the biggest weapon on the *Victory*. Each 32-pound gun weighed more than 6,000 pounds and was entirely manually operated. Between six and eight men crewed a single gun, employing 14 different tools and 11 different steps to position, fire, clean, and reload. Speed was of the essence, but even the best crews could only manage to get off two shots in a minute.

The *Victory*'s guns were awesome, but by mid-century, in the context of shell guns and breech-loaders, Nelson's smooth bores were relics. The Paixhans Gun, the first shell-firing gun that was widely adopted by the world's navies, was said to have sunk the wooden navy all by itself. An exploding shell lodged in the oak hull of a ship-of-the-line threatened to sink her with one blow. Even so, for all the hype about the Paixhans gun, it was the breech-loading shell-gun that created the armored navy.

European armies had perfected breech-loaded artillery by the 1860s, and they were quickly adopted by navies. Loading from the rear, or breech, of the barrel was easier and faster. The long barrels of these guns were also rifled to vastly increase accuracy. Breech-loaded and rifled naval guns offered greater range, higher rates of fire and improved lethality over the muzzle-loaded smooth-bore cannon of Nelson's navy. Ships like the *Victory* had to close to within a few hundred yards in order to inflict serious damage on an opponent. First generation rifled guns effectively tripled that range.

When lighter and stronger steel guns appeared in the 1870s, they became the new standard in breech-loaders. By lighter, however, I do not mean light. A steel naval gun in the late 1800s could weigh 50 tons, but it was now firing huge shells that had been upgraded to armor-piercing lethality by century's end. But accuracy only works when you can see and range what you are shooting at. By the time of Tsushima, a battleship's gun batteries were mounted with telescopes and optical range-finders.

The convergence of steel construction, steam power, and advanced gunnery would completely reconfigure the modern warship. The first generation of steam-powered ships were actually wooden. But naturally, the advent of exploding shells increased interest in armoring these ships, and by the late-1850s iron-hulled ships were coming into vogue. The first and most important of this second generation of large steam warships was the ominously beautiful HMS *Warrior*.

Back in 2000, I had the privilege of dining on the gun-deck of the *Warrior* in Portsmouth, England. (They do weddings if you are interested.) She is still intimidating, but when she was commissioned in 1860 *Warrior* was without question the fastest, the best-protected, and the most lethal warship in history. The *Warrior*-class, however, was still sail-rigged as a complement to steam.

The first all-steam warships were smaller vessels like the CSS *Virginia* and the *Monitor*. The *Monitor* also sported a turret, which gave her two big guns a broader field of fire, and the turret could be turned to protect the gun ports during reloads. Turrets offered the possibility of fewer, bigger guns, now 12-inchers, firing shells a foot in diameter. These turrets are also well protected and could pivot through that range of fire. Only a decade after her launch, the HMS *Warrior* was being out-classed by turret-mounted, steam-driven battleships.

Fewer guns, bigger holds, and advances in steam propulsion ultimately spelled the end of the steam–sail hybrid battleships like *Warrior*. In 1871, the Royal Navy launched HMS *Devastation*, exclusively steam powered and sporting a pair of two-gun turrets.

The battleships and armored cruisers that Togo had at the Battle of Tsushima were even more advanced. Togo's flagship, the *Mikasa*, represented the best of what came to be called the pre-*Dreadnought*. At over 400 ft long and displacing more than 15,000 tons, the steel-hulled *Mikasa* was half again as large as *Warrior* and *Devastation* and nearly five times the displacement of Nelson's *Victory*. And yet at 860 men, Togo's crew numbered just 10 more than Nelson's 850 tars.

Mikasa's top speed was 18 knots, which made her five knots faster than the previous generation, but *Mikasa* wasn't just fast, she had stamina. With full coal bunkers she could cruise for 7,000 nautical miles at a speed of 10 knots. To put that in perspective, *Mikasa* could steam non-stop from Tokyo to San Francisco in 19 days and still have enough coal left to cruise the California coast for more than a week.

Like *Devastation*, *Mikasa* had four 12-inch guns mounted in two turrets, one fore and one aft. These batteries were hydraulically powered, and the guns were breech-loaded and rifled. The main guns could fire three armor-piercing 800-pound shells every two minutes, and with their telescopic sights and advanced range-finders they could accurately hit targets 6,000 meters away.

That's more than three-and-a-half miles! Inaccurate fire could range as far as nine miles.

Mikasa also had what was called a mixed battery. This included smaller broad side guns and swivel guns on deck to defend against close attack, and she was armed with torpedoes. But it was the accurate big guns that were the real revolution in naval warfare. To complement its offensive punch, *Mikasa* was belted above and below the waterline with 9 inches of steel armor. Lastly, every ship in Togo's fleet was equipped with a radio–telegraph set that kept Togo in contact with his subordinates and with ground stations.

Having all that firepower, however, didn't make Togo reckless at Tsushima. Instead of running into the Russian line and trading close-in broadsides he fired from maximum distance and for maximum effect. As the battle opened, Togo was firing at a flank speed of 15 knots and landing rounds from 6,000 meters away. In contrast, Nelson collided with the French 74-gunship, the *Redoubtable*, at less than two knots and was unloading broadsides at point blank range.

It is kind of ironic that a wooden ship of the line was much more robust for its time than a steel battleship was for its. Nelson's *Victory* took a horrible beating at Trafalgar, but was still afloat. For all of their speed and armor, modern battleships were still behind the ordnance and fire-control revolutions. In the Russo-Japanese War battleships were sunk by individual mines or by a handful of well-placed 12-inch rounds. Given the small number and long production schedule of the modern battleship, Nelsonian audacity was too risky.

Cost was also a major issue. Pre-*Dreadnought* battleships were not cheap. *Mikasa* cost nearly 900,000 British pounds to build and her operating costs were also very high. Ships like *Mikasa* were very valuable commodities. Moreover, as much as gunnery was becoming concentrated on board, naval power was being concentrated in fewer, bigger ships. In 1810, the Royal Navy had 156 ships-of-the-line; in 1914 she had 72 battleships and heavy cruisers. This shift would force military and political leaders to reconsider their willingness to risk the fleet.

The modern battleship also vastly complicated the business of operating a navy. In the age of sail, barring major damage, ships needed to stop only for food and water. A steam navy, however, required elaborate logistics for coal and spare parts as well as for provisions. As much as global merchant fleets needed ports and access to coal, navies required overseas bases and dedicated coaling stations.

The new complexities of naval warfare required a new breed of naval officers. Despite some initial resistance, notably to the career advancement of filthy engineers, the world's navies were forced to embrace the new skill-sets of naval warfare and to create the training and education institutions to hone that operational edge. Japan's success at Tsushima was, of course, partly a result of the Imperial Japanese Navy's embrace of modern technology. After the Sino-Japanese War of 1894–1895, the Japanese plowed the indemnity from China into a military modernization program. This included the purchase of six British-built battleships, including the *Mikasa*, and an additional eight armored cruisers. The Japanese were also well ahead of the Russians in their embrace of the latest optical and fire-control technologies. But more than a technological revolution, the Japanese had completely adopted the model of the Royal Navy.

The Imperial Japanese Navy had a meritocratic promotion system, a culture of innovation, a strong administration, and the Japanese enjoyed excellent coordination between the military and civilian sides of the government. Above all as an island nation, Japan had a powerful motivation to go to sea and to defend its maritime empire. In other words, Japan may have bought itself a great navy, but it paid equal attention to becoming a true sea power. But as much as things had changed between Trafalgar and Tsushima, the changes in naval warfare of the decades ahead were to be even more rapid and dramatic. In fact, Tsushima might best be viewed as the last battle of a Nelsonian age. It was a one-dimensional engagement involving exclusively surface ships. The day was won by battleships firing volleys at other battleships.

A year after Tsushima, the Royal Navy commissioned the HMS *Dreadnought*. Compared to *Mikasa*, *Dreadnought* was bigger, better-armored and faster. *Dreadnought* had 10, not just four, 12-inch guns mounted in five turrets.

They were longer and more accurate than the *Mikasa*'s. Ironically, the spectacular performance of Togo's big guns at Tsushima spelled the end of the mixed battery battleship like the *Mikasa*. The age of the all big gun *Dreadnought* had begun.

That battleship was still the center of the fleet, but also in development were all manner of new ship-types and weapons systems. Destroyers, submarines, and mine-layers were advancing as rapidly as the battleship. Advanced mines, self-propelled torpedoes, and aircraft were also in the works. But I am getting ahead of myself. We'll come back to all of this new technology when we talk about the Pacific War a couple of sessions from now.

To sum up this lecture, steam and steel had transformed navies by the end of the 19th century and the pace of technological transformation was only accelerating. Yet at the same time, major naval wars were rare in the late 19th century. The Opium Wars, the Crimean War, and the American Civil War had all involved navies, but actions at sea were a sideshow to the land campaigns. In other words there was not much recent naval history from which to build new theories for the use of these new technologies.

Where Clausewitz and Jomini could look back on the Napoleonic Revolution in warfare, our next two masters were still in the midst of the sea power revolution. So as they contemplated what a major naval war of the future would look like, they had to reflect on the lessons of the past.

Alfred Thayer Mahan in the United States and Sir Julian Corbett in Britain straddled the sail-to-steam divide. They looked back to the age of sail, and particularly to Britain's Naval Wars of the 1760s through the 1810s to substantiate their analyses. At the same time they were also writing theories to guide the modern navies of the United States and Great Britain. Both theorists understood how technological revolutions and globalization impacted naval strategy.

They both appreciated that global networks of bases and coaling stations were essential to command of the sea. They both appreciated the link between global maritime trade and national power. And they both grasped the strengths and limitations of the modern battleship.

With the Russo-Japanese War of 1904–1905 they both had a test case of both the power of modern naval technology and of what they viewed as the enduring principles of naval strategy. They both found evidence there to vindicate their theories, but the Russo-Japanese War offered only a glimpse of the four decades of high-intensity naval war that was to follow. In the next three lectures we will see how well Mahan and Corbett were able to predict the future and to craft theories that were relevant beyond their lifetimes.

I'll see you next time.

Alfred Thayer Mahan
Lecture 13

In 1884, Alfred Thayer Mahan was asked to serve as a lecturer at the U.S. Naval War College, and his lectures there became the basis for two influential books on sea power. Although his writing made him a hero to foreign navies, many in the U.S. Navy were hostile to his ideas. Like Jomini, he sought to distill general and eternal principles about naval policy and warfare from his study of history. Like Machiavelli, his works were fashioned to speak to all four levels of naval war: politics, strategy, operations, and tactics. Above all, Mahan wanted to open America's eyes to the importance of sea power to the nation's destiny.

Sea Power v. Naval Power

- As we saw in the last lecture, sea power rests on a foundation of economic, institutional, geographic, technological, and cultural factors, of which naval power is only a part, albeit a key component of national power.

- Mahan's understanding of this led him to think in grand terms about America's maritime destiny. He argued that the United States must become a true sea power in all of its military, cultural, and commercial dimensions.

- In defining sea power, Mahan identifies six fundamental factors: (1) geography, (2) physical configuration, (3) extent of territory, (4) population, (5) national character, and (6) governmental institutions.

- Island, peninsular, and insular nations are preadapted to being sea powers because of their geography, but socioeconomic and political factors are also important. A people that depends on the sea is more likely to have the expertise to compete on the maritime commons, but only if the government is supportive.

- For Mahan, this becomes a virtuous cycle. Favorable geography and a "seagoing bent" among the people make for a vibrant maritime economy that, in turn, can spawn a great navy. A great navy built and supported by pro-maritime policies can strengthen the economy and society and encourage people to seek even greater fortunes on the sea. This was the story behind Britain's rise to maritime dominance.

- The fact that a nation has an affinity for the sea does not mean it is destined to be a sea power. As Mahan points out, leadership matters. Politicians who promote maritime pursuits and fund the navy are as precious as naval officers who understand the proper use of the fleet.

America as a Sea Power

- In terms of geography, physical conformation, and extent of territory, the United States is what Mahan calls an insular nation. Because it is not at immediate risk of invasion, America doesn't need a large army. But because its livelihood depends on access to the seas and it is vulnerable to having its trade routes interdicted, it does need a powerful navy.

- Mahan's assessment in the latter half of the 19th century was as follows: America faced no continental threats, but it did have three coastlines to defend. Mahan's service in the Civil War had shown him just how vulnerable the East and Gulf coasts were to blockade. But defending the coasts is not enough; a sea power needs a fleet that can preemptively take command of the seas.

- There were, however, several trends working against Mahan's arguments.
  - First, continental consolidation was drawing the energies of the American people inward, not driving them out onto the sea.

  - Second, Mahan was concerned that American democracy and American politicians were too shortsighted to appreciate sea power in all of its dimensions, especially the navy.

o A final impediment to embracing the Mahanian vision was the preference of the U.S. Navy for coastal defense and commerce raiding over fleet actions. Low-cost commerce raiders were thought to have a disproportionate impact on an enemy's economy. Mahan agreed that commerce raiding might be useful, but it was no match for the strategic effects of a battle fleet.

o As much as geography seemed to make the United States a natural sea power, the will of the population, the commitment of the government, and even the sympathies of the U.S. Navy were not in line with Mahan's thinking.

• The implications of Mahan's theory of sea power went far beyond domestic politics and military budgets, crossing the line into foreign policy. For the most part, he abided by Clausewitz's principle of subordinating the military to policy; nevertheless, his opinions on foreign policy and the fecklessness of democratic governments were well publicized.

o These policy positions derived from Mahan's strategic and operational maxims. For example, "choke points"—critical nodes in global trade—figure large in Mahan's writings. The control of choke points was the key to projecting naval power globally.

o If America was going to compete on the seas, then it needed an overseas empire, an empire comprised of strategically significant choke points. In other words, operational necessity had foreign policy implications.

o This is not imperialism simply for the sake of imperialism. To Mahan, annexation of overseas colonies had to be prudent and in America's best interests.

Mahan's Advice

• In the simplest terms, Mahan's advice for naval officers and strategists was: "Act like Nelson." But this is not as simple as it sounds. Mahan knew that Nelson could act as he had only because the full weight of British geography, society, and government enabled his actions.

- Nor was Mahan so naïve as to think that it was a good idea to try to re-fight Trafalgar. Tactics and technology had changed too dramatically, but for Mahan, "The old foundations of strategy so far remain, as though laid upon a rock." Even at the operational levels of war, some of the eternal principles still pertained.

- Still, when it came to peacetime preparations, the politicians and the military needed to be of one mind and construct the strongest naval force possible, building on the latest technological and tactical innovations.

- In addition, the battle fleet must be kept as a concentrated body. Mahan allows for other naval missions, including commerce raiding and coastal defense, but the battle line should never be drawn into those secondary pursuits.
  - o In the lead-up to war, a concentrated fleet could serve as a deterrent to a would-be challenger. A divided fleet, in contrast, was symbolic of a dangerously divided focus and could actually invite attack.

  - o In war, the massive combined firepower of the concentrated battle fleet was the surest way to send an enemy's navy to the bottom or to keep it blockaded. And defeating the enemy fleet on the high seas or bottling it up in port would give a nation an unprecedented command of the sea.

- In a shooting war, Mahan tracks with Jomini in advocating the offensive defense: Other than a few ships set aside for commerce and coastal defense, take the battle fleet into the enemy's home waters. This enables control of the lines of supply and communication and seizure of forward choke points.

- No one who devoted so much time to studying Nelson could neglect leadership and the human factor in war. Mahan was deeply impressed with the audacity shown by Nelson in his relentless pursuit of a broken enemy fleet. Great naval leaders embraced calculated risk and understood the political and strategic implications of their operations.

- The eloquence of Mahan's arguments, complemented by the passionate advocacy of civilian navalists, brought about one of the most remarkable peacetime military transformations in history: In the course of two decades, the U.S. Navy went from being a secondary service of modest capabilities to one of the leading navies of the world.

The Russo-Japanese War

- Fought in 1904 and 1905, the Russo-Japanese War was a contest of rival imperial aspirations over spheres of influence in northeast Asia. In his "Retrospect" on the war, Mahan penned a blistering critique of the Russians.

- In his estimation, the Russians had the means to build a first-class navy but not the will. The result was a hodgepodge of ship types and a shortage of training that doomed the Russians from the outset of the war.

- Further, Russia's battle line was divided into three fleets: the Baltic, the Black Sea, and the Port Arthur squadron. This gave the Japanese regional parity and emboldened them to attack Port Arthur on the first night of the war.

- Russia had also failed to set up a global network of bases and coaling stations to enable it to quickly and credibly project naval power. When the Baltic fleet sailed in October 1904, it was forced to rely on the modest support of allies. Great Britain, with its huge comparative advantages in bases, shipping, and coal, was an ally of Japan and hindered the Russian transit at every turn.

- Finally, as it negotiated 18,000 miles of transit and choke points, the Baltic Fleet quite literally telegraphed its position, progress,

The Japanese attacked the divided Russian fleet at Port Arthur on the first night of the Russo-Japanese War.

and problems to the Japanese. Russia was weak militarily and politically and did not have the control of communications required of a true sea power.

- Poor preparation was compounded by poor execution. Russian naval operations and tactics were hamstrung by an excess of caution. With the exception of a brief period in 1904, the Port Arthur squadron did not contest Japan's close blockade.

- Russian leaders were hesitant about sending the Baltic fleet to reinforce the Asian squadrons. In the end, the Port Arthur squadron was destroyed in port before the Baltic fleet could relieve the siege. This meant that Admiral Togo had the freedom to meet the exhausted Baltic fleet with the entirety of his armada.

Summing Up Mahan
- We should view Mahan's straight cause-and-effect line of decisive fleet engagements, command of the sea, and victory in war with a bit of skepticism, but his appeal is nonetheless easy to understand:

He offered readers an exceptionally clear grand strategy and naval strategy.

- As a navalist and maven of prudent imperialism, Mahan's timing could not have been better. He had powerful friends in the navy and the government, and the United States was favorably positioned to translate his theoretical prescriptions into reality.

- In another sense, however, his timing couldn't have been worse. Mahan did his best work in the 1890s, in the midst of a global transformation, not at the culmination of that transformation. Barring a full war between first-rate naval powers, Mahan was obliged to rely on the Nelsonian analogy to predict the future of naval warfare.

- For the navies of the 1890s and the first decade of the 1900s, Mahan was probably right with the Nelsonian analogy, but new technologies and tactics were on the horizon, and Mahan failed to appreciate how these might transform naval warfare.

Suggested Reading

Crowl, "Alfred Thayer Mahan."

Mahan, *The Influence of Sea Power upon History, 1660–1783.*

———, *The Influence of Sea Power upon the French Revolution and Empire, 1793–1812.*

———, *The Interest of America in Sea Power, Present and Future.*

Sprout, "Mahan: Evangelist of Sea Power."

Sumida, *Inventing Grand Strategy and Teaching Command.*

Questions to Consider

1. What were Mahan's objectives in writing maritime theory? Did he achieve those objectives?

2. What are the main elements of Mahan's critique of Russian strategy in the Russo-Japanese War? Did the Russo-Japanese War validate Mahan's theories?

Alfred Thayer Mahan
Lecture 13—Transcript

There is a Mahan Hall at the U.S. Military Academy at West Point and another one at the Naval Academy in Annapolis. The former is named for Dennis Hart Mahan, professor of Military Science and Engineering at West Point and one of America's preeminent military educators of the 19th century. The hall at Annapolis is named for his son, Alfred Thayer Mahan.

Born in 1840 and raised for 12 years at West Point, the younger Mahan had a military and an academic upbringing. A bright young man, he studied at Columbia and then transferred to the Naval Academy from whence he graduated in 1859. Mahan received his commission just in time to be a junior officer when the Civil War broke out. He served throughout that war in a variety of coastal and riverine patrols and in blockade operations.

He was already showing an interest in naval history and in naval strategy and wrote his first book on the naval dimensions of the Civil War. After the war, Mahan toyed with the idea of returning to civilian life but decided instead to pursue a naval career. By all accounts Mahan was a competent but not a popular officer. He was far too bookish for many of his peers and many of his superiors.

His long career in the navy had a lot more to do with his mentor, Admiral Stephen B. Luce. In 1884 Luce, then president of the Naval War College, asked Mahan to serve as lecturer in Naval History and Tactics. Mahan spent a year preparing a series of lectures rich, some might say too rich, in historical and tactical detail with a heavy emphasis on the British Royal Navy in the 18th and 19th centuries. Those lectures became the basis for Mahan's two best known books *The Influence of Sea Power upon History, 1660–1783*, and *The Influence of Sea Power upon the French Revolution and Empire, 1793–1812*.

Mahan had some trouble getting the first volume to print, but when it *was* published it became a global sensation. Still in uniform, Mahan was feted in the courts of Europe, his works were translated into dozens of languages, and he was offered honorary degrees from numerous colleges and universities. He even received offers of honorary commissions in foreign navies and a very lucrative job offer lecturing at the Japanese equivalent of the Naval War College. He turned these offers down.

Although Mahan was a hero to foreign navies, many in the U.S. Navy were hostile to Mahan's ideas, hostile to the study of history, and hostile to the Naval War College. Then, as now, time at sea was a naval officer's most precious professional asset. Time spent onshore studying the age of sail was time wasted in a service embracing the technology of steam power. In Mahan's eyes, Horatio Nelson, the hero of the Nile and of Trafalgar, was the embodiment of sound naval strategy and tactics, the very embodiment of the concept he called sea power. But many of Mahan's contemporaries would have wondered: What could the exploits of Nelson possibly mean to a modern naval officer?

Well, Mahan had an answer. To him, the purpose of history was to instruct contemporary naval officers and to influence national policy. Like Jomini, Mahan sought to distill general, and, in some cases, eternal principles about naval policy and naval warfare from his study of history. And like Machiavelli, the two *Influence of Sea Power* volumes and his *The Life of Nelson* are fashioned to speak to all four levels of naval war: politics, strategy, operations, and tactics. Mahan also wanted his works to have mass appeal. This was not profit motive, although he didn't mind the money. Mahan wanted to open the eyes of a democratic population of the United States to the importance of sea power to America's destiny. Mahan wanted to influence the government, the military, and the people.

When we think about sea power we shouldn't be thinking about naval power alone. We saw in the last lecture and in the Peloponnesian War that sea power rests on a foundation of economic, institutional, geographic, technological, and cultural factors of which naval power is only a part, albeit a key component, of national power. Mahan understood this and it led him to think in grand terms about America's maritime destiny. He argued that the United States had to become a true sea power, in all of its military, cultural, and commercial dimensions.

In defining sea power, Mahan identified six fundamental factors. The first was geography: Is it an island nation, an insular or peninsular nation, or a continental power? The second category is physical configuration: Does this nation have easy access to the sea? The third is the extent of its territory: Does it have long coastlines? Does it have good harbors and navigable rivers? The fourth is its population: How many citizens are there and what are they good at? The fifth is what he calls national character: Are the people active and commercial and innovative and risk-taking? And finally is the sixth factor, the governmental institutions: Does the government support maritime commerce and the navy? Does it enact enlightened maritime policies?

Some nations are pre-adapted to being sea powers. Island nations, peninsular nations, and insular nations, nations whose fates hang upon the sea, often have favorable geography, but socioeconomic and political factors matter as well. A people that depends on the sea are more likely to have the expertise to compete on the maritime commons, but only if their government is supportive.

This becomes a virtuous cycle for Mahan. Favorable geography and what he calls a "sea-going bent" among the people make for a vibrant maritime economy, which in turn can spawn a great navy. A great navy built and supported by pro-maritime policies can strengthen the economy and society, and encourage the people to seek even greater fortune upon the sea. And so on and so on. This was the story behind Britain's rise to maritime dominance.

A nation might have an affinity for the sea, but that does not destine it to be a sea power. As Mahan points out, leadership matters. Politicians who promote maritime pursuits and fund the navy are as precious as naval officers who understand the proper use of the fleet. A true sea power needs politicians like William Pitt as much as it needs admirals like Horatio Nelson.

But Mahan is writing first for an American audience. In terms of geography, physical conformation, and extent of territory, the United States is what he calls an insular nation—and insular nations and island nations are not at immediate risk of invasion. So according to Mahan, America doesn't need a big army. But since its livelihood increasingly depends on access to the sea and it is vulnerable to having its trade routes interdicted, it does need a powerful navy.

As Mahan looked around in the latter half of the 19th century, here's what he perceived: America faced no continental threats, but it did have three immense coastlines, the Atlantic, the Pacific, and the Gulf of Mexico. Mahan's service in the Civil War had shown him just how vulnerable the East and Gulf coasts were to blockade. But, defending the coasts is not enough; a sea power needs a fleet that can preemptively take command of the seas.

There were, however, several trends working against Mahan's arguments. The first was America's continental expansion. Continental consolidation of the lower 48 was drawing the great energies of the American people inward not driving them out onto the sea. Second, Mahan was concerned that American democracy and American politicians were too short-sighted to appreciate sea power in all of its dimensions, especially the navy. He warned his readers: "Popular governments are not generally favorable to military expenditure, however necessary."

A final impediment to embracing the Mahanian vision was the tradition of the U.S. Navy. The Navy favored coastal defense and commerce raiding over fleet actions. Commerce raiding, where you use individual ships to go after enemy merchants, seemed like an attractive alternative to building a big and expensive battle fleet. Low-cost commerce raiders, this theory goes, can have a disproportionate impact on the enemy's economy. Mahan agreed that commerce raiding might be useful, but it was no match for the strategic effects of a battle fleet. So, as much as geography seemed to make the United States a natural sea power, the will of the population, the commitment of the government and even the sympathies of his own service were still up in the air.

Mahan wanted America to be a whale, not an elephant. That meant a fleet of large battleships designed to fight other fleets in the style of Nelson. Moreover, the implications of Mahan's theory of sea power went far beyond domestic politics and military budgets. They crossed the line into foreign policy. Remember Clausewitz's principle of subordinating the military to policy? For the most part, Mahan abided by that principle, but his well-publicized opinions on foreign policy and the fecklessness of democratic governments pushed the subordination envelope pretty far. In other words,

Mahan was happy to serve national policy, as long as it was the national policy that he advocated. These policy positions derived from Mahan's strategic and operational maxims. For example, "choke points" figure large in Mahan's writings.

The oceans are a global commons crisscrossed by trade routes. Those routes have critical nodes, or choke points, places like Gibraltar, Suez, Hormuz, and Singapore. The control of key global choke points was the key to projecting naval power globally. This is where Mahan crosses the line into foreign policy. If America was going to compete on the seas, then it needed an overseas empire, an empire comprised of those strategically significant choke points. In other words, operational necessity, operating the fleet, had foreign policy implications. But this is not imperialism simply for the sake of imperialism. To Mahan, annexation of overseas colonies had to be prudent and in America's best interests. An empire also had to be sustainable and America needed to avoid overextension. But America needed an empire.

So, naval bases and a global network of coaling stations are integral to Mahan's grand strategy. This made Mahan an advocate for the construction of a canal across Central America and for the annexation of the Hawaiian Islands. When it came to Hawaii, the logic was that if the United States did not have a mid-Pacific naval base then the West Coast would be vulnerable to those powers that did have a mid-Pacific naval base. The study of naval history had transformed Mahan into an unabashed imperialist. On the upside, the next time you are sipping a Mai Tai on Waikiki Beach, feel free to raise a toast to Alfred Thayer Mahan.

So Mahan's grand strategic vision was to make America a true sea power both militarily and commercially. That required a commitment from the government and a network of overseas bases. This brings us to his advice for naval officers and naval strategists. In the simplest terms, Mahan's advice was "Act like Nelson." But this is not as simple as it sounds. Mahan knew that Nelson could act as he had only because the full weight of British geography, society, and government enabled his actions. Before Nelson could drive his fleet into the enemy line at Trafalgar the virtuous cycle of British sea power had to be working at full capacity.

Nor was Mahan so naïve as to think that it was a good idea to try to re-fight Trafalgar. Tactics and technology had changed too dramatically, but for Mahan: "The old foundations of strategy [so far remain, as though] laid upon a rock." They are eternal. And even at the operational levels of war some of the eternal principles still pertained. Even so, when it came to peace-time preparations, the politicians and the military needed to be of one mind and build the strongest naval force possible, building on the very latest technological and tactical innovations. In addition, the battle fleet, and by this Mahan is referring to the biggest ships (the battleships) and their auxiliaries, the battle fleet must be kept as a concentrated body. Mahan allows for other naval missions including commerce raiding and coastal defense, but the battle line should never be drawn into those secondary pursuits.

In the lead-up to war, a concentrated fleet could serve as a deterrent to a would-be challenger. A divided fleet, in contrast, was symbolic of dangerously divided focus and could actually invite attack. In war, the massive combined firepower of the concentrated battle fleet was the surest way to send an enemy's navy to the bottom or to keep them blockaded. For Mahan, the ultimate purpose of the navy was to prepare for and to engage in major fleet-on-fleet battles. Defeating the enemy fleet on the high seas or bottling it up in port would give a nation an unprecedented command of the sea, a command that would ultimately translate into victory. As a result of this core assumption, Mahan was insistent that the main battle fleet should remain concentrated in a single body.

"Never divide the fleet" is often claimed as Mahan's most famous refrain. In reality, Mahan's idea of concentration was a bit more contingent and relative. As he writes in *The Interest of America in Sea Power*, "[The navy] must be great enough to take the sea, and to fight, with reasonable chances of success, the largest force likely to be brought against it." For a second string naval power, concentration probably meant concentrating the whole battle line. A great naval power, like Britain, might be able justify separate fleets in two or more theatres, but only if they were superior to their likely opponents in each theatre.

So he's a big fan of the Royal Navy. But, as fulsome as he was in his praise for British sea power, Mahan reserved some of his harshest critique for

British failures. Nowhere was this more the case than the Royal Navy's failure to concentrate during the American Revolution. Mahan lambasted the admiralty and British politicians for letting their naval power wane in the 1760s and 1770s and assailed them for their flawed strategy in the colonial war.

Rather than bottling up the French fleet, or meeting them in battle in European waters, a divided Royal Navy allowed the French to go to sea. To make matters worse, risk-averse British admirals avoided battle in North American waters. As a result, the French fleet under de Grasse achieved temporary sea-control off Virginia, and Cornwallis was trapped at Yorktown. Game over! In Mahan's opinion, better British policy before the war and better use of the Royal Navy in the war equals no Yorktown, and that equals no American independence.

When it comes to a shooting war, Mahan is further advocating what he calls the offensive defense. At this level of war, Mahan tracks quite close with Jomini. Other than a few ships set aside for commerce and coastal defense, take the battle fleet into the enemy's home waters, go on the offense. After all, it is easier to find the enemy if he is close to his home ports. That way you can also control the lines of supply and communication and seize forward choke points. This reduces the enemy's options and hopefully forces him to meet you in a decisive engagement like Trafalgar.

Once the enemy fleet is sunk or captured you have command of the sea. With that you can wage economic warfare on the enemy. Your undisrupted trade and freedom of action can also help you recruit and support allies. To Mahan, no power that lost command of its home waters, not Carthage, not France, not the Confederacy, could survive for very long against a sea power, a nation with sea control. Subsequent generations of air-power theorists would make similar claims about the command of the air. Once that command is achieved you can starve the enemy's economy and wear down their morale.

Back to Mahan. No one who's devoted so much time to studying Nelson could neglect leadership and the human factor in war. Mahan was deeply impressed with the audacity shown by Nelson in his relentless pursuit of a broken enemy fleet. If there was anything worse for Mahan than avoiding battle, it was failing to capitalize on victory in battle. Great naval leaders embraced calculated risk.

Nelson's leadership style was equally impressive. His "band of brothers" was a cadre of like-minded officers. Nelson also was an innovator who embraced improvements in signals that allowed him to communicate with his subordinates.

Nelson also understood the political and strategic implications of his operations. Reading through Mahan's voluminous publications, it's easy to get lost in the weeds of tactical and operational minutiae, but Mahan never lost sight of the strategic and political implications of a navy properly or poorly used.

Like Clausewitz, Mahan was concerned that the very demands of being a good naval officer were actually impediments to thinking strategically.

> It is now thought, practically, more important for a naval officer to know how to build a gun, to design a ship, to understand the strength of materials, to observe the stars through a telescope, to be wise in chemistry and electricity, than to have ingrained in him the knowledge of the laws of war, to understand the tactical handling of his weapons, to be expert in questions of naval policy, strategy, and tactics.

So as much as he was seeking principles of naval warfare that could be mastered in the style of Jomini, like Clausewitz he also wants to cultivate naval officers of genius and strategic insight. With all of this in mind, we can appreciate why Mahan thought Nelson was the embodiment of the eternal principles of naval power.

Let's take a look now at Mahan's near-term influence. The eloquence of Mahan's arguments complemented by the passionate advocacy of civilian navalists like Teddy Roosevelt brought about one of the most remarkable peacetime military transformations in history. In the course of two decades, the U.S. Navy went from being a secondary service of modest capabilities to one of the leading navies of the world. On May 1st 1898 Admiral Dewey steamed four armored cruisers into Manila Bay and terminated Spain's Asian empire in the course of a morning. In 1907, the so-called Great White Fleet went on a two-year global tour. Comprising 16 battleships and their escorts, the Great White Fleet was an impressive demonstration to the world of the latest and greatest in American naval power.

But it wasn't just in the United States. In Germany a similar trend was emerging. Kaiser Wilhelm II read Mahan in English and claimed the ability to quote chapter and verse from the master. Wilhelm made the German translation required reading for his admirals and captains. Wilhelm and Admiral Alfred von Tirpitz then set about building a fleet that would match Britain's Royal Navy in the Atlantic.

It was in Japan, however, where the naval transformation was the most stunning and the most geo-strategically significant. The Japanese were avid readers of Mahan and the rapid development of their navy in the latter half of the 19th century was, in part, a testimony to his influence. In 1854 when Commodore Perry sailed into Tokyo Bay, there was no such thing as a Japanese Navy, but in 1894–1895 a new Japanese fleet shattered China's larger and heavier Beiyang fleet. A decade later they obliterated Russia's Baltic fleet at Tsushima.

Mahan was not to blame for the naval arms races that followed the publication of his books, but he did provide the eloquent rationale for those political leaders who saw a big battle fleet as crucial to national survival.

I mentioned in the last lecture that the Russo-Japanese War (1904 and 1905) was the first real test of the theories of Mahan and Corbett. What Mahan found in that war was abundant validation of his core ideas. The Russo-Japanese War was a contest of rival imperial aspirations, control over spheres of influence in Northeast Asia. In his book, a retrospect on the Russo-Japanese War, Mahan penned a blistering critique of the Russians. In his estimation, the Russians failed egregiously in satisfying the principles of naval strategy. Russian naval policy and strategy were doomed from the outset as the most serious failures had predated the war. The Russians had the means to build and exercise a first-class navy, but not the will. The result was a hodge-podge of ship types and a shortage of training.

Russia's battle line was further divided into three fleets: the Baltic, the Black Sea, and the Port Arthur squadron. This gave Japan regional parity and emboldened them to attack Port Arthur on the first night of the war. Because it was not concentrated, the Russian fleet could not readily go on the offensive. Mahan would have preferred it if the Russian battleships had been concentrated in the Baltic or at Port Arthur and he was not shy about pointing out the relevance for the United States. Russia's failure was an object lesson for America on the dangers of dividing the battle fleet.

The Russians had also failed to set-up a global network of bases and coaling stations to enable it to quickly and credibly project naval power. When the Baltic fleet did sail in October 1904 it was forced to rely on the benevolence of allies, and their support was modest at best. Great Britain, with its huge comparative advantages in bases, shipping, and coal, was an ally of Japan and hindered the Russian transit at every turn. Finally, as they negotiated 18,000 miles of transit and choke points, the Baltic fleet was quite literally telegraphing its position, progress, and problems to the Japanese. Russia was weak militarily, weak politically, and did not have the control of communications required of a true sea power.

Poor preparation was compounded by poor execution. Russian naval operations and tactics were hamstrung by an excess of caution. With the exception of a brief period in 1904, the Port Arthur squadron did not contest Japan's close blockade. Russia's naval strategy was based on the "fleet-in-being" concept, that just by its existence the Port Arthur squadron would tie down a big chunk of the Japanese fleet. Mahan called this a dangerous delusion. Russia's fleet-in-being strategy ceded the strategic initiative to the Japanese. It did tie down portions of the Japanese navy but the Japanese were otherwise free to support amphibious landings by the army and to supply that army once they were ashore.

Russian leaders also hesitated about sending the Baltic fleet to reinforce the Asian squadrons. In the end, the Port Arthur squadron was destroyed in port before the Baltic fleet could relieve the siege. This meant that Admiral Togo had the freedom to meet the exhausted Baltic fleet with the entirety of his armada and it meant that the Baltic fleet had only one place to go—

the secondary Russian base at Vladivostok—and really only one way to get there, run the Tsushima strait.

In contrast to the Russians who seemed excessively concerned with husbanding their battle fleet, to recreate the fleet-in-being at Vlad, Togo appreciated that he had to seek battle to achieve sea control, not avoid battle. After he smashed the Baltic fleet at Tsushima, Togo enjoyed absolute command of the seas. This gave Japan the appearance of being able to sustain the ground campaign indefinitely, but in reality Japan's reserves were spent and they were desperate to end the war. Naval dominance, however, allowed them to land forces on Sakhalin Island, to seize a piece of Russian territory to serve as leverage at the bargaining table. The ploy worked and Japan got the generally favorable treaty of Portsmouth.

I think that you are already getting the impression that I am not completely sold on Mahan's straight cause-and-effect relationship between decisive fleet engagements, command of the sea and victory in war. In the case of the Napoleonic Wars, there was a decade between Trafalgar and Waterloo. In the Russo-Japanese War, Togo had been able to rest, refit, and then concentrate at Tsushima because the Japanese Army had rid him of the threat of the Port Arthur squadron. It was army artillery that sank that fleet. So we need a theorist to complement Mahan's navalism, someone who looks in more depth at the interconnection between armies and navies. Fortunately, in the next lecture we will get to meet him, Sir Julian Corbett.

But returning to Mahan: Alfred Thayer Mahan was impressively prolific and remarkably influential in his own lifetime. Mahan's appeal is easy to understand. He offered his readers an exceptionally clear grand strategy and an exceptionally clear naval strategy. Mahan tells you how to secure your interests as a maritime power and he tells you in very straightforward terms how to win a naval war.

Mahan was also steady in his convictions about the eternal principles of sea power. He served in a navy that was undergoing a radical transformation, and he lived in a country that had been completely transformed in his own lifetime. Mahan, however, refused to let changes in technology and tactics crowd out principles, and he refused to be dazzled by the latest and greatest technologies.

Timing is everything, and as a navalist and maven of prudent imperialism, Mahan's timing could not have been better. He had powerful friends in the navy and the government, and the United States was favorably positioned to translate his theoretical prescriptions into sea-power reality. In another sense, his timing couldn't have been worse. Mahan did his best work in the 1890s, in the midst of a global transformation not at the culmination of that transformation. Barring a full-up war between first-rate naval powers, Mahan was obliged to rely on the Nelsonian analogy to predict the future of naval warfare.

For the pre-*Dreadnought* navies of the 1890s and the first decade of the 1900s, Mahan was probably right about that Nelsonian analogy, but new technologies and tactics were on the horizon. Torpedoes, submarines, and aircraft were still in their infancy and many have rightly pointed out that Mahan failed to appreciate how these new technologies might transform naval warfare. Two lectures from now, we'll return to Mahan in the context of the Pacific War and we'll see how well he holds up.

Sir Julian Corbett
Lecture 14

S ir Julian Corbett was a world traveler, journalist, fiction writer, and student of naval history. While Mahan gave us the strategy to win a war at sea, Corbett shows us how the whale—that nation with command of the sea—can translate its control into the defeat of the elephant. In this, Corbett was responding to the Mahanian obsession with finding and destroying the enemy's fleet. He did not disagree that fleet engagements were critical, but he viewed the fleet-on-fleet battle as only one means to a larger political end. Just as Mahan focuses primarily on winning command of the sea, Corbett concentrates on exploiting that command.

Corbett's Study of Sea Power

- Born in 1854, Julian Corbett studied law at Cambridge but practiced only for a few years. He came to the study of naval history and strategy somewhat accidentally, through an interest in Sir Francis Drake, the 16th-century explorer and naval commander.

- Corbett's first serious work of naval history, *Drake and the Tudor Navy*, brought him to the attention of Admiral Sir John Fisher, the man in charge of officer education in the Royal Navy. At Fisher's request, Corbett began lecturing at Britain's Naval War College and continued writing at a furious pace.

- Like Mahan, Corbett leaned heavily on the histories of Britain's wars against France to derive his theory of maritime war. His ability to link seemingly arcane naval history to matters of contemporary strategic significance gained him a wide audience.

- With the support of Fisher, Corbett emerged as an influential voice in pre-World War I Britain. He lobbied for closer coordination between civil and military leaders and pushed for the establishment of a joint staff, akin to the U.S. Joint Chiefs. Ever the Clausewitzian, he saw the intimate link between policy and strategy,

Corbett's Holistic Way of War

- Corbett was eager to fill in the missing components of Clausewitz's *On War* and to produce a theory of maritime strategy as a complement to, and an expansion of, Clausewitz's continental way of thinking.

- He believed that the history of British maritime power could be mined so as to deduce a general theory of how sea powers win wars. That theory was not intended to guide "conduct in the field"—it wasn't an operational manual—but it was designed to increase the strategic effects of naval operations.

- In his lectures, Corbett reminded students that naval strategy was not a "separate branch of knowledge." Naval officers were specialists in naval war, but they had to "get hold of a general theory of war, and so ascertain the exact relations of Naval Strategy to the whole."

- For Corbett, high-level strategy was designed to coordinate the actions of the different services.
  - As he wrote in *Some Principles of Maritime Strategy*, "The army and navy must be used and thought of as instruments no less intimately connected than are the three arms [artillery, cavalry, and infantry] ashore."

  - This entailed the possibility that one military branch might have to be subordinate to another in the interests of strategic success.

  - Looking at war holistically also educated officers about the abilities of the other elements of national power. A naval planner could not afford to be ignorant of the capabilities and limitations of the army or the diplomatic corps.

- Elsewhere in *Some Principles of Maritime Strategy*, Corbett offers an elegant summary of the holistic nature of strategy: "The paramount concern ... of maritime strategy is to determine the mutual relations of your army and navy in a plan of war. When this is done, and not till then, naval strategy can begin to work out the manner in which the fleet can best discharge the function assigned to it."

Functions of the Navy
- According to Corbett, the first function, or naval mission, may be exactly what Mahan prescribed: Seek out the enemy's fleet and defeat it.
  - But Corbett was skeptical about the ease with which one fleet could force an enemy fleet into a battle like Trafalgar or Tsushima. A strategist anticipating a future war should not hinge his plans on shattering the naval power of the enemy in one or two blows.

  - Nor did Corbett think that total sea control was a necessary precondition for victory. Sea control is not as absolute as Mahan implies, and the pursuit of absolute control could well lead to strategic overextension.

- The next function assigned to the navy is blockade, which has a primary and a secondary value: (1) It prevents the enemy from disrupting maritime communications or threatening the coasts, and (2) it may force the enemy to try to run the blockade and be met by the opposing fleet. Commercial blockade is another option, to disrupt the flow of the enemy's seaborne trade.

- The third and fourth naval assignments are commerce raiding and commerce defense. For Corbett, naval power is a manifestation of commercial activity. Commerce raiding can, therefore, be pursued with an eye toward its strategic effect.

- None of these various missions is an end in itself. Instead, they are means to the greater end of controlling maritime communications.
  - By "maritime communications," Corbett means not only military logistics but the entire network of maritime commerce. Because the sea is a global commons through which a portion

of every nation's prosperity travels, it is automatically a strategically critical theater.

o   Because at least a portion of the enemy's trade must travel by sea, its economy can be attacked directly. This, in turn, makes war at sea more of a zero-sum proposition than war on land.

- Corbett countered the argument that more naval assets should be shifted to commerce defense in Britain by asserting that the immensity of British seaborne commerce was in inverse proportion to Britain's strategic vulnerability to economic warfare. In other words, even the most aggressive enemy could disrupt only a fraction of British trade.

- Corbett offered up another counterintuitive argument on the fifth naval mission, homeland defense. He believed that even when absolute command of the sea was contested, local command, especially command of the English Channel, was sufficient to foil most amphibious invasions.

Role of the Navy in Operations Ashore
- Corbett's insights on the integration of land and sea power and his creation of the theory of expeditionary warfare are perhaps the most important aspects of his theory. He argued that only a sea power—isolated from the main theater of a conflict—could truly wage a limited war: a war for limited political objectives.

- Contiguous land powers were more prone to escalate a conflict to its "higher form," that is, Clausewitz's absolute. Escalation occurred because there were fewer geographical impediments keeping the two sides from throwing maximum effort into a war.

- A nation with command of the sea lines of communication, however, could more easily calibrate its intervention and could also take advantage of the maritime weakness of its continental adversary.

The Use of Sea Power

- For Corbett, the two prime examples of the Clausewitzian use of sea power were Wellington's campaign on the Iberian Peninsula and the Russo-Japanese War.

- In the Peninsular War, Britain used its command of the sea to support Portuguese and Spanish resistance to France. The war in the Iberian Peninsula induced Napoleon to commit precious resources to a protracted and inconclusive campaign of suppression. The "Spanish ulcer" not only weakened the emperor but cemented Britain's status as a leader—not just the financier—of the final coalition against Napoleon.
  - Great Britain had a long tradition of seizing colonies and occupying the overseas territories of its enemies. Closer to home, Britain engaged in maritime harassment: small-scale operations that disrupted the enemy's plans, supported allies, and strengthened Britain's strategic position.

  - But Wellington's operations in the Iberian Peninsula achieved a level of strategic significance that made them "indistinguishable from regular continental warfare."

  - Under Wellington, the British committed a "disposal force"—a modest contingent that limited the costs in blood and treasure Britain would suffer. The operations of this force were far from glamorous—conducting convoys, transporting troops, and so on—but commanding the sea on all three sides of the Iberian Peninsula proved decisive.

  - The Peninsular campaign was a perfect example of a relatively low-cost effort that achieved disproportionate strategic effects.

- As was the case with Mahan, the Russo-Japanese War was the critical test case for Corbett's theoretical concepts. While Mahan critiqued the Russian side, Corbett was primarily looking for lessons that could be relevant to an island nation. Where the Iberian

For Corbett, Wellington's campaign on the Iberian Peninsula represented a direct attack by the whale on the elephant; the British operations were, Corbett wrote, "indistinguishable from regular continental warfare."

campaign was almost perfect in execution and results, Corbett's assessment of the Russo-Japanese War was mixed.

o   The Japanese received high praise for their deft use of diplomacy to set the stage for the war. Japan's statesmen and military commanders had also thought through the specific political objectives they were trying to achieve and had determined the military objectives most likely to translate into victory.

o   In addition, army and navy leaders met as a joint staff to coordinate operations in advance. Perhaps most important, the Japanese were careful to keep the war limited, that is, not to seek the overthrow of Russia but, rather, to force the Russians to recognize Japan's sphere of influence in Korea.

o   At the same time, Corbett perceived that the Japanese also made several crucial mistakes. Most critically, they split their land operations along two axes. This division of effort lessened the offensive punch of the Japanese army and forced Togo to disperse the navy to support multiple actions.

- These missteps cost the Japanese dearly in blood, treasure, and time and threatened to undermine the entire war plan. Fortunately for Japan, the Russians failed to capitalize.

Corbett and Mahan

- As with Clausewitz and Jomini, Corbett and Mahan are more complementary than they are contradictory. The points of divergence are, however, noteworthy and illuminating.

- In addition, both theorists enjoyed near-term and long-term influence.
  - Mahan, the evangelist of sea power, became a worldwide sensation, and his works are still read widely today, especially in China.

  - Julian Corbett distilled the British way of war and profoundly influenced the works of such military visionaries as Basil Liddell Hart. Corbett was also the first to lay out the concept of joint expeditionary war.

  - In his later works, Corbett would touch on the lessons that could be learned from Britain's disastrous amphibious expedition to Gallipoli and on the promise of naval aviation.

Suggested Reading

Corbett, *Some Principles of Maritime Strategy*.

Esdaile, *The Peninsular War*.

Questions to Consider

1. How much of a Clausewitzian was Corbett?

2. What are the main elements of Corbett's analysis of the Russo-Japanese War? Did the Russo-Japanese War validate Corbett's theories?

Sir Julian Corbett
Lecture 14—Transcript

"We English have to regret that we cannot always decide the fate of empires on the sea." Those were the prescient words of Horatio Nelson. We've already seen Nelson as the architect of the greatest naval victory in the Napoleonic Wars, the Battle of Trafalgar, but even Britain's greatest admiral appreciated the limits of sea power. Obviously Admiral Nelson did not live to see Britain's ultimate victory over Napoleon, but I don't think Nelson would have been surprised that it was an Army general, Arthur Wellesley, the Duke of Wellington, who finally vanquished Napoleon.

Our master for today is Sir Julian Corbett, world traveler, journalist, fiction writer, and student of naval history. Corbett was the first theorist to systematically link Nelson's victory at Trafalgar to Wellington's triumph at Waterloo. Alfred Thayer Mahan gave us the strategy to win a war at sea. Corbett is out to show us how the whale, that nation with command of the sea, can translate that command into the defeat of the elephant. Corbett was therefore responding to Mahan and to the "Mahanian" obsession with finding and destroying the enemy's fleet. He did not disagree that fleet engagements were critical. He allowed that destroying the enemy's fleet was the best and most direct way to achieve command of the sea.

But Corbett viewed that big fleet-on-fleet battle as only one means to a larger political end. An obsession with purely naval strategy was dangerous. It was, he said, "impossible that a war can be decided by naval action alone." So, one way to parse these two sea-power theorists is to see Mahan as primarily about winning command of the sea, while Corbett is about exploiting command of the sea.

Corbett is also thinking holistically about maritime strategy. Maritime strategy comprises the army and the navy, as well as diplomacy, commerce, and economic power as equally useful instruments of war. Corbett was a big fan of William Pitt, Britain's secretary of state during the Seven Years' War, who successfully coordinated all of those different instruments.

But what was it that brought Corbett to the study of sea power? Well, it was kind of an indirect course. Whereas Mahan was a career naval officer, Sir Julian Corbett was more of a gifted amateur. Born in 1854, he studied law at Cambridge, but only practiced for a few years. He sketched and he wrote, fiction and biographies mostly. He traveled the globe, and he hunted and fished with a passion. Corbett came to the study of naval history and strategy somewhat accidentally through an interest in Sir Francis Drake, the 16th-century explorer and naval commander.

Corbett's first serious work of naval history, which he didn't begin until he was in his 40s, was called *Drake and the Tudor Navy*. Its publication brought Corbett to the attention of Admiral Sir John Fisher, the man in charge of officer education in the Royal Navy.

At Fisher's request, Corbett began lecturing at Britain's Naval War Colleges and continued writing at a furious pace. He was a really prolific author. Although Fisher himself was obsessed with the latest and greatest modern technology, he still appreciated Corbett's use of history and its relevance to the age of steel and steam. Like Mahan, Corbett leaned heavily on the histories of Britain's wars against France to derive his theory of maritime war. His students weren't always as enthusiastic about these extended reflections on the lessons from the Age of Sail, but Corbett's ability to link this seemingly arcane naval history to matters of contemporary strategic significance gained him a wide audience.

Sometimes I say to my students, in the style of Yogi Berra: "In the future you won't have the benefit of hindsight." That gets them scratching their heads, but then I explain that this is what someone like Corbett is trying to say. Corbett was a historian. He had the benefit of hindsight and the luxury of time to methodically plumb the nature of war in the past. His students, and mine, military officers, naval officers, won't have that perspective and time in the face of a future conflict. Theory and the study of history fill that gap.

With the support of Fisher, who later became First Sea Lord, Corbett emerged as an influential voice in pre-World War I Britain. Corbett also lobbied for closer coordination between civil and military leaders and pushed for the establishment of a joint staff, akin to our joint chiefs of staff. Ever the Clausewitzian, he saw the intimate linkage between policy and strategy,

Corbett was a careful student of all of the theorists of the past. But it was Clausewitz that most inspired his work. Corbett was eager to fill in the missing components of *On War* and to produce a theory of maritime strategy as a complement to and an expansion on Clausewitz's continental way of thinking. Basically, Corbett wanted to articulate a British way of war.

In the opening of his famous book, *Some Principles of Maritime Strategy*, he points out, "even the greatest of the continental strategists [that is, Clausewitz] fell short of realising fully the characteristic conception of the British [strategic] tradition."

The history of British maritime power could therefore be mined so as to deduce a general theory of how sea powers win wars. That theory was not intended to guide "conduct in the field," it wasn't an operational manual; it was designed to increase the strategic effects of naval operations.

Not much of an expert on the grammar of modern naval warfare (tactics, gunnery, navigation), Corbett was wise to shy away from claiming to offer a practical guide for action in war in the style of Jomini. He was concerned with cultivating the right habits of strategic thought. In addition, Corbett was fighting against the natural parochialism of a military service. In his lectures he reminded students that naval strategy was not a "separate branch of knowledge." Naval officers were specialists in naval war, but they had to "get hold of a general theory of war, and so ascertain the exact relations of Naval Strategy to the whole." He then went on to quote Clausewitz almost verbatim: "War is a form of political intercourse, a continuation of foreign politics which begins when force is introduced to attain our ends."

For Corbett, this Clausewitzian approach to war as a total phenomenon accustomed officers to see the interconnections between naval strategy, military strategy, and national policy. He had no reason to doubt their tactical and operational prowess, but he needed them to think strategically. At the higher level, strategy, maritime strategy, is designed to coordinate the actions of the different services. As he puts it in his work *Some Principles of Maritime*

265

Strategy: "The army and navy must be used and thought of as instruments no less intimately connected than are the three arms (artillery, cavalry, and infantry) ashore." So the navy and army need to work in the same way in a war. This often entailed the painful possibility that one military branch might have to be subordinate itself to another in the interests of strategic success. One service might have to cede its operational and strategic preferences and in Corbett's words "give way to a higher or more pressing need of the other."

Looking at war holistically also educated officers into what the other elements of national power can and cannot do. A naval planner could not afford to be ignorant of the capabilities and limitations of the army, or of the diplomatic corps.

Elsewhere in *Some Principles of Maritime Strategy*, Corbett offers an elegant summary of the holistic nature of strategy: "The paramount concern … of maritime strategy," he writes, "is to determine the mutual relations of your army and navy in a plan of war. When this is done, and not till then, naval strategy can begin to work out the manner in which the fleet can best discharge the function assigned to it."

Corbett's students knew what the steam boilers in their ships could do, and they knew what their guns and their radio telegraphs could do, but his first task was to open their eyes to what the navy could do strategically.

So what functions might be assigned to the navy? The first function, or naval mission, may be exactly what Mahan prescribed: "Seek out the enemy's fleet." Meet it and defeat it. But Corbett was skeptical about the ease with which one fleet could force an enemy fleet into a battle like Trafalgar or Tsushima. Battles like that were great when you could get them, but they were probably flukes.

A strategist anticipating a future war should not hinge his plans on shattering the naval power of the enemy in one or two blows. You can't bank on a cooperative adversary offering up his fleet for destruction, nor can you reasonably hope to have all of the necessary ships combat ready, in the right place, at the right time.

For all of Britain's glorious naval accomplishments, Corbett was no naval romantic. He warned his readers against forgetting what really happened in past wars and warned them against being blinded by "the dramatic moments of naval history" or assuming that defeating the "enemy's fleet solves all problems." Nor did Corbett think that total sea control was a necessary precondition for victory. History proves that sea control is always contingent and relative. In other words it is not as absolute as Mahan implies. Moreover, the pursuit of absolute control of the sea might very well lead to strategic overextension. The art of maritime strategy was making the most out of the level of sea control that you could reasonably hope to achieve.

The next big naval mission, or function assigned to the navy, is blockade. If it proves impossible to meet the enemy fleet at sea, Corbett argues that blockade is a viable alternative. Blockade of the enemy's navy has a primary and a secondary value. Its primary value is that it prevents the enemy from disrupting your maritime communications or threatening your coasts. Its secondary value is that it might force the enemy to try to run the blockade. Your fleet, at the peak of readiness, can then meet his, which has been bottled up and inactive for weeks, if not for months. So, naval blockade involves bottling up the enemy's navy.

Commercial blockade is another option. In a commercial blockade you use your cruisers to disrupt the flow of the enemy's sea-borne trade, and deny him the use of commercial communications. Commercial blockades have the added benefit of not tying up your battle fleet; it is "mainly an affair of cruisers." At the same time, Corbett admits that commercial blockades are protracted and attritional and they are very difficult to sustain over long periods of time. If, however, command of the sea has already been achieved, commercial blockades give you a great ability to inflict pain on the enemy. Beyond the blockade of the enemy's ports, attacking his trade at sea was also worthwhile. These are the third and fourth naval assignments: commerce raiding and commerce defense.

You'll remember that Mahan saw commerce raiding as an important, but secondary naval mission, one that should not cause a diversion of strategic assets, of battleships. For Corbett, commerce raiding stands in tandem with fleet-on-fleet battle. Remember, naval power is a manifestation of commercial activity. The two are interdependent and mutually vulnerable. Commerce raiding can, therefore, be pursued with an eye toward its strategic effect.

"Wars," Corbett says, "are not decided exclusively by military and naval force." Finance is just as important. All other things being equal, the side with more money usually wins. Therefore anything you can do to cripple the enemy's finances is a direct step toward his defeat. The most effective way to cripple the finances of a maritime state is to attack his seaborne trade.

But none of these various missions—fleet battle, blockade, and commerce raiding—are ends in themselves. Instead they are means to the greater end of controlling maritime communications. Hence, while winning command of the sea in a Nelsonian engagement was all well and good, it was what one did with that command that was the true test of maritime strategy.

"Command of the sea," Corbett argues, "means nothing but the control of maritime communications, whether for commercial or military purposes. The object of naval warfare is control of communications." By maritime communications he means not just military logistics, but the entire network of maritime commerce. Since the sea is a great global commons through which a portion of every nation's prosperity travels, it is automatically a strategically critical theatre.

In the past, land powers traditionally fought at their shared frontiers, leaving their domestic economies pretty much unharmed. The sail-to-steam revolution changed that. Since at least a portion of the enemy's trade must travel by sea, then you can attack his economy directly. This in turn makes war at sea more of a zero-sum proposition than war on land. Attacking an enemy's trade and military logistics makes him weaker and makes you stronger.

At this point in the discussion of naval missions, Corbett makes a counterintuitive argument about defending your own trade, or more specifically about defending British trade. Many in Corbett's time were arguing that the scale of British maritime trade and the empire's undeniable dependence on that trade made defending commerce a critical responsibility for the Royal Navy. More naval assets therefore, needed to be shifted to commerce defense. Corbett countered that argument by pointing out that the immensity of British seaborne commerce was in inverse proportion to Britain's strategic vulnerability to economic warfare.

In other words, even the most aggressive enemy could only disrupt a fraction of British trade. Britain's potential adversaries were another story when it came to vulnerability.

Britain's continental neighbors were less dependent on the sea, especially for food, but there were some critical commodities that they could not do without. If the Royal Navy could inflict a much higher percentage of damage on that smaller volume of maritime trade, carrying those much-needed commodities, then the pain would be acute and its strategic effects direct and immediate. The impact of U-Boats and blockades in World War I should naturally make us skeptical about Corbett's conclusions on this point, but they should not detract from the overall importance of Corbett's contributions to strategic theory.

Corbett offered up another counterintuitive argument on the fifth naval mission: homeland defense. Corbett was not dismissive of the danger of invasion, but his chapter on the subject offers a litany of reasons why the threat of invasion is low. Even when absolute command of the sea is contested, local command, especially command of the narrowest straits of the English Channel, was sufficient to foil most amphibious invasions. Even the great Napoleon gave up his plans for an invasion of England in the face of fickle weather and the inherent vulnerabilities of a slow moving invasion flotilla. The key for Corbett was not to use the big battleships and heavy cruisers to defend the British Isles against invasion. Smaller vessels would suffice.

In much the same way that he inverts Britain's relative vulnerability to commerce raiding, Corbett inverts her vulnerability to invasion. England, the island nation, is not terribly vulnerable to invasion. By contrast continental powers, especially if they have long coastlines, are acutely vulnerable to amphibious attack.

It is on this point of amphibious attack—or, specifically the role of the navy in safeguarding and enabling military operations ashore—that Corbett makes his most significant contribution to the body of strategic theory. In fact, to be perfectly honest, not much of what Corbett had to say about naval strategy that we have covered so far was particularly path-breaking, and when it came to issues like defending commerce and defending the homeland he's kind of shaky. In my opinion his insights on the integration of land and sea power and his creation of the theory of expeditionary warfare are what pushes Corbett above and beyond.

It is also here that Corbett improves most significantly on Clausewitz's concept of limited war. Corbett argued that only a sea power isolated from the main theatre of a conflict could truly wage a limited war: a war for limited political objectives. By this he meant that contiguous land-powers were more prone to escalate a conflict to its "higher form." In other words toward Clausewitz's absolute. Escalation happened because there were fewer geographical impediments keeping the two sides from throwing their maximum effort into a war. A nation with command of the sea lines of communication, however, could more easily calibrate its intervention and could also take advantage of the maritime weakness of its continental adversary. It wouldn't get sucked into that escalation cycle. Or to quote Francis Bacon: "He that commands the sea is at great liberty and may take as much or as little of the war as he will."

For Corbett, the two prime examples of the Clausewitzian use of sea power were Wellington's campaign on the Iberian Peninsula and the Russo-Japanese War. In the Peninsular War, Britain used its command of the sea to support Portuguese and Spanish resistance to France. The ugly war in the Iberian Peninsula induced Napoleon to commit precious resources to a protracted and inconclusive campaign of suppression. The "Spanish Ulcer" not only weakened the emperor, but cemented Britain's status as a leader, not just financier, of the final coalition against Napoleon.

This was nothing new. Great Britain had a long tradition of projecting land power from the sea. For one, the British had regularly and successfully seized colonies and occupied overseas territories of their enemies.

Closer to home they had engaged in maritime harassment. Something that Corbett called "descents" onto the enemy's coast. These small-scale operations disrupted the enemy's plans, supported allies, and strengthened Britain's strategic position. But Wellington's operations in the Iberian Peninsula were on a completely different scale. In Corbett's words, they achieved a level of strategic significance that made them "indistinguishable from regular continental warfare." They allowed the whale to directly attack the elephant.

In 1807, Napoleon sent an army into Portugal to force the Portuguese, Britain's oldest trading partner, to abide by the Continental System, his scheme to deny Britain markets in Europe. A year later the French overthrew the Bourbons, who had ruled Spain since 1700. In their place Napoleon put his brother Joseph. As a result, the country rose in revolt. Just in the summer of 1808 Napoleon lost 24,000 men and several capital ships to Spanish guerillas.

The situation in Portugal was just as bad. The Portuguese rose up against the French and won support from the British who landed 9,000 men in Portugal. By September, the Duke of Wellington had 30,000 British troops and a secure base area in Portugal. They could now take the war directly to the French troops occupying Spain.

The British made masterful use of the Spanish uprising to bleed Napoleon. At any one point between 1808 and 1813 Napoleon was forced to commit between 200,000 and 450,000 troops to Spain and Portugal. The "Spanish Ulcer" ultimately cost the emperor 300,000 men killed in action or lost to disease. In August 1812 Wellington marched into Madrid. A year later he had crossed the Pyrenees and invaded France. After his downfall, Napoleon admitted the scale of his blunder in Spain and Portugal: "That unfortunate war destroyed me," Napoleon said. "It divided my forces, multiplied my obligations, undermined my morale. All the circumstances of my disasters are bound up in that fatal knot."

The Peninsular War demonstrated the disproportionate strategic effect of the deft coordination of land and sea power. Under Wellington, the British committed a "disposal force"—a modest contingent that limited the costs in blood and treasure that they could suffer. Wellington could go on the offensive with that disposal force because of Nelson's Victory at Trafalgar, but the Royal Navy's operations in support of Wellington were far from glamorous or spectacular in a Nelsonian sense. Instead the Navy did convoys, resupply, troop transport, and close commercial blockades. But commanding the sea on all three sides of the Iberian Peninsula proved decisive.

The Peninsular campaign was a perfect example of a relatively low-cost effort that achieved disproportionate strategic effects. The geography was favorable to the Royal Navy. The British had safe bases of operation and resupply in Portugal. The indigenous populations were highly supportive. Above all, Napoleon was a cooperative adversary. He doubled-down on the occupation of Spain when he should have withdrawn and cut his losses. Prior to 1808, Britain had no way strike Napoleon directly. But in Spain they could exploit a peripheral theatre to wear down Napoleon's center of gravity, his army.

As a result of all of these factors, the limited war that Britain and its allies fought and won in Spain, translated directly to the unlimited objective of overthrowing Napoleon. All of that hinged on Britain's command of the sea and its control of maritime communications. Even Wellington, the Iron Duke, recognized his debt to the Royal Navy.

"If anyone," Wellington said, "wishes to know the history of this war, I will tell them it is our maritime superiority gives me the power of maintaining my army while the enemy is unable to do so." There you have Corbett's take on the history of maritime strategy, but was he able to square that with the naval wars of the early 20th century? Obviously, the answer was yes.

As was the case with Mahan, the Russo-Japanese War was the critical test case for Corbett's theoretical concepts. In fact, he wrote an entire book on that conflict. While Mahan critiqued the Russian side, Corbett was primarily looking for lessons that could be relevant to an island nation. Japan's navy had modeled itself on the Royal Navy. Britain might want to return the compliment and learn from Japan's conduct of this war.

Where the Iberian campaign was almost perfect in execution and results, Corbett's assessment of the Russo-Japanese War was decidedly mixed. The Japanese get high praise for their deft use of diplomacy to set the stage for the war. In 1902 they signed a treaty with the British that effectively meant that they would be fighting only the Russians. They also used the prewar negotiations with St. Petersburg to give them more international sympathy and potential support.

Japan's statesmen and military commanders had also thought through the specific political objectives that they were trying to achieve and had decided on the military objectives most likely to translate into victory. In addition, army and navy leaders met as a joint staff to coordinate operations in advance. Perhaps most importantly, the Japanese were careful to keep the war limited; they weren't trying to overthrow the Russian empire, but rather to force the Russians to recognize Japan's sphere of influence in Korea. Japan could not possibly have waged an unlimited war against Russia, but it could wage a limited war against a fraction of the Russian military for an object of relatively low value to St. Petersburg.

In *Some Principles of Maritime Strategy*, Corbett writes (and I quote): "Limited wars do not turn upon the armed strength of the belligerents, but upon the amount of that strength which they are able or willing to bring to bear at the decisive point." Japan's victory over Russia was a dramatic proof of this maxim.

The geography of the theatre also favored Japan. The division of Russia's Asian squadron between two naval bases, Port Arthur and Vladivostok, prevented the Russians from coordinating their naval assets to either contest sea control or to threaten the Japanese home islands. Japan's navy, on the other hand, could operate directly out of bases on the Sea of Japan and could both land and supply armies in Korea. As a result, the Japanese did not have to defeat the Russians at sea or gain absolute sea control; rather they could exploit what sea control they had and exploit their superior maritime communications from the very first day of the war.

At the same time, Corbett perceived that despite all of these favorable conditions, the Japanese made several crucial mistakes. Most critically, they split their land operations along two axes. Three Japanese armies marched into Manchuria in search of a decisive battle, while another army undertook a protracted siege of Port Arthur. This division of effort lessened the offensive punch of the Japanese army. It also forced Admiral Togo to disperse the navy to support all of these actions. For a while, it looked as if the continentalist inclinations of the army, steeped in the Prussian model, might hijack the larger strategy that hinged on what Corbett called the "sea factor." These missteps cost the Japanese dearly in blood, treasure and time and threatened to undermine the entire war plan. Fortunately for Japan, the Russians failed to capitalize. So, for all of Japan's remarkable success, Corbett viewed this case, the Russo-Japanese War, as both prescriptive and cautionary.

I hope you have enjoyed this three-lecture set on the sea-power revolution and our two sea power masters. As with Jomini and Clausewitz, Corbett and Mahan are more complementary than they are contradictory. The points of divergence, however, are noteworthy and illuminating. In addition, both theorists enjoyed near-term and long-term influence. Mahan, the evangelist of sea power became a worldwide sensation and his works are read widely today, especially in China, a nation that is pondering its future as a maritime power.

Julian Corbett distilled the British way of war and profoundly influenced the works of such military visionaries as Basil Liddell Hart. Corbett was also the first to lay out the concept of joint expeditionary war. As such he remains a favorite of the United States Marine Corps. Finally, Corbett lived to see both Britain's disastrous amphibious expedition to Gallipoli and the advent of naval aviation. In his later works, Corbett would touch on the lessons that could be learned from that abject failure at Gallipoli and on the promise of that new technology. I don't think, however, that even Corbett could imagine how dramatically naval and expeditionary warfare would develop over the next 20 years. When next we meet, we will be testing Mahan and Corbett against the greatest maritime conflict of all time: The Pacific War.

I'll see you then.

Mahan, Corbett, and the Pacific War
Lecture 15

In the strategic studies community, "Corbettian" and "Mahanian" are used as shorthand terms for the core principles of these two masters. Mahanian refers to the massing of capital ships (battleships or carriers) for a decisive fleet-on-fleet battle in order to achieve near-total command of the sea. Corbettian is shorthand for a strategy of cumulative effects, in which capital ships are deployed in an elastic configuration across a broader but still mutually supporting front and in which naval actions are integrated with amphibious landings. As we will see in this lecture, the Pacific War is rich in examples of both Mahanian and Corbettian approaches.

Origins of the Pacific War

- The origins of the Pacific War do not lie in a maritime dispute between the United States and Japan. Rather, this war began on the Asian mainland, and from a Japanese perspective, it remained primarily a continental struggle.

- Since the 1890s, Japan had been carving out an empire in east and northeast Asia. The Japanese had annexed Korea in 1910 and seized Manchuria in 1931. In 1937–1938, they seized large portions of Chinese territory, but they could not win the war in China outright. They then launched an ill-conceived war in Mongolia, where they were trounced by the Red Army.

- At this point, the Japanese navy got involved. If Japan was going to have a chance of winning the war in China, it needed secure access to raw materials from the French, Dutch, and British colonies in southeast Asia. A naval campaign was required to seize those colonies and secure sea lines of communication.
  - War against Britain and Holland was an acceptable risk, because those countries were too busy with Japan's Axis allies in Europe.

o The bigger problem was that if Japan attacked British Malaya or the Dutch East Indies, there was no guarantee that the United States would stay out of the war.

o The U.S. bases in the Philippines could potentially be used to harass the sea lines of communication between southeast Asia and Japan, which meant that Japan needed to neutralize the Philippines.

o Given that attacking the Philippines meant war with the United States, then a preemptive attack on America's fleet in being at Pearl Harbor was necessary.

• We can see in this bizarre rationalization Mahanian concepts of choke points, sea lines, and access to strategic resources. The problem was that Japan was too weak in absolute terms, too tied down on the Continent, and too short of merchant shipping to be the kind of sea power that could pull off the conflicts it planned.

• The Japanese believed that they might be able to knock the United States out with simultaneous blows against the Philippines

The strategy enacted by the Japanese in attacking Pearl Harbor was built on invalid assumptions, mislearned lessons from earlier wars, a superficial understanding of Mahan, and an almost suicidal neglect of Corbett.

and Pearl Harbor. If that didn't work, then a qualitatively superior Japanese battle line could meet a weakened U.S. fleet in a decisive engagement, much like Tsushima.

• The Japanese assumed that what they had done to Russia in 1905 would yield similar strategic and political results with the United

States in 1941. But the United States was far more economically and politically stable than Russia had been.

- Further, in the Russo-Japanese War, the Japanese had focused their finite land and sea assets on a single theater and along parallel lines of advance. In the Second World War, they scattered their navy and only a fraction of their army along multiple axes.

- As strategically flawed as Japanese thinking was, at the operational level, the first phase of Japan's Pacific War was spectacularly successful. Had they transitioned to defense, the Japanese might have been tougher to defeat, but because they were convinced that follow-on offensives were a strategic necessity, they quickly became overextended.

U.S. War Planning

- Initial U.S. war plans were very Mahanian, especially War Plan Orange, which called for massing the American fleet on the West Coast and sailing out to relieve Guam and the Philippines. These actions would be followed by a decisive battleship engagement near Japan and then a blockade of the Japanese home islands.

- Facing a possible two-front war in Europe and Asia, the United States revised Plan Orange into Plan Dog, a Europe-first strategy that called for a defensive stance in the Pacific. Between Plan Dog and the damage to the fleet at Pearl Harbor, the United States was stuck on the defensive in early 1942, but that does not mean it was inactive.

- Throughout 1942, Admiral Ernest King, the new chief of naval operations, employed what Corbett called the offensive-defensive, strategically defensive but operationally offensive when the circumstances were right.
  o This is different from Mahan's offensive-defense, in which one opponent goes on the strategic offensive. The United States could not do that at this point in the war.

o   Instead, King set up his Corbettian offensive-defensive along two lines, Hawaii to Midway and Samoa-Fiji-Australia. U.S. aircraft carriers were deployed along those two lines in an elastic configuration that allowed King to shift these precious assets from one line to the other.

o   The idea was to stem further Japanese advances and to harass and wear down the Japanese navy by forcing it to go on offensives that it could not sustain.

o   King also planned to launch the inevitable counteroffensive west and north along these two axes, which would force Japan to divide its fleet again.

o   What King envisioned was a kind of Jominian strategy at sea, a series of incremental battles, in which American and Allied forces could leverage local superiority against decisive points.

Coral Sea and Midway
•   The first test of King's offensive-defensive came at the Battle of Coral Sea in May 1942. Coral Sea evolved into a medium-scale Mahanian fleet engagement, but instead of big-gun battleships, it was a clash between two carrier groups—the first all-air battle in naval history. The Japanese won the battle at the tactical level, but at the strategic level, Coral Sea was a major setback for Japan.

•   The next Mahanian fleet-on-fleet battle to arise from the offensive-defensive was Midway in June 1942.
o   In this case, the United States was forewarned of the attack. The Japanese had also violated one of Mahan's cardinal tenets by dividing their fleet.

o   As a result, Midway was a fairly evenly matched battle, and this time, the Japanese received a Tsushima-like shellacking.

- Essentially, both Coral Sea and Midway were Mahanian surface engagements expanded into three dimensions by the addition of submarines and aircraft.

- We can also see that both of these Mahanian battles evolved out of Corbettian strategies—King's offensive-defensive—and they were fought to cover or contest amphibious landings. In fact, most of the major fleet actions of the war coincided with amphibious campaigns.

Guadalcanal

- Guadalcanal was the first tentative step in King's counteroffensive. The idea was to begin an advance up through the Solomon Islands with the ultimate goal of driving the Japanese out of New Guinea and the Bismarcks.

- U.S. Marines landed on Guadalcanal in August 1942 and seized the strategically critical air base at Henderson Field. The Japanese were compelled to contest those landings because a U.S. base on Guadalcanal would have scuttled their efforts to interdict U.S. supplies flowing to Australia.

- What followed was a complex Corbettian interaction game, with both sides trying to use their command of the local seas to enable ground operations on the island. The third dimension was in the air, with both land-based and carrier aircraft joining the fight.

- For Corbett, the key to a successful peripheral operation is local sea control, an idea we might extend into local air control. But even Corbett admitted that control is rarely absolute. In fact, at Guadalcanal, the United States did not dominate the seas or the air.

- Ideally, a peripheral operation inflicts unrecoverable damage on the enemy's critical military capabilities. Guadalcanal did exactly that to the Japanese navy.

- With the Corbettian noose tightening around Japan, there was one last flurry of Mahanian fleet action in mid- to late 1944: the battles of the Philippine Sea and Leyte Gulf, both losses for the Japanese.

The Submarine Campaign
- With submarines, smaller surface ships, and PT boats, the United States unleashed the most devastating commerce raiding campaign in history against Japan. As a result, Japan's sea lines of communication were vulnerable to interdiction throughout the Pacific War.

- The Japanese had tried to make good on their shortcomings in merchant shipping, but they neglected such simple defensive measures as convoying and antisubmarine patrols. Japan's absolute dependence on imported raw materials magnified the strategic effects of the submarine campaign. By early 1945, Japan had almost no merchant shipping.

- In contrast to America's dispersion of submarines, the Japanese built a small number of very large submarines and attached them as supports and screens for the main body of the fleet. As a result, they couldn't effectively harass the Allies' lines of communication.

- Japan's embrace of new military technology and mastery of new naval tactics, especially carrier and amphibious operations, were truly impressive. In 1941, pound-for-pound Japan had the best navy in the world, but the Japanese had wholly neglected the larger goals of maritime strategy.

The End Game
- By the summer of 1945, the fleet of Japan was mostly sunk and its merchant shipping obliterated. What should naturally follow is either a Mahanian or Corbettian end game, but that is not what happened.

- The Mahanian end game would have been a long, slow squeeze of the Japanese islands à la War Plan Orange. A Corbettian end game would have been the United States and its allies taking the war directly to Japan's center of gravity à la Wellington at Waterloo. Neither of these happened, yet Japan surrendered. Why?

- In the end, there are at least three theoretical explanations for Japan's surrender.
  - First, there is the maritime theory explanation, in which the United States destroyed the Japanese navy and its seaborne commerce.

  - Second is the Clausewitzian explanation, in which the Soviet Red Army poured into Manchuria in early August 1945 and demolished Japan's military—and, potentially, its political—center of gravity.

  - Third is the air power explanation, in which the U.S. Air Force rained destruction on every major city in Japan and closed the deal with two atomic bombs at Hiroshima and Nagasaki.

Suggested Reading

James, "American and Japanese Strategies in the Pacific War."

Marston, ed., *The Pacific War Companion.*

Questions to Consider

1. What did Guadalcanal have in common with Wellington's Peninsular campaign? Were the strategic effects similar?

2. How would Mahan and Corbett critique Japanese strategy in the Pacific War? Was Japan a cooperative adversary?

Mahan, Corbett, and the Pacific War
Lecture 15—Transcript

It is sometimes quipped that the greatest service that Alfred Thayer Mahan ever rendered to his country was to allow his books to be translated into German and Japanese. This is a snide way of saying that the adulation that Mahan received in Imperial Germany in the lead-up to World War I, and in Imperial Japan in the lead-up to World War II led those two nations into self-defeating naval arms races and into the misguided pursuit of decisive victory at sea. There is a hint of truth to this. Mahan's books were voraciously devoured in Berlin and Tokyo and did influence both grand strategy and naval tactics, but both rising powers missed the more subtle geo-strategic lessons in Mahan.

So Mahan, the "Evangelist of Sea Power," had many converts in Japan, but the same was true in the United States. Mahan is therefore very relevant to today's topic: The Pacific War. The same goes for Sir Julian Corbett. We might nickname Corbett the "Patron Saint of Jointness," jointness referring to the coordinated integration of different instruments of military power. Traditionally, this was naval and ground forces, but today we are going to add air power.

Corbett anticipated the potential that the synergistic application of multiple military instruments could have. And he presaged the advent of the amphibious doctrine that yielded such impressive results in the Pacific War. Because of their monumental influence on naval strategy and doctrine in the Modern Era, I will be using two adjectives in this lecture that you might not be familiar with: Corbettian and Mahanian. In the strategic studies community we use these two terms as shorthand for the core principles of these masters. So when I use the term Mahanian, I am referring to massing capital ships (battleships or carriers) for a decisive fleet-on-fleet battle in order to achieve near-total command of the sea.

Corbettian is short hand for a strategy of cumulative effects (wearing down an enemy), where you can deploy your capital ships (again either battleships or carriers) in an elastic configuration across a broader, but still mutually supporting front, and where you integrate naval actions with amphibious landings. That sounds like a lot to process right now, but by the end of this lecture you will be quite comfortable with these terms.

That is because the Pacific War is so rich in examples of both Mahanian and Corbettian approaches. This conflict reveals many things about the right and wrong ways to use sea power and about the relative validity of our two masters of naval strategy. Ultimately Japanese strategy was flawed from the outset and stayed so throughout the war. That strategy was built on invalid assumptions, mis-learned lessons from Japan's earlier wars, a superficial understanding of Mahan, and an almost suicidal neglect of Corbett. American prewar strategy was also built on flawed assumptions, at least at first, expecting a Mahanian outcome, but a combination of shocks, necessity, adaptability, and a cooperative adversary allowed the United States to put together a strategy that capitalized on the best of both Corbett and Mahan.

As Americans we need to realize that the origins of the Pacific War do not lie in some maritime dispute between the United States and Japan. Rather, this war begins on the Asian mainland, and from a Japanese perspective it would remain primarily a continental struggle. Since the 1890s Japan had been carving out an empire in East and Northeast Asia.

On the mainland the Japanese had annexed Korea in 1910 and were attempting to expand their sphere of influence. In the minds of Japanese leaders, Japan was not secure unless Korea was secure and Korea was not secure unless Manchuria was secure. So they laid plans for extending their sphere of influence into Manchuria, seizing it outright in 1931. But this meant that as long as China and Russia were possible enemies Manchuria was not secure.

The Japanese tried their hand at knocking the Chinese out in 1937 and 1938. They were partially successful in the sense that they drove the Chinese government into retreat and seized large portions of Chinese territory, but they could not win the China war outright and their brutality began to turn world opinion decisively against Japan. Frustrated in China, they turned their sights on the Soviet Union and launched an ill-conceived and poorly resourced war in Mongolia. In that instance they were trounced by the Red Army.

Licking their wounds, the Japanese looked for another solution to their continental conundrum. At this point the Japanese Navy got involved. If Japan was going to have any chance of sustaining and winning the war in China, they needed secure access to raw materials from the French, Dutch, and British colonies in Southeast Asia. Since there was no way to transport sufficient material overland, then a naval campaign was required to seize those colonies and to secure sea lines of communication. War against Britain and Holland was an acceptable risk, especially because they were too busy with Japan's axis allies in Europe.

The bigger problem was that if Japan attacked British Malaya or the Dutch East Indies they could not guarantee that the United States would stay out of the war. And since the United States had bases in the Philippines and could potentially harass the sea lines of communications between Southeast Asia and Japan, then Japan needed to neutralize the Philippines. And since attacking the Philippines meant war with the United States, then a preemptive attack on America's fleet at Pearl Harbor was necessary.

I know it sounds pathological, but this is how the Japanese rationalized a war with the United States as a way to win a war in China. You can also see how Mahanian concepts of choke points, sea lines, and access to strategic resources were percolating in Japanese thought. The problem was that Japan was too weak in absolute terms, too tied down on the continent, and too short of merchant shipping to be the kind of sea power that could pull something like this off. For example, in late 1941 the Japanese had one-quarter of the merchant shipping that they needed to support themselves. Let me say that again, on the eve of the war with the United States, a nation with an economy 10 times the size of Japan's, the Japanese merchant shipping could only carry enough freight to meet 25 percent of Japan's civilian and military needs.

If anything, Japan's opening gambits in the Pacific War magnified its vulnerabilities in general and specifically magnified its navy's vulnerability to both Mahanian and Corbettian counterattacks. The Japanese had essentially convinced themselves that they were on what the *Sunzi* calls death ground, no way out except to fight. This wasn't completely crazy. The United States was expanding its embargoes on Japan including steel and oil, and this created a narrow window to act before the fuel ran out. The Japanese also assumed that they could keep the war limited. America was distracted in Europe, especially if Great Britain fell, and the U.S. did not appear to have much of a stake in Asia.

Therefore Japan might be able to knock the United States out with simultaneous blows against the Philippines and against Pearl Harbor. If that didn't work, then a qualitatively superior Japanese battle fleet could meet a weakened U.S. fleet in a decisive engagement, much like Tsushima. After that the Americans would seek terms. In other words, the Japanese were assuming that what they had done to the Russians in 1905 they could do to the United States and would yield similar strategic and political results. But the United States in 1941 was not Russia in 1905. The United States was distracted by the war in Europe, but it was far more economically and politically stable at home than Russia had been, and it was on the up-slope in terms of national power, not declining.

It wasn't just Japan's enemy that was different, it was also Japanese strategy. In the Russo-Japanese War the Japanese had focused their finite land and sea assets on a single theatre and along parallel lines of advance. In the Second World War they scattered their navy and only a fraction of their army along multiple axes.

As strategically flawed as this was, at the operational level the first phase of Japan's Pacific War was spectacularly successful. In a series of lightning attacks in the winter of 1941–1942 the Japanese sent out pulses of naval, amphibious, air and ground forces into Thailand, Malaya, Sumatra, Java, New Guinea, the Philippines, Rabaul, the Gilberts, Wake, and Guam. Had the Japanese stopped there and transitioned to the defense they might have been a tougher nut to crack, but since they were convinced that follow-on offensives were a strategic necessity, satisfying that principle of continuity, they very quickly got themselves overextended. We'll come back to that in a minute.

The core U.S. assumption concerning war with Japan was that time was on our side. In particular the huge ramp up in naval construction prior to the war meant that a new fleet would soon be on line; hence we could make calculated risks and be strategically opportunistic. With the U.S. operating along secure lines of communication, the Japanese could do very little to obstruct shipping or troop transport from the West Coast to the Central Pacific.

Initial U.S. war plans were very Mahanian, especially War Plan Orange. Orange called for massing the American fleet on the West Coast, sailing out to relieve Guam and the Philippines, followed by a decisive battleship engagement near Japan, and then a blockade of the Japanese home islands. Facing a possible two-front war in Europe and Asia, Orange was revised into Plan Dog, a Europe-first strategy that called for a defensive stance in the Pacific. Between Plan Dog and the damage to the fleet at Pearl Harbor, the U.S. was pretty much stuck on the defensive in early 1942. But this does not mean that they were inactive.

Throughout 1942 Admiral Ernest King, the new chief of naval operations, the head of the U.S. navy, employed what Corbett called the offensive-defensive, strategically defensive, but operationally offensive when the circumstances were right. This is different from Mahan's offensive-defense where you defend yourself by going on the strategic offensive against your opponent. The U.S. could not do that at this point in the war. Instead King set up his Corbettian offensive-defensive along two lines, Hawaii to Midway and Samoa-Fiji-Australia. U.S. aircraft carriers were deployed along those two lines in an elastic configuration that allowed King to shift these precious assets from one line to the other. The idea was to stem any further Japanese advances, but also to harass and wear down the Japanese navy by forcing them to go on offensives, which they could not sustain. In other words it was a cost-imposition strategy.

King was also planning to launch the inevitable counteroffensive west and north along these two axes. That would force Japan to divide their fleet again. President Roosevelt (FDR) was completely on board with this strategy. What the president and Admiral King envisioned was a kind of Jominian strategy at sea, a series of incremental battles where American and Allied forces could leverage local superiority against decisive points. Taking those points was key, but in FDR's mind so, too, was sinking more ships and downing more planes than the Japanese could replace, thus making later U.S. operations more certain of achieving success.

The first test of King's offensive-defensive came at the Battle of Coral Sea in May 1942. Admiral Frank Fletcher had a carrier strike group operating north of the Fiji-Samoa line in the area of the Coral Sea, as a result, he could contest the Japanese attempt to occupy Port Moresby in New Guinea. What evolved was a medium-scale Mahanian fleet-engagement. But instead of big-gun battleships, Coral Sea was a clash between two carrier groups. It was the first all-air battle in naval history.

Technically the Japanese won the battle of the Coral Sea at the tactical level, but they were too weak to press the operational advantage or to pursue Fletcher as he withdrew. At the strategic level, however, Coral Sea was a major setback for Japan. Not only did they fail to capture Port Moresby they suffered irreplaceable losses of aircraft and pilots.

The next Mahanian fleet-on-fleet battle to arise from the Corbettian offensive-defensive was Midway in June of 1942. In this case, the U.S. was forewarned of the attack. The Japanese had also violated one of Mahan's cardinal tenets by dividing their fleet. Yamamoto sent a task force to attack the Aleutians, and at Midway he held his battleships in reserve instead of massing them forward with the carrier strike group. As a result Midway was a pretty evenly matched battle. The U.S. was able to bring three carriers, including the *Yorktown*. *Yorktown* had been heavily damaged at Coral Sea, but was ready to go a month later. Our navy had the added advantage of strike and reconnaissance aircraft flying off Midway and out of Oahu. The Japanese brought four carriers and two battleships to the main fight.

This time the Japanese were on the receiving end of a Tsushima-like shellacking. The U.S. casualties were heavy including one carrier, the *Yorktown*, and several hundred men. The Japanese losses, however, probably turned the tide of the war for good. That included four carriers, a third of Japan's active carrier fleet, and they lost almost 250 aircraft. More precious were the highly trained pilots. That loss of pilots was doubly damaging for Japan because the Japanese did not regularly rotate out experienced pilots to train new air crews.

The combined losses at Midway and Coral Sea were devastating in terms of skill and in terms of corporate knowledge among those aviators. In the spring of 1942, the air balance shifted from the qualitative edge that Japan had once held, to a quantitative and growing qualitative edge on the U.S. side.

Essentially what we have at both Coral Sea and Midway are Mahanian surface engagements but expanded into three dimensions by the addition of submarines and aircraft. Many on both sides of the conflict still thought battleships were the center-piece of naval warfare, but it was becoming increasingly clear that the bombs and torpedoes dropped from aircraft were taking the place of those shells fired from 14-, 16-, and even 18-inch guns of the battleships. We can also see that both of these Mahanian battles evolved out of Corbettian strategies. They evolved out of King's offensive-defensive, and they were also fought to cover or contest amphibious landings. In fact, most of the major fleet actions of the Pacific War coincided with amphibious campaigns.

And yet as lop-sided as it was, Midway was not followed by an all-out American counteroffensive. In fact the next major fleet engagement was still two years away. There are three main reasons for the delay: First, the U.S. was still devoting the majority of its energies to the European theatre. Second: The U.S. naval build-up was not in full swing yet, so King and Nimitz had to basically make do with what they had. This made them generally risk averse when it came to the aircraft carriers.

Third, the geography of the Western and Southwestern Pacific argued against a premature offensive. Specifically, the Japanese held dozens of islands, sporting dozens of airfields and thousands of aircraft. They also had submarines and surface ships patrolling the area. The area was not a wide-open commons; it was a hotly contested zone of layered defenses. Therefore, following the Mahanian spike of spring 1942, Corbettian incrementalism would come back to the fore. And that brings us to Guadalcanal.

Guadalcanal was the first tentative step in King's counteroffensive. The idea was to begin an advance up through the Solomon Islands with the ultimate goal of driving the Japanese out of New Guinea and the Bismarcks. U.S.

marines landed on Guadalcanal in August 1942 and seized the strategically critical air base at Henderson Field. The Japanese were compelled to contest those landings because a U.S. base on Guadalcanal would have scuttled their efforts to interdict the U.S. supplies flowing to Australia. What followed was a complex Corbettian interaction game with both sides trying to use their command of the local seas to enable ground operations on the island. This had a third dimension in the air, with both land-based and carrier aircraft joining the fight.

For Corbett the key to a successful peripheral operation, like Wellington's Peninsular War, is local sea control and if we take him farther into the 20th century a second key is local air control. But even Corbett admits that control is rarely absolute. In fact, at Guadalcanal the United States did not dominate the seas or the air, thus while they were fighting for the island, they were also fighting for control of the sea around it and the air above it.

At sea, the fight for Guadalcanal was pretty even, with both sides losing about two dozen ships. On land, the U.S. marines and their army reinforcements held a numerical advantage for most of the battle, and even when the Japanese outnumbered the Americans they could not muster enough combat power to retake Henderson field. Nearly 2,000 Americans died on Guadalcanal, but the Japanese lost 10 times as many before they were forced to withdraw in February of 1943.

On its face, the air battle also looked pretty even with each side losing over 600 aircraft, but in reality it was another catastrophic setback for Japanese air power. The United States could easily replace the planes and most of the American pilots that went down were recovered. When Japanese pilots went down, operating far from their bases, they were either killed or captured.

Ideally, what you want to do in a peripheral operation is to inflict unrecoverable damage on the enemy's critical military capabilities. Guadalcanal did exactly that to the Japanese navy. This result, however, required the Japanese to cooperate by contesting the landings and by doubling-down to retake Henderson Field. They might have been better off to cede the island. Instead, Guadalcanal burned up precious Japanese manpower, ships, aircraft, and supplies. The campaign also stressed an already overstressed Japanese logistics system and it forced the Japanese to further divide an already weakened and divided fleet.

The subsequent island-hopping campaign replicated many of the Corbettian elements of Guadalcanal, especially the close integration of air, sea, and amphibious operations. Staunch and suicidal Japanese defenses continued to prove a tactical challenge for United States and Allied troops, but for the most part they only compounded Japan's strategic overextension. This is not to say that the United States didn't get sucked into costly amphibious operations. In the Philippines and at Iwo Jima and Okinawa the Japanese found ways to force the army and marines to bleed heavily for objects of relatively low value, but by that point it was probably too late for Japan to reverse the tide.

With the Corbettian noose tightening around Japan there was one last flurry of Mahanian fleet action in mid-to-late 1944. These were the battles of the Philippine Sea and Leyte Gulf. True to the pattern so far, both battles resulted from attempts to land forces on enemy-held islands, amphibious operations. In the case of the Philippine Sea, the Allies were looking to seize air bases in the Marianas. With Leyte, it was MacArthur's long promised return to the Philippines. By this point in the war, the U.S. Navy was no longer fighting at a disadvantage or even at parity with the Japanese. At the Philippine Sea, the U.S. fleet massed 15 carriers and 7 battleships compared to Japan's 9 carriers and 5 battleships.

At Leyte, the ratios were even more lopsided: 34 carriers to Japan's four, and 34 cruisers and battleships to Japan's 23. The losses were just as uneven. In the six months between Philippine Sea and Leyte, the Japanese lost 4 big carriers, 3 smaller carriers, and 13 cruisers and battleships. The U.S. by comparison only lost a handful of ships. Among the Japanese battleships lost was the massive *Musashi,* one of the two biggest battleships ever built. At almost 900 feet long and 70,000 tons, the *Musashi* was equipped with huge 18.1-inch guns that could hurl 3,000-pound shells accurately out to 20 miles. She and her sister-ship, the *Yamato*, were conceived as the core of a new super-Mahanian battle line designed to crush the American fleet.

In reality, their contributions to the war were inconsequential and both were sunk from the air. The problem with the Japanese reading of Mahan was that it was too operational. There was too much of an obsession with decisive fleet engagement and too little attention paid to the foundations of true sea power. The Japanese also tended toward excessively complicated operational plans and all sorts of feints and deceptions that caused them to divide their forces and complicate their command and control. They also tended to be risk averse at the operational levels of war, but more than willing to accept strategic risk and strategic overextension. Given this raft of strategic pathologies, ships like the *Yamato* and *Musashi*, impressive though they were, were about as useful to the Japanese as Nelson's HMS *Victory* would have been.

Before I close, I want to take a look at one more aspect of the naval war in the Pacific: the submarine campaign. Neither Mahan nor Corbett thought much about submarines. After all, they were just beginning to mature when our two theorists were active, but both masters did talk about commerce raiding. In the Pacific, the United States unleashed the most devastating commerce raiding campaign in history. Between submarines, smaller surface ships, and PT boats, the United States obliterated Japanese merchant shipping. The U.S. used what was primarily an independent submarine fleet of individual boats to attack commercial and military shipping, already a weakness for Japan.

As a result, Japan's sea lines of communications were vulnerable to interdiction throughout the Pacific War. The Japanese had tried to make good on their shortcomings in merchant shipping, but they neglected such simple defensive measures as convoys and anti-submarine patrols. Japan's absolute dependence on imported raw materials, critical strategic commodities, magnified the strategic effects of the submarine campaign. By early 1945 Japan had no merchant shipping to speak of and U.S. and Allied submarine commanders had to factor whether or not what was left of the Japanese merchant fleet was worth a spread of torpedoes.

In contrast to America's dispersion of submarines, the Japanese built a small number of very large submarines and attached them as supports and screens for the main body of the fleet. As a result they couldn't effectively harass the

Allies' lines of communication. This was yet another shocking oversight to cap a long list of strategic blunders.

Japan's embrace of new military technology and their mastery of new naval tactics, especially carrier and amphibious operations, were truly impressive. In 1941, pound-for-pound Japan had the best navy in the world, but they had wholly neglected the larger goals of maritime strategy. Bad strategy was compounded by poor, if not completely dysfunctional, relations between Japan's Army and Navy. With a few rare exceptions, the Japanese Army had no interest in the Pacific War and was loath to lend their own navy precious manpower and materiel. Two-thirds of the army was fighting the continental war and this proved to be both a black hole of men and materiel and a drain on shipping and troop transports.

Let's contrast this to Japan's Corbettian coordination between the land and sea in the Russo-Japanese War. In World War II the Japanese Navy was fighting with one hand tied behind its back and against a mighty adversary in a life-and-death struggle about which the army cared little.

Japan held out hope for a short, sharp, and limited war against the United States. At the best this was fanciful and at the worst, insane. The United States could replace ships and aircraft with ease. At Coral Sea, Midway, and especially at Guadalcanal, Japan's one true operational advantage, well-trained aviators, had been sacrificed on the altar of ill-conceived and excessively complicated operational plans. After those disasters it was impossible for the Japanese to reach out and hurt anything of sufficient value to force the United States to negotiate. The tide had turned decisively to the Allies' advantage.

So, by the summer of 1945 we have Japan, an island nation, its fleet mostly sunk and its merchant shipping obliterated. What should naturally follow is either a Mahanian or Corbettian end game, but that is not what happened. The Mahanian end game would have been a long, slow squeeze of the Japanese islands in the style of War Plan Orange. A Corbettian end game would have been the U.S. and its allies taking the war directly to Japan's center of gravity in the style of Wellington at Waterloo. There were plans for both, but neither of these happened and yet Japan surrendered. Why?

For one, and this goes back to my discussion of the continental origins of this war, the Pacific was always a secondary theatre for the Japanese. Therefore defeat in that secondary theatre, no matter how overwhelming, was unlikely to force Japan to quit. This is not to say that the naval war was irrelevant, rather it was a necessary, but not sufficient precondition for Japan's defeat.

In the end, there are at least three theoretical explanations for Japan's surrender, none of which can explain the end game by itself. First there is the maritime theory explanation in which the U.S. destroyed the Japanese navy and its sea-borne commerce. Second is the Clausewitzian explanation in which the Soviet Red Army poured into Manchuria in early August 1945 and demolished Japan's military, its army, its political center of gravity. And third is the air-power explanation, in which the U.S. Air Force rained destruction on every major city in Japan and closed the deal with two Atomic bombs at Hiroshima and Nagasaki.

Which one tipped the scales? Honestly, we still don't know. But when we come back, we'll be looking into that last explanation: air power, air power in theory and practice. I'll see you then.

Air Power in Theory and Practice
Lecture 16

A 1936 science fiction classic called *Things to Come*, a film based on a novel by H. G. Wells, begins with an air raid on London that reduces the great city to poisoned rubble. Less than a decade later, many of the cities of Germany and Japan lay in smoldering ruins, and their populations seemed helpless before the new lords of the air, Britain's Royal Air Force and the U.S. Army Air Forces. The outcome of the war seemed to bear out many of the strategic prognostications of the early air-power theorists, but in this lecture, we'll ask whether theory and practice really aligned that closely.

The History of Air War
- In the opening phases of World War I, dirigibles and airplanes were used for reconnaissance and attached to ground and naval forces in support roles. Over the course of that conflict, however, aircraft began to play larger roles in combat.

- Even at this early point, we can see a dichotomy between tactical/operational missions and strategic missions. On the one hand, we have aircraft coordinating with land and sea campaigns. On the other hand, we have air forces beginning to operate independently and experimenting with bombing as a strategic weapon.

- Bombing raids were launched on London and on Germany's Ruhr valley. By 1918, the aircraft was a regular fixture in the skies over Europe, and while the airplane's overall role in the war was fairly modest, the war drove an overwhelming interest in aircraft and air-war doctrine.

- All the pioneers in air-power theory were veterans of the First World War, and all believed that aircraft would fundamentally transform war and strategy. At the same time, they all owed an intellectual debt to the sea-power theorists of the preceding generation.

- The air, like the sea, is mostly a vast, ungoverned space, an aerial commons. The fact that aircraft are freed from the friction of the ground and the vicissitudes of wind and tide makes air power, in theory, superior to both sea power and land power.

- Where fleets and armies are primarily operational means to political ends, an air force—again, in theory—is a strategic weapon. An air force can strike deep into the enemy's homeland at the outset of a war, without a sequence of land battles or fleet engagements.

Giulio Douhet

- General Giulio Douhet was an Italian military engineer and an early proponent of the rapid mechanization of the Italian military. Even before the outbreak of World War I, Douhet was sold on the strategic significance of air power.

- Although the strategic impact of air power had not yet been tested, Douhet was convinced of several basic theoretical assumptions:
  - All wars in the future would be total wars; hence, from the start, all strategies should be geared toward maximum strategic effect.

  - The third dimension of air war rendered ground and naval forces subordinate, if not superfluous, to strategy.

  - Air power is innately offensive, and the vastness of the aerial commons means that no effective air defense can be mounted against a massed flight of heavy bombers.

  - The goal of strategic bombing is to shatter the morale of the civilian population and, with it, the enemy's means and will to continue the war.

- The first phase of an air war required seizing command of the air. With this, the air force, comprised exclusively of self-defended heavy bombers, would completely ignore tactical support roles and even military targets, focusing instead on bombing the adversary's industry and population centers.

- In the meantime, ground forces would hold the enemy's army in place. A Clausewitzian battle was no longer required; an enemy would simply implode under relentless battering from the air.

- In Douhet's conception, no means would be spared; poison gas, incendiaries, and explosives were all on the table. Ironically, as ghastly as this vision seemed, anything else would have been inhumane and immoral.

Sir Hugh Trenchard
- In Great Britain, one key element of Douhet's vision had already been realized: the Royal Air Force (RAF), created in 1918, was a wholly independent military service. Great Britain also had its own air-power visionary in the person of Sir Hugh Trenchard, the first commander of the RAF.

As first commander of the Royal Air Force, Hugh Trenchard carved out a place for the RAF in policing the far-flung British Empire from the air.

- Trenchard echoed and amplified Douhet's argument that without command of the air, ground and naval forces were doomed. But Trenchard's theory of air war was not simply about the indiscriminate bombing of urban areas. He identified vital infrastructure nodes and key industries that should be targeted for maximum strategic effects.

- The physical destruction and logistical disruptions caused by effective targeting would be amplified by psychological shock. Such operations would, however, require highly detailed economic and logistical intelligence on the enemy.

- Trenchard shared many theoretical assumptions with Douhet:
  - Command of the air was the key to victory.

  - Command of the air could be seized only by going on the offensive at the earliest possible moment in the war.

  - Physical destruction is desirable, but it is psychological shock that will break the enemy's will to fight.

- Although Trenchard and other British air-power theorists maintained a primary focus on offensive strategic strike, they tried to balance those demands with air defense of the homeland and tactical support to ground and naval forces.

General William Mitchell
- Across the Atlantic, General William "Billy" Mitchell was America's leading air-power advocate. Working on the British model, Mitchell advocated dividing U.S. air forces into tactical and strategic missions, although he remained convinced that strategic strike against the enemy's homeland was the primary mission of the air force.

- After the war, Mitchell began lobbying both for an independent air force and for Congress to appropriately fund the air services.

Mitchell was also convinced that the airplane had fundamentally undermined the utility of big battleships.

- Despite his repeated condemnations of the U.S. Navy, Mitchell was still a Mahanian at heart. He saw the same virtuous cycle in air power that Mahan saw in sea power. A nation blessed with geographical advantages, home to a technologically advanced and air-minded population, and enjoying the benefits of unabashed political support must become a true air power.

- Mitchell shared with Douhet and Trenchard the belief in the offensive to gain command of the air, deep strikes against the enemy's vital centers, and the preeminence of psychological shock over physical destruction.

- Mitchell did not live to see the U.S. Air Force become an independent service, but a young cadre of Mitchell protégés, known as the "Bomber Mafia," began to have a major influence on air-power doctrine.
  - The members of the Bomber Mafia were the progenitors of the concept of daylight precision bombing—a way to destroy or disrupt critical nodes in the enemy's "industrial web."

  - This was the doctrine that the Army Air Force had on hand when the United States entered World War II.

Air Power in Action
- The Combined Bomber Offensive (CBO) was a joint Anglo-American strategic bombing campaign against the Luftwaffe and the industrial web of Germany. Although it was an Allied effort, the campaign was divided primarily into the American Eighth Air Force launching daylight precision attacks and the RAF engaged in nighttime area/saturation bombing.

- The CBO began in June of 1943 as an attempt to focus round-the-clock bombing on Germany's war-making capacity. What followed was the largest and costliest air campaign to date, yet its effects diverged dramatically from the strategic predictions of prewar theorists.

- The early air-power theorists had fairly simple, almost mechanistic views of how strategic bombing would work. Theoretically, if enough bombs were put on the right targets, then the enemy would cave. But what was missing from that theoretical perspective was an appreciation of interaction and adaptation in war.
  o Early air-power theorists also tended to overemphasize the blessings of the air and disregard such challenges as wind and weather.

  o Further, the idea that an effective defense against a massed air assault was impossible proved untrue. Massed bomber attacks were relatively easy to track, and fighter planes could approach a slow-moving mass of bombers from any angle.

  o It was only when the Allies were able to provide long-range fighter escorts that this problem was solved. Even then, the strategic bombing campaign fell short in several categories, including accuracy, bomb damage, and psychological effects.

- As much as the theorists had underestimated the power of air defense, they had also grossly overestimated the ability of bombers to find and hit targets. Inflicting damage on Germany's industrial web took time; it was not until late in the war that core German military industries were decisively degraded.

- Ironically, the most important effects of the strategic bombing campaign in Europe were tactical and operational.
  o Bombing raids were interdicted by the Luftwaffe at great cost to the bomber fleets, but when the Allied bombers got long-range escorts, the Luftwaffe was nearly wiped out. This changed the operational air balance on the Eastern and Western fronts, making Allied and Soviet advances easier.

o The Germans were forced to divert thousands of their antitank guns and hundreds of thousands of personnel to antiaircraft missions, further easing the Allied operational advance.

o Finally, the damage done to German industry, especially the oil industry, and the destruction of the German rail system made German armies less maneuverable in the face of Allied armies, who had unmolested interior lines of supply.

Air Campaigns against Japan

- In the Pacific theater, the Boeing B-29 Superfortress was a significant improvement over the previous generation of bombers in terms of range and bomb loads.

- Starting in March of 1945 and for the next five months, B-29s dropped tens of thousands of tons of explosives and incendiaries on Japan and thousands of mines in Japan's coastal and inland waters. By the summer of 1945, nearly every major city in Japan had been destroyed from the air.

- Still, the intercepts of signal traffic in June and July of 1945 showed that the Japanese remained well armed and prepared to defend the home islands. Their means and will were as yet unbroken, even in the face of the most ferocious bombing campaign ever conceived. The promise of air power had fallen short.

- That conclusion, however, doesn't take into account the atomic bombs. For all of their apparent shortcomings, it might be the case that the air-power theorists were only a bit premature when it came to predicting the impact of air-power technology. The marriage of Superfortresses with super-weapons, which took place over Hiroshima and Nagasaki, approached the realization of Douhet's vision: the short, sharp, will-shattering blow that leads directly to capitulation.

Suggested Reading

Emerson, "Operation Pointblank."

MacIsaac, "Voices from the Central Blue."

Meilinger, ed., *The Paths of Heaven*.

Pape, *Bombing to Win*, chapter 4.

Warner, "Douhet, Mitchell, Seversky."

Questions to Consider

1. What are the principal tenets of early air-power theory?

2. Based on the strategic bombing campaigns of World War II, which early air-power assumptions were the most valid? Which assumptions were the most flawed?

Air Power in Theory and Practice
Lecture 16—Transcript

There is this 1936 science fiction classic called *Things to Come*, a film based on the novel by that early air-power visionary H. G. Wells. The movie begins with a shocking air raid on London. In short order, the great city is reduced to poisoned rubble and the British people are reduced to a barbaric struggle for survival.

This was science fiction, but less than a decade later many of the cities of Germany and Japan lay in smoldering ruins, and their populations lay helpless before the new Lords of the Air, Britain's Royal Air Force and the United States Army Air Forces. *Things to Come* was produced at the peak of speculation about the decisive effects of this terrifying and fascinating new weapons system, strategic bombing. And it captured the spirit of the day. The outcome of the war a decade later seemed to bear out many of the strategic prognostications of the early air power theorists, but did theory and practice really align that closely?

Before we get to that question and to the strategic effects of the bombing campaigns of the Second World War, let's start by reviewing the early history of air war and the first generation of air-war theorists. In the opening phases of World War I we have aircraft, both dirigibles and airplanes, being used for reconnaissance and generally attached to the ground and naval forces in a support role. Over the course of that conflict, however, aircraft began to play larger and larger combat roles. Even at this early point we can see a dichotomy between the tactical and operational missions and strategic missions. On the one hand we have aircraft coordinating with land and sea campaigns, providing close air support, interdicting enemy forces, and attacking enemy aircraft. The successful Allied offensive against the St. Mihiel salient in September 1918 was supported by a combined air fleet of nearly 1,500 planes and dirigibles.

On the other hand we have air forces beginning to operate independently and experimenting with bombing as a strategic weapon, striking directly at enemy homelands.

Bombing raids were launched on London and on Germany's Ruhr Valley. By 1918, the aircraft was a regular fixture in the skies over Europe, and while the airplane's overall role in the war was fairly modest, the war drove an overwhelming interest in aircraft and air-war doctrine. In fact, all of the early theoretical pioneers were veterans of the First World War and all believed that these slow and fragile aircraft were about to fundamentally transform war and strategy.

But before we get to our air power theorists, I do want to point out that all of them owed an intellectual debt to the sea-power theorists of the preceding generation. If we step back and think about it for a second, this makes a lot of sense. After all the air, like the sea, is mostly a vast ungoverned space, a kind of great aerial commons. Thus to paraphrase Francis Bacon, he who commands the air can take as much or as little of the war on land as he wants. But the aerial commons has an advantage over the maritime commons: it is above rather than adjacent to land. Maritime powers, those whales we have been talking about, have always struggled to make their power felt against elephants. How does a whale grow legs? Meanwhile the elephant faces the reverse problem. How does the elephant grow fins to compete with the sea power? Air power on the other hand eliminates these problems of asymmetry because now you can take the war directly to the enemy's homeland without regard for geographical or materiel impediments.

Aircraft are freed from the friction of the ground and the vicissitudes of wind and tide. Air power, again in theory, is therefore an order of magnitude superior to both sea power and land power. Where fleets and armies are primarily operational means to political ends, an air force, in theory at least, is a strategic weapon.

From very early in their history, aircraft, and especially bombers, have been thought of as a way to derive immediate strategic effects. In theory, an air force can strike deep into the enemy's homeland at the very outset of the war. It can strike with unprecedented speed and lethality. And it can strike without having to bother with a sequence of land battles or fleet engagements. In the modern era of total war, and especially in the aftermath of World War I, the mass carnage of that conflict, air power was alternately appealing and terrifying.

Our first air-power theorist is General Giulio Douhet. Douhet was an Italian military engineer and an early proponent of the rapid mechanization of the Italian military. Even before the outbreak of World War I, Douhet was also sold on the strategic significance of another machine: the airplane. Douhet saw air power as the ultimate strategic weapon.

Douhet was, therefore, intensely critical of Italy's use of aircraft to support ground operations. Air power was too potentially decisive a weapon to be shackled to parochial ground commanders and their tactical obsessions. As early as 1911–1912 Douhet was lobbying for the establishment of an entirely independent Italian air force, an air force whose core mission was to be the strategic bombing of enemy cities. Even though the strategic impact of air power had never been tested, Douhet was convinced of several basic theoretical assumptions: All wars in the future will be total wars, hence from the start all strategies should be geared toward maximum strategic effect. The third dimension of air war has rendered ground and naval forces subordinate, if not superfluous, to strategy. Airpower is innately offensive and the vastness of the aerial commons means that no effective air defense could be mounted against a massed flight of heavy bombers: the bomber would always get through.

The goal of strategic bombing is to shatter the morale of the civilian population and with it the enemy's means and will to continue the war. In practice this meant that the first phase of an air war required seizing command of the air. With command of the air in hand, the air force, comprised exclusively of self-defended heavy bombers, would completely ignore tactical support roles and even military targets, including the enemy air force, and instead focus on bombing the foundations of the adversary's national power, in other words its industry and its population centers.

In the meantime, the ground forces would hold the enemy's army in place while the nation was hollowed out from within. A Clausewitzian battle was no longer required; an enemy would simply implode under relentless battering from the air.

I should point out here that in Douhet's conception, no means would be spared, poison gas, incendiaries, and explosives were all on the table.

Ironically, as ghastly as this vision seemed, anything else would have been inhumane and immoral. "The direct attack against the people," Douhet said, "will hasten the decision, and shorten the war."

True to his engineering background, Douhet offered a raft of mathematical formulas for predicting both the physical and psychological impact of X number of bombers, dropping Y number of type-Z bombs on a major urban area. At the same time he was cognizant of the limitations of the aircraft available in his own day. His was a prophetic vision, but one which any reasonable political leader or military commander had to take seriously.

Douhet was not shy in his criticism of Italian policy and strategy in the First World War, and he was court-martialed for insubordination. He was eventually cleared of the charges and promoted to general, but his later career was dedicated primarily to publishing his theories. Douhet's writings, especially his oft-translated *The Command of the Air*, found an immediate global audience, partly out of horror, partly out of curiosity, but primarily because Douhet's was the first lucid and comprehensive treatment of the new air weapon. In short order, air-power theorists in the militaries of all of the great powers were forced to engage with Douhet's theories.

In Great Britain, one key element of Douhet's vision had already been realized. The Royal Air Force (RAF), created in 1918, was a wholly independent military service. Great Britain also had its own air power visionary in the person of Sir Hugh Trenchard, the first commander of the RAF. Like Douhet, Trenchard was a veteran of the First World War, but unlike the Italian theorist, Trenchard had trained as a pilot.

During the First World War Trenchard rose through the ranks of the rapidly forming British Air forces. For the most part, his energies were devoted to reconnaissance and tactical air support to British units operating in France and Belgium. Trenchard wasn't opposed to strategic air missions in theory, but at that point in the war he believed that tactical support was a better use of Britain's limited air assets. In 1918, however, Trenchard was reassigned to the strategic arm of the air force where he oversaw operations against Germany's industrial heartland.

After the war, Trenchard was appointed chief of staff of the new Royal Air Force and so began a 20-year struggle to keep the RAF an independent service. In between these bureaucratic battles, Trenchard proved to be an innovative air-power theorist and practitioner. In a foreshadowing of American unmanned aerial vehicle operations today, Trenchard carved out a place for the RAF in policing the far-flung British empire from the air, including over Iraq, and in what are now the lawless border regions of Pakistan and Afghanistan, where the RAF supported the army's counterinsurgency campaigns. Closer to home, Trenchard became a strident advocate of offensive strategic air strikes to shatter the enemy's economy and society, but above all to shatter its will.

Douhet argued that without command of the air, ground and naval forces were doomed. Trenchard echoed and amplified those sentiments for a British audience still reeling from the First World War. But Trenchard's theory of air war was not simply about the indiscriminate bombing of urban areas; he was looking for the maximum strategic effects. As a result, he began the process of identifying vital infrastructure nodes (rail yards, bridges, and ports) and key industries (coal, steel, and armaments) that should be targeted for those maximum strategic effects.

The physical destruction and logistical disruptions that this caused would be amplified by psychological shock. Effective targeting, however, would obviously require highly detailed economic and logistical intelligence on the enemy. Air strategy hinged on knowing the enemy, or more precisely, knowing how his economy, society, and political system functioned.

It is not surprising then that air planners regularly pored over railway schedules, industrial output records, and commodity price reports. Predicting an air assault's effect on these tangible elements of national power was hard enough, predicting the psychological and human effects was another thing entirely.

Operating in a senior position within the British government and military, Trenchard was not nearly as hyperbolic as Douhet, but he did share many of the same theoretical assumptions. Command of the air was the key to victory. Command of the air can only be seized by going on the offensive at the earliest possible moment in the war. Physical destruction is important, but it is the psychological shocks that will break the enemy's will to fight.

Nonetheless, Trenchard and other British air-power theorists, especially Trenchard's brilliant protégé Jack Slessor, managed to walk air-power theory back a few steps from Douhet's extremist zealotry. For one, while they maintained a primary focus on offensive strategic strike, they tried to balance those demands with air defense of the homeland and tactical support to ground and naval forces.

Trenchard and Slessor both accepted that the air force was not likely to win the war all on its own, and as a result would have to coordinate with and support the army and the navy. Leave it to the British to develop theorists who thought about air power in the same ways that Sir Julian Corbett had thought about sea power.

Across the Atlantic it was General William "Billy" Mitchell, who was America's leading air-power advocate. A privileged but restless young man, Mitchell joined the army at the outbreak of the Spanish-American War and between 1898 and 1901 served in Cuba, the Philippines, China, and Alaska. He grew into a cosmopolitan army officer with a global outlook. He was also fascinated by the promise of the aircraft and he earned his wings just in time to ship off to France in 1917.

In France, Mitchell made the acquaintance of Hugh Trenchard, and working on the British model he advocated dividing U.S. air forces into tactical and strategic missions. Trenchard would remain a major influence on Mitchell's thinking about air power.

Even at this early point Mitchell saw the air service operating in these two realms, first by strategic strike directed at the destruction of the enemy's air forces and homeland, and second in a support role to surface forces. It was Mitchell who coordinated the American piece of the massive air assault for the St. Mihiel offensive in 1918. He remained convinced, however, that strategic strike against the enemy's homeland was the primary mission of the air force, and as such it had to be a separate service free from the tactical and operational imperatives of the army.

After the war, Colonel Mitchell returned to the states and began lobbying both for an independent air force and for Congress to appropriately fund the air services. To Mitchell, if America was to remain a great power it needed to become a great air power, an air power in military, civilian, and technological terms. Mitchell was also convinced that the airplane had fundamentally undermined the utility of big battleships. Building battleships was a waste of resources, resources better committed to building an air force.

Remember, this is in 1920 and we are only 15 years past Tsushima and less than a generation into the *Dreadnought* era, and yet this upstart claimed that wood and canvas planes could sink a battleship. But that is exactly what happened in July 1921 when bombs dropped from six of Mitchell's wood and canvas planes sank the German battleship, the *Ostfriesland* in a demonstration off the Chesapeake Capes.

Mitchell took the *Ostfriesland* test as a vindication of his vision and accelerated his lobbying for an independent air service. The air forces, not the navy, should be America's first line of defense. Aircraft, which would soon be able to reach anywhere on the planet, could only be stopped by other aircraft. This made both technological sense and economic sense. Mitchell did the math for his readers: If a $20,000 dollar bomber could sink a $45 million dollar battleship, why was the navy ordering new battleships?

But despite his repeated condemnations of the U.S. Navy, Mitchell was still a Mahanian at heart. He saw the same virtuous cycle in air power that Mahan saw in sea power. A nation blessed with geographical advantages, home to a technologically advanced and air-minded population and enjoying the benefits of unabashed political support must become a true air power.

During the 1920s, the period of his greatest activity, Mitchell struck up a friendship and a long correspondence with Douhet and saw to it that translations of Douhet's book, *The Command of the Air*, were circulated among his fellow officers. To be honest, Mitchell did not add much of substance to early air-power theory. If anything, what we see here are primarily variations on similar themes.

Mitchell shared with Douhet and Trenchard the belief in the offensive to gain command of the air, deep strikes against the enemy's vital centers, and the preeminence of psychological shock over physical destruction.

On the other hand, Mitchell argued that bomber fleets could and should have escort fighters. Moreover, with the *Ostfriesland* test, Mitchell actually demonstrated the promise of air power, and his books, articles, and opinion pieces anticipate a whole range of air capabilities, such as remotely piloted drones, capabilities that we now take for granted.

Mitchell's vanity and arrogance caused him to run afoul of his superiors and he was found guilty in a well-publicized court martial in 1925; Gary Cooper played Mitchell in the movie version three decades later. Mitchell died a civilian in 1936, but was posthumously reinstated and promoted to the rank of major-general.

He did not live to see the United States Air Force become an independent service, but a young cadre of Mitchell protégés, known as the "Bomber Mafia," began to have a major influence on air-power doctrine. The aptly named Bomber Mafia were the progenitors of the concept of daylight precision bombing: A way to destroy or disrupt critical nodes in the enemy's "industrial web" so as to paralyze his ability to wage war and to shatter his will to resist. This was the doctrine that the Army Air Force had on hand when the United States entered World War II.

Now that we have gone over the basics of early air-power theory, let's take a look at air power in action in the European and Pacific theatres. In particular, I want to contrast what strategic bombing promised in theory over against what it actually delivered in World War II.

First, let's consider the Combined Bomber Offensive, or CBO. This was a joint Anglo-American strategic bombing campaign against the Luftwaffe and the industrial web of Germany. While an Allied effort, the campaign was divided primarily into the American Eighth Air Force launching daylight precision attacks and the Royal Air Force engaged in nighttime area, or saturation, bombing.

The CBO began in June of 1943 after a deal was struck at the Casablanca conference to focus round-the-clock bombing on Germany's war-making capacity. What followed was the biggest and costliest air campaign to date. In numbers of planes and tons of bombs it dwarfed even the loftiest prescriptions of the prewar theorists, and yet in both near and long-term effects it diverged dramatically from their strategic predictions.

The early air-power theorists had fairly simple, almost mechanistic, views of how strategic bombing would work. Theoretically, if you put enough bombs on enough of the right targets then the enemy would cave. But what was missing from that theoretical perspective was an appreciation of interaction and adaptation in war. And early air-power theorists also tended to overemphasize the blessings of the air and to disregard the challenges of the air. In the first place, the heavens are a tough place to operate. It turns out that wind and weather are to air power what terrain is to land power.

Secondly, the same logic that was employed to claim that an effective defense against a massed air assault was impossible actually proved the opposite. Massed bomber attacks were relatively easy to track, especially after the introduction of radar and ground tracking stations. In addition, the three-dimensional nature of the aerial commons meant that fast and lethal fighter planes could approach a slow-moving mass of bombers from any angle. This was the reason why the British shifted from daytime operations to nighttime operations when the bombers were less vulnerable to German fighters,but also less accurate in their strikes.

When the U.S. Eighth Air Force entered the fray, they stuck with daytime precision bombing. This proved to be costly and premature. In the daylight raid on the ball-bearing plants at Schweinfurt in October 1943, Eighth Air Force sortied 228 aircraft. Of those 62 were lost and 138 were damaged. Nearly 600 airmen lost their lives and another 65 were taken prisoner. This was just one bloody vignette in a long and costly interaction game in the skies over Germany.

In total, Eighth Air Force suffered 47,000 casualties and thousands of aircraft lost. Eighth Air Force accounted for close to 10 percent of all the Americans killed in the Second World War. The bomber did not always get through. It was only when the Allies were able to provide long-range fighter escorts, that the Luftwaffe problem was solved. Even then, the strategic bombing campaign still fell short in several critical categories, especially in terms of accuracy, bomb damage, and psychological effects.

As much as the theorists had underestimated the power of air defense, they had grossly overestimated the ability of bomber to find and hit targets, to cause enough damage to shut factories or to sever rail-lines, and they overestimated the psychological fragility of German society. German morale did take a beating, but the German people were not going to rise up and demand an end to the war.

What about the damage to Germany's industrial web? That took time and it was not until very late in the war that the core military industries were decisively degraded. What then were the effects of the strategic bombing campaign in Europe? Ironically, the most important effects of strategic bombing were tactical and operational. Bombing raids were interdicted by the Luftwaffe at great cost to the bomber fleets, but when the Allied bombers got long-range escorts, like the P-51 Mustang, the Luftwaffe was pretty much wiped out.

This changed the operational air balance on the Eastern and Western fronts, making Allied and Soviet advances easier. The Germans were also forced to divert thousands of their big anti-tank guns and hundreds of thousands of personnel to anti-aircraft missions, further easing the Allied operational advance. Finally, the damage done to German industry, especially the oil industry, and the destruction of the German rail system made German armies less maneuverable in the face of Allied armies who had unmolested interior lines of supply.

If there were strategic effects, they were largely unintentional. For example, the bombing campaign drove Hitler to accelerate the V1, V2, and V3 programs to exact vengeance on England. That was a waste of German resources, but such a wasteful strategic distortion was not what air-power theory promised. In both the European and Pacific theatres it was the tactical and operational contributions of aircraft that were the most impressive, aircraft carriers and integrated close air support to amphibious and ground attacks swung the operational balance to the Allies' favor.

But let's return to strategic bombing and the air campaigns against Japan. In the Pacific theatre, Curtis LeMay's XXIst Bomber Command had a new wonder weapon, the Boeing B-29 Superfortress. For all of its technical glitches, the B-29 was a significant improvement over the previous generation of bombers in terms of range and in terms of bomb-loads. Weighing in at over 100,000 lbs, a B-29 could carry 15,000–20,000 lbs of bombs, three to four times the load of a B-17, and it had a combat range of 3,200 miles. B-29s operating out of the Marianas could be over Tokyo in seven hours.

From November 1944 to March 1945 XXIst Bomber Command had engaged in high-altitude daytime bombing of Japanese military and industrial targets. In the early morning hours of March 10th, 1945, however, 300 Superfortresses hit Tokyo with over 3 million pounds of incendiary bombs. In the conflagration that followed 260,000 buildings were destroyed and perhaps as many as 100,000 people were killed.

Over the next five months, masses of B-29s dropped tens of thousands of tons of explosives and incendiaries on Japan. They also dropped thousands of mines in Japan's coastal and inland waters. By the summer of 1945 every major city in Japan, with the exception of the spiritual center at Kyoto, had been destroyed from the air. XXIst Bomber Command then turned to smaller cities and Japan's dispersed industries.

By his own calculations, LeMay believed the war would be over sometime in October after he had destroyed the last of Japan's surviving industry on or around the first of that month. In all, the costs of the air campaign over Japan were relatively light, relative that is to other theatres, with 2,600 airmen killed and around 400 planes lost. Many of those planes succumbed to malfunctions, not enemy fire, since the Japanese had few means to defend against the raids. Over Japan, the bomber almost always got through.

The damage to Japan was therefore epic, and yet our intercepts of Japanese signals traffic in June and July of 1945 showed that the Japanese were still well-armed and well-prepared to defend the home islands and were capable of inflicting hundreds of thousands of casualties on an invasion force. Their means and will were as yet unbroken even in the face of the most ferocious bombing campaign ever conceived. The promise of air power had fallen short yet again.

But that was before the atomic bombs. For all of their apparent shortcomings, it might be the case that the air-power theorists were just a bit premature when it came to predicting the impact of air-power technology. Maybe when you marry Superfortresses with super-weapons, as the United States did at Hiroshima and Nagasaki, you might get close to realizing Douhet's vision. In other words, that short, sharp, will-shattering blow that leads directly to capitulation.

At the same time, we need to realize that while the atomic bombs certainly influenced Hirohito's decision to surrender, we are talking about two weapons dropped on an already exhausted and devastated nation, a nation facing military defeat on land, at sea, and in the air. How the scales were weighted to tip Hirohito toward surrender is still not clear, even decades after the fact.

Ultimately, when it comes to total war, a war waged for unlimited objectives, a war against states motivated by perverse ideologies, a war contested on a global scale, when it comes to that kind of war no single theorist or single theoretical paradigm can adequately explain the outcome.

From Rolling Thunder to Instant Thunder
Lecture 17

We ended our last lecture by alluding to the specter of the atomic bomb, but in this lecture, we will put nuclear weapons aside for the moment and instead look at the thinking of American air-power theorists in relation to the use of conventional bombing in the decades after World War II. We will then analyze a few examples of conventional air power in action: Robert McNamara's Rolling Thunder campaign against North Vietnam, John Warden's Instant Thunder plan for the 1990–1991 war against Iraq, and the NATO air operations over Yugoslavia and Libya.

Conventional Air Power after World War II

- Even with the introduction of nuclear weapons, Americans quickly learned that conventional air power still had an important role to play. The second generation of air theorists continued to stress the value of independent strategic strikes and to highlight the psychological impact of bombing over destruction of the enemy's means to fight.

- Early Air Force doctrine enshrined the centrality of strategic bombing, both nuclear and conventional. While the Air Force continued to support surface operations, its core mission remained strategic. Air power, even conventional air power, still promised the most direct means to compel the enemy to do one's will.

- In an era of nuclear weapons and superpower rivalry, there was much to justify this focus. Strategic air power also satisfied the American predilection for high technology and strategies that leveraged America's wealth over investment in large standing militaries.

Rolling Thunder

- The first big test of conventional air power against a Maoist-style people's war took place in Vietnam. Initial Air Force plans for the bombing campaign in Southeast Asia focused almost exclusively on strategic strikes against North Vietnam, not attacks on the insurgency in the South.

- The air plan remained true to the tenets of early air-power theorists in that the campaign was designed to be intense and massive in order to maximize strategic shock and speed the capitulation of the North. This would be accomplished by rapidly destroying both North Vietnam's means and its will to continue the struggle.

- The Johnson administration modified these initial plans in favor of a more graduated air strategy that would inflict calibrated pain on North Vietnam but prevent Chinese intervention. The compromise was the Rolling Thunder campaign envisioned by Secretary of Defense Robert McNamara.

- As a former Air Force officer, McNamara was as convinced of the strategic efficacy of air power as his superiors, but as Secretary of Defense, he felt obliged to balance the "go-big, go-early" inclinations of the Air Force against the need to avoid a repeat of Korea.
  - o A major Chinese intervention in Vietnam was not likely, but it was certainly a possibility, and such a scenario had daunting nuclear repercussions.

  - o Rolling Thunder, therefore, was primarily directed toward convincing North Vietnam to stop its support of the insurgency in South Vietnam. Such strategic persuasion hinged as much on what targets the bombers avoided as on those they hit.

  - o Given that the United States could destroy almost any target it chose, the assumption was that it could hold hostage those targets of particularly high value to North Vietnam by not bombing them. The idea was that restraint would induce cooperation.

  - o Secondarily, Rolling Thunder would devastate the industry and infrastructure of the North so as to deny Hanoi the ability to support the Vietcong.

o   It soon became apparent, however, that strategic persuasion was not working and that the air interdiction side of the campaign should become the primary focus.

- Between 1965 and 1968, U.S. planes dropped more tons of bombs on North Vietnam than they had on Japan during World War II, yet Rolling Thunder was an abject failure. The United States could not inflict sufficient pain on the North to force it to renounce the objective of overthrowing the Saigon government.

- Air-power advocates regularly point to Rolling Thunder as an object lesson in how not to run an air war. Excessive political meddling, restrictive targeting lists, and gradualism all prevented the air weapon from achieving its strategic potential.

- Vietnam offers mixed lessons on the strategic utility of air power. Better targeting, better technology, and stealth aircraft promised to bring conventional strategic bombing a step closer to its theoretical promise.

Instant Thunder

- The plan for air-power use in the Gulf War of 1991, Operation Instant Thunder, was a product of the lessons learned from Rolling Thunder's failure. Designed by U.S. Air Force Colonel John Warden, it was also meant to serve as proof of concept of the strategic paralysis that air power can deliver.

- Warden's concept of air power hinged on the innate superiority of air power as a strategic instrument.
  o   At best, land and naval forces can strike only operational centers of gravity, the enemy's armed forces.

  o   By contrast, properly targeted and sufficiently destructive air strikes against the enemy's strategic centers of gravity can directly contribute to victory and can do so at relatively low cost and low risk.

- Warden parsed these different centers of gravity at the different levels of war as a system of five concentric rings. They are, in increasing levels of importance from the outer ring to the inner: the enemy's armed forces, civilian population, infrastructure, "system essentials" (food, fuel, electricity, and communications), and leadership.

- If we think of an adversary as an organism, then striking the brain (the leadership) and the nervous system (system essentials) will naturally have a more direct and paralyzing result than hacking away at the limbs, or outer rings.

- Given the conventional wisdom on the failures of Rolling Thunder, in particular, the negative connotations of civilian "meddling," it is ironic that Warden's air-power doctrine demanded a high degree of political oversight. But the more strategic the target, especially an enemy head of state, the more essential it is to have senior civilians give the final approval.

- The first draft of Instant Thunder called for a week of attacks on 84 targets almost exclusively in the inner two rings of Saddam Hussein's regime.
  o Over time and under pressure from his superiors, Warden modified the plan to include strikes that would physically paralyze the Iraqi army.

  o In the end, a modified version of Instant Thunder became just one phase of a four-phase air plan that targeted essentially everything of any military, economic, or communications significance in Iraq and Kuwait.

- Precision-guided munitions, the centerpiece of Instant Thunder, represented just a fraction of the ordnance dropped on Iraq. Nonetheless, Warden and many in the Air Force were convinced that the rest of the air and ground war were sideshows to the paralyzing effects of Instant Thunder.

- Others, however, remained skeptical. Robert Pape, a specialist in international security affairs, challenged many of Warden's core assumptions. For Pape, air strikes in Warden's outer rings—against the enemy's armed forces and national infrastructure—can also win wars.

Air War over Yugoslavia

- In March of 1999, NATO initiated a campaign of air strikes against the government and military of Yugoslavia. The objectives of the campaign were to force Yugoslav president Slobodan Milosevic to stop the ethnic cleansing of the Albanian population in Kosovo, withdraw his forces from Kosovo, accept UN peacekeepers, and abide by the terms of the Rambouillet Accords.

- Targeting of the campaign corresponded to four of Warden's five rings: leadership, regime infrastructure, national infrastructure, and the Yugoslav military.

- The NATO strategy was initially coercive, aiming to punish Milosevic and the Serbian military and force them to accede to NATO demands. Very quickly, however, it evolved into a denial strategy, with the aim of denying Milosevic the means to conduct purges.

- The early bombing campaign stiffened support for Milosevic, but over time, economic pain and popular unrest started to wear on the regime. The strikes on the Yugoslav military proved particularly effective against large bases and columns of heavy machinery, but they did not stop small groups of Yugoslav infantry from terrorizing Albanians or driving them out of Kosovo. Milosevic ultimately caved to NATO demands in June of 1999.

- In the final analysis, Kosovo looks like a partial vindication of strategic bombing as a decisive instrument in war. With NATO in complete control of the air, a mix of coercion and denial seemed to work against a weak and isolated regime and in a war fought for limited objectives.

Air Campaign over Libya

- NATO air strikes against the regime of Muammar Qaddafi began in mid-March 2011 in response to Tripoli's bloody crackdown against protestors. From the outset, the goal of the NATO campaign seems to have been regime change.

   o The early air plan was a mix of coercion to convince Qaddafi to stop attacking the anti-regime elements and denial to prevent him from attacking the rebels.

   o As in Kosovo, the strategy evolved into something more aggressive. Here, it became a campaign of brute force against the regime and the Libyan military.

- Denial strikes against the Libyan army and its mercenary allies were ostensibly about protecting the protestors, but in reality, they were primarily designed to help the rebels make the transition from guerilla tactics to conventional operations.

- When it became clear that Qaddafi was not going stop his campaign of repression, then forceful regime change became the only option. At that point, coercion and denial were transformed into brute force.

- In the face of Qaddafi's recalcitrance and the relative military weakness of the rebels, NATO air power decisively altered the balance of power and allowed the Libyan resistance to go on the offensive. The rebels on the ground never did become particularly powerful or militarily proficient, but they were strong enough to defeat an army that had been driven back from rebel strongholds and pummeled relentlessly from the air.

Modern Theories of Conventional Air Power

- Contemporary theorists have given us three basic approaches to modern conventional air power:

   o Warden: Paralyze the enemy regime with targeted strikes in the inner rings.

○ Pape: Coerce the enemy with a mix of strikes designed to affect both its means and will.

○ Libya: Employ full-spectrum targeting with the aim of aiding a local surrogate and toppling the enemy regime.

• It's likely that future air campaigns will end up being a combination of all three. The ratio of approaches in that combination will depend on the nature of the war, the strategy of the adversary, and the type of operational environment.

Suggested Reading

Byman and Waxman, "Kosovo and the Great Air Power Debate."

Lake, "The Limits of Coercive Airpower."

Pape, *Bombing to Win*, chapters 6 and 7.

Warden, "The Enemy as a System."

Questions to Consider

1. What were the critical assumptions about air power that informed Rolling Thunder?

2. How would you modify air-power theory based on the lessons learned from Kosovo and Libya?

From Rolling Thunder to Instant Thunder
Lecture 17—Transcript

At the end of our last lecture we talked about the atomic bomb. We'll explore the strategic issues surrounding nuclear warfare in the next lecture. But in this lecture we are going to put nuclear weapons aside for the moment and instead look at how American air-power theorists thought about the use of conventional bombing in the decades after World War II.

We will then look at a few examples of conventional air power in action. In particular, we'll analyze Robert McNamara's Rolling Thunder campaign against North Vietnam, John Warden's Instant Thunder plan for the 1990–1991 war against Iraq, and the NATO air operations over Yugoslavia and Libya.

Even with the introduction of nuclear weapons, Americans quickly learned that conventional air power still had an important role to play. In the Korean War, the newly independent U.S. Air Force fought a hotly contested air war over the peninsula. B-29s, those Superfortresses that LeMay had used against Japan, were rolled out early in Korea to attack industrial targets in the North. When the Chinese and Soviets intervened to rescue the North from certain defeat, the air war morphed into high-speed dogfights between Soviet and American fighter jets. For the most part, the air forces of both sides engaged in a slugfest to achieve enough air superiority to attack ground forces. The tactical and operational nature of the air war in Korea did not, however, deflect the second generation of air-power theorists from the core strategic tenets of Douhet, Trenchard, and Mitchell.

In almost every way the second generation of air theorists kept close theoretical faith with the first. They continued to stress the value of independent strategic strike and continued to highlight the psychological impact of bombing, destroying the enemy's will to fight, over and above the destruction of the enemy's means to fight. This is not surprising given that almost all of the post war leadership of the Air Force were members of the Bomber Mafia.

Air Force generals like Hap Arnold and Ira Eaker carried the Bomber Mafia concept forward. They enshrined the centrality of strategic bombing, both nuclear and conventional, in early Air Force doctrine. While the Air Force continued to support surface operations, its core mission remained strategic. Air power, even conventional air power, still promised the most direct means to compel the enemy to do our will.

In an era of nuclear weapons and superpower rivalry there was a lot to justify this focus. Strategic air power also satisfied the American predilection for high technology and strategies that leveraged America's wealth over investment in large standing militaries. Americans prefer throwing money and technology—not bodies—at strategic problems. But at the same time as we see this growing love affair with high technology, the early Cold War was also an era of low-tech wars: insurgencies and counterinsurgencies in the Third World. The Air Force, with its focus on compelling industrialized states, was intellectually unprepared to respond to the challenges posed by the likes of Mao Tse-tung and Ho Chi Minh.

The first big test of conventional air power against a Maoist style people's war took place in Vietnam. Initial Air Force plans for the strategic bombing campaign in Southeast Asia focused almost exclusively on strategic strikes against North Vietnam, not attacks on the insurgency in the South.

The air plan also remained true to the tenets of early of air-power theorists in that the campaign was designed to be intense and massive so as to maximize strategic shock and speed the capitulation of the North. This would be accomplished by rapidly destroying both North Vietnam's means and its will to continue the struggle.

Still smarting from the Chinese intervention in the Korean War, the Johnson administration modified these initial plans in favor of a more graduated air strategy that would inflict calibrated pain on North Vietnam, but prevent Chinese intervention. The compromise was the Rolling Thunder campaign as envisioned by Secretary of Defense Robert McNamara.

McNamara, a former president of the Ford Motor Company, is often savaged as a civilian know-it-all who tried in vain to inject business concepts into the world of military strategy. In reality, he was as much a product of the United States Air Force as he was of American business culture. During the Second World War, McNamara had been a statistical analyst for XXth and XXIst Bomber Commands in Asia. In other words, he was Curtis LeMay's number cruncher.

As an air force officer, McNamara was as convinced of the strategic efficacy of air power as his superiors, but as Secretary of Defense he felt obliged to balance the "go-big go-early" inclinations of the Air Force against the need to avoid a repeat of Korea. Given what we now know about Chinese calculations in the mid-1960s, such caution was warranted. A major Chinese intervention in Vietnam was not likely, but it was certainly a possibility. Such a scenario had daunting nuclear repercussions. In fact, since the 1950s the American military had assumed that war with China would involve nuclear weapons. Johnson and McNamara did not want to test that assumption.

Rolling Thunder, therefore, was primarily directed toward convincing North Vietnam to stop its support to the insurgency in South Vietnam. This is what we call compelling or coercing an enemy. Such strategic persuasion hinged as much on what targets the bombers did *not* hit as what targets they did hit. The assumption was that since the United States could destroy pretty much any target then the United States could hold hostage those targets of particularly high value to North Vietnam by not bombing them. The idea was that restraint would induce cooperation. Secondarily, Rolling Thunder would devastate the industry and infrastructure of the North so as to deny Hanoi the ability to support the Vietcong, or VC. It soon became apparent, however, that strategic persuasion was not working and that the air interdiction side of the campaign should become the primary focus.

Between 1965 and 1968, U.S. planes dropped more tons of bombs on North Vietnam than they had on Japan during World War II, and yet Rolling Thunder was an abject failure. The U.S. could not figure out how to inflict sufficient pain on North Vietnam to force them to renounce their objective of overthrowing the Saigon government.

Nor did Rolling Thunder significantly restrict the flow of men and materiel to the South. The Ho Chi Minh trail snaked through Laos and Cambodia, sovereign nations, which at this point in the war were off-limits to U.S. air strikes. In the end, the damage that Rolling Thunder wreaked on North Vietnam was great, but Hanoi had allies in Beijing and Moscow that could replace the food and materiel that had been destroyed by American bombs.

Air-power advocates regularly point to Rolling Thunder as an object lesson in how not to run an air war. Excessive political meddling, restrictive targeting lists, and gradualism all prevented the air weapon from achieving its strategic potential.

Instead they point to the massive, sudden, and unrestrained Linebacker I and II campaigns of 1972 as a better proof of the air-power concept. Linebacker I took place over the summer of 1972 and targeted North Vietnamese port facilities and transportation infrastructure. Linebacker I also involved the first widespread use of precision-guided munitions, weapons that enabled the United States to demolish several strategic targets in short order.

Linebacker II, or the Christmas Bombings, so named because they took place in December of 1972, involved over 200 B-52s and some 20,000 tons of bombs. The destruction wrought by the two Linebacker operations was immense and in the weeks that followed Hanoi was more accommodating at the negotiating table. The Paris Peace Accords were signed at the end of January 1973. As a result, Linebacker looks like a perfect example of coercion in practice, the gloves come off and the enemy is forced to accede. But we need to remember that what were at stake were minor negotiating points, not the renunciation of the North's overarching political objectives.

From Rolling Thunder to Linebacker I and II, Vietnam offers mixed lessons on the strategic utility of air power. In the aftermath of Vietnam, American air-power theorists struggled to rescue the legitimacy of conventional strategic bombing. In their minds, many things had gone wrong in Vietnam. Gradualism, signaling, and targeting restrictions often topped the list, but so, too, did the limits of technology. The Air Force understood the significance of precision-guided bombs, but the overwhelming majority of the bombs dropped in Vietnam, were still "dumb bombs," virtually identical to those dropped on Germany and Japan. Bombing was therefore inaccurate and indiscriminate. And since it required massive attacks by multiple bombers to take out a single target, bombing was disproportionately costly. Better targeting, better technology, especially precision-guided munitions, and stealth aircraft promised to bring conventional strategic bombing a step closer to its theoretical promise.

U.S. Air Force Colonel John Warden was the leading theorist of this post-Vietnam generation and his plan for air-power use in the Gulf War of 1991 was called Operation Instant Thunder. Instant Thunder was a product of the lessons learned from Rolling Thunder's failure and was designed as Warden's proof of concept of the strategic paralysis that air power can deliver. Warden served as a fighter pilot in Vietnam and later as commandant of the Air Command and Staff College, the Air Force equivalent of the Naval War College. Warden's concept of air power hinged on the innate superiority of air power as a strategic instrument: at best, land and naval forces can only strike operational centers of gravity, the enemy's armed forces.

By contrast, properly targeted and sufficiently destructive air strikes against the enemy's strategic centers of gravity can directly contribute to victory, and can do so at relatively low cost and low risk. Warden carried forward many of the core tenets of early air-power theory, but differed from his predecessors by de-emphasizing economic and civilian targets.

Warden parses these different centers of gravity at the different levels of war as a system of five concentric rings. They are, in increasing levels of importance: The enemy's armed forces are the fifth or outer ring. The enemy's civilian population is the fourth ring. His infrastructure (transportation and industry) is the third ring. His "system essentials," essentially food, fuel, electricity, and communications, form the second ring.

At the center is the first ring, comprising the enemy's leadership. If you think of an adversary as an organism, then striking the brain, i.e., the leadership, and striking the nervous system, the second ring, will naturally have a more direct and paralyzing result than hacking away at the limbs—or outer rings.

"Countries," Warden says, "are inverted pyramids that rest precariously" on the inner ring, "their leadership." If their leadership and communications can be paralyzed, then the country is defeated even though its armed forces are "fully intact."

To appreciate Warden's theoretical approach, we need to recognize that there was something of a turf war going on in the years leading up to the first Gulf War. Warden was worried that the Air Force was being hijacked by the army to make operational support its core mission.

To Warden, fighting an enemy's military was in his words "at best a means to an end and at worst a total waste of time and energy." It was the job of the Air Force to target primarily those two center rings, not the outer rings, not the enemy's military, with the paired goals of decapitation and strategic paralysis. Given the conventional wisdom on the failures of Rolling Thunder, in particular the negative connotations of civilian "meddling," it is pretty ironic that Warden's answer was an air-power doctrine that actually demanded a very high degree of political oversight. The more strategic the target, especially an enemy head of state, the more essential it is to have the senior civilians, the president, give the final approval. In all of America's air campaigns since the 1980s every American president has been involved in strategic targeting.

For example, on the morning before Operation Iraqi Freedom kicked off, President George W. Bush was personally involved in the decision to bomb the Dora Farms compound, where it was believed Saddam Hussein was visiting his family. This is how it should be, the president should be involved in decisions with that much strategic significance, but it seems 180 degrees out from what most people think went wrong in Vietnam.

But let's get back to Warden and to the first Gulf War. In the summer of 1990, Warden was working in a strategic planning group at the Pentagon named Checkmate. After the Iraqi invasion of Kuwait, Checkmate was tasked with coming up with a plan to liberate Kuwait and to punish Saddam Hussein. The product that Warden's team came up with was Operation Instant Thunder, an unsubtle dig at McNamara's Rolling Thunder.

The first draft of Instant Thunder called for a week of attacks on 84 targets almost exclusively in the inner two rings of Saddam's regime:

command bunkers, presidential palaces, Ba'ath party head-quarters and telecommunications. The Iraqi troops occupying Kuwait were largely irrelevant. In other words, Instant Thunder was exclusively strategic.

Over time and under pressure from his superiors, Warden modified the plan to include strikes that would physically paralyze the Iraqi Army, but he was soon shunted out of the war planning. In the end, a modified version of Instant Thunder became just one phase of a four-phase air plan, a plan that targeted essentially everything of any military, economic, or communications significance (even the most marginal significance) in Iraq and Kuwait. We pretty much bombed everything.

In the end as well, precision-guided munitions, the centerpiece of Instant Thunder represented just a fraction of the ordnance dropped on Iraq. Nonetheless, Warden and many in the Air Force were convinced that the rest of the air and ground war were sideshows to the paralyzing effects of Instant Thunder.

Others, however, remained skeptical. The leading air-power skeptic is Robert Pape, whose 1996 book, *Bombing to Win: Air Power and Coercion in War*, challenged many of Warden's core assumptions. In particular, Pape questioned whether regime paralysis was a sufficient precondition for victory. In contrast to Warden, Pape advocated a two-hand approach. On the one hand you have coercion, strikes aimed at targets of high value to the regime to affect the enemy's will. But since even modern high-tech war is still primarily about destroying the enemy's military forces, you need the other hand.

The other hand is called "denial." In other words, denying the enemy the means to fight. For Pape air strikes in Warden's outer rings can also win wars, strikes against the enemy's armed forces and his national infrastructure, not just the air strikes in the inner rings. Pape was convinced that the destruction of the Republican Guard and the ground advance into Kuwait were what won the first Gulf War, not the strategic strikes against leadership targets.

Since the 1990s we have had numerous opportunities to test all sides of the paralysis, coercion, and denial debate. In our remaining time, we will look at two of these cases. The 1999 air war over Yugoslavia and the 2011 NATO air campaign over Libya.

In March of 1999 NATO initiated a campaign of airstrikes against the government and military of Yugoslavia. The objectives of the campaign were to force Yugoslav president Slobodan Milosevic to stop the ethnic cleansing of the Albanian population in Kosovo, to withdraw his forces from Kosovo, accept UN peacekeepers, and abide by the terms of the Rambouillet Accords. Over the next two and a half months NATO aircraft and cruise missiles struck a dizzying array of targets in Yugoslavia.

Targeting corresponded to four of Warden's five rings: leadership, regime infrastructure, national infrastructure, and the Yugoslav military. There were some inadvertent strikes against civilians, but NATO scrupulously avoided targeting the general population.

The NATO strategy was initially coercive in concept. In other words, it aimed to punish Milosevic and the Serbian military and to force them to accede to NATO demands. Very quickly, however, it evolved into a denial strategy. The aim then, was to deny Milosevic the means to purge Kosovo of Albanians. An additional benefit was to breed enough dissatisfaction among the population that the Yugoslavian people might force Milosevic to seek terms.

Ironically, the early bombing campaign actually stiffened support for Milosevic, but over time economic pain and popular unrest started to wear on the regime. As to the strikes on the Yugoslav military, they proved particularly effective against large bases and columns of heavy machinery, but they did not stop small groups of Yugoslav infantry from terrorizing Albanians or from driving them out of Kosovo.

In other words, Milosevic's preferred strategy was not particularly vulnerable to denial attacks. Milosevic's strategy of ethnic cleansing depended on small, light units that were difficult to target and to destroy. His regime on the other hand seemed highly vulnerable to leadership strikes.

Milosevic ultimately caved to NATO demands in June of 1999. The people, and especially the elites, seemed to have had enough. It might be counterintuitive, but the less totalitarian a regime is, then the more vulnerable it will probably be to strikes in Warden's inner rings. Milosevic's government was just centralized enough and just authoritarian enough to be held responsible for the disruption of public services, like communications, transportation, electricity, and food. At the same time, it was not sufficiently authoritarian to survive without elite and grassroots support.

A final factor that may have pushed Milosevic toward capitulation was the growing threat of a ground invasion. By June, the degradation of Yugoslavia's heavy forces may have convinced Milosevic that a NATO ground campaign was more likely. Some argued that an invasion was necessary because the Kosovo Liberation Army was not enough of a viable local surrogate to challenge the Yugoslav Army on its own, even with outside air support. The invasion never materialized, but it had become more credible and the possibility might have forced Belgrade's hand, but there is little evidence to support this assertion. In the end it appears that the threat of further denial attacks from the air, in combination with the leadership strikes and regime infrastructure strikes, were enough to coerce Milosevic to capitulate.

In the final analysis then, Kosovo looks like a partial vindication of strategic bombing as a decisive instrument in war. With NATO in complete control of the air, a mix of coercion and denial seemed to work against a weak and isolated regime and in a war fought for limited objectives. In other words, it may be a proof of the coercion concept, but the circumstances were almost ideal.

Let's turn now to Libya. I was mid-way through preparing this lecture when the news broke that Muammar Qaddafi had been captured and killed, thus bringing to an end the war between Qaddafi's regime and the combined forces of NATO and the Libyan Transitional National Council. Given that I was already hip-deep in air-power theory and practice, I couldn't very well ignore the question of how to best explain the success of NATO's air campaign over Libya. Was it paralysis? Was it coercion? Was it denial? Was it something else? The answer is yes.

329

NATO air strikes against the Qaddafi regime began in mid-March 2011 in response to Tripoli's bloody crackdown against protestors. From the outset the goal of the NATO campaign (and this is just my opinion) was regime change. Qaddafi needed to go, but exactly how that was going to happen was still unclear. The early air plan was therefore a mix of coercion to convince Qaddafi to stop attacking the anti-regime elements, and denial to prevent him from attacking the rebels. As in Kosovo, the strategy evolved into something more aggressive. Here it became a campaign of brute force against the regime and against the Libyan military.

Leadership and regime infrastructure strikes were designed to disrupt, blind, and paralyze the regime while denial strikes against the Libyan army and its mercenary allies were ostensibly about protecting the protestors. In reality, they were primarily designed to help the rebels make the transition from guerilla tactics to conventional operations. If the rebellion was going to succeed, the rebels had to seize and hold major socioeconomic and political centers. NATO air cover helped them do that and also protected the rebels from counterattack.

When it became clear that Qaddafi was not going stop his campaign of repression, then forceful regime change became the only option. At that point coercion and denial were transformed into brute force. That Qaddafi was willing and able to fight to the end should not have come as a surprise. He had been in power since the late 1960s and the fate of the Egyptian President Hosni Mubarak probably didn't encourage him to step down peaceably.

Qaddafi had also fully entrenched his immediate family and his tribe into all elements of the Libyan government. It wasn't just Qaddafi, but his entire clan that was on death ground. Therefore, high-profile defections of some senior officials were unlikely to affect his resolve. He couldn't be coerced.

Among regime loyalists it was also relatively easy for Qaddafi to deflect blame for the economic and communications disruptions onto NATO. In other words Qaddafi was not as susceptible to elite or popular opinion as Milosevic had been in the Kosovo War: he couldn't be coerced.

In the face of Qaddafi's recalcitrance and the relative military weakness of the rebels, NATO air power decisively altered the balance of power and allowed the Libyan resistance to go on the offensive. In both Kosovo and Libya, we need to appreciate that while outside military intervention was almost exclusively from the air, there was also a ground war going on. Given the unlimited objective of regime change, a ground campaign to seize the regime's political centers of gravity, Tripoli and Qaddafi's hometown of Sirte, was required. In Libya, much more than in Kosovo, there was a potentially potent local ally for NATO to coordinate with.

At the same time, the rebels did not have to worry about command of the air, that had been secured by NATO. What they did need was an operational mass big enough to contend with Qaddafi loyalists. That contest was evened by a mix of air strikes and by the arms embargo against Tripoli. The rebels never did become particularly powerful or militarily proficient, but they were strong enough to defeat an army that had been driven back from rebel strongholds and pummeled relentlessly from the air.

By August–September of 2011, NATO was engaged in close and coordinated air support for the operational and tactical movements of the Libyan rebels. They were also engaged in 24/7 aerial surveillance of the theatre. It was in those paired roles of surveillance and strike that NATO aircraft located and attacked Qaddafi's convoy fleeing Sirte on October 20, 2011.

In Libya as they had had in Kosovo, NATO enjoyed complete command of the air. They and their rebel allies were also facing an adversary who was isolated domestically and internationally. Qaddafi had also been militarily weakened to a significant extent. Given the unlimited objective and Qaddafi's death-grip on power, a highly muscular form of denial—in other words brute force—was required. That campaign in turn supported a viable internal rival. All of those things needed to be in place to effect regime change. It's not surprising that it took six months.

So if we look back at our contemporary theorists, Warden and Pape, and at the case of Libya, we have three basic approaches to modern conventional air power. The A. option is Warden: paralyze the enemy regime with targeted strikes in the inner rings. Option B. is Pape: coerce the enemy to do your political will with a mix of strikes designed to affect both his means and his will. And in Libya we have the C. option: full-spectrum targeting with the aim of aiding a local surrogate and toppling the enemy regime.

In the end, the Warden versus Pape versus Libya approach is a bit simplistic. And it would be misguided and dangerous to assume that victory hinges on either A or B or C. As you probably suspect, future air campaigns will invariably end up being a combination of all three. The A to B to C ratio of that combination will depend on the nature of the war, the strategy of the adversary being attacked, and the type of environment (physical and political) in which you are operating.

There's that pesky "It depends!" answer again! As to what kind of air power will prove most decisive, if Gulf War I or Kosovo or Libya are any model, then the jury will be out for a very long time, if not indefinitely. As a result, I would be very cautious about drawing too many direct lessons from either Kosovo or Libya. A lot changed between those two air campaigns, not the least of which was technology—the maturation of stealth, precision-guided munitions, and Unmanned Aerial Vehicles (UAVs). This technological shift made targeting and battle damage assessment much easier in Libya, but it did not make the process of matching air strategy to NATO policy easy.

Today there are some pundits as well who look to Libya as proof of concept for what they, not the president, call The Obama Doctrine: multinational, stand-off, humanitarian intervention against odious regimes. This sounds good in theory, and in both Kosovo and Libya I believe that the United States and its allies did the right thing.

But in both cases the air campaign was virtually cost-free. Sure it cost money, but neither Milosevic nor Qaddafi had the means to inflict significant operational or strategic costs on NATO. We cannot guarantee that future adversaries will be as militarily impotent as those two.

Nuclear Strategy
Lecture 18

To this point in the course, we've talked about strategy as the use of military force to achieve political objectives. The threat of nuclear war turns that concept entirely on its head. Nuclear strategy is primarily about not resorting to force because the costs of a nuclear exchange dwarf all conceivable political gains that might be sought. At the same time, preventing nuclear war means thinking openly and at length about how such a war might be waged. In this lecture, we'll look at three theorists who have tried to make sense of this paradox.

Key Terms in Nuclear Strategy
- The core concept in nuclear strategy is deterrence, which hinges on the capability to inflict unacceptable costs on an adversary, as well as the ability to credibly communicate the intent to do so. The key words here are: capability, credibility, and communication.

- Under the heading of credibility is the concept of proportionality. The scale of reprisal must be proportional to the value of the object that is threatened. If the possible reprisal either is not costly enough or could be classified as overkill, then it does not represent credible communication of intent.

- Deterrence can take many forms, including immediate deterrence (responding to a specific, near-term threat), general deterrence (a more comprehensive strategy to prevent a range of threats), direct deterrence (convincing an adversary not to attack), extended deterrence (convincing an adversary not to attack an ally), minimum deterrence (maintaining a second-strike capability), or limited deterrence (maintaining the ability to strike an enemy's military assets to control escalation).

- Counter-value strikes are attacks on civilian targets, and counter-force strikes are attacks on military targets.

- Mutual assured destruction (MAD) is the capability of two or more adversaries to sustain an initial strike and retain the ability to retaliate with a massive counterstrike.

- Flexible response refers to a range of options between capitulation and mutual annihilation.

- Arms limitation or disarmament is the reduction of the nuclear arsenal on both sides.

Bernard Brodie

- Bernard Brodie was the first and most enduring of America's nuclear theorists. He was also among the first generation of American academics to study the interconnections among policy, strategy, and war.

- To Brodie, the advent of nuclear weapons represented a strategic revolution comparable to the revolution in Napoleonic warfare. Absolute war was now possible, but that fact was actually a cause for guarded optimism.
  - Although irrationality and inadvertent escalation could never be eliminated, Brodie believed that they would be remote possibilities. Rationality would stay the hand of world leaders when it came to pushing the nuclear button.

  - Given that nuclear retaliation was the almost certain response to nuclear aggression, leaders had to realize that no political object was worth the risk of nuclear war. This was the core assumption of deterrence, and Brodie was the first to articulate it in these terms.

- Almost immediately after Brodie sketched out the basics of deterrence, another school, known as the war-fighters, began exploring how nuclear weapons might actually be used in the event of a war. Among the questions they pondered were these: Was limited nuclear war possible? Could escalation to all-out war be controlled?

- In the 1950s, Brodie answered both of those questions in the affirmative. Nuclear weapons, he said, might be useful at the tactical level, and they could be used in ways short of total annihilation. But that was only if the political and military leadership had identified ways to control escalation.

- For Brodie, the larger question was: Could a nuclear war be won? And his answer to that was also a tentative yes. A belligerent could achieve its political objectives, but probably not at acceptable costs.

- Brodie concluded that limited nuclear war was preferable to massive retaliation. In preparing for such a war, he believed that the United States would gain tactical and operational nuclear capabilities that could also further deterrence by demonstrating credibility and capability across a range of conflict scenarios.

- Although he later repudiated the idea of limited nuclear war, Brodie did lay the theoretical groundwork for flexible response. But flexible response was always in tension with massive retaliation.

Thomas Schelling

- Thomas Schelling, a Nobel Prize winner in Economics, brought to nuclear strategy a general interest in conflict, competition, and competitive bargaining.

- Because most bargaining is more variable sum than zero sum (one side's gain is the other side's loss), Schelling looked for ways to use the threat of nuclear weapons as a variable-sum bargaining tool.
  - To Schelling, the advent of nuclear weapons did as much to transform international relations as it did to transform warfare.

  - The ability of a nuclear power to instantaneously reach out and hit an enemy's homeland made coercive diplomacy much more likely.

- Schelling likened coercive bargaining in a nuclear context to a game of chicken: The winner is the one who might be just crazy enough to drive the car off the cliff.
  - One player wins in this game when the other player balks. In a political crisis, the best way to get one player to balk is to credibly commit to driving both players off the cliff.

  - Massive retaliation could only be credible if one adversary thinks the other might risk nuclear war over a small chunk of territory or the fate of an ally.

  - Nuclear chicken is not only a winning strategy in specific crises (immediate deterrence), but it also helps in developing a "bargaining reputation," a consistent commitment to playing hardball that satisfies long-term or general deterrence.

  - In other words, Schelling was trying to figure out how to make fear and irrationality serve the rational ends of deterrence.

- Schelling was also interested in making the nonrational dimensions of chance and probability serve rationality. He came up with the idea that a threat that left something to chance could be an effective bargaining tool.
  - Even if the enemy is not entirely convinced that its adversary is crazy enough to push a crisis to the nuclear brink, the closer both players get to the brink, the higher the risk that some unforeseen accident will push both over the edge.

  - The enemy is forced to make the rational decision to back down by fear of the unknown and fear of the adversary. In other words, fear can be exploited and manipulated to enhance bargaining. This was how Schelling rationalized brinksmanship.

- Winning in a game of nuclear chicken obviously hinges on controlling the play of probability and chance and on possessing greater intelligence than the enemy. These are difficult requirements to meet in practice and present a significant risk if either is wrong.

- Schelling believed that in peacetime, a player should sell itself as the one least likely to try to change the status quo; in a crisis, that player should sell itself as the one most likely to escalate. The limits of restraint are signaled by establishing the outer limits of the player's nuclear umbrella and populating that defensive perimeter with its own troops.

- Schelling penned some of the foundational works on arms control theory and practice. He didn't believe that arms control was an end in itself—the nuclear genie would never be put back in the bottle—but arms control, if applied to the right kinds of weapons, could enhance stability, promote greater communications with the Soviet Union, and increase mutual deterrence.

Vasily Sokolovsky

- Vasily Sokolovsky had a distinguished career in the Soviet military and, after his retirement, became an important military theoretician. His most famous work, *Military Strategy*, sought to integrate competing Soviet military schools of thought in one authoritative volume.

The book *Military Strategy*, compiled by Vasily Sokolovsky, a Soviet army commander and military theoretician, offers a frightening look at Soviet nuclear theory in the early 1960s.

- Frighteningly, Sokolovsky's book includes nothing about deterrence, and there is a heavy emphasis on nuclear warfare, including preemption, and on massive and simultaneous nuclear strikes on both counter-force and counter-value targets. Above all, there is a high degree of optimism that the Soviet Union could fight and win a nuclear war.

337

- Sokolovsky and his co-authors assumed that any war between the superpowers would escalate almost immediately to a global thermonuclear war. Therefore, going on the offensive early and overwhelmingly would be the best way to make the inevitable communist victory less costly.

- The core Soviet political assumption was that the capitalist world was out to destroy communism; thus, despite whatever minor proximate crisis might lead to war, the true objectives of the United States were unlimited. Such a war would be an act instigated by the capitalists out of desperation, but it was a war that the Soviets would ultimately win.

- The key to nuclear strategy was to limit the costs the Soviets and their allies would suffer in the course of the war. This translated into massive, multidimensional attacks on American targets around the globe. The idea was to completely disrupt all elements of America's war-making potential: weapons systems, the economy, command and control, and so on.

- In such a strategy, there could be no illusions about economy of force, such as more precise attacks to deliver disproportionate strategic effects. Overkill was the dominant concept. This naturally meant that the Soviets had no interest in nuclear arms control and were relatively unconcerned with limited nuclear war and conventional war between the superpowers.

- It's important to note that *Military Strategy* was produced for public consumption inside and outside the Soviet Union. For this reason, it might be regarded as a sort of strategic communication designed to rattle the West.

- It's also significant that the book was written almost exclusively by Soviet military officers, whose organization was absolutely subordinate to the Communist Party. Their goal was not to influence policy but to be prepared if called by their leadership to wage a nuclear war. The Kremlin's nuclear stance was actually more about deterrence than victory in nuclear war.

Nuclear Strategy in the 21st Century

- As we look forward into the 21st century, we should note that almost all of the foundational thinking about nuclear weapons is a product of the Cold War, an anomalous period of global bipolarity between two massively nuclear-armed superpowers.

- A lot less ink has been spilled on the nuclear strategies of middle powers or on the dynamics of counter-proliferation against rogue nations, but these are precisely the nuclear challenges that we now face.

Suggested Reading

Bayliss and Garnett, eds., *Makers of Nuclear Strategy*.

Freedman, "The First Two Generations of Nuclear Strategists."

Gray, "Strategy in the Nuclear Age."

Questions to Consider

1. How did the radically different natures of the United States and the Soviet Union influence American and Soviet thinking about nuclear weapons?

2. Did nuclear deterrence work in the Cold War? If so, will it work on powers with small nuclear arsenals, such as North Korea, China, and possibly, Iran?

Nuclear Strategy
Lecture 18—Transcript

To this point in the course, we've been talking about strategy as the use of military force to achieve political objectives. The threat of nuclear war turns that concept entirely on its head. Nuclear strategy is primarily about not resorting to force because the costs of a nuclear exchange dwarf all conceivable political gains that might be sought. It is Clausewitz's "Absolute War."

And yet at the same time, preventing nuclear war means thinking openly and at length about how you might wage such a war. The mental exertion involved in trying to make sense out of this paradox is probably the main reason why the field of nuclear strategy is so relatively small.

Napoleon Bonaparte once said that even Isaac Newton would quail at the complexities of modern war. Only a few theorists have successfully wrestled with the complexities of nuclear war. Today, we're going to look at three of those theorists: two Americans and one Soviet. But before we do I'd like to start by defining some of the key terms that are used when people talk about nuclear strategy.

The core concept in nuclear strategy is deterrence. Clausewitz talked about war by algebra, but he was pretty skeptical that great powers could be deterred by algebraic calculations of relative strength. Some leaders would always be willing to roll the dice.

In the nuclear age, however, it became an imperative to explore the strategic aspects of deterrence. But how do you deter a nation that looks like it might want to upset the status quo or impinge on your interests? Deterrence hinges on your capability to inflict unacceptable costs on that adversary as well as the ability to credibly communicate your intent to inflict those costs. The key words there are capability, credibility, and communication.

Under the heading of credibility is the concept of proportionality. The scale of reprisal has to be proportional to the value of the object that is threatened. If the possible reprisal is not costly enough, if it is only a slap on the wrist, then you are not credibly communicating your intent. If the possible reprisal is overkill, for example, global thermonuclear war over a chunk of frozen wasteland, then your deterrence is also not credible.

But if only it were that simple! In fact, deterrence can take many forms. For example, we might be talking about immediate deterrence, that is, responding to a specific near-term threat. Or, we might be talking about general deterrence, a more comprehensive strategy to prevent a range of threats from arising.

To complicate matters even further we might be talking about direct deterrence, convincing that troublemaker not to attack you, or we might be talking about extended deterrence, that is convincing him not to attack one of your allies. A state might pursue a strategy of minimum deterrence, which means having just enough nuclear weapons so that even if the enemy nukes you first, you still retain a painful second-strike capability. Hopefully that will convince him not to attack in the first place. You might move up to limited deterrence, which requires all of the elements of minimum deterrence with the added ability to strike or threaten the enemy's military assets so as to control escalation in a conflict. In other words the enemy's initial strike is not a freebie.

So let's suppose you have a modest nuclear arsenal and you are considering either a strategy of minimum deterrence or limited deterrence. You then have to determine if you want to focus on countervalue strikes, attacks on the civilian targets, or if you want to focus on counterforce strikes, attacks on military targets. If you embrace minimum deterrence you are probably going to lean toward countervalue strikes. Destroying Los Angeles will carry a greater psychological weight than destroying an Air Force base. If you move up to limited deterrence, then you will start moving toward a mix of countervalue and counterforce targeting.

Let's say that neither minimum deterrence nor limited deterrence meets your strategic requirements. Then massive retaliation is your next option. No matter what the cause of the war, your retaliation will be huge, sudden; it will involve counterforce and countervalue attacks. And more than likely it will be out of all proportion to the proximate cause of the war.

When two or more belligerents pursue massive retaliation and can sustain an initial nuclear strike, then you have an unavoidable condition known as mutual assured destruction, or MAD. MAD is the capability of both adversaries to sustain an initial strike and still have the ability to retaliate with a massive counterstrike on the adversary. In other words, it is Armageddon.

Optimally, MAD sets a very low threshold for efforts by either side to upset the status quo, but it also strains credibility. Are you really going to use massive retaliation if your enemy upsets the status quo by invading some frozen wasteland in the middle of nowhere? If you don't like the option of either caving on that territorial spat or launching an all-out nuclear barrage, then you might like something like flexible response, a range of options between capitulation and mutual annihilation. The trick is figuring out what mix of conventional capabilities and nuclear capabilities allows you to contest aggression and also control escalation from a conventional spat to a nuclear splat.

If the neighborhood is still too dangerous, you might want to improve relations with your neighbors. For example, you might try to convince your enemy that your intentions are good and that you are willing to reduce your nuclear arsenal if he is. In other words, you might want to try détente, arms limitations, or maybe even disarmament.

Finally, if you don't like the idea of living with the fact that the enemy's initial strike will always get through, then you can try to do something about it. This was the logic of the strategic defense initiative, or SDI, in the 1980s. Reagan's dream was a missile shield so effective that it would render offensive nuclear weapons obsolete and end the arms race with an eye to the total abolition of nuclear weapons.

Others thought of SDI as only a partial solution and primarily as a way to make America's second-strike capability that much more survivable and intimidating. Yet others took SDI as a belief that a nuclear war was winnable for the United States. If SDI worked, it might allow the United States to launch a preemptive nuclear war without fear of retaliation.

These three disparate interpretations of SDI get right to the heart of the problems of perception and interaction inherent in strategy in general and nuclear strategy in particular. I take Reagan at his word that he wanted to permanently eliminate the evil of nuclear weapons, but how likely was it that the Soviets would take him at his word?

Well now that we've had an overview of some of the key terms and issues relating to nuclear deterrence let's turn to our three theorists. Bernard Brodie was the first, and the most enduring of America's nuclear theorists. His career spanned the era from low-yield atomic bombs dropped from B-29s to that of jet bombers, ballistic missile submarines, and intercontinental ballistic missiles topped with up to a dozen warheads. As a matter of fact, Brodie would have been quite at home teaching this course. He was among the first generation of American academics to study the interconnections between policy, strategy, and war.

When the atomic bombs were detonated over Hiroshima and Nagasaki, he immediately recognized the significance of those events. And, given his teaching background he came at the issue with a decidedly Clausewitzian view. To him, the advent of nuclear weapons represented a strategic revolution comparable to the revolution in Napoleonic warfare. Absolute war was now possible, but this was actually a cause for guarded optimism. While irrationality and inadvertent escalation could never be eliminated, Brodie believed that they would be remote possibilities. Rationality would stay the hand of world leaders when it came to pushing the nuclear button. Since nuclear retaliation was the almost certain response to nuclear aggression, then leaders had to realize that no political object was worth the risk of nuclear war. This was the core assumption of deterrence and Brodie was the first to articulate it in these specific strategic terms.

Brodie then expanded on the nature of nuclear war: Nukes were fundamentally strategic; they are inherently superior in strategic effects to conventional land and naval forces; there is no realistic defense against them (the bombs will always get through); and finally, nukes can decide a war by themselves. This sounds a lot like air-power theory, right? The U.S. Air Force didn't miss the parallels and hired Brodie for a brief time.

But Brodie did not share the Air Force's belief in the indiscriminate bombing of cities. He preferred to figure out what specific targets, what strategic centers of gravity, would deliver the biggest deterrent effect. He was even more concerned that Air Force thinking about the use of nuclear weapons wasn't coordinated with senior civilians. In the nuclear age, few things were more dangerous than a breakdown in the civil–military dialogue.

Brodie's brief employment with the Air Force was filled with unpleasantness and frustration. Whether inside the government or out, however, Brodie showed a remarkable analytical flexibility. He started in 1946 by declaring that nukes represented "the ultimate weapon" and that the old conception of strategy was completely overturned. Almost immediately after he sketched out the basics of deterrence, another school called the "war-fighters" started exploring how nukes might actually be used in the event of a war. At that point, the numbers and destructiveness of the early Soviet and American arsenals were limited enough for the war-fighters and strategists to ponder some very interesting questions:

Was limited nuclear war possible? Could escalation to all-out war be controlled? In the 1950s, Brodie answered both of those questions in the affirmative. Nuclear weapons, he said, might be useful at the tactical level and there were ways that nuclear weapons might be used short of total annihilation. That was only if the political and military leadership had come up with ways to control escalation. In a moment of prescience, Brodie pointed out that for a superpower to fight and win a limited war, it had to figure out how to make do with one hand tied behind its back.

The bigger question was, could a nuclear war be won? Brodie's answer to that was also tentatively yes. Yes, a belligerent could achieve his political objectives, but probably not at acceptable costs.

All of these discussions sprung from Brodie's dislike of Eisenhower's massive retaliation concept. He wanted the United States to have more strategic options short of pushing the button. He also didn't like the nuclear brinkmanship that went along with massive retaliation. These two policies threatened general war any time the Soviets or their proxies got out of line.

At that point, Brodie concluded that limited nuclear war was preferable to massive retaliation. In preparing for such a war, he believed, the United States would gain tactical and operational nuclear capabilities that could also further deterrence by demonstrating credibility and capability across a range of conflict scenarios. Although he later repudiated limited nuclear war, Brodie did lay the theoretical groundwork for flexible response. But flexible response was always in tension with massive retaliation.

It was up to Thomas Schelling to make sense out of massive retaliation and make sense out of the strategic utility of threatening global thermonuclear war over minor superpower competition. Schelling was an economist, not a specialist on strategic theory or military technology. In fact he shared the 2005 Nobel Prize for Economics. Schelling brought to nuclear strategy a general interest in conflict, competition, and especially competitive bargaining.

Schelling's critics often point out that his work on nuclear strategy and deterrence was too abstract and too theoretical. In other words Schelling was operating in a contextual vacuum, but he had no illusions that he was describing reality. Rather, like Clausewitz, he believed that beginning with the abstract was the first step to understanding reality. Game theory allowed Schelling to engage in elaborate and interactive thought experiments that produced decision-making models: models to guide real world strategies.

Since most bargaining was more variable sum than zero-sum, one side's gain is the other side's loss, Schelling looked for ways to use the threat of nukes as a variable sum bargaining tool.

Most critically to Schelling, the advent of nuclear weapons did as much to transform international relations as it did to transform warfare. The ability of a nuclear power to instantaneously reach out and hit an enemy's homeland made coercive diplomacy much more likely. The United States needed the mental preparation and the bargaining strategies for prevailing in diplomatic bargaining when general nuclear war was on the line.

I mentioned earlier that massive retaliation strains credibility; it was Schelling's job to make it credible. Schelling likened coercive bargaining in a nuclear context to a game of chicken. The guy who wins is the guy who might be just crazy enough to run his car off the cliff. He wins when the other guy balks. In a political crisis, the best way to get the other guy to back down might be to credibly commit to driving both of you over the cliff. Massive retaliation could only be credible if your adversary thought you might be just crazy enough to risk nuclear war over a small chunk of territory or more importantly over the fate of an ally.

Nuclear chicken is not only a winning strategy in specific crises, that is, immediate deterrence, it helps you develop a "bargaining reputation," a consistent commitment to playing hardball that satisfies long-term, or general deterrence. In other words, Schelling was trying to figure out how to make fear and irrationality serve the rational ends of deterrence.

Schelling was also interested in making the non-rational dimensions of chance and probability serve rationality. He came up with the idea that a threat that left something to chance could be an effective bargaining tool. Even if your enemy is not entirely convinced that you are crazy enough to push a crisis to the nuclear brink, still the closer you get to the brink increases the risk of some unforeseen accident pushing you both over the edge. His fear of the unknown and his fear of you force the enemy to make the rational decision to back down. Fear can be exploited and manipulated to enhance bargaining. This was how Schelling rationalized brinksmanship.

But let's think about this. Winning in a game of nuclear chicken obviously hinges on controlling the play of probability and chance. It also hinges on knowing more about the enemy than he knows about you. These are difficult requirements to meet in practice, and you run a huge risk if you get these assessments wrong. Especially because you can't be sure that your value of the object exceeds the value of that same object for your enemy.

Another problematic element of Schelling's strategy for general and extended deterrence was long-term and irrevocable commitments to allies. This can be a hard sell for politicians who want flexibility and tend to vary their level of commitment based on the relative value of that political object in its current context.

But before you start thinking that Schelling is a nut, a mad theoretician itching for opportunities to play nuclear chicken with the Soviets and their proxies, let's remember that he is just talking about crisis situations. At all other times Schelling called for restraint in American foreign policy. In a crisis you sell yourself as the guy most likely to escalate. In peace, you sell yourself as the guy least likely to try to force a crisis, the guy least likely to try to change the status quo. You establish your red lines and you stay within them. But how do you signal the limits of your restraint? Those red lines help; those are your defense perimeters, the outer limits of your nuclear umbrella. You also want to populate that defensive perimeter with your own troops. Overseas deployments at the edges deter aggression.

U.S. forces in West Berlin and South Korea, and carrier battle groups in the Taiwan straits are all trip wires. They aren't designed to stop an attack at the operational level of war. They are there to demonstrate commitment and in the event that the enemy does attack these forces, then their deaths will trigger the resolve of the American people to play hardball. Paradoxically, these trip wires can also reassure the enemy. Think about U.S. forces in Korea today. They are a triple deterrent. They deter the North Koreans from launching an attack and killing Americans. They deter the South Koreans from engaging in anything too risky that might endanger those Americans. They are also a self-deterrent on the Unites States, which reassures Pyongyang. In other words, the U.S. will not risk the lives of those troops by pushing the North aggressively on minor issues.

It was in the context of this general American restraint that Schelling penned some of the foundational works on arms-control theory and practice. Arms control was not idealistic to Schelling, but it was practical. He didn't think that arms control was an end in itself (the nuclear genie would never get put back in the bottle), but arms control, if applied to the right kinds of weapons, could enhance stability, promote greater communications with the Soviet Union, and increase mutual deterrence.

Was Schelling right about this? Was he right about bargaining and deterrence in general? To answer that question we have to turn to the Soviet side. Vasily Danilovich Sokolovsky is the only military man in our brief survey of the nuclear masters. Sokolovsky had a distinguished military career. In fact, he commanded one of the Soviet army groups that stormed Berlin in 1945 and toppled the Third Reich. He retired at the rank of marshal of the Soviet Union in 1960 and began a new career as a military theoretician. Sokolovsky's most famous work, simply titled, *Military Strategy*, is also unique because it was a collaborative enterprise that tried to integrate competing Soviet military schools of thought in one authoritative volume.

For good reasons, we tend to view the Soviet Union as our polar opposite in the Cold War: radically different society, economy, and political system. Different societies and different political systems will obviously come up with different paradigms and different sets of strategic inclinations. So when we look at *Military Strategy* it is not surprising that many of these early discussions of nuclear weapons are pretty scary.

In *Military Strategy* nuclear weapons are treated as primarily a new and more lethal weapon. As a result, there is nothing about deterrence and instead there is a heavy emphasis on nuclear warfare, including preemption, on massive and simultaneous nuclear strikes on both counterforce and countervalue targets, and above all there is a high degree of optimism that the Soviet Union could fight and win a nuclear war.

Sokolovsky's authors assumed that any war between the superpowers would escalate almost immediately to a global thermonuclear war. Therefore going on the offensive early and overwhelmingly would be the best way to make the inevitable communist victory less costly.

The core Soviet political assumption was that the capitalist world was out to destroy communism, thus despite whatever the minor proximate crisis that might have led to war, the true objectives of the United States were unlimited. Such a war was therefore an act instigated by the capitalists out of desperation, but it was a war that the Soviets would ultimately win.

That's right, Sokolovsky and his fellow officers were true believers and they embraced the ideological optimism about communism's inevitable victory over capitalism. Hence the key to nuclear strategy was to limit the costs that the Soviets and their allies suffered in the course of that war. Early soviet nuclear strategy, therefore, involved massive, multi-dimensional attacks on

American targets across the globe, buttressed by defense of the homeland and of Soviet command and control. The idea was to completely disrupt all elements of America's war-making potential: weapons systems, the economy, command and control, everything.

In such a strategy there could be no illusions about economy of force, such as more precise attacks to deliver disproportionate strategic effects. Overkill was the dominant concept. This naturally would mean that the Soviets would have no interest in nuclear arms control, as any reduction in the quantity of their nuclear arsenal might increase the pain that the United States could inflict on them.

Sokolovsky and his co-authors were relatively unconcerned with limited nuclear war and conventional war between the superpowers. True, later generations would pay more attention to those types of scenarios, but for most of the 1950s, 1960s, and 1970s Soviet nuclear theorists were looking almost exclusively at how to win an all-out nuclear war.

You see now why this looks pretty scary. On the other hand there are several reasons not to start digging that bomb shelter. First, *Military Strategy* was produced for public consumption inside and outside of the Soviet Union. Therefore, it might be regarded as a sort of strategic communication, designed to rattle the West. It might, therefore have been a uniquely Soviet form of deterrence. In fact, later editions of *Military Strategy* backed away from the more strident and preemptive ideas, indicating that the Soviets were sensitive that such public discussions could be counterproductive to U.S. Soviet relations.

Second, Sokolovsky's *Military Strategy* is a little less scary because it was written almost exclusively by Soviet military officers. Why is this significant? The American nuclear theorists that we have looked at were civilians and their analyses embraced not just war-fighting, but also the moral justness and political wisdom of nuclear war. Their goal was to influence policymakers and the authors of strategy. In the Soviet Union, the military was absolutely subordinate to the party. Therefore, the military were unfettered by moral or political considerations.

After all as faithful servants of the party they might be called upon by the leadership to wage a nuclear war. They needed to be prepared for that contingency. Ironically, their absolute subordination to the party made them relatively free to engage in intellectual experiments and creative thinking about winning a nuclear war, including bandying about ideas like preemptive first strikes. All of that was done in a policy-free context. In all honesty, what the Soviet military was thinking about was not that much different from the nuclear scenarios discussed by U.S. military planners.

But at the end of the day, while the Soviet military may have been giving the leadership military options in a nuclear war, they could not dictate the actual nuclear policy and strategy of the party. Sokolovsky's collection of strategic options was not synonymous with the Kremlin's nuclear stance, which was actually more about deterring nuclear war than winning a nuclear war.

The Soviets were never itching for a nuclear war. Nuclear war was unlikely, but possible. If it did happen it would come at the instigation of the United States. Therefore the Soviet military did not focus their main efforts on reducing the likelihood of a nuclear war, that was the job of the party. The military's job was to prepare for the worst.

This level of military preparation had an unexpected result: as good soldiers and as good Marxist-Leninists, the Soviet military did a lot of number crunching on the destructiveness of nuclear weapons, as the reality of human and environmental costs filtered up through the levels of planning, the Soviets began to have serious reservations about the logic of waging, much less winning, a nuclear war. When Brezhnev was briefed on the hard realities of nuclear war, he was visibly shaken.

It was also a good thing that Soviet threat perceptions highlighted the desire of the capitalist world to try to reverse the inexorable tide of history that had the Soviet Union coming out on top. For much of the Cold War the Soviets were convinced that they were winning the global struggle against capitalism. By the 1980s, as the tide seemed to reverse, the party leadership of the Soviet Union reasserted its dominance in public discussions of nuclear strategy. That was also a good thing. A regime that was increasingly convinced that it was losing the global contest and one that still embraced the irrational optimism of Sokolovsky's nuclear strategy would have been very dangerous indeed.

In the end, there was no conclusive proof of any of these theoretical concepts of deterrence or nuclear strategy. To be sure we can try to figure out what prevented nuclear war, but it is still unclear how to weight any single strategic approach. As to winning a nuclear war, well, thankfully we have no evidence against which to test Sokolovsky's strategic injunctions.

As we look forward into the 21st century we should finally note that almost all of the foundational thinking about nuclear weapons is a product of the Cold War: an anomalous period of global bipolarity between two massively nuclear armed superpowers. A lot less ink has been spilled on the nuclear strategies of middle powers or on the dynamics of counterproliferation against rogue nations, but these are precisely the nuclear challenges that we now face.

Are we prepared to deal with powers like Iran and N. Korea when it comes to their pursuit of nuclear weapons? Can you threaten massive retaliation as a response to their development or use of nuclear weapons? Is that threat credible? Is it proportional? How do nuclear weapons figure in U.S.–China relations? Does China's minimum deterrence trump American capabilities of massive retaliation? Would we be willing to trade Los Angeles for Taiwan?

These are the issues that confront strategic theorists and practitioners today. I do not envy them.

Mao Tse-tung in Theory and Practice
Lecture 19

M̲ao Tse-tung is unique among our masters for the scale of his own political and military achievements. In the course of the Chinese Civil War, Mao led the Chinese Communists back from abject defeat in the mid-1930s to the military conquest of most of China in 1949. His success is largely explained by his theory of insurgent war and his ability to put it into practice. In this lecture, we'll examine that theory and see it in action in the Chinese Civil War. We'll also discuss why Mao's theories are still viewed as relevant by insurgents and counterinsurgents alike.

Background on Mao

- Mao was born into a modestly prosperous peasant family in 1893 and first exposed to Marxist-Leninist thought at Peking University. In 1921, Mao attended the founding meeting of the Chinese Communist Party and later joined the Kuomintang, or Chinese Nationalist Party, as part of the First United Front.

- In 1927, the United Front collapsed, and Chiang Kai-shek ordered a purge of Communists from within his Nationalist Party. Mao was ordered by the central Communist Party to lead an uprising against the Nationalists in Hunan, but it failed, and Mao was forced to seek refuge in the countryside. Mao and a few remnants of the shattered Chinese Communist Party ultimately established a base area in the mountains of Jiangxi Province.

- The Communists were eventually forced out of Jiangxi and onto the Long March, which brought them to the even more remote and barren environs of Yenan. There, Mao began to write at length about strategies in China's revolutionary war.
  - He embraced the Marxist idea that all socioeconomic systems throughout history contained within themselves the seeds of their own destruction.

- o At the same time, he was profoundly Leninist in his emphasis on the need for a disciplined and ideologically pure party to lead the revolution and to prevent the movement from losing focus.

- At the beginning of Mao's career, China was still semi-feudal. By Marxist orthodoxy, it was not yet ready for socialism or communism. But Mao argued that the contradictions in the Chinese socioeconomic system were sufficiently explosive that a Communist-led revolution would speed China through Marx's phases of history.

"On Protracted War"

- Mao's essay "On Protracted War" lays out a three-phase formula for revolutionary warfare: (1) strategic defense, (2) strategic stalemate, and (3) strategic counteroffensive. As a good Marxist and a good student of Clausewitzian interaction, Mao emphasizes the dialectics of each phase, in other words, the balance and interaction between the two belligerents.

- In the first phase, strategic defense, the invader or the counterrevolutionary is on the offensive and the insurgent is on the defensive.
  - o But Mao's first phase is not just an operational defensive. It is designed to lure the enemy past its culminating point of attack, at which point, small insurgent bands can overwhelm overextended and isolated enemy units.

  - o These small offensives within the larger strategic defense are an important source of arms and ammunition. They are also designed to push the population toward more active support of the revolutionary movement.

- In the second phase, strategic stalemate, the enemy has essentially ceded large swaths of territory, and the insurgency moves from relying on the generosity of the population to building a government to lead the population. At the same time, the army is gaining in competence and continuing to capture supplies and weapons.

- Ideally, the third phase, strategic counteroffensive, is the shortest phase of a protracted war. The rebels have the manpower, materiel, and training necessary to meet the enemy in a conventional campaign. Ultimately, the conventional defeat of the counterrevolutionary army in the field compounds the internal weaknesses of the now-hollow regime and convinces its allies to abandon it.

- Note that "On Protracted War" actually relates to two distinct struggles: the war of national liberation against the Japanese and the revolutionary war against Chiang Kai-shek's Nationalist Party. This is particularly relevant to phase III, because the scale of the final counteroffensive will vary depending on whether the rebels are dealing with a foreign occupier or an indigenous government.
  - The value of the object, that is, maintaining power over occupied territory, will likely be lower for a foreign invader. An indigenous government will probably value its hold of national territory much more highly and will be much more strategically focused on suppressing the revolution within.

  - A single offensive victory might be sufficient to convince a foreign power that the costs of the war have exceeded the value of the object. But when it comes to overthrowing the national government, a series of offensive campaigns will be needed.

- Phase III is certainly appealing in theory, but it is a challenge to implement in practice. A premature leap into a strategic counteroffensive may actually play to the strengths of the incumbent regime. Mao was aware of this problem, and his answer was for the rebels to fall back on a robust phase II or even phase I.

Mao on Civil-Military Relations
- On the subject of civil-military relations, Mao takes Clausewitz's subordination of the military to the political to an extreme. In a revolutionary war, everything the military does has political ramifications; thus, political oversight must be highly invasive.

- Ultimately, maintaining absolute subordination of the military is essential to winning the war against what Mao calls the "enemies with guns," as well as consolidating the revolution against the "enemies without guns" (the secret counterrevolutionaries).

Mao in Practice
- The Chinese Civil War breaks down into three fairly clear phases, but Mao's elegant script is much more messy and contingent in practice than in theory.

- Phase I corresponds to the period from 1927–1937, with Chiang Kai-shek on the offensive and the Chinese Communists on the defense. Following the demolition of the urban base of the Communist Party in 1927, the remnants fell back to isolated base areas in the hinterland, the largest and best organized of which was in Jiangxi Province.
  - o Over the next six years, the Communists in Jiangxi gradually expanded that base and were able to occupy towns and some small cities. At the same time, they experimented with different approaches to land and social reform, and Mao cobbled together a modest military force that he called the Red Army.

  - o In 1933–1934, Chiang Kai-shek encircled and strangled the Communists' base in Jiangxi, forcing them to break out and undertake the Long March. Chiang tried to repeat the encirclement strategy at the Communists' new refuge in northwest China, but most of his accomplishments were undone by the Japanese invasion in 1937.

- The outset of phase II is marked by the Japanese invasion, which provided some relief for the Communists, allowing them to build more base areas and sell themselves as fighting a foreign invader. In reality, after 1941, neither the Japanese nor Chiang Kai-shek could muster enough energy to oust the Communists from their bases.

- When Japan surrendered in 1945, the Communists were far stronger than they had been in the 1930s and had a higher domestic and international profile.

- They were, however, still at a significant disadvantage relative to the Nationalists. The territory they controlled was desolate and remote, and they faced desperate shortages of weapons, tanks, and trucks.

- By 1947, the Communists, now armed with captured Japanese and American weapons and supplied by the Soviet Union, transitioned to phase III. By late 1948, 600,000 Red Army troops fought an equal number of Nationalist troops for a critical railway junction in Anhui Province.
  - In a battle that lasted more than two months, the Communists achieved victory through mechanized maneuver warfare and their new mastery of artillery. By the end of January 1949, Chiang Kai-shek had lost all of North China to the Communists.

  - On October 1, 1949, Mao proclaimed the founding of the People's Republic of China.

The Three Phases in Manchuria

- In 1945, both Chiang and Mao took a huge gamble and committed significant forces to Manchuria. In the short term, the gamble didn't pay off for Mao.

- Essentially, the Communists rushed into a premature phase II in Manchuria, trying to seize and govern three provinces. Chiang Kai-shek capitalized on their overextension and drove them back into a combination of phase I in southern Manchuria and phase II in some parts of the north.

- In the process, however, Chiang became overextended. By early 1947, the Nationalists were past their culminating point of attack, but Chiang could not accept the political risks of ceding territory.

The Communists were able to gradually wear down isolated garrisons and seize their weapons and vehicles.

- This sounds like a classic transition from phase I to phase II, but the Communists didn't have time to win the loyalty of the population. Instead, they conducted a systematic campaign of mass murder to terrorize the people into support.

- Backed up by the ruthless exploitation of the people and enabled by unprecedented levels of manpower and materiel, Mao's Red Army leapt into phase III.

- In 1948, the Communists completed the conquest of Manchuria and threw their full strength into the conquest of those areas south of the Great Wall. At this point, they could claim the political legitimacy they had lacked as rural guerillas.

- Mao's three phases worked in Manchuria, but the conditions there may well have been too ideal to repeat. Manchuria thus represents a problematic proof of Mao's theory.

Mao's Legacy

- In his youth, Mao had envisioned the Communist Party's role as harnessing a whirlwind of popular dissatisfaction. By 1948–1949, after 20 years of brutal struggle, the only way Mao could defeat the Nationalists was by shifting to a systematic campaign to exploit the peasant masses.

- This is Clausewitz's trinity in the making. Mao saw that the use of violence by the party could mobilize the passions of the people. Popular passion and support would strengthen the party but also give it the military means to contend with the Nationalists in the realm of chance and probability. By dominating that realm militarily, Mao defeated his enemies and achieved his ultimate political purpose.

- Mao's stunning victory in China made him something of an icon among communists in the developing world. By the 1950s, insurgent leaders were hungrily devouring Mao's writings, and China was sending aid and advisors to movements around the globe.

- But Mao's legacy goes far beyond the Cold War. From the Shining Path in Peru in the 1980s and 1990s to the communist movement that took power in Nepal in 2008, Mao's prescriptions for revolution have maintained their appeal and their apparent effectiveness.

Suggested Reading

Beckett, "Mao Tse-tung and Revolutionary Warfare."

Mao Tse-tung, "On Protracted War."

Marks, ed., *Maoist Insurgency since Vietnam*.

Questions to Consider

1. What are Mao's three phases? What is the critical vulnerability of each phase?

2. Is Mao more of a Sunzian or a Clausewitzian?

Mao Tse-tung in Theory and Practice
Lecture 19—Transcript

Reflecting on the Vietnam War, Henry Kissinger famously asserted, "The guerrilla wins if he does not lose. The conventional army loses if it does not win." But for Mao Tse-tung, history's most preeminent theorist of guerilla war and insurgency, nothing could be further from the truth.

For Mao, a revolution is an act of violence by which one class, in his case the peasants, overthrows another class, the landlords. A revolutionary war therefore requires a sustained campaign of organized violence to unseat the entrenched power of the dominant class, a class that holds immense material and military advantages and will certainly not give up without a fight. Mao's thesis was that the guerilla band cannot win unless it evolves into a conventional army. That proposition is the basis of Mao's theory of insurgent warfare and his ability to put it into practice largely explains why Mao's Communists won the Chinese Civil War.

Mao is therefore unique among our masters for the scale of his own political and military achievements. In the course of the Chinese Civil War Mao led the Chinese Communists back from abject defeat in the mid-1930s to the military conquest of most of China in 1949.

Today I will be framing my talk around three main topics: The first is Mao in theory, and specifically a discussion of Mao's 1938 essay "On Protracted War." The second topic is to see how well the Communist victory in the Chinese Civil War, or more simply put, Mao in Practice, conforms to Mao's theory. And we'll close with a short discussion of how and why Mao's theories have endured and why they are still viewed as relevant by insurgents and counterinsurgents alike.

I have a grudging respect for Mao as a strategic theorist and as a successful revolutionary, but let me say here that Mao was also one of the most evil and deranged rulers in history. He relentlessly purged his own party to guarantee his definition of ideological purity. His land reform campaigns in the early 1950s targeted 2 million landlords for persecution and murder. And in the Great Leap Forward of the late 1950s, Mao's botched economic policies resulted in the deaths of as many as 50 to 60 million people. So as we discuss Mao's strategic genius, let's not lose sight of his genocidal depravity.

Mao was born into a modestly prosperous peasant family in 1893. That his family was fairly well-to-do afforded Mao the opportunity for an education. He graduated from the Hunan provincial teachers college and served briefly as an assistant librarian at Peking University, where he was first exposed to Marxism and Leninism. In 1921, Mao attended the founding meeting of the Chinese Communist Party and later joined the Kuomintang, or Chinese Nationalist Party, as part of the First United Front.

It was at this point in 1926 and 1927 that Mao developed an interest in the revolutionary potential of China's poor peasants, penning a famous report on peasant uprisings in his home province of Hunan. The United Front collapsed in 1927 and Chiang Kai-shek ordered a purge of Communists from within his Nationalist Party. Mao was ordered by Communist Party central to lead an uprising against the Nationalists in Hunan, but it failed miserably and Mao was forced to seek refuge in the countryside. Mao and a few remnants of the shattered Chinese Communist Party ultimately established a base area, or Soviet, in the mountains of Jiangxi province.

The Communists were eventually forced out of Jiangxi and onto the Long March, which brought them much weakened, but with Mao now firmly in command, to the even more remote and barren environs of Yenan. It was in Yenan, where Mao began to write at length about strategies in China's revolutionary war.

Mao may have been a product of a traditional Chinese background and steeped in Chinese popular culture, but he was also a devout Marxist-Leninist, and this had a profound impact on his strategic insights. In his views of history, Mao was a true Marxist. In particular, he embraced the idea that all socioeconomic systems throughout history contained within themselves the seeds of their own destruction. He was also profoundly Leninist in his emphasis on the necessity of a disciplined and ideologically pure party to lead the revolution and to prevent the movement from losing track.

This was why Mao was critical of the great rebellions of the Chinese past. They were born out of the fundamental contradictions of the Chinese socioeconomic system, the injustice and inequality of traditional society, but even when they were successful in toppling a dynasty, they simply recreated traditional society with former rebels now in the roles of emperors and Mandarins. A vanguard party was essential to prevent that from happening again. Lenin had also highlighted the importance of wars of national liberation in the developing world as part of the larger struggle against capitalist imperialism. Mao naturally gravitated toward that concept.

While Mao was certainly a devout Communist, he also held some distinctly heterodox views. Most importantly he viewed the poorest peasants in China as the wellspring of revolution, not the small and generally well-paid Chinese industrial proletariat. China was still semi-feudal rather than capitalist. In other words by Marxist orthodoxy it was not yet ready for socialism or communism like say the industrialized societies of Western Europe. But Mao argued that the contradictions in the Chinese socioeconomic system were sufficiently explosive that a Communist-led revolution could speed China through Marx's phases of history. This reinforced the centrality of the party as the vanguard of the revolution.

Mao was also innovative in his focus on the human will. As he writes in *On Protracted War*: "Weapons are ... important ... but not ... decisive ... ; it is people ... that are decisive. [War] is not only a contest of military and economic power, but also a contest of human power and morale." In this regard, Mao was directly and indirectly influenced by Clausewitz. Directly because *On War* was available in Chinese and Mao read it in the late 1930s and indirectly because many of Mao's lieutenants had studied Clausewitz in China and abroad—and also because Lenin had lifted extensively from Clausewitz. We will see a good deal of Clausewitz's influence in a moment, when we explore the elements of Mao's strategic theory.

Some have seen Sunzian inspiration in Mao. I am not convinced. Mao was certainly familiar with the *Sunzi*, and passages from it appear throughout his writings, but they tend to be at the tactical and operational levels of war. As a revolutionary Mao viewed the *Sunzi* as a feudal relic. Moreover, Mao's views on the nature of revolutionary war convinced him that the most famous of Sunzian maxims, "the acme of skill is to win without fighting," was inconceivable.

Turning now to the core elements of the theory as laid out in *On Protracted War* (kind of a riff on Clausewitz's *On War*), Mao is very straightforward and almost scientific. We can also see why Mao is popular among insurgent groups. Mao argues that weakness, defeat, and retreat are necessary starting points for a successful revolution, and I am sure this has provided solace to a lot of insurgents hiding in caves.

On Protracted War lays out a three-phase formula for revolutionary warfare. The first phase is the strategic defense. The second phase is the strategic stalemate and the third is the strategic counteroffensive. As a good Marxist and a good student of Clausewitzian interaction Mao emphasizes the dialectics of each phase, in other words the balance and interaction between the two belligerents.

Let's look at each phase in turn, starting with phase I: Strategic defense. This is where the invader, or the counterrevolutionary, is on the offensive and the insurgent on the defensive. Mao's Red Army trades space for time, taking advantage of China's immense geography and huge population. But Mao's first phase is not just an operational defensive, it is a strategic defensive. It is designed to lure the enemy in deep, to drag him past his culminating point of attack, where small insurgent bands can overwhelm over-extended and isolated enemy units.

These small offensives within the larger strategic defense serve as morale boosters and are an important source of arms and ammunition. At this point, Mao is trying to use the enemy's military strengths against him. Ideally the guerillas are like fish in the sea of a friendly population. The counterinsurgent in contrast is forced into ham-handed methods and has a hard time telling friend from foe. Hopefully this will push the population toward more active support of the revolutionary movement. This is critically important since at this point the revolutionaries are totally beholden to the generosity of the population.

But as much as Mao is trying to convert weaknesses into strengths, the movement is still very weak in the absolute terms of military power, materiel capacity, and political legitimacy. Which brings us to the second phase: Strategic stalemate.

With the enemy frustrated and overextended, the insurgency shifts from military operations to actually trying to build a civilian government. The enemy has essentially ceded large swaths of territory and the insurgency moves from relying on the generosity of the population to actually governing the population. This builds legitimacy for the movement, and it puts them in control of material resources. Nor is phase II completely civil, the army is gaining strength and competence and critically it is continuing to capture supplies and weapons, and hopefully it is also capturing or recruiting enemy soldiers who know how to use these weapons.

As in the first phase, there's a big propaganda element to phase II. The rebels need to sell their message, but they also find themselves on the horns of a dilemma. This is a traditional and conservative society. If the Communists push their ideological agenda and land-reform campaigns too aggressively they run the risk of alienating the population. On the other hand, if they temper their message too much they run the risk of losing revolutionary steam and of undermining their ideological purity.

A successful phase II also assumes that the counterrevolutionaries have reached, or passed, their culminating point of attack. But if the government can go back on the offensive, then the base area becomes a great target. Ultimately phase II is about competent governance and using time to your advantage. Governance builds credibility and capacity, time allows you to hone and spread your message. Time also works against an overextended invader and creates opportunities to cultivate friends abroad. With phase II well underway, the base areas are sufficiently prosperous and the populace sufficiently loyal. The time is now ripe for the transition to Phase III: the strategic counteroffensive.

Ideally phase III is the shortest phase of a protracted war. The rebels have the manpower, materiel, and training necessary to meet the enemy in a conventional campaign. Instead of relying on dispersed guerilla attacks,

Mao's Red Army undertakes the massive and coordinated use of organized violence. They can do this because their secure base areas are providing resources and manpower. The Red Army is also steeped in all of the mechanisms of modern war: training, tactics, doctrine, logistics, intelligence, operational art, and command and control. In phase III, the strategic focus also shifts from the countryside to the cities. Capturing cities increases the political legitimacy of the movement and puts it in control of major economic centers.

But this isn't all homegrown. An insurgency entering phase III often has the active and open support of a foreign benefactor, a comrade like Stalin, who supplies weapons and training and offers the movement political legitimacy. Recent events in Libya are a good example of this dynamic, where NATO played the role of military benefactor to the anti-Qaddafi forces, enabling them to go into phase III. Ultimately the conventional defeat of the counterrevolutionary army on the field compounds the internal weaknesses of this now hollow regime and convinces its allies to abandon it.

At this point, I should point out that *On Protracted War* actually relates to two distinct struggles: the war of national liberation against the Japanese and the revolutionary war against Chiang Kai-shek's Nationalist Party. This is particularly relevant to phase III because the scale of the final counteroffensive will vary depending on whether you are dealing with a foreign occupier or an indigenous government.

The value of the object, maintaining power over occupied territory, will likely be lower for a foreign invader, and in the case of Japan, China was but one of many theatres. Japan faced threats from China, from the allies in India, from the U.S. in the Pacific, and from the Soviet Union. Japan's strategic energies and strategic focus were therefore divided.

An indigenous government on the other hand will probably value its hold of the national territory much more highly and will be much more strategically focused on suppressing the revolution within. In other words a single offensive victory, like say the Battle of Yorktown, might be sufficient to convince a foreign power that the costs of the war have exceeded the value of the object. But when it comes to overthrowing the national government and toppling the ruling class, a series of offensive campaigns will be needed.

While this move to a decisive and overwhelming phase III is certainly appealing in theory, it is a real challenge to implement in practice. A premature leap into a strategic counteroffensive may actually play to the strengths of the incumbent regime and it might even make some sense for the regime to lure the insurgency into phase III. Mao is aware of this problem, not surprising given the beating that the Communists took from the Japanese in 1940 after attempting a premature phase III offensive. But Mao has an answer. If phase III fails, the rebels can fall back on a robust phase II, or even back into phase I. The size of China along with the support of the people and the help of foreign governments gives this movement tremendous depth and flexibility.

So those are the three phases in a nutshell, but before I move on to Mao in practice, I want to take a minute to see what Mao has to say about one of my favorite topics: civil–military relations. On this subject Mao takes Clausewitz's subordination of the military to the political to an extreme. It is pretty much Elliot Cohen's "unequal dialogue" on steroids and the complete antithesis of the normal theory and of the Sunzian general's autonomy. To Mao, politics is war without bloodshed, and war is politics with bloodshed. Where Clausewitz admits that war has a unique grammar, Mao denies that it is unique in any way from politics.

In a revolutionary war everything that the military does has political ramifications, so political oversight must be highly invasive. Political indoctrination of the rank and file pumps up morale and prevents desertions. But there is much more to it than that. Mao grew up in an era of warlordism, when those with the guns dictated to the politicians. Naturally he wants to reverse that and guarantee that the party always controls the gun. Ultimately, maintaining the absolute subordination of the military is essential to winning the war against what Mao calls "the enemies with guns" as well as consolidating the revolution against the "enemies without guns" (the secret counterrevolutionaries).

Given the elegant simplicity of Mao's three-phase script, many people assume that the Chinese Civil War has a very straightforward storyline. Communists build base areas, get proficient at guerilla and then mobile war, spread a message to the masses, and then topple a hopelessly corrupt and incompetent Nationalist regime ruled by the hopelessly corrupt and incompetent Chiang Kai-shek.

The speed of Chiang Kai-shek's collapse in the late 1940s was so shocking that it led generations of historians and strategic analysts to seek macro-explanations for his reversal of fortune. For example, some spoke of the insurmountable flaws in the Nationalist regime, while others offered Marxist explanations of revolutionary inevitability. There were even conspiracy theories that blamed Communist infiltrators in the Roosevelt and Truman administrations for selling out Chiang Kai-shek.

But those explanations completely ignore the "war" part of the Chinese Civil War. And they ignore critical questions, such as: How do you turn a million farm boys into an army? How do you supply such an army? How do you protect such a force until they can shift over to the offense? How do you mechanize a peasant army? How do the Communists go from their nadir of power and legitimacy in 1935 to a point in 1947 where they can go toe-to-toe with Chiang Kai-shek's American trained and armed troops?

So let's step back and look at the actual progress of the Chinese Civil War. Interestingly, what we find is that the war breaks down into three fairly clear phases. The fact that theory and practice generally line up should come as little surprise—since the Chinese Civil War is the reality that generated Mao's three-phase theory. But we are also going to see that Mao's elegant script is a lot more messy and contingent in practice.

Let's start with phase I. Phase I corresponds to the period from 1927–1937 with Chiang Kai-shek on the offensive and the Chinese communists on the defense. Following the demolition of the urban base of the Communist Party in 1927, the remnants fell back to isolated base areas in the deep hinterland, the largest and best organized of which was the Jiangxi Soviet.

Over the next six years the Communists in Jiangxi gradually expanded that base and were able to occupy towns and even some small cities. At the same time they were experimenting with different approaches to land and social reform, and Mao and his military mentor, Marshal Zhu De, cobbled together a modest military force that they grandiosely called the Red Army.

But building a base area requires you to stay in one place and Jiangxi was close to Chiang Kai-shek's core of political power. This made the Jiangxi Soviet vulnerable to encirclement and strangulation. This is exactly what Chiang Kai-shek did in 1933 and 1934 when he forced the Communists to break out of Jiangxi and go on a desperate retreat: The Long March.

By all accounts the Long March was an unmitigated disaster. Unable to systematically extract resources or indoctrinate new supporters, the Communist forces, about 100,000 total, dwindled rapidly. When they finally found refuge in a remote and desolate backwater in northwest China, only 10,000 or 12,000 had survived the ordeal. Chiang Kai-shek tried to repeat this encirclement strategy by sending one of his most powerful domestic rivals, the former Manchurian warlord, to quarantine the Communists in their desolate base area in the Northwest.

But most of Chiang's accomplishments were undone by the Japanese invasion in 1937. Chiang tried to seize the initiative against the Japanese, but his army was no match for the invaders. In short order, he lost most of best-trained military and with it control over eastern China. He was forced to carry on the war from the remote Southwest.

This brings us to phase II. The Japanese invasion provided some relief for the Communists, allowing them to build more base areas in the interstices of an uneven Japanese occupation. The Communists could also play the nationalism card, advertising that they were in the fight against a brutal foreign invader. In reality, after 1941, neither the Japanese nor Chiang Kai-shek could muster enough energy to oust the Communists from their base areas. When Japan surrendered in 1945 Mao had had nearly five years to consolidate in phase II. The Communists were far stronger than they had been in the 1930s and had a higher domestic and international profile. They were, however, still at a significant disadvantage relative to the Nationalists.

They controlled more territory at the end of the war than they did in 1937, but it was far from the best real estate. Additionally, despite large numbers of men in their ranks they faced desperate shortages of weapons, especially standardized light arms and they had almost no tanks, trucks, or artillery.

Over the next two years, however, relative military strength shifted in favor of the Communists and with it came a shift in the balance of power within China. By 1947, the Communists, now armed with captured Japanese and American weapons, and also supplied by the Soviet Union, transitioned to a full-up phase III and by late 1948 600,000 Red Army troops fought an equal number of Nationalist troops for a critical railway junction in Anhui province. In a battle that lasted over two months, the Communists achieved victory through mechanized maneuver warfare and through their new mastery of artillery. By the end of January 1949 Chiang Kai-shek had lost all of North China to the Communists.

On October first, 1949, Mao stood atop the Gate of Heavenly Peace in Beijing and proclaimed the founding of the People's Republic of China. So that pretty much tracks exactly with what Mao describes in *On Protracted War*, but I am actually skipping over a big part of the story, that is the three phases as they operated in Manchuria. And it is useful to take a step back and see what role that theatre played in the power shift in China.

In 1945, both Chiang and Mao took a huge gamble and committed significant forces to Manchuria. We really can't blame them. There was a power vacuum in Manchuria after the fall of the Japanese puppet regime. The three provinces up there were resource rich and had some fairly advanced industrial capacity.

For Mao it looked good because Manchuria was chock-full of surrendering Japanese soldiers and Manchurian puppet troops who were giving up their arms. At this point Manchuria was also occupied by the Soviets and surrounded on three sides by either the Soviet Union or by Soviet proxies. So Mao bet the farm on Manchuria. He basically threw all of his best soldiers and best political mobilizers into the region. In the short term, however, the gamble did not pay off.

Essentially, the Communist rushed into a premature phase II in Manchuria, trying to seize and govern three entire provinces. Chiang Kai-shek seized on their overextension and drove them back into a combination of phase I in southern Manchuria and phase II in some parts of the north.

In the process, however, Chiang got himself overextended. Chiang's army was heavy and mechanized with a lot of offensive punch, but it was also difficult to supply. The further north it advanced the more vulnerable it became. By early 1947 the Nationalists were past their culminating point of attack, but Chiang could not accept the political risks of ceding territory. This meant that the Communist could gradually wear down isolated garrisons and ultimately seize their weapons and vehicles. In the process, Chiang lost many of his best men and best equipment to the Communists. This accelerated the larger political power shift.

This sounds like a classic phase I to phase II move, but the Communists didn't have time to win the loyalty of the population. Instead they decided to shatter local society and go after the "enemies without guns" first, in other words, the landlord class. What followed was a systematic campaign of mass murder to terrorize the people into supporting the Communists.

Backed up by the ruthless exploitation of the people, and enabled by unprecedented amounts of well-trained manpower (captured and dragooned) and mountains of materiel (Japanese, Soviet, and American), Mao's Red Army leapt into phase III. What we see at this point is a mechanized war that bears more than a passing resemblance to the Eastern Front in World War II.

In 1948 the Communists completed the conquest of Manchuria and then threw their full strength into the conquest of those areas south of the Great Wall. At this point the Communists could claim the political legitimacy that they had lacked as rural guerillas. So Manchuria both validates and calls into question Mao's theory. The three phases worked in Manchuria, but at the same time an awful lot of things broke Mao's way. And the conditions might be too ideal to repeat. In other words Manchuria is a problematic proof of Mao's theory.

So let me close with a few reflections on Mao's legacy. Back in his idealistic youth, Mao had envisioned the Communist Party's role as harnessing a whirlwind of popular dissatisfaction. By 1948–1949, after 20 years of brutal struggle, Mao had shifted to a systematic campaign to exploit the peasant masses. That was the only way he could defeat the Nationalists.

This is Clausewitz's trinity in the making. Mao saw that the use of violence by the party could mobilize the passions of the people. Popular passion and popular support would strengthen the party, but also give it the military means to contend with the Nationalists in that realm of chance and probability. By dominating that realm militarily, Mao defeated his enemies and achieved his ultimate political purpose. Mao proved Kissinger wrong, the only way for the guerilla to win, is by winning.

Mao's stunning victory in China made him something of an icon among and a potential strategic model for communists in the developing world. By the 1950s, insurgent leaders were hungrily devouring Mao's writings, and China was sending aid and advisors to movements across the globe. Hanoi was Mao's most important client.

But Mao's legacy goes far beyond the Cold War. From the Shining Path in Peru in the 1980s and 1990s to the Communist movement that took power in Nepal in 2008, Mao's prescriptions for revolution have maintained their appeal and their apparent effectiveness. As we will see in the next lecture, Mao's works are also required reading among counterinsurgency theorists and practitioners.

Even today, our students at the War College, get very animated when they read Mao. Mao is at once novel and alien given how little they tend to know about China and the Chinese Civil War, but at the same time it is also approachable in the simplicity of the three phases and it is intuitively familiar given the U.S. military's recent obsession with counterinsurgency.

For better or for worse and almost four decades after his richly deserved death, Mao lives.

Classics of Counterinsurgency
Lecture 20

The wave of insurgencies that erupted in the 1950s and 1960s forced many political and military leaders to develop responses to Mao's theory of revolutionary war. While the British, French, and Americans all experimented with a range of strategies, it was not until the early 1960s that these experiences were codified in theory. Of the early treatises on counterinsurgency, those by David Galula and Roger Trinquier, both seasoned military professionals with experience in the Algerian War, have proven enduring and influential, especially in the context of America's wars in Iraq and Afghanistan.

Background on Algeria
- Algeria had been conquered in the 1830s and incorporated into metropolitan France soon after; as such, Algeria wasn't considered a colony but an integral part of France.

- In the 1950s, small cells of Algerian nationalists began an insurgency to overturn French rule and to release the grip of the European settlers, known in Algeria as the *pieds noirs*.

- By 1954, Paris was confronted by a major nationalist rebellion led by the Front de Libération Nationale (FLN).
  - This rebellion was an expression of the grievances of a native Algerian population long denied full citizenship and economic opportunity.

  - Much of the FLN effort was concentrated in the cities along the Mediterranean coast, where the nationalist forces conducted a campaign of terrorism.

- The French were initially united in their opposition to Algerian independence, and the French government deployed more than 400,000 troops to Algeria.

- o Starting in Algiers, the French tried to crush the FLN using a mixture of population control, psychological operations, resettlement, and intensive military operations.

- o But when the harsh methods of the elite French paratrooper units (*paras*) became publicly known, the legitimacy of France's claims over Algeria came into question.

- The situation in Algeria, especially in Algiers, was further complicated by the *pieds noirs* and their allies in the French military and Algerian government.
  - o The *pieds noirs* declared their own war against the FLN and were even less restrained than the *paras* in their tactics.

  - o Further, the *pieds noirs* were willing to retaliate against the government and the military when it looked as if French policy was softening toward Algerian independence. The situation devolved into a multidimensional civil war.

- Despite impressive military successes in the period from 1957–1960, the French president, Charles de Gaulle, came to the conclusion that the value of retaining Algeria was not equal to the projected costs in blood, treasure, and French prestige. In the early 1960s, de Gaulle opened negotiations with the FLN, and Algeria gained its independence.

David Galula

- In the mid-1950s, David Galula was a company commander in the rural Kabylie region of northern Algeria. He later became a research fellow at Harvard and was in high demand at the RAND Corporation, where his works were translated into English for an American audience contemplating a major U.S. commitment to Vietnam.

- Galula's theoretical observations on counterinsurgency derived from his own professional experience, as well as his reading of military history and strategic theory. His operational memoir, *Pacification in Algeria, 1956–1958*, offers unflinching criticism of his colleagues in the French army, who relied on counterproductive military solutions to what he understood to be essentially a political problem.

- According to Galula, to wage a successful counterinsurgency, it's necessary to embrace Mao's demolition of the distinction between the political and the military. In other words, in counterinsurgency, all military actions have political implications and vice versa.

- That realization led Galula to the conclusion that the "essence [of counterinsurgency] can be summed up in a single sentence: Build (or rebuild) a political machine from the population upward." Because a Maoist first phase hinges on the population giving material support to the guerillas, the key for the counterinsurgent is controlling the population, not controlling territory.
  - Popular support for either the insurgent or the counterinsurgent is rarely spontaneous or overwhelming, but the insurgent desperately needs material support from the people, while the counterinsurgent needs local allies.

  - In rural Algeria, the French were the outsiders. They needed a local ally to help them win over the population or at least to deny popular support to the insurgency.

  - Such allies are gained through "clear-hold-build" operations, that is, finding and eliminating insurgents, protecting the local population, and rebuilding the infrastructure.

  - In Galula's scheme, once one base of popular support is cleared, held, and rebuilt, the process is repeated in progressively larger areas. The fact that the counterinsurgent has more military power and more resources than the insurgent means that the general population gradually moves from passivity to active support of the counterinsurgency.

  - When that level of popular support is achieved, the counterinsurgent can then move into areas of the country

373

where the insurgency is in a Maoist phase II, trying to hold and govern territory.

- Galula attacks the vulnerabilities of Mao's phase I and phase II to deny the insurgents the ability to progress to the decisive phase III. His solution demands a massive and sustained commitment in time, treasure, and troops, as well as a firm hand to command local respect and reassure local allies of the seriousness of the counterinsurgents.

Roger Trinquier

- Roger Trinquier served in Indochina in the mid-1930s and for 10 years in China. He brought a wealth of insurgency and counterinsurgency experience with the Viet Minh to his assignment in Algeria.

- According to Trinquier, modern war is fundamentally different from traditional war; it is "an interlocking system of actions—political, economic, psychological, military—that aims at the overthrow of the established authority in a country and its replacement by another regime." His fellow officers, however, failed to recognize this change and instead insisted on waging traditional war.

- Trinquier argued that the center of gravity of an insurgency is not the army of the enemy or even the population; it is the "armed clandestine organization" that is trying to impose its will on the population. Modern wars are wars of subversion, not wars of conventional arms. The goal of the counterinsurgent is, therefore, complete destruction of the clandestine organization.

- The problem with urban counterinsurgency is that the enemy can readily hide within the civilian population and exploit the illusion of civil law and order, what Trinquier called the "fiction of peace." The insurgents exploit the fiction of peace to cover the fact that they are waging a war and to prevent the government from responding appropriately. The crisis in Algiers was not a law enforcement problem; it was a war.

The Crisis in Algiers

- Algiers in 1956 was a city of nearly a million people and the political and cultural center of French Algeria. As such, the city was overwhelmingly pro-French. If the FLN were to achieve independence, then French control of Algiers had to be shaken.

- In the heart of Algiers was the Casbah, a densely packed neighborhood of some 80,000 Muslim Algerians. The 1,500-man Algiers command of the FLN enmeshed its clandestine organization within the fabric of the Casbah, from which it could reach out and launch acts of terrorism on the various European districts of the city.

The FLN's campaign of terrorism and murder in Algiers was designed to jumpstart a revolution and strike directly at the heart of French control.

- As intelligence chief and second-in-command of the elite 10th Paratrooper Division in Algiers, Trinquier understood that he had to pierce the veil of the Casbah to get the upper hand over the FLN. Ordinarily, that task would have fallen to the city's police force, but Trinquier assessed that the police in Algiers were not up to the task.

- The French declared martial law in Algiers, creating what Trinquier considered the necessary preconditions for a successful urban counterinsurgency. French *paras* conducted aggressive and highly militarized sweeps of the Casbah, summarily executed insurgents, and used torture to gain intelligence and build a picture of the leadership structure of the FLN.
  - Trinquier knew that torture violates the traditional laws of war, but in his view, it is a necessary evil to combat a war of subversion. French torture was perceived to be so effective that no one in the membership of the FLN could resist.

o The use of torture made an already nervous and highly suspicious FLN see potential French spies everywhere. An added benefit was that the paired threats of indiscriminate sweeps and torture induced many Algerians to spontaneously inform on the FLN.

- Because of his views on torture, Trinquier is not mentioned in the U.S. Army's *Counterinsurgency* field manual, but many elements of his theory are included there in spirit, in particular, his methods for controlling the population and dismantling the insurgent command structure.

- In the end, Trinquier's injunctions on how to fight and win a modern war seem vindicated by the results of the Battle of Algiers. By the summer of 1957, the FLN's Algiers command and control structure was in ruins and its senior leadership was either dead or cooperating with the French.

- At the same time, the national and international blowback that followed the revelations of *para* methods undermined the legitimacy of French rule in Algeria and toppled the government of the Fourth Republic.

The French Defeat as a U.S. Model?

- The U.S. military looked at the Algerian War as a model for the wars in Iraq and Afghanistan because Algeria offered many elements present in those conflicts: a mix of urban and rural theaters, religious and nationalistic motivations, and the successful use of terrorism by an insurgency.

- On the counterinsurgency side, the Algerian War shows us a highly professional but largely conventional French military struggling to respond to a radically different type of war and being called on to perform the functions of both a civilian government and a military occupation.

- Further, Algeria lets us explore the problematic nature of employing tactical and operational expedients, such as torture, forced resettlement, and counterterror, which may enable military success but can also have significant strategic and political blowback.

- It remains to be seen whether a counterinsurgency doctrine based explicitly on the French model of Algeria—a war characterized by the counterinsurgent's use of torture, racial profiling, and extrajudicial executions—makes good political sense in the context of the global war on terror.

Suggested Reading

Aussaresses, *The Battle of the Casbah.*

Galula, *Counterinsurgency Warfare.*

———, *Pacification in Algeria, 1956–1958.*

Horne, *A Savage War of Peace.*

Pontecorvo (director), *The Battle of Algiers* (film).

Trinquier, *Modern Warfare.*

U.S. Army, *Counterinsurgency* (FM 3-24).

Questions to Consider

1. What are the core elements of Galula's and Trinquier's theories of counterinsurgency?

2. Why is it so difficult for counterinsurgents to translate their military superiority into their desired political outcome—the restoration of a stable political order?

Classics of Counterinsurgency
Lecture 20—Transcript

In May 2007 President Bush invited the British historian Alistair Horne to a meeting at the White House to talk about Horne's definitive history of the war for Algerian independence, *A Savage War of Peace*. Given that France lost that war to a stubborn Algerian insurgency, the President was eager to avoid similar mistakes in the wars in Iraq and Afghanistan. Bush may also have wanted to avoid a political implosion like the one that occurred on the French homefront in the early 1960s.

This wasn't the first time that the Algerian analogy had come up. As early as the summer of 2003, only six months into the Iraq War, the film *The Battle of Algiers*, was being screened at the Pentagon. That film chronicles the cycle of terrorism and counterterrorism that gripped Algiers in the mid-1950s and follows France's tactically successful but strategically counter-productive campaign of urban counterinsurgency. For all the talk about the lessons of Vietnam it seemed that the lessons of Algeria were a better match to the global war on terrorism.

The wave of insurgencies that erupted in the 1950s and 1960s forced many political and military leaders to develop responses to Mao's theory of revolutionary war. While the British, French, and the Americans all experimented with a range of strategies, it was not until the early 1960s that these experiences were codified in theory. Of these early treatises on counterinsurgency, those of David Galula and Roger Trinquier have proven enduring and influential especially in the context of America's wars in Iraq and Afghanistan. In fact, the U.S. Army's counterinsurgency manual (FM 3-24), which was overseen by General David Petraeus, owes a lot to the works of these two French officers.

Galula and Trinquier were seasoned military professionals with experience in China and in Indo-China. Both men spoke Chinese and were familiar with Mao's strategy for winning a protracted insurgency. Trinquier's service in Indo-China in the years before the French defeat and Galula's observations of Indo-China and the Huk uprising in the Philippines, gave them additional insight into the potential vulnerabilities of the Maoist Model. It was in

Algeria, however, that they honed their respective theories and attempted to put counterinsurgency theory into practice.

Algeria had been conquered in the 1830s and incorporated into metropolitan France soon after; as such, Algeria wasn't considered a colony, but rather an integral part of France.

Algeria's proximity and the settlement of a million Europeans in the territory made for especially strong political and cultural ties. In the 1950s, however, small cells of Algerian nationalists began an insurgency to overturn French rule and to release the grip of the European settlers, known in Algeria as the *pied-noirs*.

By 1954, the same year as the defeat at Dien Bien Phu in Indochina, Paris was confronted by a major, nationalist rebellion led by the *Front de Libération Nationale* (FLN). This rebellion was an expression of the grievances of a native Algerian population long denied full citizenship and economic opportunity.

French policy, on the other hand, supported the political and economic dominance of the European minority. That policy largely disenfranchised and systematically discriminated against the Arabs and Berbers that made up almost 90 percent of the population.

The FLN took some strategic cues from Mao, but they deviated from the Maoist game plan in significant ways. Insurgency in the countryside generally followed the phase one to phase two progression that we discussed last time, but much of the FLN effort was concentrated in the cities along the Mediterranean coast. There a campaign of terrorism and the murder became a way to jump-start the revolution and to strike directly at the heart of French control.

The French were initially united in their opposition to Algerian independence. Political parties from the far left to the far right all insisted that Algeria was part of France. Backed by popular passion, the French government deployed more than 400,000 troops to Algeria, about half of the regular army. What began as a relatively conventional response to the rebellion had by 1957 been reframed by the French military as a counterrevolutionary struggle against the FLN.

Starting in Algiers, the French tried to crush the FLN using a mixture of population control, psychological operations, resettlement, and intensive military operations. But French counterinsurgency tactics, especially those employed by the elite paratrooper units, or *paras*, started to backfire. The *paras* had been called in to restore order in Algiers, and they employed torture, summary executions, and collective reprisals. The *paras* shattered the urban base of the FLN, but when their methods became public the legitimacy of France's claims over Algeria came into question.

The situation in Algeria, and especially in Algiers, was further complicated by the *pied-noirs* and their allies in the French military and the Algerian government. *Pied-noir*, remember, refers to the European settlers in Algeria. What essentially happened was that the *pied-noirs* declared their own war against the FLN and were even less restrained than the *paras* in their tactics. The *pied-noirs* were also willing to retaliate against the government and the military when it looked as if French policy was softening toward Algerian independence. There was also a violent power struggle going on between rival factions of Algerian nationalists. Algeria devolved into a multidimensional civil war.

Despite impressive military successes in the period from 1957 to 1960, the French were unable to translate that into political success. The French president, Charles de Gaulle, came to the conclusion that the value of retaining Algeria was not equal to the projected costs in blood, treasure, and French prestige. In the early 1960s De Gaulle opened negotiations with the FLN. Despite numerous coup attempts by extremists in the French army and a *pied-noir* terrorism campaign in Algeria and in France, De Gaulle made a deal with the FLN and Algeria became independent.

So what do our two theorists, David Galula and Roger Trinquier, have to say about the lessons of Algeria? Let's start with David Galula. Galula was born in French Tunisia and graduated from the French Military academy at St Cyr in 1939. As a Jew he was expelled from the French military under the Vichy government, but later joined De Gaulle's Army of National

Liberation in 1944 and saw action in the final stages of the European War. In 1945, he was assigned to the French Embassy in Beijing at the height of the Chinese Civil War. He also served in the Philippines and Hong Kong and was a UN observer in the Balkans. A brilliant and intensely active staff officer, Galula pored over the works of Mao and over the Western literature on counterinsurgency, and he brought a great deal of energy to his service in the Colonial Infantry in Algeria in the mid-1950s.

He was a company commander in the rural Kabylie region of northern Algeria and later worked on various headquarter staffs. In the 1960s Galula was a research fellow at Harvard and was in high demand at the Rand Corporation, where his works were translated into English for an American audience contemplating a major U.S. commitment to Vietnam. In fact, at one point Henry Cabot Lodge, the U.S. Ambassador in Saigon, argued to President Johnson that Westmoreland's strategy was misguided and that Galula was a better model for pacifying South Vietnam. Despite that high-level endorsement, Galula had little influence on U.S. counterinsurgency in the 1960s.

Galula's theoretical observations on counterinsurgency derived from his own professional experience as well as his reading of military history and strategic theory. Galula's operational memoir, *Pacification in Algeria 1956–1958*, is a detailed account of his service and is the basis for the theory he presents in his later book *Counterinsurgency Warfare*. In *Pacification in Algeria* Galula offers unflinching criticism of his colleagues in the French Army who relied on counterproductive military solutions to what he understood to be essentially a political problem.

According to Galula, if you are going to wage a successful counterinsurgency then you have to embrace Mao's demolition of the distinction between the political and the military. In other words, in counterinsurgency everything you do militarily has political implications and vice versa. That realization led Galula to the conclusion that, and I quote, the "essence [of counterinsurgency] can be summed up in a single sentence: Build (or rebuild) a political machine from the population upward."

Since a Maoist first phase hinges on the population giving material support to the guerillas, the key for the counterinsurgent is controlling the population, not controlling territory. In addition, insurgencies are forced to start from weakness because their cause enjoys little overt support from the masses and might even engender outright hostility from some of the population.

Popular support for either the insurgent or the counterinsurgent is rarely spontaneous or overwhelming, but the counterinsurgent desperately needs material support from the people. What the counterinsurgent needs are local allies. In rural Algeria the French are outsiders. They need a local ally to help them win over the population or at least to deny popular support to the insurgency.

But how do they get such allies? We can find Galula's answer in David Petraeus's FM 3-24. The answer lies in "clear-hold-build operations": You clear by finding and eliminating the insurgents; you hold by protecting the local population; and you build by rebuilding the infrastructure, increasing the legitimacy of the local government, and bringing the rule of law to that area.

Denying the insurgent the ability to control large segments of the population forces them to remain in phase I and prevents the movement from building military momentum or political legitimacy. The counterinsurgent, on the other hand, has to avoid overly aggressive and overly offensive pacification. Using too heavy a hand and or pushing your operations too far run the risk of alienating the population and pushing you past your culminating point. In other words, those mistakes might help the insurgent's transition to phase two.

In Galula's scheme, once you have cleared, held, and built one base of popular support, you repeat the process in progressively larger areas. The fact that the counterinsurgent has more military power and more resources than the insurgent, means that the general population gradually moves from passivity to active support of the counterinsurgency.

Galula puts it this way: "The counterinsurgent reaches a position of strength when his power is embedded in a political organization issuing from, and firmly supported by, the population." When that level of popular support is achieved, the counterinsurgent can then move into areas of the country where the insurgency is in a Maoist phase two, where the insurgent is trying to hold and govern territory.

As we can see Galula is attacking the vulnerabilities of Mao's phase I and phase II to deny the insurgents the ability to progress to the decisive phase III. For an insurgency struggling in phase I, Galula prescribes denying them moral and material support. If they are in Phase II, then you mass against their conventional and guerilla units to drive them out of their base areas, dismantle their government apparatus, and replace it with one that you and your local allies have built.

But before you start thinking that Galula has come up with an easy answer to the counterinsurgency dilemma, keep in mind the costs of his strategy. If you are going to defeat a Maoist insurgency you need to out-protract the protractor. We are talking then about a massive and sustained commitment in time, treasure and troops. Galula thinks it is possible in Algeria because of the scale of the French military commitment (4000,000 men), the relative ease with which Algeria's borders can be sealed, and because the FLN lacks a ready base of spontaneous popular support. If you change any one of those factors you might dramatically alter the counterinsurgent's chances of success.

In addition, if you spend any time reading Galula you are quickly disabused of the idea that he is some warm and fuzzy, win the hearts and minds kind of guy. What he is talking about early in the counterinsurgency is population control, not population security. A firm and resolute hand is needed to command respect and to reassure local allies of your seriousness. This may involve the forced resettlement of the population into fenced camps. Nor is Galula opposed to immediate, merciless, and very public punishment of rebels and he is not shy about saying that this is the only thing these "people" understand.

Galula is also asking the army to take on the role of civilian government. Consider this passage from *Pacification in Algeria*:

To confine soldiers to purely military functions while urgent and vital tasks have to be done, and nobody else is available to undertake them, would be senseless. The soldier must then be prepared to become a propagandist, a social worker, a civil engineer, a schoolteacher, a nurse.

Whether or not the French government, the French People, or the French Army had the will and capacity to sustain this kind of effort is another matter entirely.

Finally, while Galula might be on to something when it comes to winning the war in the countryside, we are only talking about a single snapshot of a large and diverse war with multiple theatres and multiple insurgent centers of gravity. Galula might have the answer for the population as one center of gravity, but we also need to look at Roger Trinquier's strategy for going after the FLN's leadership, especially in Algiers.

Trinquier was a decade older than Galula and had a good deal more combat experience. Trinquier served in Indo-China in the mid-30s, and then served for 10 years in China. Despite the fact that he had served under the Vichy government, Trinquier stayed in the army and spent much of the late 1940s and early 1950s in Indo-China. There Trinquier led airborne commando units that operated behind Viet-Minh lines to disrupt the insurgency and shake their hold over the population. In fact, at one point Trinquier was running his own anti-communist insurgency with as many as 10,000 local fighters.

He therefore brought a wealth of insurgency and counterinsurgency experience to his assignment in Algeria. Trinquier was a hard-boiled operator, but he was also a careful student of the theory and history of insurgency and counterinsurgency. In fact he was a very prolific author. He wrote nearly a dozen books, the most famous of which is *Modern Warfare: A French View of Counter-insurgency*. Trinquier wrote on all aspects of counterinsurgency, urban and rural, but in the interests of time I am just going to focus on urban counterinsurgency and on the Battle of Algiers: the 1956 to 1957 struggle in Algeria's largest city. In Algiers, Trinquier served as intelligence chief and second in command of the elite 10th Paratrooper Division.

According to Trinquier, modern war is fundamentally different from traditional war, which in his view had been rendered obsolete. Modern war was, as he put it, "an interlocking system of actions—political, economic, psychological, military—that aims at the overthrow of the established authority in a country and its replacement by another regime." War in the style of Clausewitz or Jomini, was well and truly dead. But in his mind, Trinquier's fellow officers had failed to realize this sea-change and instead insisted on waging traditional war. That and political weakness had cost the French the war in Indo-China and might cost them the war in Algeria.

In conducting modern warfare, Trinquier argued that the center of gravity of an insurgency is not the army of the enemy, or even the population, it is the "armed clandestine organization" that is trying to impose its will on the population. Modern wars are wars of subversion, not wars of conventional arms.

The goal of the counterinsurgent is therefore the complete destruction of the "clandestine organization." The problem with urban counterinsurgency is that the enemy can readily hide within the civilian population and it can exploit the illusion of civil law and order. This is what Trinquier called the "fiction of peace." The insurgents exploit the fiction of peace to cover the fact that they are actually waging a war and to prevent the government from responding appropriately. The crisis in Algiers was not a law enforcement problem; it was a war.

Algiers in 1956 was a city of nearly a million people. The overwhelming majority were European *pied-noirs*. Algiers was also the political and cultural center of French Algeria. As such, the city was overwhelmingly pro-French and if the FLN were to achieve independence, then French control of Algiers had to be shaken.

In the heart of this most French of Algeria's cities was the Casbah, a densely packed neighborhood of some 80,000 Muslim Algerians. The 1,500-man Algiers command of the FLN enmeshed its clandestine organization within the fabric of the Casbah. The Casbah was a perfect base for the FLN, as Algerian Muslims they blended in naturally in this anonymous crush of humanity. In addition, French civilian governance generally stopped at the perimeter of the Casbah, and this Algerian ghetto was smack dab in the middle of Algiers. As a result, the FLN could reach out and launch spectacular acts of terrorism on the various European districts of the city.

Trinquier understood all of this and as an intelligence officer he understood that if the *paras* were going to get the upperhand over the FLN then he had to pierce the veil of the Casbah. Ordinarily that task would have fallen to the city's police force, but Trinquier assessed that the police in Algiers were not up to the task. For one, they were understaffed. Secondly, the police were dominated at the top by *pied-noirs*, some of whom had gone rogue and were involved in a campaign of violent reprisals against the Algerians. At the lower level, local Algerian cops couldn't be trusted not to be FLN spies.

Let's stop a moment to think about the nature of a police force. Local police are effective because they have a lot of local knowledge. They know the people and they know the streets, they are also not very disruptive, they can gather intelligence through more subtle and discriminate methods. On the other hand, local police are constrained by civilian law. In addition both the police and the justice system work very slowly and most of all police and judicial work tends to be reactive. The police generally investigate crimes that have already taken place and try to catch the perpetrators.

To Trinquier and his superiors in Algiers the innate strengths of the local police had been rendered moot and their innate vulnerabilities were what the FLN was trying to exploit. The *paras* had to step in to do the job of the civilian police, which was made possible when the French declared martial law in Algiers. Martial law creates what Trinquier considers the necessary preconditions for a successful urban counterinsurgency, but it also creates a few paradoxes.

In the first place declaring war on the FLN actually increases the FLN's prestige, and it heightens national and international scrutiny of the events in Algiers. In the second place, calling on the military to do police work may be counterproductive. The military are outsiders, and they don't have that local knowledge. As a result, they are going into this thing at a distinct intelligence disadvantage. They are also far less discriminate and far more disruptive than the police. Most importantly Trinquier wants to go on the offensive against the FLN. To do that he needs preemptive intelligence gathering, not reactive police work to punish the perpetrators.

There is a really fascinating scene in the film *Battle of Algiers* where the French *para* commander, Col. Mathieu, who was partly based on Trinquier, explains this very challenge. The army has been called in to do police work, but they have neither the time nor the skills to do ordinary police work. They have to rely on what they are good at.

Trinquier and his alter-ego Col. Mathieu accept the paradoxical nature of what they are doing and are unapologetic about the aggressive and highly militarized sweeps of the Casbah, the summary execution of insurgents, and the widespread use of torture. Torture in particular was critical to winning the intelligence battle. (These are Trinquier's opinions, not mine.) Once an insurgent was captured whatever information he had would only be useful for a short period of time. The FLN was a highly compartmentalized clandestine organization. Each prisoner potentially had a snapshot of one part of the FLN organization. Trinquier needed to amass enough of those snapshots to get a clear picture of the whole leadership structure so that he could strike at the heart of the FLN. Each bit of actionable intelligence extracted by torture led to further strikes and sweeps, which yielded a bigger intelligence picture of the FLN's command and control apparatus. In fact, there are lots of organizational charts in Trinquier's book *Modern Warfare* and if you watch the movie *Battle of Algiers* you'll see similar charts on easels around Colonel Mathieu's headquarters, on which the *paras* were trying to graph their enemies. U.S. forces in Afghanistan engaged in almost identical charting of Al Qaeda and the Taliban.

But you'll rarely hear U.S. counterinsurgency experts mention Trinquier by name. Why not? Well, torture. Trinquier is almost clinical about torture. He knows it violates the traditional laws of war, but in his view torture is a necessary evil to combat a war of subversion. Nor does he hold any animosity toward the FLN's gunmen and bomb-throwers. They are soldiers just like him and once they give up their information they should be treated as normal POWs. To Trinquier, torture has the added benefit of accelerating the implosion of the FLN. French methods of torture are so shocking (not surprising given that the French *paras* had learned them from the Nazis, the

Japanese, and the Viet-minh), they are so shocking and so well-known in the Casbah that they sow distrust within FLN ranks. French torture is perceived to be so effective that no one, not even the most loyal FLN member, can resist.

What Trinquier did through his use of torture then was to make an already nervous and highly suspicious FLN see potential French spies everywhere. The FLN rank and file started to suspect each other and to inform on and murder their comrades. An additional benefit was that the paired threats of indiscriminate sweeps and torture induced many Algerians to spontaneously inform on the FLN. (Again, these are Trinquier's conclusions, not mine.)

Understandably, many people fixate of Trinquier's endorsement of torture, and it is probably good that General Petraeus' Counterinsurgency Manual makes no mention of Roger Trinquier. But many elements of his theory are there in spirit. In particular Trinquier's *Modern Warfare* provides very detailed discussions of how the counterinsurgent controls the population through grid patterns staffed by hierarchies of departments that put state agents in direct contact with the population, highly accurate census taking to map the human terrain, ID cards, and checkpoints.

American techniques for securing neighborhoods in Baghdad and Fallujah bore more than a passing resemblance to Trinquier's techniques. In addition, Trinquier's approach to dismantling the insurgent command structure through superior intelligence and superior firepower strongly resembles the approach of U.S. Special Forces in Iraq and Afghanistan.

In the end, Trinquier's injunctions on how to fight and win a modern war seem vindicated by the results of the Battle of Algiers. In January 1957, the *paras* had a clear enough intelligence picture of the FLN to disrupt a planned general strike; this was a major blow to the prestige of the FLN. By the summer of 1957 the FLN's Algiers command and control structure was in ruins and its senior leadership was either dead or cooperating with the French.

But at the same time the national and international blowback that followed the revelations of *para* methods undermined the legitimacy of French rule in

Algeria and toppled the government of the Fourth Republic. De Gaulle came to the presidency deeply conflicted about Algeria. In the end he decided that France would be better off without its North African territories. Many of the *paras* understandably viewed this as a betrayal and an admission of defeat in a war that they believed that they had won.

The fact that France lost this war might raise legitimate questions about why we are looking at it in this course and why the United States military looked at it as a model for the wars in Iraq and Afghanistan. But it is an important case. For one, winners don't have a monopoly on strategic wisdom; there is a lot to learn from failure. Secondly, the Algerian War offers a mix of urban and rural theatres, it introduces religious and nationalistic motivations into insurgency and it highlights the successful use of terrorism by an insurgency. Does any of this sound familiar? It should, because many of our contemporary adversaries take their cues from the FLN in Algeria.

On the counterinsurgency side, the Algerian War shows us a highly professional, but largely conventional, French military struggling to respond to a radically different type of war and at the same time being called upon to perform the functions of both civilian government and of a military occupation. One can only wish that our interest in Algeria had begun before the wars in Afghanistan and Iraq rather than beginning in the midst of those two conflicts. Algeria also lets us explore the problematic nature of employing tactical and operational expedients like torture, forced resettlement, and counter terror, which may enable military success, but can also have huge strategic and political blowback.

Ultimately what David Petraeus and the other authors of FM 3-24 were trying to do was to replicate French counterinsurgency successes and at the same time avoid their mistakes. It remains to be seen, however, whether a counterinsurgency doctrine based explicitly on the French model of Algeria, a war characterized by the counterinsurgent's use of torture, racial profiling, and extra-judicial executions makes good political sense in the context of the global war on terror.

Just-War Theory
Lecture 21

Questions regarding the morality of war are as old as war itself, and all serious scholars and practitioners of war need to take such issues into account. This is why just-war doctrine—which has grown out of centuries-old religious and secular writings concerning the morality of war—is an important part of the curriculum at military academies, war colleges, and security studies programs and an invaluable complement to our study of the classics of strategic theory. In fact, as we'll see in this lecture, the language and principles of just-war theory have become pervasive and inescapable in the study and conduct of warfare.

An Ancient Tradition

- In *The City of God*, St. Augustine addressed a fundamental paradox of the western Roman Empire: It was a Christian state committed to peace, but it was also a territorial entity beset by enemies. To Augustine, Christians could be pacifists as individuals, but a Christian state required a legitimate recourse to war. In wrestling with this paradox, Augustine laid the foundations for *jus ad bellum*, the just recourse to war.

- In his *Summa theologica*, Thomas Aquinas expanded on Augustine to resolve some of the lingering questions about morality and war. For a war to be just, Aquinas argued, it had to meet three criteria: (1) The decision for war must be exclusively reserved to the ruler; (2) war must be fought for a just cause and to reestablish justice; (3) the intentions of the ruler in going to war, not merely the rationale for war, must be just.

- Hugo Grotius, a 17th-century Dutch jurist, began the process of translating just-war theory into modern international law. Among his most important contributions was advancing the rules that govern *jus in bello*, the just conduct of war.

- The contemporary scholar Brian Orend has proposed a third category within just-war theory: *jus post bellum*, the just termination of war.

Jus ad bellum

- The lynchpin of *jus ad bellum* is that war is waged for a just cause—for example, to right a wrong, resist aggression, or defend the innocent.

- The second criterion of *jus ad bellum* is right intention, meaning that a belligerent must be sincere in its claims to seek justice and right wrongs.

- The third criterion stresses that only the proper authorities of a sovereign state may declare war and that the declaration must be made public.

For the 17th-century Dutch jurist Hugo Grotius, as much as the justness of the cause matters, so too does the justness with which states wage war.

- The fourth criterion is that war must be a last resort; it is justified only when all other peaceful means have been exhausted.

- The fifth criterion posits that a just war must stand a reasonable chance of success. Committing national suicide, even in the pursuit of a just cause, is not just.

- The last criterion of *jus ad bellum* is proportionality. The inevitable costs in death and destruction that a belligerent is likely to inflict and to suffer must be proportional to the magnitude of the injustice being rectified.

- The concepts and vocabulary of *jus ad bellum* are deeply entrenched in international law, in the teachings of the Catholic Church, and in the charter of the United Nations.

Jus in bello

- *Jus in bello* concerns the actions that a belligerent takes in war itself. These standards are codified in international conventions, such as The Hague and Geneva conventions. Deviation from these strictures makes even the most justifiable wars immoral.

- The first key principle of *jus in bello* is that military operations must distinguish between combatants and noncombatants and, to the greatest extent possible, minimize noncombatant casualties.

- The second principle is that military actions cannot be disproportionately costly relative to the military value of the target being attacked. This involves an assessment of the likely costs suffered by both sides.

- Third, operations must be guided by military necessity, targets must be legitimate military targets, and their destruction or capture must contribute measurably to the military defeat of the enemy.

- Fourth, prisoners of war can no longer be treated as active combatants. They must be looked after humanely and repatriated at the earliest possible moment.

- Finally, no means may be used in war that are *mala in se*, that is, evil in and of themselves. This includes rape, torture, the recruitment of children, collective reprisals, and the use of any technology that is by its nature indiscriminate, especially weapons of mass destruction.

- In addition to the standards covering military operations, some just-war scholars argue that a state at war should not infringe on the rights of its own population. Internment of suspect minorities, press censorship, and the suspension of elections and legal rights may all call into question the just conduct of a war.

Jus post bellum

- As mentioned earlier, *jus post bellum*, the just end of war, is a relatively new idea, but we can still identify several characteristics of a just peace.

- First, a just war, justly waged, is justly won only if the terms of the peace vindicate the original grievances. In other words, the peace doesn't simply restore the status quo ante but establishes a better and more just state of peace.

- The demands of the victors must be proportional in a just peace. They must not be excessively punitive relative to the injustice that was the cause of the war.

- Further, peace terms must distinguish between soldiers and civilians and between the government and the population. The weight of the punishment must fall on the decision-makers, not the people.

- A just peace also includes fair systems of compensation. The victims of aggression might have their losses made good. This is often at the discretion of the victor, who may choose to forgo reparations.

- Fair and public trials must be held for the senior leaders who violated *jus ad bellum* and for the military commanders who violated *jus in bello*.

- Finally, a victor may bear a heavy responsibility to rehabilitate a defeated foe and rebuild its institutions of government.

Jus ad bellum in Iraq

- In 2003, President Bush asserted that the war in Iraq was a just cause. His rationale was twofold: first, self-defense against the possibility of an attack by Iraq and, second, the illegitimacy and brutality of Saddam Hussein's regime.

- Bush also claimed that the United States and its allies had right intentions. In his address to the American people on the first night of the war, the president said, "We have no ambition in Iraq, except to remove a threat and restore control of that country to its own people."

- The president made these justifications public and believed he had proper authority as elected representative of the American people. He also had the consent of Congress and international support. On the other hand, the lack of a final UN resolution meant that Bush's rhetorical position was not unassailable.

- War against Iraq was claimed as a last resort. Bush offered Hussein and his two sons a 48-hour window to leave Iraq and prevent a war, thus shifting the moral burden for the war to the Iraqi leader.

- Proportionality and the probability of success were bound up in the war plan that applied "decisive force" and would "not be a campaign of half measures." But it was also a plan that targeted the regime, not the population.

Jus in bello in Iraq

- Regarding *jus in bello*, Bush's speech at Camp Lejeune in 2003 noted that the standard operating procedures of the Iraqi military were *mala in se*, but the liberators did not sink to those depths.

- American and allied troops treated civilians kindly, tried to spare noncombatants from harm, and showed respect to soldiers who surrendered. They were also careful to distinguish between soldiers and civilians. For example, the extensive use of precision guided munitions was intended to satisfy proportionality and to limit civilian casualties.

- Target selection in Operation Iraqi Freedom was also based on the *jus in bello* standard of military necessity.

Lecture 21: Just-War Theory

394

- The incredible performance of the allied military forces in March and April 2003 set a new standard for abiding by the stringent requirements of *jus in bello*.

Jus post bellum in Iraq

- It is easy to find fault with the planning and execution of the post-combat phase of Operation Iraqi Freedom, but the Bush administration did pay significant attention to many of the criteria of *jus post bellum* in the lead-up to the war.

- As we said, the peace terms that conclude a just war should establish better conditions than those that existed prior to the conflict, and for President Bush, the status quo ante was unacceptable. The key rationale and goal of the war was to replace Hussein's regime with a democratic Iraq, but that set the bar of expectations and postwar responsibilities high.

- Nonetheless, when it became clear that Hussein had lost hold of the reins of power, President Bush made a public declaration that the aims of the war had been accomplished. The United States and Great Britain claimed the authority of occupying powers in accordance with international laws and conventions.

- Again, although critical elements of postwar planning were lacking, the administration had made extensive preparations for near-term humanitarian crises, such as famine and a crush of refugees.

- During the occupation, the Coalition Provisional Authority tried to discriminate in its pursuit of the Iraqi leadership. The subsequent decisions to disband the Iraqi army and purge all Ba'athists from the government were further attempts to hold only a portion of the population responsible and to reform dysfunctional institutions.

- The United States did not seek compensation for itself or its allies, and although it held international criminal tribunals, it urged the new Iraqi government to publicly try Hussein and his inner circle.

- The jury is still out on how well the United States and its allies met the *jus post bellum* criteria in Iraq, but the standards were clearly considered.

The Moral Element in Strategy
- Many of the strategists we have talked about in this course have been rightly obsessed with maximizing efficiency and effectiveness in war. In contrast, abiding by just-war principles is decidedly inefficient.

- Furthermore, in making the just-war argument, a state runs the risk of ceding the moral high ground to its critics and opponents. No state can possibly meet all of the just-war criteria, and any failure threatens to undermine the moral legitimacy of the entire war.

- Despite these persistent problems, the efforts of the Bush administration to meet the just-war standards in Operation Iraqi Freedom reveal just how deeply these concepts are ingrained in 21st-century military strategy.

Suggested Reading

Orend, *The Morality of War*.

Walzer, *Just and Unjust Wars*.

Questions to Consider

1. What are the three aspects of just-war doctrine?

2. Which just-war strictures are the most difficult to satisfy? Was Operation Iraqi Freedom a just war?

Just-War Theory
Lecture 21—Transcript

In an address to the Marines at Camp Lejeune in April 2003, President George W. Bush characterized U.S. actions in Iraq in the following way:

> By our actions, we serve a great and just cause. ... In combat, Saddam's thugs shield themselves with women and children. They have killed Iraqi citizens who welcome coalition troops. They force other Iraqis into battle, by threatening to torture or kill their families. ... In stark contrast, the citizens of Iraq are coming to know what kind of people we have sent to liberate them. American forces and our allies are treating innocent civilians with kindness, and showing proper respect to soldiers who surrender.

Regardless of what you may think about the rationales for and conduct of the Iraq War, what I find really interesting in this speech is the invocation of so many of the elements of the just-war tradition. It may be boilerplate, it may be sincere, but it is remarkable that here we have the most powerful man in the world obliged to frame his discussion of a 21st-century war in the vocabulary of medieval theologians and 17th-century jurists.

While the masters we've studied so far have focused primarily on the operational, strategic, and political levels of warfare, their works do deal with moral issues from time to time. For example, the *Sunzi* asserts that the use of the military is governed by five fundamental factors, one of which is "the moral law which causes the people to be in complete accord with their ruler."

Clausewitz places even greater emphasis on moral factors, arguing that "moral elements are among the most important in war." Indeed, he warns that the "loss of moral equilibrium must not be underestimated" because "it can attain such massive proportions that it overpowers everything by its irresistible force."

The moral dilemmas posed by warfare are also captured in Thucydides' famous Melian dialogue where the Athenians dismiss to the pleas of the

Melians for fairness and justice by warning them that "the strong do what they can and the weak suffer what they must."

And in our last block, we confronted the moral qualms and the political blowback aroused by the French Army's use of torture in Algeria.

Questions regarding the morality of war are, therefore, as old as war itself and all serious scholars and practitioners of war need to take these issues into account. This is why just war doctrine is an important part of the curriculum at military academies, war colleges, and security studies programs. It is an invaluable complement to our study of the classics of strategic theory. In fact, as we'll see today the language and principles of just-war theory have become pervasive and inescapable.

Just-war theory grows out of centuries-old religious and secular writings concerning the morality of war. It draws on ancient Greek philosophy and principles found in the Koran. But perhaps most notably the just war tradition grew out of the writings of St. Augustine and Thomas Aquinas— who, as theologians, could not afford to be as cavalier or cold-blooded about war as some of our masters.

Both Augustine and Aquinas offered ethical criteria for judging whether a war was just and whether it was fought by just means.

In *The City of God* Augustine addressed a fundamental paradox of the Western Roman Empire. It was a Christian state committed to peace, but it was also a territorial entity beset by enemies. To Augustine, Christians could be pacifists as individuals, but a Christian state required a legitimate recourse to war. In wrestling with this paradox, Augustine laid the foundations for *jus ad bellum*, the just recourse to war. He writes: "It is the wrongdoing of the opposing party which compels the wise man to wage just wars."

In his *Summa Theologica*, Thomas Aquinas expanded on Augustine to resolve some of the lingering questions about morality and war. For a war to be just, Aquinas argued, it had to meet three criteria: The decision for war was exclusively reserved to the ruler; war must be fought for a just cause, to punish a wrong, and to reestablish justice; the intentions of the ruler in going to war, not merely the rationale for war, must be just.

Augustine and Aquinas were not naïve idealists. The world of man was an imperfect place and they did not delude themselves into thinking that war could be perfectly just. But they did strive to create standards of justice in war based on the Judeo-Christian tradition. And their ideas took hold: Just think of the horror that Machiavelli inspired with his over-the-top realism. By the time of the Renaissance notions of Just War had spread to the secular world.

Hugo Grotius, the 17th-century Dutch jurist, began the process of translating just war theory into modern international law. Among his most important contributions was the third volume of *On the Laws of War and Peace*. This work moves beyond *jus ad bellum* and advances the rules that govern *jus in bello*, the just conduct of war.

As much as the justness of the cause matters, for Grotius so too did the justness with which states waged war. Barring a body of rules of conduct, war could become so depraved that (as Grotius puts it) "even barbarous races should be ashamed." More recently, the political philosopher Michael Walzer, has refined these philosophical precepts and applied them to contemporary warfare. Walzer's work has influenced the last three decades of the just-war debate.

So the just-war tradition is very old, but it is also growing and maturing. Just in the last decade the scholar Brian Orend, has proposed a third category within just-war theory. Orend calls this *jus post bellum*, the just termination of war.

So we have just-war doctrine divided into three categories. *Jus ad bellum* (the just recourse to war) establishes the ethical criteria by which political leaders determine whether or not a war should be declared. *Jus in bello* (the just conduct of war) provides ethical guidelines for the manner in which combatants should carry out a war. And *jus post bellum* (the just termination of war) concerns justice after a war, including peace treaties, reconstruction, war crimes trials, and reparations.

I'd like to go into a little bit of detail on each of these three categories and hopefully prove to you why the just-war school matters through illustrations from history. All three elements of the tradition establish exceedingly rigorous and detailed criteria. Obviously in practice pure justice is illusory, but I suppose it is better to have lofty standards to shoot for than no standards at all.

So let's begin with *jus ad bellum*, the just recourse to war. The lynchpin of *jus ad bellum* is of course that the war is waged for a just cause—for example, to set right a wrong, or to resist aggression, or to defend the innocent. Legitimate regimes are expected to eschew wars of aggression, but if they pursue them other states have just cause to resort to war to punish them and to restore international harmony and justice.

To see a terrific argument for just cause, we only need to look to our own Declaration of Independence. Jefferson offers a litany of injustices perpetrated on the colonies. And he asserts:

> [W]hen a long train of abuses and usurpations, pursuing invariably the same object evinces a design to reduce them under absolute despotism, it is [the people's] right, it is their duty, to throw off such government, and to provide new guards for their future security.

Just cause is also enshrined in Article 51 of the United Nations charter, which upholds the right of all nations to self-defense.

The second criterion of *jus ad bellum* is right intention. Basically this means that a belligerent is sincere in its claims to seek justice and right wrongs. Such claims have to be more than pretense. They can't just be top-cover for a land grab or the seizure of a critical asset. In the first Gulf War, the Bush administration was at great pains to avoid any hint that we were after anything more than the just causes of liberating Kuwait and punishing Iraq.

The third criterion stresses that only the proper authorities of a sovereign state may declare war and that the declaration must be made public. For example, on the morning of December 7th 1941, just after the attack on Pearl Harbor, Emperor Hirohito promulgated an official declaration of war against the United States and Great Britain. The declaration also articulated Japanese grievances. Even though they had launched a surprise attack, the Japanese still felt obliged to abide by the international standard of a formal public declaration.

The fourth criterion is last resort. War is justified only when all other peaceful means have been exhausted. Again the Declaration of Independence establishes a tradition for U.S. governments to exhaust, or at least claim to exhaust, all means short of war prior to making this momentous decision. As Jefferson put it, "In every stage of these oppressions we have petitioned for redress in the most humble terms: our repeated petitions have been answered only by repeated injury."

Criterion five posits that a just war must stand a reasonable chance of success. Committing national suicide even in the pursuit of a just cause is not just.

Finally we have proportionality. The inevitable costs in death and destruction that a belligerent is likely to inflict, and to suffer, must be proportional to the magnitude of the injustice being rectified. This standard of proportionality requires a belligerent to judge whether it is worth it to humanity to right this particular wrong.

To be considered just, a decision to go to war must meet all of these criteria. The concepts and vocabulary of *jus ad bellum* are inescapable. For example, they are deeply entrenched in international law, in the teachings of the Catholic Church and in the charter of the United Nations.

Once a decision for war is made, its conduct is also governed by highly demanding standards. *Jus in bello* concerns the actions that a belligerent takes in war itself. These standards are codified in international conventions, such as the Hague and Geneva Conventions. Deviate from these strictures and even the most justifiable wars become immoral. It is the criteria of *jus in bello* that weigh heaviest on our military planners and operators and that are most obvious in our Rules of Engagement.

The five key principles of *jus in bello* are: 1) Military operations must distinguish between combatants and non-combatants and to the greatest extent possible minimize non-combatant casualties. This standard of distinction raises serious questions about actions like the firebombing of Tokyo and Dresden. 2) Military actions cannot be disproportionately costly relative to the military value of the target being attacked. Again, this involves an assessment of the likely costs suffered by both sides. A nuclear exchange is not a proportional response to a dispute over a border crossing. 3) Operations must be guided by military necessity, targets must be legitimate military targets, and their destruction or capture must contribute measurably to the military defeat of the enemy. Again, bombing civilians in the hopes that they might rise up and overthrow their government would fail this test. 4) Prisoners of war are out of the fight and can no longer be treated like active combatants. They must be looked after humanely and repatriated at the earliest possible moment. After September 11th, the Bush administration struggled to show that this standard did not apply to the "unlawful enemy combatants" that were captured in Afghanistan. 5) No means may be used that are *mala in se*, evil in and of themselves. This includes rape, torture, recruiting children, collective reprisals, and the use of any technology that is by its nature indiscriminate, especially weapons of mass destruction.

Abiding by *jus in bello*, becomes all the more complicated when the adversary does not abide by the same norms. Counterinsurgency operations in Iraq and Afghanistan confront movements that intentionally blur the distinctions between combatants and non-combatants. They seek to induce indiscriminate overreactions and reprisals, but this is nothing new.

Theologians, statesmen, and military planners have been confronting this dilemma for decades if not centuries. In fact, the U.S. counterinsurgency field manual, FM 3-24, is laden with references to all the core elements of *jus in bello*. Restraint and discrimination come to the fore as keys not merely to justly waging the war, but to winning the war.

In addition to the standards covering military operations, some just-war scholars argue that a state at war should not infringe on the rights of its own population. Internment of suspect minorities, press censorship, and the suspension of elections and of legal rights may all call into question the just conduct of a war.

I pointed out earlier that the idea of *jus post bellum*, the just end of war, is a relatively new idea. It is not as deeply intertwined in international law as the standards expected in the declaration and the conduct of war. Nonetheless, just in the past 60 years, from occupied Germany and Japan, to Korea, to the Balkans, to Afghanistan and Iraq there are abundant examples, both good and bad, of post-war settlements.

From these historical experiences we can identify several characteristics of *jus post bellum*. A just war, justly waged is justly won only if: The terms of the peace vindicate the original grievances. This means that the peace doesn't just restore the status quo, but actually establishes a better and more just state of peace.

The demands of the victors are proportional. They are not excessively punitive relative to the injustice that was the cause of the war. Obviously the more depraved and dangerous the regime, the more invasive and transformative the peace terms may have to be.

Peace terms must distinguish between soldiers and civilians, and between the government and the population. The weight of the punishment must fall on the decision makers, not the people. This was an issue of great controversy in the 1990s, especially as regards UN sanctions against Iraq. In fact, while no fan of Saddam Hussein, Osama bin Laden pointed to the human costs of sanctions as just cause for his declaration of jihad against the United States. I don't endorse that view, but it is illustrative of the universality of just war vocabulary.

There are fair systems of compensation. The victims of aggression might have their losses made good. This is often at the discretion of the victor, who may choose to forego reparations.

Fair and public trials are held for the senior leaders who violated *jus ad bellum*, and for the senior military commanders who violated *jus in bello*. Nuremberg and the trials of former Serbian leaders fall into this category, but these are invariably problematic efforts. In the interests of post-war stability, a victor might want to avoid long and public trials that dredge up too many painful memories.

Finally, a victor may bear a heavy responsibility to rehabilitate a defeated foe, to rebuild his institutions of government. This may extend to remaking his society and re-socializing the defeated nation into the family of nations. As we have learned from our own national experience of occupation from the 1940s to this decade, such fundamental fixes are neither easy, nor cheap, nor quick. And yet the alternative of premature withdrawal, as we have heard in debates about our draw-downs in Iraq and Afghanistan, may very well undermine the long-term peace.

So there are the three categories of just war. Traditionally the responsibility for *jus ad bellum* has been borne by the political leadership. Just conduct in war has been the purview of the military. As you can probably guess, I would advocate challenging that hard distinction by drawing more military input into the declaration of war and demanding more political oversight of the conduct of the war. When you add *jus post bellum* into the mix, it becomes even more dangerous to try to neatly divide the categories. You can't have the politicians simply hand authority over to the military at the declaration of war and then have the military simply hand it back when you are ready to transition to post war. Abiding by just war strictures adds another layer of complexity to the already challenging civil–military relationship.

So let's apply what we've just learned about just war learned to a recent conflict—the war in Iraq: Operation Iraqi Freedom. At the top of the lecture I offered a quote from a 2003 speech delivered by President Bush at Camp Lejeune. In that speech Bush asserted that, "By our actions, we serve a great and just cause." But why was the war in Iraq a just cause? What was the president's claim to have *jus ad bellum*—a just recourse to war?

Essentially, the president's rationale was two-fold: first, self-defense against the possibility of an attack by Iraq, and second, the illegitimacy and brutality of Saddam Hussein's regime. Grotius advocated sovereign legitimacy as based on respect for universal human rights. By extension a government that is a threat to its own population is a threat to all of mankind. That regime has therefore lost its sovereign legitimacy and can justly be removed from power. It was further claimed that the U.S. and its allies had right intentions. In his address to the American people on the first night of the war, Bush said: "We have no ambition in Iraq, except to remove a threat and restore control of that country to its own people."

The president made these justifications public and believed he had proper authority as elected representative of the American people. He also had the consent of Congress to use force to disarm Saddam Hussein. Proper authority was further strengthened by international support, the Coalition of the Willing. On the other hand, the lack of a final UN resolution meant that this rhetorical position was not unassailable.

War against Iraq was also claimed as a last resort. The nation was reluctant to enter this war, Bush said, but all other means had been exhausted. Bush also offered Saddam Hussein and his two sons a 48-hour window to leave Iraq and prevent a war, thus shifting the moral burden for the war to the Iraqi leader. Proportionality and the probability of success were bound up in the war plan that applied "decisive force" and would "not be a campaign of half measures." But it was also a plan that targeted the regime not the population.

As to *jus in bello* the Lejeune speech offered a study in contrasts. Bush claimed that Saddam's forces "shield themselves with women and children … killed Iraqi citizens who welcome coalition troops … and … forced Iraqis into battle, by threatening to torture or kill their families." "They have executed prisoners of war, waged attacks under the flag of truce and concealed combat forces in … schools, hospitals and mosques." In other words the Iraqi military's standard operating procedures were *mala in se*, evil in and of themselves, but the liberators would not sink to those depths. According to Bush, American and Allied troops treated civilians kindly, did everything they could to spare non-combatants from harm, and showed respect to soldiers who surrendered.

Allied forces were also careful to distinguish between soldiers and civilians. For example, the extensive use of precision-guided munitions was intended to satisfy proportionality and to limit civilian casualties. Target selection in Operation Iraqi Freedom was also based on the *jus in bello* standard of military necessity. Bush spoke of "striking selected targets of military importance to undermine Saddam Hussein's ability to wage war."

To be honest, when it came to just conduct of war, the Bush administration was operating at a distinct advantage. Anyone who has served in or worked with the U.S. military will appreciate just how deeply *jus in bello* criteria are ingrained in American military doctrine and culture. Even though these criteria undermine military efficiency and effectiveness and increase the risks to our forces, the president did not need to tell the military to act in accordance with the laws of war. They were going to do that anyway. Ultimately the incredible performance of the Allied military forces in March and April 2003 set a new standard for abiding by the stringent requirements of *jus in bello*.

Turning finally to *jus post bellum* in Iraq, it is very easy to find fault with the planning and execution of the post-combat phase of Operation Iraqi Freedom. In fact, at the point that I am recording this lecture, nine years after the start of the war, the *post bellum* situation is still highly fluid. All of that being said, the Bush administration did pay significant attention to many of the criteria of *jus post bellum* in the lead-up to the war.

Remember that the peace terms that conclude a just war should establish better conditions than those that existed prior to the conflict. For President Bush, the status quo ante was unacceptable. The key rationale and goal of the war was the replacement of Saddam Hussein with a democratic Iraq, but that set the bar of expectations and post-war responsibilities very high. Nonetheless, when it became clear that Saddam had lost hold of the reins of power, President Bush made a public declaration on board the Aircraft Carrier *Abraham Lincoln* that the aims of the war had been accomplished. At exactly the same time, the United States and Great Britain claimed the authority of occupying powers in accord with international laws and conventions. In addition, while critical elements of post-war planning were lacking, the administration had made extensive preparations for near-term humanitarian crises such as famine and a crush of refugees.

During the occupation, the Coalition Provisional Authority also tried to discriminate in their pursuit of the Iraqi leadership. The famous deck of cards, with its 55 most-wanted Iraqis, might be seen as a less than elegant attempt to discriminate between an evil regime and those who suffered under it. The subsequent decisions to disband the Iraqi Army and purge all Ba'athists from the government were further attempts to hold only a portion of the population responsible and to reform dysfunctional institutions. Unfortunately, however well-intentioned these decisions may have been, they ultimately proved to have destabilizing effects.

Interestingly, the United States did not seek compensation for itself or its allies. I suspect that this was because the administration did not want to taint America's right intentions. As to punishments, although they did not hold international criminal tribunals, the United States nonetheless urged the new Iraqi government to publicly try Saddam and his inner circle. Those trials also served as a test of the rehabilitation and reform of Iraqi government institutions. In fact, the Allied forces that occupied Iraq after Saddam's fall were not just there to contain an insurgency. They were also pursuing a fundamental structural and cultural transformation of Iraqi society and political institutions. Obviously, the jury is still out on how well the United States and its allies met the *jus post bellum* criteria in Iraq, but they were clearly considered.

To recap: Today I have introduced yet another element of the environment in which strategy is planned and executed: The moral element. And even though you may never have heard of just-war theory before, I hope that I have convinced you that this seemingly arcane concept can exercise an incredible influence on all phases of war.

Many of the strategists we have talked about in this course have been rightly obsessed with maximizing efficiency and effectiveness in war. Some have fully embraced the notion that all is fair in war. In contrast, abiding by just principles is just about the most inefficient thing that you can do.

So why did President Bush and other U.S. government and military officials make such extensive use of just-war language when they spoke about the war in Iraq? Why did they try to meet moral standards that invariably raise the bar for justifying, waging, and terminating a war? Doesn't this just get in the way of good strategy?

Given the number and severity of these strictures, and the near-impossibility of meeting them all, why were they so explicit? By self-consciously and repeatedly making reference to the tenets of just war, didn't the Bush administration put itself into a rhetorical trap?

This is the ultimate just war paradox. As soon as you try to make a just war argument, you run the risk of ceding the moral high-ground to your critics and to your opponents. No state can possibly meet all of the just-war criteria, and any failure threatens to undermine the moral legitimacy of the entire war. And it raises the specter that you are just cynically parroting this language to cover more Machiavellian motivations.

In fact, couching Operation Iraqi Freedom (OIF) in these terms might have done even more long-term damage to America's moral legitimacy than the alternative of taking an explicitly realist approach, because it provided its own "unjust war" counterargument.

I don't have answers to any of these questions, but ultimately my point is not whether the United States met all of the just-war standards, or whether the results vindicated the justness of America's actions in Iraq. Regardless of what you think about the Iraq War or about the value of just-war theory, it is impressive and illuminating to see just how hard the Bush administration tried to clear this moral bar. It shows just how deeply just-war concepts are ingrained in 21st-century military strategy and why issues of morality and legality figure so prominently in the strategies to which we now turn: terrorism and counterterrorism.

I'll see you next time.

Terrorism as Strategy
Lecture 22

Horrific though it may sound, there is an undeniable strategic logic to terrorism. In fact, terrorism might be the most strategic of all instruments of war. The tactical or operational significance of most terrorist acts is inconsequential, but their psychological impact can be enormous. In this lecture, we'll look at a model for objectively and strategically understanding terrorism and for measuring the likelihood that a terrorist movement will achieve its political objectives. We'll then use this model to explain how the Irish Republican Army was able to achieve partial Irish independence in the 1920s.

Defining Terrorism
- The first element of a definition of terrorism is that it is a tool used by political movements, primarily non-state actors.

- The second defining characteristic is that these political movements are weak; they seek strategic and political effects that are completely out of proportion both to their political legitimacy and to their relative economic and military strength.

- Finally, these movements must make direct and explicit connections between their acts of terrorism and their desired strategic and political effects.

Terrorism as Theater
- The five audiences model is premised on the idea that terrorism is first and foremost a form of political theater. Terrorists try to influence five audiences: (1) the incumbent government, (2) constituent population, (3) nonconstituent population, (4) members of the terrorist organization itself, and (5) international public opinion.

- Terrorist strategy is a matter of planning and executing attacks to elicit the desired responses from each targeted audience. The additional challenge or advantage is that individual acts will affect different audiences in different ways. Because they affect multiple audiences simultaneously, individual terrorist acts can be highly cost effective.

- The chances that a terrorist movement will succeed hinge on how well its acts of violence are crafted to have the desired effects on the five audiences and on favorable conditions in the general operating environment.

The Five Audiences
- With the incumbent government as an audience, terrorist attacks can have psychological, political, and practical effects. For example, an attack may be designed to paralyze a government to make it look weak in the eyes of other audiences, force incumbent leaders to make political concessions, or create some practical operating room for the terrorist movement.

- Within the constituent population, a terrorist movement seeks to narrow the range of identity choices so that the only identity available is the one the movement chooses for members of its natural constituency. Attacks here may threaten individuals directly or those with similar identities, or they may be designed to induce the government to launch an indiscriminate counterterrorism campaign.

- With regard to the nonconstituent population, terrorists seek to induce horror with the aim of making nonconstituents critical of the government or making them pressure the government to accede to terrorist demands.

- Successful terrorist attacks can also motivate or intimidate the rank and file of the terrorist movement itself. Threats of reprisals and demonstration killings of traitors keep the membership in line.

- From the fifth audience, international public opinion, terrorists seek to solicit support, both material and moral. The aim here is to get the international community to condemn the actions of the incumbent government.

The Anglo-Irish War of 1919–1921

- The story of the Anglo-Irish War begins in 1916 with the so-called Easter Rising, a badly planned revolt launched by Irish nationalists in central Dublin. Not only did the rising fail to spark a nationwide rebellion, but the actions of the rebels horrified the majority of their natural constituency.

- In the aftermath of the rising, the British placed hundreds of participants in a largely self-policing prison camp at Frongoch in Wales. There, the prisoners held lectures and seminars on the theory and practice of insurgency. The smartest "graduate" of Frongoch was Michael Collins.

- In late 1918, Collins ran on the Sinn Féin ticket and won election to the House of Commons. But Collins and the other 73 Sinn Féin candidates who had won seats refused to be seated in the British Parliament. Instead, they formed an Irish Parliament, proclaimed an Irish Republic, and declared war on Britain.

- Over the next two years, Collins served as the chief financier, chief intelligence officer, and a chief strategist for the Irish Republic. At the end of the war, he served as the lead negotiator with the British government, accepting a compromise settlement that left the six counties of Ulster under British control.

Collins and the Five Audiences

- In dealing with the incumbent government—the British—Collins knew that Ireland was too politically and strategically valuable for London to give it up without a fight. He also knew that the British had essentially two means of holding on to Ireland, civilian governance and military occupation.

411

o   London was unlikely to opt for military occupation at first because that would legitimize Sinn Féin. By standing up as a republican government and a republican army, Sinn Féin was claiming sovereignty and legitimacy that were out of all proportion to its actual power.

o   If the British rose to that bait and either declared war or opted for a highly militarized response, they would have tacitly accepted the Irish claims of statehood.

- Collins recognized that the most effective counterintelligence unit the British had was civilian law enforcement, the Royal Irish Constabulary (RIC) and the Dublin Metropolitan Police (DMP).

o   The Irish police were well staffed, well resourced, and highly professional and had both English and Irish officers with local knowledge and sources within Sinn Féin's constituent population. In terms of both manpower and assets, the police had the upper hand in the intelligence battle. Collins was out to shift that balance and to attack the British strategy by declaring war on the police.

o   In 1919, Collins set up the Squad, also known as the Twelve Apostles. The Squad set about intimidating and murdering the most effective officers in the DMP and RIC and murdering civilians who cooperated with the police. This campaign of terror gave the IRA operating room in Dublin.

o   Collins also recruited agents inside the police to alert him to counterintelligence operations and police spies within his own camp.

o   By incapacitating the intelligence service, denying it new Irish recruits, and infiltrating the organization with IRA agents, Collins undermined London's faith in the police force and denied intelligence-intensive solutions to the Irish problem. Collins's victory in the intelligence war left the British with only coercive and indiscriminate options.

- In 1920, the British began beefing up the ranks of the RIC and DMP with "auxiliaries" recruited from English, Scots, and Welsh veterans of the Great War. Unfamiliar with police work and hostile to the Irish, these auxiliaries became famous for their indiscriminate attacks on innocents in the name of flushing out the IRA.

  - Across the board, the Squad succeeded in having precisely the effect Collins wanted on the British government: It forced the British into a cycle of violence and induced them to militarize the conflict.

- Collins was also sensitive to the nonconstituent population as an audience, especially the people back in England. He wanted to calibrate the terrorism campaign to keep this population largely neutral or critical of the British conduct of the war.
  - The nonconstituent population in Ireland, however, was another matter. The Ulstermen presented a tactical and operational problem, especially with their private army and their attacks on the IRA and Sinn Féin members.

  - But the excesses of the Ulstermen were a strategic asset that drove neutral Irishmen closer to Sinn Féin and tarnished the image of British rule.

- With regard to the constituent population, Collins was brilliant and brutal. He tolerated neutrality among the constituent population but tried to overcome it with an aggressive propaganda campaign. Pro-British sympathies and active support for British rule, however, were not tolerated; Irish "collaborators" were murdered.

- Collins was equally strategic when it came to the rank-and-file members of the IRA itself. He worked hard to keep morale up and advertised the exploits of the Squad to highlight IRA successes. He also made sure that traitors within the IRA were rooted out and dealt with summarily and publicly.

- As to the last audience, international public opinion, there, the IRA did not have to work too hard. Sinn Féin had a large and loyal constituency in the United States, and Woodrow Wilson's call for national self-determination made the international environment even more favorable to the Irish cause.

The IRA and al-Qaeda
- Before making a comparison between the IRA and al-Qaeda, it's important to look at the context in which Collins was operating.
  - Collins's adversary, the incumbent government, was weary and distracted. It was fresh out of a costly and protracted war but still enmeshed in a number of small wars and imperial policing operations.

  - The British people were also weary, distracted, and conflicted about the Irish crisis. Meanwhile, the nonconstituent population of Ulster, like the British government, proved to be a highly cooperative adversary, basically acceding to Collins's strategic script.

  - Sinn Féin offered a political objective—an Irish republic—that had wide appeal to a large natural constituency in Ireland.

  - The rank and file of the IRA was smart, motivated, well informed, and well led. Their institution was also highly resistant to penetration by counterintelligence.

  - Finally, the sympathies of a major foreign power, the United States, were with the cause of Irish independence.

- We can note some parallels and differences with the global war on terror.
  - The United States may be tired, cash-strapped, and distracted, but its situation is nowhere close to that of Britain in 1920.

  - The nonconstituent population, the vast majority of Muslims that do not ascribe to bin Laden's vision, are implacably hostile

As Americans learned on September 11, 2001, small groups of terrorists can temporarily paralyze advanced societies, but in the near term, these movements will likely be unable to radically alter the global balance of power.

to al-Qaeda. The natural constituency of al-Qaeda is actually a very narrow subgroup of Sunni Islam.

o Some rank-and-file members of al-Qaeda have been frighteningly impressive, especially the perpetrators of the September 11 attacks, but post–9/11, al-Qaeda is not nearly as impressive or disciplined and, like all terrorist groups, is prone to infighting and implosion.

o Finally, with the exception of certain military and intelligence services in a few countries, international public opinion is also hostile to al-Qaeda.

• It's not the case that terrorists and strategies of terrorism are a thing of the past, but in the near term, these movements are unlikely to enjoy conditions that are sufficiently favorable to allow them to radically alter the regional or global balance of power.

Suggested Reading

Crenshaw, "The Logic of Terrorism."

Gray, "The Anglo-Irish War, 1919–21."

National Commission on Terrorist Attacks upon the United States, *The 9/11 Commission Report.*

Townshend, *The British Campaign in Ireland, 1919–1921.*

Questions to Consider

1. Describe the five audiences of terrorism.

2. What were Michael Collins's greatest strengths as a strategist? Can al-Qaeda replicate the success of the IRA/Sinn Féin?

Terrorism as Strategy
Lecture 22—Transcript

Horrific though it may sound, there is an undeniable strategic logic to terrorism. In fact, terrorism might be the most strategic of all instruments of war. I say this because the tactical or operational significance of *most* terrorist acts are inconsequential. But their psychological impact, both on the enemy and on the terrorists' would-be supporters, can be enormous. It is equally shocking to realize that movements like Al Qaeda can draw on an abundant literature by and a detailed historical record about strategically successful terrorists.

In the aftermath of September 11th there was a lot of interest in working more terrorism into our curriculum at the Naval War College. Given the passions aroused by those attacks we knew we had to figure out a way for students and faculty to approach the topic objectively.

The first thing we needed to do was to find a stand-in for the global war on terrorism in the same way that Thucydides had originally been a stand-in for Vietnam and the Cold War. That was the easy part.

Unfortunately terrorism has a long and bloody history. Instead of Al Qaeda we could train our analytical energies on the Irish Republican Army (IRA), Algeria's FLN, and Peru's Shining Path. We could also lean on our masters, Clausewitz, Sunzi, and especially Mao to try to understand the strategic logic of terrorism. But it was a colleague of mine, Professor Bill Fuller, who came up with what I believe to be the best model for objectively and strategically understanding terrorism and for measuring the likelihood that a terrorist movement will achieve its political objectives. Professor Fuller called the model the five audiences of terrorism.

In our opening section, I will go into each of those five audiences to better understand the purpose and strategic utility of terrorism. Then I will profile one of history's most cunningly successful terrorists, Michael Collins, and use the five audiences' matrix to explain how and why Collins and the IRA were able to achieve partial Irish Independence. At the end, we will look at what the five audiences' concept and the Irish case might tell us about Al Qaeda's chances for achieving their political objectives.

But, what is terrorism? First, I am treating terrorism as distinct from simply terror, like terror bombing, and terrorism as distinct from insurgency or revolutionary war. Terrorism may be used in combination with other means of war, or it may characterize a phase of a conflict, but I want to narrow our discussion down to pure terrorist groups.

Therefore the first element of the definition is that terrorism is a tool used by political movements, primarily non-state actors. Now, we could be talking about very, very small movements, but they are still political movements pursuing political objectives. The main strategic instrument employed by these movements are acts of violence directed primarily at civilians.

The second defining characteristic is that these political movements are weak; they are seeking strategic and political effects that are completely out of proportion both to their political legitimacy and to their relative economic and military strength. This is not a Maoist approach of gradually building military power and political legitimacy to go toe-to-toe with the government.

Finally, to meet my definition of terrorism these movements must make direct and explicit connections between their acts of terrorism and their desired strategic and political effects. They must think strategically about this instrument.

Terrorists have political aims and terrorism is their primary strategic means to achieve those aims. With that definition in mind, let's turn to the five-audiences' model I mentioned a moment ago. Let me say again, how beholden I am to my brilliant colleague Bill Fuller for allowing me to use it in this lecture.

The five audiences' model is premised on the idea that terrorism is first and foremost a form of political theatre. In the words of Sean MacStiofain, the one-time chief of staff of the Provisional IRA in the 1970s: "Terrorists are actors ... [and] ... their activities are performed as an operational drama with the world as an audience."

There are five audiences that terrorists are trying to influence: the incumbent government, constituent population, non-constituent population, the members of the terrorist organization itself, and international public opinion. We'll define and analyze each of these five audiences individually in a moment. But first, let's make sure we understand what we mean when we say that terrorism is a form of theatre or communication. This is not to be glib.

Terrorist strategy is a matter of planning and executing attacks that are supposed to elicit the desired responses from each targeted audience. The additional challenge or advantage is that individual acts will affect different audiences in different ways. This is a challenge because one or more audiences might be affected in a desirable way, but with others the effects might be counterproductive. This can also be an advantage. Because they affect multiple audiences simultaneously individual terrorist acts can be highly cost effective.

The chances that a terrorist movement will succeed will hinge on how well their acts of violence are crafted to have the desired effects on these audiences and also on how favorable the general audience environment actually is. In other words, as much as a successful terrorist needs to be a smart strategist he also needs a favorable operating environment. He needs a fair degree of spontaneous support from the constituent population, he needs physical and political room to maneuver locally, and he needs at least moral support on the international stage.

So let's look at the first of our five audiences: the incumbent government. In the case of Algeria in the 1950s, the incumbent government was of course the French government. Now if you're a terrorist, what kinds of messages do you want to communicate to the government and what kinds of responses do you want to get? Well, your attacks can have psychological, political, and practical effects. For example, psychologically you can paralyze a government with fear to make it look weak in the eyes of other audiences. You may be trying to force incumbent leaders to make some political concession by inflicting unacceptable pain or by threatening more pain if they don't concede. Or you might attack the government to create some practical operating room for your movement. Your attacks might be geared toward preventing the government from doing some aspect of its core mission, usually law enforcement and local governance. This can open up areas where you can operate relatively unmolested. Conversely, you might want the government to come after you with everything it's got. You might want to induce an overreaction. There is a perverse logic here: terrorists don't have a lot of means and can't really take the time to develop those means in the style of Mao, so instead they try to use the strength of the incumbent government against itself.

Let's turn now to our second audience: the terrorist's constituent population. Within any constituent population there is a range of identity choices. Say I live in Algiers in the mid-1950s. I can be a Muslim, I can be proud of my Algerian heritage, I can also like French movies and poetry and be a proud citizen of a greater French state. The terrorist movement wants to narrow that range of choices so that as a member of what they view as their natural constituency, my only choice is to be an Algerian nationalist and an Algerian nationalist of their definition.

How can they narrow those choices? Well, they can threaten me directly and that often works, but that might also backfire. They can assassinate an Algerian working for the French, which might intimidate me. They can assassinate a French official who is famously corrupt. That might get me to identify with their cause and look upon them as a benefactor. Or they might do something that induces the French government to launch an indiscriminate counterterrorism campaign, a campaign that draws no distinction between pro-French, neutral, and pro-FLN Algerians. I might have once enjoyed life under French rule and didn't believe what these extremists were saying, now I believe them and find life under French rule to be unbearable.

What about our third audience—the non-constituent population? In Algiers in the '50s this would have been the European settlers—the *pied noirs*. If you're a terrorist you want to horrify this population. You also might want to make them critical of their government or to pressure the government to accede to your demands. Alternately you might want to induce them to overreact and take the law into their own hands. We saw in Algeria the *pied noirs* joining the fight against the FLN and we'll see in Ireland the Protestant Irish, the Ulstermen, driving part of the escalation cycle.

Moving now to the fourth audience: the rank and file of the terrorist movement. Sometimes you may want to motivate your members. At other times you may want to intimidate them. Successful attacks can boost morale and motivate them. But you also need to maintain intense discipline and prevent infiltration, so threats of reprisals and demonstration killings of traitors can keep the membership in line.

And finally we have the fifth audience: international public opinion. From this audience you might want to solicit support, foreign friends who will send you guns and money. In other cases, moral support might be enough, but you probably want a little of both. Ideally you want to get the international community to condemn the actions of the incumbent government. You want international bodies to call for an end to hostilities and for negotiations. International recognition of your cause is a huge boost: remember you are still a poor and weak movement, but if you get a foreign government or the UN to treat you as a player then you are punching way above your weight.

As a terrorist, you're more likely to succeed if you can get outside audiences to view what you are doing as a necessary evil, or as an understandable outgrowth of the policies of the incumbent government. Your tactics are extreme and morally reprehensible, but they draw attention to what must be an unbearable situation to have forced some among this population to such extreme actions.

Turning now to our case study, the Anglo-Irish War of 1919–1921, through which the Irish Free State was established. A key figure in this conflict was Michael Collins, a brilliant strategist for whom I have a lot of respect. But, Michael Collins *was* a terrorist, and both his political organization, Sinn Fein, and its military arm, the Irish Republican Army, achieved their political objectives primarily through a campaign of purposeful and terror-inducing violence against Irish civilians and the British government.

In the two years between the Irish Declaration of Independence in January 1919 and the signing of the Anglo-Irish treaty of December 1921, a small and lightly armed group of Irish nationalists (perhaps 5,000 die-hards total), compelled the most powerful nation on Earth to grant independence to the 26 counties of Southern Ireland. Handguns, dynamite, and propaganda achieved things for the cause of Irish independence that could not possibly have been achieved by conventional military action or through the ballot box.

Major Irish rebellions go back centuries, but our story begins in 1916 with the so-called Easter Rising. Launched by Irish nationalists, the Easter Rising proved to be a badly planned and poorly resourced revolt in central Dublin. Not only did it fail to spark a nationwide rebellion, but the actions of the rebels actually horrified the majority of their natural constituency.

In the aftermath of the Rising, however, the British committed an even more egregious and strategically significant mistake. The British took hundreds of the young members of the Irish volunteers who had participated in the rising and put them in a huge and largely self-policing prison camp at Frongoch in Wales. As a result, what came to be known as the Irish Republican Army had its first War College. At Frongoch, the prisoners held lectures and seminars on the theory and practice of insurgency and on the lessons learned from the Easter Rising. Frongoch's smartest graduate was Michael Collins.

Collins was 26 at the time of the Rising; a brash, vain, and brilliant young man, he was from a long line of Irish nationalists. At the age of 16, Collins had moved to England and worked in the postal service for nearly a decade. His time in England sharpened his acuity for numbers and he later raised funds and served as finance minister for the Irish Republic. That decade also gave him an intense familiarity with the British government and with British politics. Collins knew his future enemy very, very well.

After the Rising, Collins was imprisoned for six months before returning to Ireland in late 1916. In late 1918 Collins ran on the Sinn Fein ticket and won election to the House of Commons. But Collins and the other 73 Sinn Fein candidates who had won seats refused to be seated in the British parliament. Instead they formed an Irish parliament, proclaimed an Irish Republic, and declared war on Britain. Over the next two years Collins served as the chief financier, the chief intelligence officer, and a chief strategist for the Republic. At the end of the war, he got the additional job of serving as the lead negotiator with the British government. On the other side of the table was Winston Churchill. Yes, Winston Churchill negotiated with terrorists.

Something of an instinctive Clausewitzian, Collins realized that by the summer and fall of 1921, the IRA was at or past its culminating point of attack. There was very little else that they could do militarily. He also knew that they were probably at the culminating point of victory. In other words if they pushed London too hard for more political concessions the British might walk away (David Lloyd-George had said as much) and the British might restart a war that the Irish were destined to lose.

So Collins accepted a compromise settlement that left the six counties of Ulster under British control (the province of Northern Ireland). Maximalists within Sinn Fein/IRA hated this compromise, and as is often the case with insurgencies and terrorist movements, a civil war broke out between the maximalists and the pragmatists. The Irish civil war of 1922–1923 turned out to be far bloodier than the war against the British. Collins was among the casualties, he was gunned down in an ambush in August 1922. If you are interested there is a pretty good movie, *Michael Collins*, starring Liam Neeson.

The story of Collins' life and career is pretty gripping and makes for fine cinema, but that is not what has drawn me to him. Fortunately, we don't have a master of terrorism, but if someone were to write the book on how to be a strategically effective terrorist, it would have been Collins. He is a particularly dangerous and strategically imaginative individual. We have every reason to fear the next Michael Collins.

So, let's look at how Collins managed the five audiences of terrorism. First, the incumbent government—in this case, the British government and its instruments of rule in Ireland. Terrorism is a violent negotiation, in order to win in those negotiations you need to have good idea how your adversary is going to react. Collins knew that Ireland was too politically and too strategically valuable for London to give it up without a fight. Collins also knew that the British had two means of holding on to Ireland, civilian governance and military occupation.

London was unlikely to opt for military occupation at first because that would legitimize Sinn Fein. As grandiose as it was, by standing up a Republican government and a Republican Army, Sinn Fein was claiming sovereignty and legitimacy that were out of all proportion to its actual power. If Britain rose to that bait and either declared war or opted for a highly militarized response then they would have tacitly accepted the Irish claims of statehood.

Collins knew that the British probably wouldn't militarize the conflict in 1919 and he knew that the IRA weren't likely to beat the British militarily. He also knew that the most effective counterintelligence unit the British had was civilian law enforcement, the Royal Irish Constabulary (RIC) and the Dublin Metropolitan Police (DMP). The RIC and DMP in 1919 were everything the Algiers police force wasn't in 1956. The Irish police were well-staffed, well-resourced, and highly professional and had both English and Irish officers with lots of local knowledge and lots of sources within Sinn Fein's constituent population. In terms of manpower and assets the police had the upper hand in the intelligence battle. Collins was out to shift that balance and to attack the British strategy by declaring war on the police.

In 1919, Collins set up "The Squad" also known as the "Twelve Apostles." The Squad set about intimidating and murdering the most effective officers in the DMP and the RIC and murdering civilians who cooperated with the police. That campaign of terror did a lot to give the IRA operating room in Dublin. Collins claimed that he could sit right next to police officers in pubs and on city trams and they would be too terrified to do anything.

In November 1920 "The Squad" boldly gunned-down several British officers, a move that did as much to shift the intelligence balance as it did to advertise the power and pervasiveness of the IRA. As much as he blinded the police, Collins recruited inside agents to alert him to counterintelligence operations and to police spies within his own camp. As if that weren't enough, in April 1919 Collins broke into police intelligence headquarters and spent hours poring over the details of what the police knew about the IRA and more importantly how they knew it.

By incapacitating the intelligence service, denying them new Irish recruits, and infiltrating the organization with IRA agents, Collins undermined London's faith in the police force and denied them intelligence-intensive solutions to the Irish problem. Collins' victory in the intelligence war left the British with only coercive and indiscriminate options.

Collins famously argued that the worse the reprisals that the British visited upon the Irish, the better it was for the Irish cause of independence. He had already induced some members of the police into murderous counter terror and in 1920 the British doubled down and began beefing up the ranks of the RIC and DMP with "auxiliaries" recruited from English, Scots, and Welsh veterans of the Great War.

Unfamiliar with policework and hostile to the Irish, these auxiliaries became famous for their indiscriminate attacks on innocents in the name of flushing out the IRA. Their dark tunics and khaki trousers earned them the nickname "Black and Tans." For that reason, never order a Black-and-Tan in a proper Irish pub, ask for a half-and-half instead.

Across the board "The Squad" succeeded in having precisely the effect Collins wanted on the British government. For the price of a few hundred guns, a few thousand rounds of ammunition, and some cases of dynamite, Collins had attacked British strategy, forced them into a cycle of violence, and induced them to militarize the conflict.

We have also seen that Collins was careful not to push things too far. Earlier in the war, Collins had toyed with the idea of higher profile assassinations and major attacks in London, but by the end of the war he was much more cautious and at one point he vetoed a mustard gas attack on the London underground. Collins was looking for the perfect balance of frustration and exhaustion from London, not blood vendetta. As such, he was very sensitive to the non-constituent population, especially the people back in England. He wanted to calibrate the terrorism campaign to keep them largely neutral or at best critical of the British conduct of the war. Collins knew enough about English society to know that the British press would advertise the gory details of the Irish crisis to a population tired of war and bloodshed.

The non-constituent population in Ireland was another matter. The Ulstermen were a tactical and operational problem, especially with their private army and their attacks on the IRA and Sinn Fein members, but their excesses turned out to be a strategic asset that drove neutral Irishmen closer to Sinn Fein and tarnished the image of British rule.

When it came to the constituent population, Collins was brilliant and brutal. Among the Irish there was a huge variety of identities. In fact, at the time of the Rising most Irish citizens were somewhat sympathetic to the cause of independence, but not passionately so. As a result Sinn Fein in 1915–1916 was a fringe political party. By 1921, however, it was the only party recognized as the voice of Irish nationalism. That shift had not been spontaneous.

Collins could tolerate neutrality among the constituent population but tried to overcome it with an aggressive propaganda campaign. What he could not tolerate were pro-British sympathies and active support for British rule. Irish "collaborators" were murdered in high-profile ways to frighten anyone with pro-British sympathies. Young women who dated policemen or British soldiers had their heads shaved. Many Irish came to fear and respect the IRA more than the British government. Even when the police nabbed one of "The Squad" no witnesses would come forward to support the government's case.

Collins was equally strategic when it came to the rank and file members of the IRA itself. He worked hard to keep morale up and advertised the exploits of "The Squad" to highlight IRA successes and power. He also made sure that traitors within the IRA were rooted out and dealt with summarily and publicly.

As to the last audience, international public opinion, there the IRA did not have to work too hard. Sinn Fein had a large and loyal constituency in the United States. Eamon de Valera, President of the Irish Republic, had been born in New York and spent much of 1919 and 1920 in the United States raising over $5 million dollars, $500,000 of which Sinn Fein plowed back into both sides of the 1920 U.S. presidential election.

These activities notwithstanding, the international environment was exceptionally favorable to Sinn Fein, especially with Woodrow Wilson's calls for national self-determination. In one of his least strategic moments, Collins proposed kidnapping President Wilson and forcing the Irish Issue at Versailles, fortunately for the Irish cause, cooler heads prevailed.

So here we have the strategic logic of terrorism as carried out by one of history's greatest strategic terrorists, Michael Collins. In fact, it is his strategic brilliance that, in part, makes Collins such a scary individual. He gets even scarier when you realize that terrorists study other terrorists and learn from their successes and failures. But before we start panicking about Al Qaeda finding their Michael Collins, let's think about the context in which Collins was operating.

His adversary, the incumbent government, was weary and distracted. It was fresh out of a horrifically costly and protracted war. At the same time the British Empire was larger in 1919 than at any time in its history. As a result, the army and navy were distracted by a raft of small wars and imperial policing missions from Palestine, to Iraq, to India, to Afghanistan. British means and British will were divided. Ireland may have been valuable, but how valuable relative to all of those competing demands?

Like their government, the British people were weary, distracted, and conflicted about the Irish crisis. Meanwhile, the non-constituent population of Ulster, like the British government, proved to be a highly cooperative adversary, basically acceding to Collins's strategic script. When it comes to the Irish people, Sinn Fein offered a political objective, an Irish republic, which had wide appeal to a large natural constituency. And the rank and file of the IRA was smart, motivated, well-informed, and well-led. Their institution was also highly resistant to penetration by counterintelligence. Finally, the sympathies of a major foreign power, the United States, were with the cause of Irish independence.

Fast forward to the global war on terror and we definitely see some parallels. Yes, the United States may be tired, cash-strapped, and distracted, but nowhere close to the situation that the British found themselves in in 1920. Furthermore, we've seen that bin Laden's assumptions about the United States and its allies were deeply flawed.

The non-constituent population, the vast majority of Muslims that do not ascribe to bin Laden's vision, are implacably hostile to Al Qaeda. Al Qaeda's objectives are grand and appealing to some in the Muslim world, but their natural constituency is actually only a very narrow sub-group, of a sub-group of Sunni Islam. Pro-independence elements in Ireland tracked very closely with the ultimate geography of the Irish Free State. Al Qaeda's territorial fantasies are out of all proportion to its very narrow base. In addition, the narrowness of Al Qaeda's appeal is evident in the fact that Al Qaeda in Iraq was betrayed and destroyed by their fellow Sunnis.

What about the rank and file? Well some members of Al Qaeda have been frighteningly impressive, especially the perpetrators of the September 11th attacks, but post 9-11 Al Qaeda is not nearly as impressive or disciplined, and like all terrorist groups is prone to infighting and implosion.

Finally, with the exception of certain military and intelligence services in a few countries, which I will not name, international public opinion and all of the great powers are also implacably hostile to Al Qaeda.

I am not saying that terrorists and strategies that employ terrorism are a thing of the past. Terrorism, and here I mean the individual acts of violence, is actually pretty easy. Small groups of highly motivated terrorists can temporarily paralyze the most advanced societies while other terrorist movements can still wrest concessions from great powers. But in the near term these movements, even if they do find their Michael Collins, are unlikely to enjoy conditions that are sufficiently favorable to allow them to radically alter the regional or the global balance of power.

I'll see you next time.

Strategies of Counterterrorism
Lecture 23

I n the last lecture, we looked at terrorism as a strategy for accomplishing specific political objectives, but in this lecture, we ask: What are the theories of counterterrorism? When we set out to answer this question, we're likely to find a number of grand and fairly ambiguous policy objectives, as well as counterterrorist tactics, techniques, and technologies, but little in the way of counterterrorism strategy. Further, there seems to be an analytical gulf between the tactics of counterterror and their larger political purpose. Fortunately, we don't have to reinvent the wheel when it comes to thinking strategically about counterterrorism; we can turn to our strategic masters.

Unique Challenges of Counterterrorism Strategy

- Whatever the counterterrorist does along the spectrum from capitulation and political concession to mass retaliation and militarization will invariably result in negative repercussions.

- Suppose we start at one end of the spectrum, with an incumbent government simply ignoring a terrorist problem and hoping it goes away. In that case, the government has ceded the struggle and the initiative to the terrorists.

- Moving a little further along the spectrum, the incumbent government might decide to accede to a terrorist demand, for example, to grant some concession by freeing a group of political prisoners or rescinding some odious decree. This action means that the government has bent to intimidation; any concessions prove that terrorism works, serve as an admission that the government is wrong, and embolden terrorists.

- Moving from concessions to the use of law enforcement, we've seen that this option is often reactive—law enforcement can't do much until an act is perpetrated. Further, because police officers are often lightly armed, they are relatively easy to outgun and intimidate.

- o If the terrorist movement has a loyal constituency, then law enforcement will find it difficult if not impossible to conduct effective investigations and apprehend perpetrators.

- o Local law enforcement may also be too local; it may be more loyal to the terrorist's cause than to the national government.

- o If a terrorist is caught and brought to trial, he or she may use the courtroom as a grandstand for advertising the cause, railing against the inequities of the system, and inspiring a new generation of believers. It's also unlikely that law enforcement will catch the leaders of the movement.

- o Beefing up the police and the law enforcement response—giving the police better weapons, loosening the rules of engagement, and so on—implies a failure of normal procedures and could result in criticisms related to constitutional rights.

- The next step on the spectrum of counterterrorism options is the paramilitary response: bulking up the police to a greater degree, distancing police officers from legal constraints, and recruiting local allies into paramilitary groups and community policing. The problem here is that such groups are difficult to control and can quickly devolve into vigilantism and rogue behavior.

- The next step is the declaration of martial law, but militarizing the conflict is an admission that civil institutions have failed and may legitimize the terrorists' cause. In addition, military techniques are likely to be disruptive and may drive some constituents into the terrorist camp.

- Finally, at the extreme active end of the counterterrorism spectrum, the government can establish full militarization, including curfews, checkpoints, resettlement, border fences, 24/7 street and air patrols, regular sweep-and-screen operations, and so on. This option might promise the highest level of preemptive security, but the associated

Options for counterterrorist strategy run the spectrum from capitulation and political concession to mass retaliation and militarization.

activities are expensive, are largely indiscriminate, and can alienate domestic and international opinion.

The Five Audiences for Counterterrorism
- Like the terrorist, the actions of the counterterrorist must be crafted toward a range of audiences.

- Given that the counterterrorist is the incumbent government, the counterpart audience for the government is the command and control nexus of the terrorist movement. Actions designed to address this audience might seek to induce a strategic blunder.

- The terrorist's nonconstituent population is the incumbent government's natural constituency. The government might take actions to make this audience feel safer and to enhance its own legitimacy. It might also attempt to prevent this audience from giving material and moral support to the terrorists.

- To address the terrorist's constituent population, the government might consider physically and psychologically isolating its members from the movement and looking for allies within the population.

- The fourth audience is the same for the government and the terrorists: the movement's rank and file. The government's aim here is to shock, terrorize, or demoralize the members. The government may also seek to turn some of them into intelligence assets, to make their leadership look bad, or to induce them to attempt unsanctioned attacks that defy the orders of their superiors.

- Finally, the government must calibrate all its actions under the scrutiny of the fifth audience—international public opinion.

- As politicians and military leaders think about counterterrorism options within this five-audience framework, they need to identify which combination of actions and reactions gives them the greatest chance of achieving their political objectives with the lowest probability of negative strategic and political consequences.

Crime v. War

- Whether terrorism is treated as a law enforcement problem or as a war depends on the context in which it takes place and the capabilities available to address it.

- Terrorism may be treated as a law enforcement issue if robust and capable law enforcement mechanisms are in place, the terrorist movement is vulnerable to disruption and intelligence penetration, and the legal system can handle the unique challenges of a terrorism trial. The operations of the New York City Police Department's counterterrorism unit represent a good example of this approach.

- If, on the other hand, the terrorist network operates largely in ungoverned space, where law enforcement is not robust or might be corrupted, where the terrorists mass in identifiable locations, and where the negative repercussions of military actions are manageable, then terrorism may be treated as a war. The highly militarized campaign of the Sri Lankan government against the Tamil Tiger terrorist group serves as an example here.

Strategic Counterterrorism Options

- Regardless of how depraved and horrific their acts of terrorism may be, the most dangerous terrorists are the ones who keep these acts subordinate to political purpose. The counterterrorist's response must be even more strategic.

- From the *Sunzi*, one approach might be to attack the terrorists' strategy by refusing to be a cooperative adversary or to attack their alliances to deny them external support. These options require a high degree of intelligence and all five types of spies, especially turned spies.

- If sufficient intelligence isn't available, another approach might be to focus counterterrorist energies on a Jominian or Clausewitzian decisive point. Afghanistan in 2001, where the Taliban and al-Qaeda tried a stand-up fight, and Sri Lanka are probably the best examples of this sort of approach.

- Galula's approach represents another option. Are there ways to resolve longstanding grievances and rebuild political institutions from the population up?

- If Galula's approach is too costly and time consuming, the government might opt for a direct strategy—going after the people, materiel, and money that constitute the enemy's means. Even more direct is to attack the command and control functions of the movement; this was what Trinquier had in mind.

- Alternatively, a counterterrorist might want to consider a more Corbettian approach. This would involve using the incumbent government's greater strategic mobility to open a new theater in the struggle, which might induce the enemy to commit a strategic blunder.

- In thinking about the approaches of our masters of strategy, it becomes apparent that a war on terrorism, like all other wars, requires us to think interactively and jointly.
  - In the Anglo-Irish War, the British were right to rely on law enforcement in Ireland, but the vicious attacks of Collins forced adaptation of that strategy.

  - In terms of joint action, the British were also right at first not to overwhelmingly militarize the crisis in Ireland. The army had a role to play but as an adjunct to law enforcement.

- If a conflict escalates and if the value of the object justifies it, the government might have to migrate from the intelligence-intensive law enforcement end of the spectrum to the firepower-intensive population control end of the spectrum. But as it builds security and institutional capacity, the government may migrate back toward intelligence-intensive operations.

Allies
- There is one constant across the spectrum of counterterrorism responses: allies.

- International allies can bring advantages in capabilities or may provide access to a particular theater. Local allies may offer better local intelligence and the opportunity to be more strategically effective.

- At the same time, and as we have seen repeatedly in the decade since 9/11, both state and sub-state allies can be problematic. They can both expand and limit strategic options. Allies can also embroil the government in regional squabbles and tribal vendettas that divert attention from its policies and strategies.

Political Objectives
- In the end, whatever counterterrorism strategy is chosen, it must serve the government's political objectives.

- Such objectives might be unlimited—complete destruction of the movement and the repudiation of its political aims—or limited—degradation of the movement and no significant alteration in the status quo.

- If both terrorist and counterterrorist have maximalist objectives, then a negotiated settlement is unlikely. But if there is a possibility of convergence, then the approach to counterterrorism should contemplate terminating the war short of the total defeat of the enemy.

- In some circumstances, negotiating with terrorists, as Winston Churchill did in the Anglo-Irish War, may be an option. The government may also choose to make concessions without negotiating to undercut the grievances of the terrorists' constituent population.

- It may even be possible to ignore the actions of a particular terrorist group and hope the group goes away. Some movements are so fringe and isolated that they are not worth government attention.

- Even if a struggle against a terrorist movement is not a war in the strict and legal sense of the term, terrorism and counterterrorism are both means to bend an enemy to one's political will, and as such, both are still amenable to the types of strategic analysis we have seen throughout this course.

Suggested Reading

Dickey, *Securing the City*.

Ganor, *The Counter-Terrorism Puzzle*.

Smith, "Understanding Sri Lanka's Defeat of the Tamil Tigers."

Trinquier, *Modern Warfare*.

1. How can counterterrorists avoid blowback with one or more audiences?

2. When is law enforcement an effective counterterrorism strategy? When is military action an effective counterterrorism strategy?

Strategies of Counterterrorism
Lecture 23—Transcript

In our last lecture we looked at terrorism as a strategy for accomplishing specific political objectives. And in particular we profiled one of history's most successful terrorists—Michael Collins. So today we ask ourselves: Who are the great theorists of counterterrorism? Is there a master out there who is the yin to the yang of Michael Collins?

Well, if you set out to answer those questions what you're likely to find today are a lot of grand, ambitious, and fairly ambiguous policy objectives. This is understandable. The horror and revulsion elicited by terrorism invariably induces political leaders to invoke the noblest values and grandest political objectives in counterterrorism. You'll also find a lot of counterterrorist tactics, techniques, and technologies. If you have been in an airport in the past 10 years you have had first-hand knowledge of some of these techniques and technologies.

What you probably won't find, however, is very much in the way of counterterrorism *strategy*: A strategy to link counterterrorism tactics to those lofty political objectives. Why is this the case? For one, the very nature of terrorism as a strategic instrument seems to defy conventional strategic analysis. In the period immediately following September 11th it was difficult to posit the relevance of a Sunzi or a Clausewitz to this new kind of war. Moreover, the intensity of emotions aroused by September 11th and the highly charged debates that have followed tend to distract us from the types of analysis that we should be doing. We need to be thinking about the connections between the tactical, operational and strategic levels of the war against Al Qaeda and its Associated Movements (AQAM).

But what we tend to get instead are discussions and debates about their tactics and about our tactics. You also get a lot of discussion and debate over exactly what Al Qaeda wants to achieve politically. What are their political objectives? And we wrestle with what our political objectives are. Are we trying to eliminate the root causes of extremism, or are we trying to eliminate Al Qaeda? These are all important discussions, but strategy gets lost in the yawning gulf between tactics and political objectives.

Case in point, many have criticized the declaration of a global war on terrorism as strategically meaningless. At best, it is a declaration of war against a tactic, the same as declaring war against land mines or amphibious landings. Others have argued, in many cases rightly, that declaring a war is exactly what Al Qaeda wanted. They wanted that level of credibility and legitimacy that comes with the United States declaring war. More recently, critiques of the Obama administration have pointed to the White House's "strategy of tactics"; in other words, substituting tactical strikes against terrorist targets for a larger strategy for defeating terrorism.

I don't adhere to any of these views, but I am worried about that analytical gulf between the tactics of counter terror and their larger political purposes. On the other hand, I can take some comfort in the fact that we don't have to reinvent the wheel when it comes to thinking strategically about counterterrorism. We have ready at hand a host of masters to whom we can turn.

Just a few lectures back we spent time with Roger Trinquier, who came close to the kind of cool, strategic objectivity that we need when confronting terrorists. On the other hand, Trinquier may be a little *too* cool and detached. Trinquier was the kind of guy who could torture a prisoner for several hours and then offer him a cigarette and a ride home. Trinquier was also thinking in an operational bubble. He was very good on the local contest in Algiers between the *paras* and the clandestine organization of the FLN, but the larger national and international contexts were missing. So while we can borrow from Trinquier's menu of options, we need to salt in a few more of the masters.

I am not coming down on either side of the questions of whether this is a war, whether it should be called a war, or whether it should be waged primarily like a war. Instead, what I am saying is that regardless of what you call it and regardless of the mix of means you use to wage it, a campaign against a movement that uses terrorism as its primary strategic instrument is still amenable to classical strategic analysis.

But before we hear what our masters have to say, let's address some of the unique challenges that face someone trying to come up with a counterterrorism strategy. This is the counterterrorist's conundrum. "Whatever we do we are sure to be wrong." That was General Sir Nevil Macready's assessment of England's strategic options in Ireland. Macready was Britain's last military commander in the Anglo-Irish War, and there is a lot of truth to his lament—not only as it related to the specifics of the Irish case but also as it relates to the counterterrorist's conundrum in general. Whatever the counterterrorist does along the spectrum from capitulation and political concession at the one end, to mass retaliation and militarization at the other end, will invariably result in negative repercussions.

Let's examine why that is the case: Suppose we start at one end of the spectrum and the incumbent government simply ignores the problem and hopes it goes away. Well, in that case the government has ceded the struggle and the initiative to the terrorists.

Moving a little farther along the spectrum, the incumbent government might decide to accede to a terrorist demand—to grant some concession by freeing a group of political prisoners or rescinding some odious decree. But if the government does this, then it has bent to intimidation. If you make concessions you have proven that terrorism works and have admitted that the government is somehow in the wrong. And concessions embolden terrorists. For example, in the American colonies the British backed down in the face of resistance from Sam Adams and the Sons of Liberty. What did Sam Adams do in response to those political concessions? He escalated the crisis! Ultimately, confining your actions to this more passive or conciliatory end of the spectrum does little to prevent or to deter terrorist acts.

Let's move along the spectrum from concessions to the use of law enforcement. As we saw in Algeria, law enforcement is often very reactive and can't do much until an act is perpetrated. Also, because the police are often lightly armed they are relatively easy to out-gun and intimidate. If the terrorist movement has a loyal constituency, then law enforcement will find it difficult, if not impossible, to do effective investigations and to apprehend perpetrators. Local law enforcement may be too local; it may be more loyal to the terrorist's cause than to the national government. For example, in the 1950s and 1960s, the Ku Klux Klan was allied with local law enforcement in the South. The local police were enabling and even participating in the

Klan's acts of terrorism. And even if you do catch one of the perpetrators and bring them to trial, they may use the courtroom as a grandstand for advertising their cause and railing against the inequities of the system and inspiring a new generation of believers.

In addition, the people you're likely to catch are probably not the leaders of the movement. Think back to Trinquier. Arresting the gunmen and bomb throwers cannot be an end in itself, it has to get you access to the higher-ups, the senior leadership. The problem becomes all the more complex when you are dealing with cross-border attacks and transnational groups. The tacticians and operators are in your territory, but the strategists are somewhere beyond the reach of your law enforcement.

Let's say then that you start to beef up the police and your law enforcement response. Give the cops bigger and better guns, armored vehicles, and helicopters. Loosen the rules of engagement and the requirements for search warrants and wiretaps to beef up their intelligence gathering capabilities. Expand their abilities to detain suspects indefinitely. And because the normal courts don't work in terrorism cases, you set up special courts and special judicial procedures. This is certainly appealing, but it implies a failure of normal procedures and opens you up to accusations that you are playing fast and loose with the Constitution. We have certainly heard these kinds of accusations in America since 9/11.

The next step on the spectrum of counterterrorism options is the paramilitary response. Bulk-up those police forces even more; distance them more from police procedures and legal constraints. This option might also involve recruiting local allies into paramilitary groups and community policing. But how do you control these groups, what is the chain of command? The Black and Tans and the extremist *pied noirs* are two cautionary examples of how quickly the paramilitary option can devolve into vigilantism and rogue behavior.

Well, then government might step it up another notch. They might turn to the professional military and declare martial law. That was what Trinquier thought was the crucial first step to winning this kind of war. But as we can see in both Ireland and Algeria, militarizing the conflict might actually legitimize the terrorists' cause. A declaration of martial law is also an admission that civil institutions have failed. In addition, military techniques are likely to be much more disruptive and more off-putting and may drive some constituents into the arms of the terrorists.

Finally, at the extreme, active end of the counterterrorism spectrum, the government can go with the full-up militarized option. Curfews, check points, resettlement, border fences, 24/7 street and air patrols, regular sweep and screen operations, all of those things. These can look appealing and might promise the highest level of preemptive security, but they are expensive, largely indiscriminate, and can alienate domestic and international opinion.

So Macready was right. No matter what the counterterrorist does, they are sure to be wrong. But that can't be taken as an excuse for political and strategic paralysis. As with many things in war and strategy what we have here is a menu of the least bad options. But we also have something else. We actually have a useful framework within which to explore our options.

In the last lecture we saw just how important the environment, and especially the five audiences' environment was, to explaining Sinn Fein's success. That larger strategic and political environment might be even more enabling or disabling to the counterterrorist. Like the terrorist, the actions of the counterterrorist must be crafted toward a range of audiences.

Since the counterterrorist is the incumbent government, his counterpart audience will be the command-and-control nexus of the terrorist movement. Can you figure out how to change their rational calculus? Can you induce them to commit a strategic blunder? The terrorist's non-constituent population is the incumbent government's natural constituency. Can you do things to make this audience feel safer, things that enhance your legitimacy in their eyes, things that maintain their morale for a long, hard slog? Conversely, do you need to do things that prevent them from giving material or moral support to the terrorists?

Then there is the terrorist's constituent population. How can your actions have maximum impact on this third audience? You might consider isolating them physically and psychologically from the movement. And you might look for local allies within that population—allies who can help you carry the fight to the enemy. You might even give them the starkest of choices, "you are either with us or against us," and let their choice decide their fate. Or maybe you're willing to accept a large number of fence sitters?

As for the signals that you send to the fourth audience—namely, the terrorist movement's rank and file. You might want to shock, dismay, terrorize, or demoralize them. You might want to turn some of them into intelligence assets. You might also want to do things that make their leadership look bad. In some cases you might actually want to induce them to break ranks, to go rogue and attempt un-sanctioned attacks that defy the orders of their superiors and that tarnish their brand. Trinquier and the French paratroopers were very good at inducing this sort institutional implosion.

Finally, you have to calibrate all of these actions under the scrutiny of the fifth audience that we've talked about—international public opinion. As politicians and military leaders think about their counterterrorism options within this five-audience framework, what they need to do is figure out which combination of actions and reactions gives them the greatest chance of achieving their political objectives with the lowest probability of negative strategic and political consequences. In other words, the counterterrorist must determine a realistic political objective and then must figure out the combination of political, diplomatic, and military actions that are best suited to achieving that political objective.

This leads me to the least useful argument that we have had in the last two decades: Should we treat terrorism as a law enforcement problem or should we treat it as a war? The answer is "It depends!" It depends on context and on capabilities. When you have robust and capable law enforcement mechanisms, when the terrorist movement is vulnerable to disruption and intelligence penetration, and your legal system can handle the unique challenges of a terrorism trial, then you treat it as a law enforcement issue.

The New York City Police Department's counterterrorism unit is a good example of how this might work. You take New York police officers who know the city and the people. Salt into that experts on how individuals become radicalized and recruited into terrorist networks, add 600 linguists who can read the literature, roam the websites, and interact with the immigrant communities. Then you take that task force and at the top end you recruit people familiar with the CIA and FBI: folks who interface with federal agencies, the military, and with foreign law enforcement. At the bottom end you reach out to the precincts across the city to tap into their street-level intelligence. The New York approach is a really interesting model: a mix of capabilities built on voracious intelligence consumption and institutionalized intelligence information sharing.

This, however, is a very tough model to replicate and it can't effectively address many levels of terrorist operations. So sometimes you need an option that goes beyond law enforcement. If the terrorist network is largely operating in ungoverned space, where law enforcement is not robust, or might be corrupted, where the terrorists mass in identifiable locations and where the negative repercussions of your military actions are manageable, then you can treat it more like a war.

Operations against Al Qaeda cells in Yemen, their base camps in Afghanistan and Pakistan, and the Abu Sayyaf enclaves in the southern Philippines are all good examples of the utility of the military approach. But one of the best recent cases is in Sri Lanka. In 2009 the Sri Lankan government launched a highly militarized and ultimately decisive campaign against the Tamil Tiger terrorist group. That campaign succeeded for a number of reasons. First, the Sri Lankan government gradually retreated from policies that alienated the Tamil minority. Second, Sri Lankan President Mahinda Rajapaska worked assiduously to get the government, the military, and the people behind the campaign. Third, the Tamil Tigers's command-and-control system had already started to implode and, during the ensuing conflict, the Tigers proved to be a cooperative adversary—fighting for base areas which could be quarantined by government forces. And finally, the Sri Lankan government enjoyed the covert, but significant support of the United States and India and the overt military support of China and Pakistan.

While there was some out-cry from the larger international community about Sri Lankan tactics, the combination of a very effective media black-out and the Tamil Tigers's already badly tarnished international image meant that the Tigers could count on little in the way of international moral or material support. End result? The Tamil Tigers were obliterated. So there are some circumstances where treating terrorism as a war will give the best results. But that doesn't mean you should *never* treat terrorism as a law enforcement problem. It just depends on capabilities and context.

Now at this point, it would be a useful exercise to turn directly to our masters. What do they have to tell us about the strategic options available to the counterterrorist? We have already noted that regardless of how depraved and horrific the acts of terrorism may be, the most dangerous terrorists are the ones that keep these acts subordinate to political purpose. The counterterrorist's response has to be even more strategic.

Can you, like the Sunzi, attack their strategy by refusing to be a cooperative adversary? Can you attack their alliances to deny them external support? To do those two things requires a high degree of intelligence and all five varieties of spies, especially the turned spies. Do you have that clarity of intelligence? For example, federal law enforcement was able to penetrate the Ku Klux Klan with agents; can we or our allies get agents into Al Qaeda? If you can't bank on intelligence you might want to gamble on a Jominian or Clausewitzian decisive point and focus the bulk of your energies there. Afghanistan in 2001, where the Taliban and Al Qaeda tried a stand-up fight, and Sri Lanka in 2009, as we've just seen, are probably the best examples of this sort of approach.

How about Galula? Are there ways to resolve long-standing grievances and rebuild political institutions from the population up? If that is too costly and time consuming, the government might opt for a direct strategy—going after the men, materiel and the money that constitute the enemy's means. Even more direct is to attack the command-and-control functions of the movement: This was what Trinquier had in mind. And for examples of this kind of action, we might look at the decapitation strikes such as the raid that nabbed bin Laden. That still leaves you with a disgruntled constituent population and hundreds of dangerous rank-and-file members, but in the near term you have significantly disrupted the terrorist organizational structure.

Alternatively, a counterterrorist might want to consider a more Corbettian approach. This would involve using your greater strategic mobility to open a new theatre in the struggle. Opening that new theatre might induce the enemy to commit a strategic blunder. This was not the initial intent of the 2003 invasion of Iraq, but during the conduct of the war and in the context of the unfortunately phrased "bring it on" comments, President Bush made a sound strategic point.

Fighting radicalized Islamists in Iraq, where the U.S. held conspicuous advantages in firepower and military intelligence and had very loose rules of engagement was superior to fighting this enemy in Europe or in North America where very different rules applied. But who made the bigger mistake? Did Al Qaeda commit a strategic blunder by contesting the occupation of Iraq? Did the defeat of Al Qaeda in Iraq outweigh the political and strategic consequences of our decision to oust Saddam Hussein? We won't know those answers for a long time to come.

So when we start thinking about our masters, we have to realize that this war, like all others, requires us to think interactively and jointly. You are not stuck with your first option for the duration of a conflict. Interaction and adaptation will happen and you need to respond. If your initial strategy fails, be ready to admit your mistakes and reassess. If your initial strategy works a smart enemy will figure out ways to attack it.

For example, the British were right to rely on law enforcement in Ireland. The Irish police were their most effective instrument for gathering intelligence on and disrupting the activities of the IRA. That was why Collins went after the police so viciously. Now, if the enemy attacks your chosen strategy and undermines its effectiveness, do you abandon that strategy? In some cases you might have to. In other cases, the best strategy will be to do what is necessary to get your original strategy back on track. In Ireland the British needed to protect the police enough to allow them to do their jobs and to stay in the intelligence battle.

What about jointness? At first, the British were also right not to overwhelmingly militarize the crisis in Ireland. The army had a role to play, but as an adjunct to law enforcement. Remember what Corbett said about the army and the navy? Using them as mutually reinforcing instruments of war? We can say the same about the military and law enforcement. One service might have to cede its operational and strategic preferences and give way to a higher or more pressing need of the other. But, which service gives way will depend on the context.

As you can well imagine this raises cultural, institutional, and communications hurdles that are very difficult to surmount. Nevil Macready refused joint command of the British Army and the Irish Police. That was probably a mistake. Had there been unity of command, better intelligence sharing and a single strategic vision, the British might have stood a better chance of success against Michael Collins.

If the conflict escalates and its nature changes and if the value of the object justifies it, you might have to migrate from the intelligence intensive, law enforcement end of the spectrum to the firepower intensive, population control end of the spectrum. But as you build security and institutional capacity you want to migrate back toward intelligence intensive operations. This was the less provocative later part of Trinquier's strategic script: use the military as the first step toward restoring civilian governance. You migrate it back to a law enforcement issue.

Across the spectrum of responses I've been talking about, there's one constant that I should mention: Allies matter a great deal in counterterrorism campaigns. International allies can bring advantages in capabilities or they might provide you with access to a particular theatre. Local allies can give you better local intelligence and they can make you more strategically effective. At the same time, and as we have seen repeatedly in the decade since 9/11, both state and sub-state allies can be very problematic. Allies can expand your strategic options, but they can also limit your strategic options. Allies can also suck you into regional squabbles and tribal vendettas that deflect you away from your policies and strategies. As we like to say, the only thing worse than working with allies, is not having any allies to work with.

At the end of the day, whatever counterterrorism strategy you and your allies choose has to serve your political objectives. Your objectives might be unlimited, complete destruction of the movement and the repudiation of its political aims. Or they might be more limited: degrade the movement and prevent it from significantly altering the status quo, or do just enough to compel the terrorists to relent. You also have to think about the possible ways to end the conflict—and indeed to end it in a better state of peace. Obviously if both terrorist and counterterrorist have maximalist objectives, then a negotiated settlement is unlikely. But if there is a possibility of convergence, then your approach to counterterrorism has to contemplate terminating the war short of the total defeat of the enemy.

The primordial passions and hatred and the extremes of behavior that characterize terrorism and counterterrorism make this very difficult. In the Algerian War, the negotiated settlement threatened civil war in France and directly led to a bloody civil war in Algeria. And I appreciate the rhetorical value of "we will never negotiate with terrorists," but as a student of strategy I have to think that in some circumstances negotiating with terrorists might be an option. After all, if Winston Churchill could sit face-to-face with Michael Collins, anything is possible.

There is another way that an incumbent government can make political concessions without negotiating with terrorists. The government can simply make concessions unilaterally. True, this threatens to legitimate the use of terrorism and may reveal you as weak, but if it undercuts the grievances of the terrorists' constituent population then that might be to your advantage.

Last on the list of options for ending this kind of war is actually an option I mentioned in passing before: ignore the problem and hope it goes away. That's a terrible option, right? Maybe not! What if you don't have any means to respond? Or what if the only means at your disposal are destined to provoke unacceptable blowback? What if a terrorist movement is so fringe and so isolated that it is not worth your attention? Well, you might decide to quarantine them. Let them terrorize the local population and ultimately implode. Pakistan tried this approach when dealing with the Taliban in the Swat Valley. In fact, some pundits suggested that the United States do exactly that at the height of the sectarian violence in Iraq. Stand back and let the civil war burn itself out.

That would have been a terrible choice in Iraq, but I have to think that in some scenario that it might be a least bad option. In the end, even if a struggle against a terrorist movement is not a war in the strict and legal sense of the term, or even if for a wide variety of reasons a government can't or won't call it a war, terrorism and counterterrorism are both means to bend an enemy to your political will. As such, and with due attention paid to the unique character of this style of warfare, terrorism and counterterrorism are still amenable to the types of strategic analysis that we have been talking about throughout this course. The lessons of our masters extend even to the most contemporary forms of conflict. Tactics and technologies change, the enduring principles of strategy do not.

From the Jaws of Defeat—Strategic Adaptation
Lecture 24

In the past 23 lectures, we've covered a great deal of ground, from the hoplites and triremes of ancient Greece, to marines and aircraft carriers in World War II, to nuclear weapons in the Cold War, and terrorism and counterterrorism in the 21st century. Along the way, we have stuck close to our first definition of strategy: the process by which political purpose is translated into military action. In this final lecture, we'll look at the second definition of strategy: a process of adapting, of seizing opportunities in the midst of a war to link unanticipated military opportunities to desired political outcomes.

The Battle of Long Island, August 1776
- In the spring of 1776, after the colonists had driven the British out of Boston, George Washington set his mind to the defense of New York. Based on the lessons of Bunker Hill, Washington assumed that the Continentals could hold their ground against the Redcoats and inflict unacceptable costs on the British.

- In a sense, Washington was predicting how the American Revolution might play out: If he could offer a staunch enough defense of New York, the war might end there, with the British offering terms. But Washington was also guilty of script-writing, that is, assuming that an adversary will act in predictable ways.

- What advice might our masters have offered to Washington?
  - o Sun Tzu might have asked him whether he really knew himself, the enemy, and the terrain he would be fighting on.

  - o Machiavelli would have admired Washington's citizen-army but warned him about going toe-to-toe with British and Hessian professionals.

- o Clausewitz would probably have agreed that the British army was the strategic center of gravity but questioned whether Washington would have enough mass at the decisive point.

- o Corbett would have warned him that Britain had complete command of the sea and the strategic mobility that comes with that level of command.

- As it turned out, the British were anything but a cooperative adversary. Washington's 10,000 Continentals and 9,000 militiamen were no match for the huge force of British and Hessians massed in New York.

- Only by a stroke of good fortune was Washington able to evacuate his army from Brooklyn and wage a fighting retreat. The Americans lost two more battles in quick succession, and by December 1776, Washington's army was reduced to about 3,000 men.

- Washington's script for some kind of Jominian or Clausewitzian decisive battle turned out to be a colossal failure. But it was also the turning point of the war, because Washington had the ability to reassess his strategic options and adapt his strategy from one that sought a decisive result in the near term to something more akin to Mao: play for time, wear down the means and will of the enemy, and try to get some outside assistance.

- In the end, Washington's strategic adaptation paid off. His well-executed Fabian strategy, along with luck, great operational and strategic leadership, and French assistance, culminated in the Battle of Yorktown in 1781, where Washington finally achieved the decisive blow that shattered Britain's political will.

- Washington and his aide at the time, Alexander Hamilton, serve as examples to illuminate what the British strategic theorist Colin Gray meant when he said that strategy is the bridge between politics and war. The best strategists from the policy side are conversant in military operations—Pericles, Lincoln, FDR, and Churchill. The

The colonial victory at Yorktown in 1781 represented the culmination of a successful strategic adaptation on the part of George Washington, forced by the Battle of Long Island in August 1776.

best strategists from the military side are conversant in policy—Washington and Hamilton, Ulysses Grant, and Eisenhower.

The Civil-Military Nexus

- In the comparative lecture on Clausewitz and Jomini, we touched on Eliot Cohen's "unequal dialogue," in which, contrary to normal theory, the political leader engages in judicious supervision of war. One of Cohen's archetypes of civilian leadership in war was Abraham Lincoln, a president who relentlessly pestered his military commanders and offered his own operational and sometimes tactical suggestions.

- We saw FDR engaged in unequal dialogue when he overruled General Marshall on Operation Torch. In the end, Torch vindicated the president's strategic opportunism, delivering on everything FDR had argued to justify the decision and more: Hitler committed precious resources to a secondary theater, and the Mediterranean evolved into a theater of strategic opportunity that opened up another avenue of advance on Axis-dominated Europe.

- In the Pacific War, the Europe-first strategy and the damage wrought at Pearl Harbor demanded strategic adaptation, but there, FDR didn't have to overrule the military. The goal of the offensive-defensive, on which the president and Admiral King agreed, was not merely holding on the defensive but capitalizing on opportunities to weaken Japan by sinking more ships and downing more planes than the Japanese could replace.

- In Korea, the dispute between President Truman and General MacArthur over both political objectives and the means necessary to achieve them represented a breakdown of the civil-military dialogue and threatened a total collapse of the strategy bridge.

- In Vietnam, the military and civilians talked past each other, squandering opportunities for reassessment and adaptation. Our failure there was the result of violating the Clausewitzian maxim of understanding the nature of the war and, in contrast to popular thought, too little civilian oversight.

The Weinberger-Powell Doctrine

- In 1984, Secretary of Defense Caspar Weinberger laid out the argument that the United States should commit to a war only in situations in which its core interests were threatened, the political and military objectives were clear and attainable, military force could be overwhelming and unfettered, the will of the American people was robust, and there would be a clear idea of when victory was achieved. General Colin Powell later expanded on this list of metrics in what has come to be called the Weinberger-Powell Doctrine.

- Such a set a metrics is a good place to start thinking about strategy, but if it becomes a checklist, it can stifle strategic imagination and deny the interactive nature of war. We know, for example, that clear and attainable military objectives are a good place to start, but no plan survives first contact with the enemy.

- This linear linking of policy, to strategy, to operations, to tactics is the essence of war planning, and it is absolutely critical, but in the end, it is not the entirety of strategy. Policy and strategy must match each other and the context, but the conduct and outcome of any war rarely correspond to what either belligerent predicted.

America's Recent Wars

- Washington, Lincoln, and FDR were all forced to adapt based on the hard realities of their circumstances. In the Iraq War, it took several years of creeping uncertainty about the appropriateness of U.S. strategy before President Bush was forced to reassess and adapt; the result was the "surge."

- The surge wasn't a product of the civil-military dialogue within the administration; it was the brainchild of Fred Kagan, an analyst at the American Enterprise Institute and the son of the Thucydides scholar Donald Kagan. In translating Kagan's strategic vision into operational reality, Bush was able to rely on General David Petraeus.

- In this instance, we see a system at work in engaging the energies of the best and the brightest on both sides of the strategy bridge and forcing reassessment and strategic adaptation in the midst of war.

The Strength of the Strategy Bridge

- The damage to civil-military relations caused by the war in Iraq seems to have resulted in the weakening of "strategy" as a unifying concept between the professional military and senior civilians.
  - o The general sense among the military was that the Bush administration ignored military advice and punished those officers who raised concerns about mismatches between political ends and military means. This characterization is not entirely accurate, but it is pervasive.

o The most troubling effect of that may be that new officers, having seen the fate met by their superiors, may now demure on most strategic issues and prefer to limit themselves to their comfort zone: the tactical and operational levels of war.

o At the same time, we might also see the next generation of senior civilians staying in their professional comfort zone and shying away from the messy and contingent business of strategy. In the aftermath of bruising civil-military clashes, the civilians might opt to defer to the military on the application of force.

• This mutual dereliction of duty could be catastrophic, but it seems unlikely. There is a vibrancy of strategic education in the United States. In peacetime, building strategic literacy depends on the three-way dialogue among academics, policymakers, and military officers, and in many ways, that trinity is quite robust.

The Charms of Technology
• Strategy has to adapt to technology, both in terms of new threats and new capabilities, but technology is not likely to transform strategy into a science.

• The embrace of technology and innovative doctrine in America is wonderful, but at the same time, we must avoid assuming that the high-tech instruments used in recent conflicts will provide a formula for winning the next war.
  o As we saw, early air-power theorists made bold predictions about future wars based on scant evidence from World War I that came up conspicuously short.

  o Cyber-war theorists are engaged in a similar kind of prognostication today and may be overselling the technological transformation of war.

• Many of the classics of strategy were written in response to dramatic institutional, social, and technological changes that transformed warfare. The great strategic thinkers appreciated technological and tactical innovations but were not seduced or blinded by innovation. They were aware of what had changed and knew what had endured.

Summing Up Strategic Thinking

- A close study of the classics of strategic theory overlaid on a foundation of military and political history is rewarding in and of itself. It is also the best way to cultivate those habits of strategic analysis that are most precious for our senior military and civilian decision makers.

- As citizens, understanding classic strategic thought gives us the confidence to become informed and insightful participants in future debates over policy and strategy.

- The ultimate benefit of studying strategic theory lies not in providing pat answers to the questions pondered by politicians, soldiers, and citizens but, rather, in equipping us all with habits of critical thought that allow us to turn a clear eye on the infinite complexity of our current and future struggles.

Suggested Reading

Fischer, *Washington's Crossing*.

Gray, *Fighting Talk*.

International Security (Journal).

Journal of Strategic Studies.

McPherson, *Tried by War*.

Questions to Consider

1. Has "strategy" lost its meaning?

2. Which two or three masters of strategy should the president of the United States keep on his nightstand? Why? Which two or three masters should the president of China keep on his nightstand? Why?

From the Jaws of Defeat—Strategic Adaptation
Lecture 24—Transcript

Welcome back to Masters of War and to our final lecture in this series. We've covered a lot of ground in the last 23 sessions, from the hoplites and triremes of ancient Greece, to marines and aircraft carriers in World War II, to nuclear weapons in the Cold War, and finally to terrorism and counterterrorism in the 21st century. Along the way, we have stuck close to our first definition of strategy: the process by which political purpose is translated into military action.

When we look at war that way we have a linear approach. You begin with your desired end-state, your political objectives, and then you factor what combination of military actions will be sufficient to compel your enemy to do your political will. So in that scheme tactical objectives derive from operational objectives. Operational objectives derive from strategic objectives. And strategic objectives derive from political objectives. That is where we want to start.

That's why I began this course talking about Pearl Harbor. That was a brilliantly executed military action, but it was also a colossal strategic blunder in the sense that not only did it not further the achievement of Japan's political objectives, but also it set that nation on the path to total defeat.

But while thinking through the linkages between military objectives and political objectives is certainly where we want to start, that is rarely where we end up. Helmuth von Moltke, the chief of the Prussian General Staff and the architect of Prussia's stunning military victories over Austria and France in the 1860s and 1870s, once said, "No plan survives first contact with the enemy." Unless your adversary is a potted plant, war never tracks along the linear script like I just laid out.

And that's why I want to spend some time today talking about the other definition of strategy that I covered in the first lecture. That second definition looks at strategy as the process of adapting, of seizing opportunities in the midst of a war to link unanticipated military opportunities to desired political outcomes.

And to explore that definition, let's take another page from American military history and see how George Washington adapted and rescued the cause of American independence from the jaws of defeat. After the colonists had driven the British out of Boston, Washington set his mind to the next phase of the campaign, the defense of New York City. Based on the lessons of Bunker Hill, Washington assumed that the Continentals could hold their ground against the Red Coats and inflict unacceptable costs on the British. This is how strategy is supposed to work, right? You start with your political objective, in this case independence, and then figure out ways to inflict enough pain on your enemy to force him to accept those terms.

So Washington was predicting how the American Revolution might play out: if Washington could offer a staunch enough defense of New York, the war might culminate there and the British might offer terms. He based this on his personal experiences and on his reading of history. Washington was doing what we want a strategist to do. But Washington was also guilty of what we call scriptwriting, assuming that an adversary will act in predictable ways so if I do A, he will do B, and then C and D will follow from there. These were dangerous assumptions.

At this point we might want to imagine what sort of advice our masters might have offered Washington in the spring of 1776. Sunzi might have asked him if really knew himself and knew the enemy, and did he really know the terrain that he was going to be fighting on. Machiavelli would have admired Washington's citizen-army, but warned him about going toe-to-toe with British and Hessian professionals. Clausewitz would probably have agreed that the British Army was the strategic center of gravity, but questioned whether Washington was going to have enough mass at the decisive point. And Mahan and Corbett would have warned him that Britain had complete command of the sea and the critical strategic mobility that comes with that level of command.

As it turned out, the British were anything but a cooperative adversary at New York. In the summer of 1776, the British massed a huge expeditionary force to face Washington's Army at New York City, that force included some 70 warships, 10,000 sailors, 23,000 Red Coats, and another 10,000 Hessian mercenaries. What followed was the largest battle of the American

Revolution, the Battle of Long Island in August of 1776. Despite what he thought he had learned in Boston, Washington's 10,000 Continentals and 9,000 militiamen were no match for the British and Hessians. They were outmaneuvered and outfought at every turn. Only by a stroke of good fortune was Washington able to evacuate his army from Brooklyn and wage a fighting retreat along Manhattan Island. The Americans lost two more battles in quick succession at White Plains and Fort Washington. Between the hundreds killed, the thousands captured and the countless desertions, Washington's Army had been reduced to about 3,000 men by December of 1776.

Washington's script for some kind of Jominian or Clausewitzian decisive battle turned out to be a colossal failure. But it also turned out to be the turning point of the war, because Washington had the ability to reassess his strategic options and adapt his strategy from one that sought a decisive result in the near-term, to something more akin to Mao. To wage what is called a Fabian strategy, play for time, try to wear down the means and the will of your enemy, and try to get some outside assistance, in this case from the French; before going back on the strategic offensive when the time was ripe.

So at Pearl Harbor we had a spectacular tactical and operational success that led to strategic disaster. New York, an operational and tactical disaster, forced a successful strategic adaptation.

If you want a wonderfully written and eminently strategic treatment of Washington's reassessment after the New York debacle, you can't go wrong with *Washington's Crossing* by David Hackett Fischer. It is a fascinating exploration of the dynamic interaction and adaptation games that took place between the summer of 1776 and Washington's attacks on Trenton and Princeton in the winter of 1776–1777. Reading it you can't help but conjure up echoes of Sunzi, Machiavelli, Clausewitz, and Mao.

In the end, Washington's strategic adaptation paid off. A well-executed Fabian strategy, along with a lot of luck, some great operational and strategic leadership, and an awful lot of French help culminated in the Battle of Yorktown in 1781, where Washington finally got that decisive blow that shattered Britain's political will.

But back in 1776 it took vision and moral courage to change course so radically. It also took a favorable environment and steadfastness on the part of the Continental Congress. It is hard to imagine in this day and age, a military commander coming out of a disaster like New York and still having a job.

And what if Washington had been relieved of command? What was the alternative? Well, one alternative was a partisan or guerilla war advocated by General Charles Lee. Lee had something akin to the Kissinger thesis I talked about in our discussion of Mao: the guerilla wins by not losing and gradually by frustrating the enemy to the point that he gives up. But for Washington, keeping the Continental Army intact in order to ultimately transition to the counteroffensive was the only way to hurt the British enough to make them concede. Had Lee won the argument, we might very well imagine the entire movement for American independence dying on the vine. But that didn't happen, and that had a lot to do with Washington's stature, but it also had a lot to do with the fact that Washington and his subordinates thought strategically and were able to make cogent and sound arguments in favor of their strategic preferences. Fortunately, Washington wasn't just an adaptable strategist blessed with Machiavelli's *virtu*; he was also blessed with having Alexander Hamilton on his staff.

Even after Washington's victories at Trenton and Princeton, there was a lot of unease about the Fabian strategy. In June of 1777, Hamilton, Washington's aide, wrote to Robert Livingston, a powerful member of the Continental Congress. The purpose of the letter was to justify the Fabian strategy and to sell it to the skeptics. Hamilton, only 20 years old at the time, his letter was a masterpiece of strategic analysis. Hamilton assessed the strengths and weaknesses of both sides and showed how the Fabian strategy played to American strengths and attacked British weaknesses. In other words he understood the contest between Britain and the Colonies. Hamilton also assessed the larger international context within which the war was being fought. Hamilton was the exactly kind of officer that I want to have come through my seminar: strategically minded, politically savvy, and eloquent. And this is really the key to successful strategy and to successful strategic adaptation, individuals like Washington and Hamilton.

To borrow a metaphor from the British strategic theorist, Colin Gray, strategy is the bridge between politics and war. It spans the gulf between policy and military operations. The best strategists coming from the policy side are confident and conversant on the military end of the bridge. Pericles, Abraham Lincoln, FDR, and Winston Churchill are good examples of that kind of strategically minded politician. The greatest strategists from the military side are confident and conversant on the political end of the bridge. In that category we could place Washington and Hamilton, Ulysses Grant, Dwight Eisenhower, and maybe David Petraeus. And that brings us to another theme that we have been talking about throughout this course, which is critical to strategic adaptation: getting the civil–military nexus to function properly.

In our comparative lecture on Clausewitz and Jomini I mentioned a book by Eliot Cohen, *Supreme Command: Soldiers, Statesmen and Leadership in Wartime.* In contrast to the normal theory that posits a sharp line of division between soldiers and statesmen, Cohen's "unequal dialogue" has the statesman engaging in the judicious supervision of the war: Maintaining the subordination of strategy to policy by questioning and even second-guessing the military judgments of the soldiers.

One of Cohen's archetypes of civilian leadership in war was Abraham Lincoln, a president who relentlessly pestered his military commanders and offered his own operational and sometimes tactical suggestions. And Lincoln kept this up even after he found Ulysses S. Grant, a general who shared the president's strategic vision. If you don't want to take Cohen's word on the importance of the "unequal dialogue" in the Civil War I can recommend another outstanding book: James McPherson's *Tried by War.* That book offers an in-depth examination of how Abraham Lincoln, a president with almost no military experience, taught himself the essentials of strategy and how he ultimately managed to impose his political and strategic vision on a resistant U.S. Army. It is a profile in strategic genius and strategic adaptability from the unlikeliest of candidates.

Moving forward, we saw FDR exercise this kind of unequal dialogue when he overruled General Marshall on Operation Torch. Remember that FDR viewed Torch as a way to support Britain militarily in North Africa and to help Churchill politically at home. Torch would also build credibility with the Soviets who were impatient with the lack of action in Western Europe. And for America, Torch would keep our energies focused on the European theatre and provide the U.S. military with some much needed combat experience. Marshall acceded to Roosevelt's logic, and in the end Torch vindicated the President's strategic opportunism. Torch delivered on everything that FDR had argued to justify the decision, and much more. Hitler ended up committing precious resources, Panzer divisions, to that secondary theatre, resources better spent against the Soviets or in the defense of France. And, starting with Torch, the Mediterranean evolved into a theatre of strategic opportunity that opened up yet another avenue of advance on Axis-dominated Europe.

In the Pacific War, the Europe-first strategy and the damage wrought at Pearl Harbor demanded strategic adaptation, but there FDR didn't have to overrule the military. Roosevelt and Admiral King were in full agreement on the merits of the Corbettian offensive-defensive. Where the goal was not merely holding on the defensive, but also to capitalize on every opportunity to weaken Japan by sinking more ships and downing more planes than the Japanese could possibly replace.

That sort of healthy and productive civil–military dialogue, which is so critical to adaptation and to staying ahead of the violent interaction game that is war, was completely absent on the Japanese side. There was simply no way for the Japanese to reassess and adapt once the decision for war was made. But even the United States is not immune to this sort of breakdown.

In Korea, the dispute between President Truman and General MacArthur over both political objectives and the means necessary to achieve them threatened a total collapse of the strategy bridge, that is until Truman reasserted his primacy and relieved MacArthur.

In Vietnam the military and civilians were talking past each other. In that war the United States violated the Clausewitzian maxim of understanding the nature of the war on which they were embarking. Instead the U.S. attempted to fight that war in ways that suited American strategic and operational preferences, not in a way that suited the unique nature of the conflict.

That was a terrible mistake, but it was not unrecoverable. But the fact that the civilians and military were talking past each other meant that the abundant opportunities for reassessment and adaptation were squandered until it was too late. That failure of strategic imagination and mental agility was what gave rise to the type of course that I teach at the Naval War College and the one that I have been privileged to offer here.

But that was not the only response to the failure in Vietnam. One explanation for our defeat was that we stumbled into a war with a lack of clear political objectives, a lack of popular will and unacceptable limits on the use of the military. That was an appealing argument, but it wasn't entirely true. Rather than too much civilian oversight of the war, there wasn't enough, especially of the ground war in which General Westmoreland had a very free hand. President Johnson failed to interrogate Westmoreland's assumptions, and Westmoreland lacked the strategic vision to realize that his strategy was counterproductive. There was a dereliction of duty on both sides. And yet one of the pervasive mis-learned lessons of Vietnam, was that soldiers and statesmen should confine themselves to their respective sides of the bridge.

Yet another response to Vietnam was the understandable desire to return to linear thinking about strategy, and there were some very smart people who made this argument. In the 1980s that included Secretary of Defense Caspar Weinberger. In 1984 Weinberger laid out the argument that United States should only commit to a war when its core interests were threatened, where the political and military objectives were clear and attainable, when military force was overwhelming and unfettered, where the will of the American people was robust, and where there was a very clear idea of when victory would be achieved.

General Colin Powell later amplified and expanded on this list of metrics, in what has come to be called the Weinberger-Powell Doctrine. In defense of these two esteemed public servants, such a set a metrics is a good place to start thinking about strategy, but if it becomes a checklist then very quickly we can see a doctrine like this stifling strategic imagination and trying to deny the interactive nature of war.

For one, no matter how hard we might wish them to be, political objectives are rarely crystal clear or concrete. They will always retain some degree of ambiguity and flexibility. Likewise, clear and attainable military objectives are a good place to start, but no plan survives first contact with the enemy. In addition, overwhelming and unfettered force is an appealing way to dominate Clausewitz's realm of chance and probability, but there will always be limits on what you can do militarily. And again, unless your enemy is a potted plant, he will always get a vote. And finally, while it is good idea to think about what the end of the war will look like, it is almost always the defeated side who decides when it is over.

This linear linking of policy to strategy, to operations, to tactics is the essence of war planning, and it is absolutely critical, but in the end, it is not the entirety of strategy. Policy and strategy need to match each other and they need to match the context. But the conduct and outcome of any war rarely corresponds to what either belligerent predicted.

Only in the rarest cases, for example in the Iraq War of 1990–1991, where one side had an overwhelming military advantage, was able to play to its military strengths, and fought an adversary who was both strategically cooperative and politically isolated can you hope to neatly match policy-to strategy-to operations. Once interaction kicks in, you realize just how important it is to have robust and continuous civil–military dialogue.

And this brings us to America's recent wars. Washington and Lincoln and Roosevelt were all forced to adapt based on the hard realities of their circumstances. In the Iraq War it took several years of creeping uncertainty about the appropriateness of U.S. strategy before President Bush was forced to reassess and adapt: the result was the "Surge."

Interestingly enough, the Surge wasn't a product of the civil–military dialogue within the administration. The Surge wasn't Bush's idea or David Petraeus's idea; it was the brainchild of Fred Kagan, an analyst at the American Enterprise Institute and the son of the Thucydides' scholar Donald Kagan. It was Kagan's advice, not the advice of the U.S. military, that President Bush followed. In fact, the military had to scramble to translate Kagan's strategic vision into operational reality. But in that translation process, Bush was fortunate to have the services of General Petraeus, an officer steeped in exactly the kinds of historical and theoretical study that we have been engaged in for the past two-dozen lectures.

So it would seem that the system worked, albeit slowly, a system that engaged the energies of the best and the brightest on both sides of the strategy bridge and that forced reassessment and strategic adaptation in the midst of a war. But, even as I record this lecture nine years after the start of the Iraq War and two months after the last U.S. combat troops left Iraq, it is still not clear that Bush and Kagan and Petraeus succeeded in snatching victory from the jaws of defeat.

So as we think about successful and unsuccessful examples of strategic adaptation in the past, what issues should we be on guard for in the future? Under this category, I see two things that might be enablers of or impediments to our ability to remain adaptive strategists. The first has to do with the strength of the strategy bridge and the other with the seductive charms of technology.

First, the strategy bridge. I am somewhat concerned by the weakening of "strategy" as a unifying concept between the professional military and senior civilians. The war in Iraq damaged civil–military relations in this country and I can predict that there will be lots of books casting blame for that breakdown. But, I am less concerned about the causes than about the effects. The general sense among the military was that the Bush administration ignored military advice and punished those officers who raised concerns about mismatches between political ends and military means. This characterization is not entirely accurate, but it is a pervasive sense. The most troubling effect of that may be that up-and-coming officers, having seen the fate that met their superiors, may now demure on most strategic issues and prefer to limit themselves to their comfort zone: the tactical and operational levels of war.

This is doubly concerning because at the same time we might also see the next generation of senior civilians staying in their professional comfort zone and shying away from the messy and contingent business of strategy. In the aftermath of bruising civil–military clashes, the civilians might opt to defer to the military on the application of force.

That could amount to a catastrophic combination, a mutual dereliction of duty. But I think that this is unlikely. Between my students at the War College and from what I hear from my colleagues out in the civilian world, I don't see many shrinking violets who are excessively wary of stepping out of their comfort zones.

There is a vibrancy of strategic education in the United States. In peacetime, building strategic literacy depends on the three-way dialogue between academics, policy makers, and military officers. In many ways in the United States that trinity is quite robust.

The service academies and the war colleges all teach the classics of strategic thought and use historical case studies in their curriculum. This accustoms future military leaders to think it terms similar to their civilian counterparts. In the civilian sector, Yale University's Grand Strategy program is producing hard-charging future strategists. Similar programs are available at MIT, Tufts, Duke, Johns Hopkins, and Georgetown. To paraphrase Clausewitz, we are cultivating a generation of future statesmen and military commanders who understand both the logic and the grammar of war.

We are talking about a pretty small group, and I don't know if the United States is still producing strategists on par with Washington and Hamilton, but the baselines look pretty good. And then we have technology. America has had a long love affair with technology, especially in war.

Strategy has to adapt to technology, both in terms of new threats and new capabilities. But technology is not likely to transform strategy into a science. The embrace of technology and of innovative doctrine is great; it's critical. In 2011 alone high-tech surveillance and precision strikes yielded out-sized strategic results. The super-human work of navy special operators in bagging bin Laden and the remarkable coordination of the NATO air war over Libya may very well herald a new way of war.

Cyber-threats, too, are especially troubling, and it is essential to assess to potential strategic effects of cyber-attack. At the same time, we should avoid assuming that the ways these instruments have been in recent conflicts will provide a formula for winning the next war. We saw that based on scant evidence from World War I, early air-power theorists made bold predictions about future wars that came up conspicuously short. Cyber-war theorists do a lot of this kind of prognostication today and I predict that they are also overselling the technological transformation of war.

Studying the past and studying strategic theory alerts us to the importance of change, but also to stubborn continuities. As we have seen, many of the classics of strategy were written in response to dramatic institutional, social, and technological changes that transformed warfare. The great strategic thinkers appreciated technological and tactical innovations but were not seduced or blinded by innovation. They were aware of what had changed and they knew what had endured. Compared to the introduction of gunpowder; the French *levée en masse*, the steam battleship, airpower, and nuclear weapons—well, compared to those innovations, drone strikes and cyber-attacks look pretty pale. Strategy will continue to be much more of an art than a science.

Over the course of these lectures, I hope that I have convinced you that strategic thinking matters. I also hope that you are convinced that a close study of the classics of strategic theory overlaid on a foundation of military and political history is both rewarding in and of itself and is also the best way to cultivate those habits of strategic analysis that are most precious for our senior military and civilian decision makers.

I further suspect that this course has already begun to have an insidious effect on the way you think about policy, strategy, and war. By this point I can bet that you are no longer able to watch the nightly news or read the daily paper without thinking about Thucydides or Machiavelli or Mao. If I have done that much, then I think that I can count this course a success.

But more importantly, I would hope that you as citizens will take what you have learned in this course and have the confidence to become informed and insightful participants in future debates over policy and strategy.

466

As you reflect back on this course I hope you will see the enduring relevance of classical strategic thought especially to the most comprehensive and far-reaching tasks that we face today: assessing and reassessing the nature of the wars upon which we have embarked or are soon to embark.

The ultimate benefit of studying strategic theory lies not in providing pat answers to the questions pondered by statesmen, soldiers, and citizens, but rather in equipping them with the habits of critical thought, habits that allow them to turn a clear eye upon the infinite complexity of our current and future struggles. Our masters have enormously important things to say to us in the 21st century, but only if we listen.

Finally, my ability to teach this course has been immeasurably enhanced by the thousands of military officers that have attended my lectures and participated in my seminars. I have learned a lot more from these implementers of strategy than they have ever learned from me, a mere student of strategic thought. In the end, if you have enjoyed this course, then that is one more reason to be grateful to our men and women in uniform.

As for me, I'd like to take this last opportunity to thank them for their service, and to thank you for your interest in the Masters of War.

Bibliography

Aussaresses, Paul. *The Battle of the Casbah: Terrorism and Counter-Terrorism in Algeria, 1955–1957.* Translated by Robert L. Miller. New York: Enigma Books, 2002. Aussaresses, who worked closely with Trinquier's intelligence section, is unapologetic about the operational, strategic, and psychological value of torture during the Battle of Algiers.

Bayliss, John, and John Garnett, eds. *Makers of Nuclear Strategy.* New York: St. Martin's Press, 1991. In the spirit of the earlier *Makers* volumes, Bayliss and Garnett offer several top-notch essays on the major American, British, French, and Soviet nuclear theorists. The chapter on Sokolovsky is very eye-opening.

Beckett, Ian F. W. "Mao Tse-tung and Revolutionary Warfare." In *Modern Insurgencies and Counter-Insurgencies: Guerillas and Their Opponents since 1750,* chapter 4. London: Routledge, 2001. There is an essay on revolutionary war in the second edition of *Makers of Modern Strategy* that is well worth a read, but I prefer Beckett's overview of Mao in theory and practice. The Beckett volume also includes important comparative cases.

Brinton, Crane, Gordon A. Craig, and Felix Gilbert. "Jomini." In *Makers of Modern Strategy: Military Thought from Machiavelli to Hitler,* edited by Edward M. Earle, 77–92. Princeton: Princeton University Press, 1943 (1971, 1973 paperback editions). Like many of the other chapters in the Earle anthology, this is one of the best short introductions to this enigmatic Swiss theorist.

Brodie, Bernard. *Sea Power in the Machine Age.* Princeton: Princeton University Press, 1941. Brodie, a political scientist with a head for technological details (whom we meet in our discussion of nuclear strategy), penned this classic of the sail-to-steam genre very early in his career. His survey covers everything from steam propulsion and gunnery advances to the strategic and political implications of the steam battleship navy.

Byman, Daniel L., and Matthew C. Waxman. "Kosovo and the Great Air Power Debate." *International Security* 24, no. 4 (2000): 5–38. Two RAND analysts test the validity of several schools of air-power theory, including those of Pape and Warden, and find all lacking in satisfactorily explaining Milosevic's decision to concede to NATO's demands in 1999.

Calhoun, Mark T. "Clausewitz and Jomini: Contrasting Intellectual Frameworks in Military Theory." *Army History* PB 20-11-3, no. 80 (2011): 22–37. Calhoun tends to fall into the camp of Clausewitz fans, but this is still a concise overview of both masters' analytical superstructures and theoretical contributions.

Chandler, David G. *The Campaigns of Napoleon: The Mind and Method of History's Greatest Soldier.* New York: Macmillan, 1966. Of all the ink that has been spilled on Napoleon, Chandler's single comprehensive volume is hard to beat among the English-language scholarship. Chandler covers all of the major campaigns of revolutionary and Napoleonic France and keeps his focus at the strategic and operational levels of war.

———. *Jena 1806: Napoleon Destroys Prussia.* Oxford: Osprey, 1993. This exceptionally concise and nicely illustrated volume is ideal for those looking for an approachable account of the pivotal campaigns of 1806, those that figure so singularly in the strategic prescriptions of Jomini and Clausewitz. The other volumes in Osprey's *Campaign Series,* such as the ones on Marengo, Austerlitz, and Waterloo, are also worth a look.

Clausewitz, Carl von. *On War.* Translated and edited by Michael Howard and Peter Paret. Princeton: Princeton University Press, 1989. English translations of *On War* have been available since the 19th century, but this is a truly exceptional version that revolutionized Clausewitz studies in the United States. The Princeton version comprises an elegant translation of Clausewitz's often-turgid prose and includes introductory essays, an index, and an appendix of chapter-by-chapter summaries.

Cohen, Eliot. *Supreme Command: Soldiers, Statesmen, and Leadership in Wartime.* New York: Free Press, 2002. Cohen leans heavily on Clausewitz's book 8, chapter 6, to argue that the normal theory represented a dangerous dereliction of the duties of political leaders in wartime. In contrast to letting the generals exercise professional autonomy, it was incumbent on the politicians to be knowledgeable about military affairs, to question, and even to second-guess the military judgments of the soldiers. *Supreme Command* was reportedly on President Bush's reading list the summer before the Iraq War began.

Corbett, Julian S. *Maritime Operations in the Russo-Japanese War, 1904–1905*. Annapolis, MD: Naval Institute Press/Newport, RI: Naval War College Press, 1994. Corbett's real-time assessment of what went right for Japan and what went terribly wrong for Russia in the Russo-Japanese War of 1904–1905. Where Mahan's essay is a short critique of Russian mistakes, Corbett's analysis covers two volumes. I suggest the closing summary in volume II, specifically pages 382–411.

———. *Some Principles of Maritime Strategy*. Annapolis, MD: Naval Institute Press, 1988. In a terrible oversight, Corbett was not judged to be worthy of a chapter in either edition of *Makers of Modern Strategy*; fortunately, the 1988 reprint of *Principles* contains a fine overview of Corbett's life and work by the British naval historian Eric Grove. Corbett's classic is divided into three parts: "Theory of War," "Theory of Naval War," and "Conduct of Naval War." *Principles* is a delight to read in its entirety, but the sections on limited war in parts I and II and the closing section on support to operations ashore in part III stand out for their brilliance.

Crenshaw, Martha. "The Logic of Terrorism: Terrorist Behavior as a Product of Strategic Choice." In *The Origins of Terrorism: Psychologies, Ideologies, Theologies, States of Mind*, edited by Walter Reich, 7–24. Washington, DC: Woodrow Wilson Center Press, 1998. With determined objectivity, Crenshaw digs past the horror of terrorism to interrogate its coldly rational political purpose. Her essay is a classic in the field and a real eye-opener for students.

Crowl, Philip A. "Alfred Thayer Mahan: The Naval Historian." In *Makers of Modern Strategy from Machiavelli to the Nuclear Age*, edited by Peter Paret, 444–477. Princeton: Princeton University Press, 1986. Provides the necessary background on Mahan's career, his writings, and his remarkable celebrity.

Cubbage, T. L. "German Misapprehensions Regarding Overlord: Understanding Failure in the Estimative Process" and "The Success of Operation Fortitude: Hesketh's History of Strategic Deception." In *Strategic and Operational Deception in the Second World War*, edited by Michael I. Handel, 114–174 and 327–346. London: Routledge, 1987. Cubbage details the inner workings of Operation Fortitude and the reasons why the Nazis fell so completely for this masterpiece of military deception.

Dickey, Christopher. *Securing the City: Inside America's Best Counterterror Force—the NYPD*. New York: Simon & Schuster, 2009. Dickey, a veteran Middle East journalist, offers a multilayered view of the NYPD's counterterrorism unit as a local, national, and international actor. CBS's *60 Minutes* also had a recent feature on the unit.

Earle, Edward M., ed. *Makers of Modern Strategy: Military Thought from Machiavelli to Hitler*. Princeton: Princeton University Press, 1973. No course on the evolution of Western strategic thought is complete without Earle's brilliant compendium. Its framework of historical context, key elements of theory, and long-term influence for each "maker" was the inspiration for many of these lectures.

Emerson, William. "Operation POINTBLANK: A Tale of Bombers and Fighters." Lecture 4 in the *Harmon Memorial Lecture Series*, 1962. http://www.usafa.edu/df/dfh/harmonmemorial.cfm. Emerson's Harmon Lecture is the single best treatment of the operational and strategic effects of the Combined Bomber Offensive over Europe. It is a valuable "reality check" on early air-power theory.

Esdaile, Charles J. *The Peninsular War*. London: Penguin Books, 2003. There is no shortage of excellent scholarship on Napoleon's disaster in Spain. Among the newest "classics" is Esdaile's sweeping account of the seemingly endless war that ground down Napoleon's grand army. This book is a useful primer for our discussion of Sir Julian Corbett. Esdaile goes into rich detail on the land operations side of the war in Spain and Portugal. It is an essential complement to Corbett's maritime focus.

Fischer, David Hackett. *Washington's Crossing*. New York: Oxford University Press, 2004. David McCullough's terrific *1776* garnered the bulk of attention and praise back in 2004–2005, but for my money, *Washington's Crossing* is the better account of the strategic duel that took place across New York and New Jersey in that pivotal year.

Freedman, Lawrence. "The First Two Generations of Nuclear Strategists." In *Makers of Modern Strategy from Machiavelli to the Nuclear Age*, edited by Peter Paret, 735–778. Princeton: Princeton University Press, 1986. Freedman provides a concise overview of American nuclear strategy debates and highlights Brodie and Schelling as key figures on opposite sides of critical issues.

Galula, David. *Counterinsurgency Warfare: Theory and Practice*. New York: Praeger, 1964. Covers Galula's general theories derived from personal experience and his reading of military history and strategic theory.

———. *Pacification in Algeria, 1956–1958*. Santa Monica, CA: RAND Corporation, 2006. A detailed account of Galula's service in Algeria; unflinching in its criticism of French army doctrine.

Ganor, Boaz. *The Counter-Terrorism Puzzle: A Guide for Decision Makers*. New Brunswick, NJ: Transaction Publishers, 2005. Ganor makes a noble effort to cover the immense array of options available to the counterterrorist and the mix of potentially productive and counterproductive strategic effects they may carry. His work is a good test of the "five audiences" framework from the counterterrorism perspective.

Gilbert, Felix. "Machiavelli: The Renaissance of the Art of War." In *Makers of Modern Strategy from Machiavelli to the Nuclear Age*, edited by Peter Paret, 11–31. Princeton: Princeton University Press, 1986. Gilbert's essay, updated from the first version in the Earle edition of *Makers*, covers the humanist origins and summarizes the content and influence of the only major text published during Machiavelli's lifetime. It is a balanced evaluation of Machiavelli's strengths and weaknesses as a military thinker.

Bibliography

Gray, Colin S. "The Anglo-Irish War, 1919–21: Lessons from an Irregular Conflict." *Comparative Strategy* 26, no. 5: 371–394. Gray makes a 28-point case for what contemporary counterinsurgents and counterterrorists can learn from this little-known conflict. He also provides a clear narrative of the causes, conduct, and termination of the Anglo-Irish War, as well as the pivotal role of Michael Collins.

———. *Fighting Talk: Forty Maxims on War, Peace, and Strategy.* Washington, DC: Potomac Books, 2009. Pithy and provocative, Gray's 40 short essays make a persuasive case for the classics of strategic theory and for the rigorous study of military and political history.

———. *The Leverage of Sea Power: The Strategic Advantage of Navies in War.* New York: Free Press, 1992. A comprehensive overview of the relative advantages in strategic mobility and resiliency enjoyed by sea powers. Gray posits that the strategic trends that prevailed in the 19th and 20th centuries will endure into the future.

———. "Strategy in the Nuclear Age: The United States, 1945–1991." In *The Making of Strategy: Rulers, States, and War*, edited by Williamson Murray, Alvin Bernstein, and MacGregor Knox, 579–613. Cambridge: Cambridge University Press, 1996. Gray situates the nuclear strategy debate within the larger framework of American strategic inclinations. He argues that U.S. nuclear strategy is best seen in the context of protecting the Eurasian periphery as an American sphere of influence.

Hale, John R. *Lords of the Sea: The Epic Story of the Athenian Navy and the Birth of Democracy.* New York: Viking, 2009. Hale discusses the dialectical relationship between Athens' political institutions and its maritime power. This is a gripping inside examination of the foundations of Athenian sea power. Hale's account also covers the period of Athenian recovery after the disasters of the late 5th century B.C.

Handel, Michael I. *Masters of War: Classical Strategic Thought.* London: Frank Cass, 2001. The final edition of Handel's brilliant survey of Sun Tzu, Machiavelli, Clausewitz, Jomini, and Mao. Handel emphasized the universality of strategic thought even when its leading authors were divided by huge gulfs of time and culture. This course is an homage to Handel's legacy, and this book is an invaluable reference for the study of strategic thought.

Hanson, Victor D. *A War Like No Other: How the Athenians and Spartans Fought the Peloponnesian War*. New York: Random House, 2005. Hanson's blow-by-blow account of the tragic implosion of ancient Greece stands as a metaphor for the contemporary United States.

Heuser, Beatrice. *The Evolution of Strategy: Thinking War from Antiquity to the Present*. Cambridge: Cambridge University Press, 2010. Heuser offers a rich and provocative survey of the foundations of Western strategic culture and its evolution from ancient Greece and Rome, through the Middle Ages, to the age of Napoleon, and on to the contemporary world.

———. *The Strategy Makers: Thoughts on War and Society from Machiavelli to Clausewitz*. Santa Barbara, CA: Praeger/ABC-CLIO, 2010. True to her title, Heuser provides the bridge between European military theorists of the late Renaissance and the age of Napoleon. It is a valuable corrective to the idea that our small roster of masters stands alone in an intellectual wasteland.

Horne, Alistair. *A Savage War of Peace: Algeria, 1954–1962*. New York: New York Review Books, 2006. In 2007, President Bush invited Horne to a face-to-face meeting at the White House to discuss *A Savage War of Peace*, the definitive history of the war for Algerian independence.

Hornqvist, Mikael. "Machiavelli's Military Project and the *Art of War*." In *The Cambridge Companion to Machiavelli*, edited by John M. Najemy, 112–127. Cambridge: Cambridge University Press, 2010. A brief but illuminating essay from the *Cambridge Companion*, this chapter links Machiavelli's prescriptions in the *Art of War* to his experiences recruiting and training the Florentine militia in the late days of the republic.

Huntington, Samuel P. *The Soldier and the State: The Theory and Politics of Civil-Military Relations*. Cambridge, MA: Harvard University Press, 1995. No discussion of civil-military relations would be complete without a reference to Huntington's classic of the late 1950s. Generations of civil-military theorists have had to engage with Huntington's discussion of the theory of objective civilian control of the professionally autonomous military: the so-called "normal theory" of civil-military relations.

International Security. http://belfercenter.ksg.harvard.edu/project/58/quarterly_ journal.html. If you want to continue your self-education on the classics of strategy and their real-world applications, you cannot go wrong in regularly perusing this consistently excellent journal.

James, D. Clayton. "American and Japanese Strategies in the Pacific War." In *Makers of Modern Strategy from Machiavelli to the Nuclear Age*, edited by Peter Paret, 703–732. Princeton: Princeton University Press, 1986. This is the single best theory-centric overview of the competing naval strategies of these two belligerents.

Jomini, Antoine-Henri. *The Art of War.* Translated by G. H. Mendell and W. P. Craighill. Philadelphia: J. B. Lippincott & Co., 1862. Although a bit dated and heavy on military terminology, this early translation of Jomini has stood up remarkably well for more than a century and a half.

―――. *Jomini and His Summary of the Art of War: A Condensed Version.* Edited by J. D. Hittle. Harrisburg, PA: Stackpole Books, 1987. The overwhelming volume of Jomini's military writings is difficult to cover in any comprehensive way. His *Summary of the Art of War* is widely available in translation, and e texts of it are readily available online.

Journal of Strategic Studies. http://www.tandf.co.uk/journals/titles/01402390. asp. If you want to continue your self-education on the classics of strategy and their real-world applications, you cannot go wrong in regularly perusing this consistently excellent journal.

Kagan, Donald. *The Peace of Nicias and the Sicilian Expedition.* Ithaca, NY: Cornell University Press, 1981. You cannot go wrong with Kagan on the events in the Peloponnesian War. His interpretation, however, is often at odds with that of Thucydides himself. Nowhere is this more the case than with their competing takes on the Sicilian expedition.

————. *The Peloponnesian War*. New York: Penguin Publishing, 2003. This single volume is a condensed version of Kagan's epic four-volume treatment of the Peloponnesian War. Impeccably sourced and masterfully written, it is a favorite of students and faculty.

————. *Thucydides: The Reinvention of History*. New York: Viking, 2009. If you don't have the time to dig through Kagan's larger works, this shorter version is a lucid and critical evaluation of where Kagan sees Thucydides's pro-Periclean biases most fully on display.

Lake, Daniel R. "The Limits of Coercive Airpower: NATO'S 'Victory' in Kosovo Revisited." *International Security* 34, no. 1 (2009): 83–112. Lake argues that it was primarily the indirect erosion of Milosevic's domestic power base and elite dissatisfaction as a result of the bombings that drove him to capitulate, not the direct effects of the NATO air campaign itself.

Machiavelli, Niccolò. *The Chief Works and Others*. Translated by Allan H. Gilbert. Durham, NC: Duke University Press, 1965. There are many different versions of Machiavelli's works, but the Gilbert collection is notable both for its quality and for the fact that it includes *The Art of War*, along with *The Prince* and the *Discourses on Livy*.

MacIsaac, David. "Voices from the Central Blue: The Airpower Theorists." In *Makers of Modern Strategy from Machiavelli to the Nuclear Age*, edited by Peter Paret, 624–647. Princeton: Princeton University Press, 1986. The first section of MacIsaac's essay is an extended review of the Warner chapter below, to which he adds a brief section on Trenchard, a discussion of strategic bombing in World War II, and a concise examination of the theory and practice of air power in the Cold War.

Mahan, Alfred Thayer. *The Influence of Sea Power upon History, 1660–1783*. Boston: Little, Brown, 1890. Mahan was a remarkably prolific and popular author during his lifetime, and it would take years to work through all of his writings. The two *Influence* volumes represent Mahan at his most historically focused. This work covers the rise of Britain as the world's dominant sea power.

———. *The Influence of Sea Power upon the French Revolution and Empire, 1793–1812*. Boston: Little, Brown, 1912. This volume details the exercise of British sea power during the titanic struggle with Napoleonic France.

———. *The Interest of America in Sea Power, Present and Future*. Boston: Little, Brown, 1897. Showcases Mahan the grand strategist and full-throated advocate of embracing America's sea-power destiny.

———. "Retrospect upon the War between Japan and Russia." In *Naval Administration and Warfare*, 133–173. Boston: Little, Brown, 1918. Mahan's real-time assessment of what went right for Japan and what went terribly wrong for Russia in the Russo-Japanese War of 1904–1905. Where Mahan's essay is a short critique of Russian mistakes, Corbett's analysis covers two volumes.

Mao Tse-tung. "On Protracted War." In *Selected Military Writings of Mao Tse-tung*, 143–144. Peking: Foreign Languages Press, 1967. For all of its political jargon and ideological baggage, "On Protracted War" is justifiably pointed to as a classic of insurgency. Writing in the late 1930s, Mao lays out a three-stage strategy by which an initially weak non-state actor can overthrow the incumbent government and seize absolute power.

Marks, Thomas, ed. *Maoist Insurgency since Vietnam*. London: Frank Cass, 1996. Unfortunately, the Marks volume covers Mao's influence only through the 1990s. If you're interested in mining more recent news, anything on the Unified Communist Party of Nepal, the most "successful" Maoist movement of the last decade, is well worth your attention.

Marston, Daniel, ed. *The Pacific War Companion: From Pearl Harbor to Hiroshima*. Oxford: Osprey, 2005. This collection of 13 wonderful essays that cover all the major land, air, sea, and amphibious operations in the Asian theater was published on the 60th anniversary of the end of the Pacific War. Pay particular attention to the chapters on Japanese and American naval strategies and to chapter 13, "Ending the Pacific War." That last chapter figures prominently in the second half of the lecture on air power.

McPherson, James M. *Tried by War: Abraham Lincoln as Commander in Chief*. New York: Penguin, 2008. We might re-title this new classic of military history *The Strategic Education of Abraham Lincoln*. A president with almost no military experience teaches himself the essentials of strategy and succeeds in imposing his vision on a resistant U.S. Army. You may want to read it in tandem with Eliot Cohen's chapter on Lincoln in *Supreme Command*.

Meilinger, Philip S., ed. *The Paths of Heaven: The Evolution of Airpower Theory*. Maxwell AFB, AL: Air University Press, 1997. The first seven essays in this rare survey of air-power theorists cover the leading theoretical lights of the air-power debates in the interwar period. The second half of the volume covers air theory and doctrine since 1945.

Meyer, Andrew, and Andrew R. Wilson. "*Sunzi Bingfa* as History and Theory." In *Strategic Logic and Political Rationality: Essays in Honor of Michael I. Handel*, edited by Bradford A. Lee and Karl F. Walling, 99–118. London: Frank Cass, 2003. This essay offers an expanded discussion of why historical context is so critical to understanding the analytical strengths and weaknesses of the *Sunzi*.

Murray, Williamson, Alvin Bernstein, and MacGregor Knox, eds. *The Making of Strategy: Rulers, States, and War*. Cambridge: Cambridge University Press, 1996. This volume is more on the practice of strategy than on strategic theory. It contains rich and illuminating case studies on nations at war.

Najemy, John M. "Society, Class, and State in Machiavelli's *Discourses on Livy*." In *The Cambridge Companion to Machiavelli*, edited by John M. Najemy, 96–111. *Cambridge*: Cambridge University Press, 2010. This is a short but thorough introduction to the main tenets of Machiavelli's republican vision as reinforced by his reading of Livy. Najemy is one of the leading Machiavelli experts active today. His *Cambridge Companion* is an invaluable desk reference for fans and detractors of the Florentine.

National Commission on Terrorist Attacks upon the United States. *The 9/11 Commission Report: Final Report of the National Commission on Terrorist Attacks upon the United States.* New York: W. W. Norton, 2004. No discussion of terrorism is complete without a clear understanding of the nature and motivations of al-Qaeda. *The 9/11 Commission Report* is one of the best ways to know this enemy.

Orend, Brian. *The Morality of War.* Peterborough, Ontario, Canada: Broadview Press, 2006. Widely considered the Walzer of his generation, Orend expands upon and codifies the concept of *jus post bellum*, the just termination of war. Orend applies all three elements of just war to Afghanistan, Iraq, and the broader war on terror.

Pape, Robert A. *Bombing to Win: Air Power and Coercion in War.* Ithaca, NY: Cornell University Press, 1996. In chapter 4, Pape attempts to weight the relative impact of conventional bombing, the atomic bombs, and the Allied land and the sea campaigns in driving Japan to seek terms in August 1945. He concludes that it was the combination of the atomic bombs and the Soviet invasion of Manchuria that tipped the scales. Nonetheless, he offers four potential alternative explanations of the outcome that view the impact of air power differently. Throughout, Pape returns to Douhet and looks forward to a theorist from the nuclear strategy lecture, Thomas Schelling. Pape also has a good chapter on the air campaign against Germany that complements the Emerson essay. In chapter 6, Pape critiques the flawed assumptions about North Vietnamese morale that undergirded the Rolling Thunder and Linebacker air campaigns. As the leading skeptic of the Warden school of air power, Pape is equally critical of the assumptions and execution of the air campaign against Iraq (chapter 7).

Paret, Peter. "Clausewitz." In *Makers of Modern Strategy: Military Thought from Machiavelli to Hitler*, edited by Edward M. Earle, 186–213. Princeton: Princeton University Press, 1943 (1971, 1973 paperback editions). For those in the market for a quick overview of the life, writings, and influence of Clausewitz, the two *Makers* volumes are a great place to start.

————, ed. *Makers of Modern Strategy from Machiavelli to the Nuclear Age*. Princeton: Princeton University Press, 1986. Paret's updated version of *Makers* is as much a classic as its predecessor. In addition to the chapters on individual masters, later chapters are more thematic and cover types of warfare: air power, nuclear strategy, insurgency, and so on. These two volumes could be considered the baseline texts for our course.

————. "Napoleon and the Revolution in War." In *Makers of Modern Strategy from Machiavelli to the Nuclear Age*, edited by Peter Paret, 123–142. Princeton: Princeton University Press, 1986. Written for the second edition of *Makers*, Paret's essay is designed as a lead-in to the two subsequent essays on Jomini and Clausewitz in that volume. It is an excellent synthesis of the major tactical, technological, organizational, and political changes that took place during the French Revolution and the wars of Napoleon.

Plutarch. *The Rise and Fall of Athens: Nine Greek Lives*. Translated with an introduction by Ian Scott-Kilvert. New York: Penguin, 1960. Thucydides died before he completed his great history. Plutarch's biographies of the leading Athenian and Spartan strategists of the war's last decade fill in what the master could not.

Pocock, J. G. A. *The Machiavellian Moment: Florentine Political Thought and the Atlantic Republican Tradition*. Princeton: Princeton University Press, 1975. The classic treatment of the context and content of the *Discourses*. Machiavelli's search for inspiration in the early Roman Republic was also undertaken by his contemporaries. Pocock provocatively links those thinkers to the "Atlantic republican tradition" that includes notable American founders.

Pontecorvo, Gillo, director. *The Battle of Algiers*. Algeria: Casbah Films, 1966. Beginning in 2000, Pontecorvo's classic was being screened at the Pentagon. The film chronicles the cycles of terrorism and counterterrorism that gripped Algiers and follows the tactically successful but strategically counterproductive French counterinsurgency campaign.

Rothfels, H. "Clausewitz." In *Makers of Modern Strategy: Military Thought from Machiavelli to Hitler*, edited by Edward M. Earle, 93–113. Princeton: Princeton University Press, 1943 (1971, 1973 paperback editions). One of the leading German scholars of his day, Rothfels explores the connections between Clausewitz's theories and the transformation of European warfare and clarifies some of the thornier concepts in *On War.*

Sawyer, Ralph. *The Seven Military Classics of Ancient China.* Boulder, CO: Westview Press, 1993. Sawyer includes translations of seven classics and situates the *Sunzi* within the canon of Chinese/Asian strategic literature.

Shy, John. "Jomini." In *Makers of Modern Strategy from Machiavelli to the Nuclear Age*, edited by Peter Paret, 143–185. Princeton: Princeton University Press, 1986. While these classic overview essays are a bit suspicious of Jomini's motivations and dismissive of his theoretical insights, they nonetheless are a fine introduction to the life and works of our Swiss master.

Smith, Niel A. "Understanding Sri Lanka's Defeat of the Tamil Tigers." *Joint Forces Quarterly* 59 (2010): 40–44. Smith highlights the rare convergence of domestic and international factors that explain the success of Sri Lanka's highly militarized campaign against the Tamil Tigers.

Sprout, Margaret Tuttle. "Mahan: Evangelist of Sea Power." In *Makers of Modern Strategy: Military Thought from Machiavelli to Hitler*, edited by Edward M. Earle, 415–445. Princeton: Princeton University Press, 1973. Provides the necessary background on Mahan's career, writings, and remarkable celebrity.

Strachan, Hew. *Clausewitz's On War: A Biography.* New York: Atlantic Monthly Press, 2007. The immense popularity of the Howard and Paret version of *On War* has motivated a new generation of scholars to revisit the original and to question critical interpretive points. Among the best of these "revisionists" is the British military historian Hew Strachan. In particular, most people consider Clausewitz an advocate of the idea that war should be a rational instrument of policy. Strachan shows that for Clausewitz, real war could never be truly rational or absolutely subordinate to political purpose.

Strassler, Robert B., ed. *The Landmark Thucydides*. New York: Free Press, 1996. There are many versions of Thucydides, but the *Landmark* is the gold standard. The translation is an update of Richard Crawley's masterful 19th-century version with the invaluable addition of maps, a running summary, and illuminating appendices on everything from Greek naval warfare to Spartan politics. Pages 350–357 of Book V cover the Melian Dialogue, and Books VI and VII detail the decision to go to Sicily and the disaster that befell the Athenians at Syracuse.

Strauss, Barry. "Sparta's Maritime Moment." In *China Goes to Sea: Maritime Transformation in Comparative Historical Perspective*, edited by Andrew S. Erickson, Lyle J. Goldstein, and Carnes Lord, 33–61. Annapolis, MD: Naval Institute Press, 2009. Strauss is one of the few classicists to treat seriously Sparta's effort to match Athens' maritime dominance.

Strauss, Leo. "Thucydides: The Meaning of Political History." In *The Rebirth of Classical Political Rationalism: An Introduction to the Thought of Leo Strauss*, edited by Thomas L. Pangle, 72–102. Chicago: University of Chicago Press, 1989. Strauss is often tarred with the broad brush of neoconservatism. This short essay is a good introduction into what he actually thought about Thucydides rather than what many think he thought.

Sumida, Jon Tetsuro. *Inventing Grand Strategy and Teaching Command: The Classic Works of Alfred Thayer Mahan Reconsidered*. Baltimore: Johns Hopkins University Press, 1999. Sumida's great achievement lies in rescuing Mahan the grand strategist and innovative strategic theorist from the battle-fleet-obsessed caricature that he has become.

Sun Tzu. *The Art of War*. Translated by Samuel B. Griffith. Oxford: Oxford University Press, 1980. There are several excellent translations of the *Sunzi*, among which Griffith's classic version stands out. Griffith's translation is written from the perspective of a general officer in the U.S. Marine Corps (and a former member of the Naval War College faculty), who had seen combat in World War II and had lived and studied in China. This is a scholarly and approachable version.

Bibliography

————. *The Art of Warfare*. Translated by Roger Ames. New York: Ballantine Press, 1993. This is the first English translation to incorporate archaeological evidence unearthed in the 1970s. Stylistically, Ames is quite spare in his rendering of the text, and he omits the later commentaries that appear in many other versions. For those familiar with Chinese, the counter-position of the original text with the translation is welcome. Ames's introductory essay situates the *Sunzi* within both the military ethos and the philosophical universe of Warring States China.

Townshend, Charles. *The British Campaign in Ireland, 1919–1921: The Development of Political and Military Policies.* Oxford: Oxford University Press, 1975. Where Gray emphasizes the remarkably effective IRA strategy, this classic by Townshend offers a competing view of the innate weaknesses of the IRA and the efforts of the British to exploit those critical vulnerabilities.

Trinquier, Roger. *Modern Warfare: A French View of Counterinsurgency.* Translated by Daniel Lee. Westport, CT: Praeger Security International, 2006. Trinquier was a prolific theorist and commentator, but this is his best work. *Modern Warfare* is particularly strong on the interrelation between terrorism and insurgency, as well as the unique ability of urban insurgents to exploit the institutions of civilian governance. Trinquier is very good on how to get inside and shatter the clandestine organization of a terrorist movement, but the question remains whether his methods inevitably carry negative strategic and political repercussions.

Tucker, Spencer C. *Handbook of 19th Century Naval Warfare.* Annapolis, MD: Naval Institute Press, 2000. In this well-written and nicely illustrated volume, Tucker covers all of the military-technological changes in the transition from sail to steam. The concluding chapter contains a useful summary of the major operations of the naval wars at the turn of the last century, including the Spanish-American and the Russo-Japanese wars.

U.S. Army. *Counterinsurgency* (FM 3-24). www.fas.org/irp/doddir/army/fm3-24.pdf. I do not recommend trying to grind through all the jargon and acronym-laden detail of FM 3-24, but even a cursory survey will reveal the unmistakable influence of Galula and Trinquier.

Walling, Karl F. "Thucydides on Democratic Politics and Civil-Military Relations." In *Strategic Logic and Political Rationality: Essays in Honor of Michael I. Handel*, edited by Bradford A. Lee and Karl F. Walling, 139–163. London: Frank Cass, 2003. Walling, a second-generation student of Leo Strauss, sees valuable lessons in Thucydides for the future of American democracy and the health of American civil-military relations.

Walzer, Michael. *Just and Unjust Wars: A Moral Argument with Historical Illustrations.* 4th ed. New York: Basic Books, 2006. In print for three and a half decades, this is the seminal study of the core tenets of the just-war tradition, elegantly laid out and systematically applied to a series of case studies.

Warden, John A. "The Enemy as a System." *Airpower Journal* 9, no. 1 (1995): 40–55. As a counterpoint to Pape, I will let Warden make his own case.

Warner, Edward. "Douhet, Mitchell, Seversky: Theories of Air Warfare." In *Makers of Modern Strategy: Military Thought from Machiavelli to Hitler*, edited by Edward M. Earle, 485–503. Princeton: Princeton University Press, 1973. Warner counterpoints Douhet's career and writings with those of Mitchell. Given that it was written at the height of World War II, the essay's conclusions are tentative at best, although the overview of the theorists is very good.

Warner, Michael. "The Divine Skein: Sun Tzu on Intelligence." *Intelligence and National Security* 21, no. 4 (2006): 483–492. At the time that Warner wrote this essay, he was a historian in the Office of the Director of National Intelligence. I had the pleasure of contributing feedback and translation advice on early drafts.

Bibliography

Notes

Notes

Notes

Notes